THE REV

LOVE'S VICTORY

LADY MARY WROTH

edited by Alison Findlay, Philip Sidney
and Michael G. Brennan

MANCHESTER
UNIVERSITY PRESS

Introduction, critical apparatus, etc.
© Alison Findlay, Philip Sidney and Michael G. Brennan 2021

The rights of Alison Findlay, Philip Sidney and
Michael G. Brennan to be identified as the editors of
this work have been asserted by them in accordance with the
Copyright, Designs and Patents Act 1988.

This edition published by Manchester University Press
Oxford Road, Manchester M13 9PL

www.manchesteruniversitypress.co.uk

British Library Cataloguing-in-Publication Data
A catalogue record for this book is available from the
British Library

ISBN   978 1 7849 9320 7   hardback
ISBN   978 1 5261 6717 0   paperback

First published 2021
Paperback published 2022

Typeset
by New Best-set Typesetters Ltd

Dedicated to the memory of William Philip Sidney, 1st Viscount De L'Isle VC KG, who first brought this manuscript of Lady Mary Wroth's play to a public readership; to Gillian Mary Hayton, a wonderful mother; and to Henrietta Maybanks, a well-beloved niece.

Contents

List of illustrations

General Editors' Preface

Clifford Leech conceived of the Revels Plays as a series in the mid-1950s, modelling the project on the New Arden Shakespeare. The aim, as he wrote in 1958, was 'to apply to Shakespeare's predecessors, contemporaries, and successors the methods that are now used in Shakespeare's editing'. The plays chosen were to include well-known works from the early Tudor period to about 1700, as well as others less familiar but of literary and theatrical merit. 'The plays included', Leech wrote, 'should be such as to deserve and indeed demand performance'. We owe it to Clifford Leech that the idea became reality. He set the high standards of the series, ensuring that editors of individual volumes produced work of lasting merit, equally useful for teachers and students, theatre directors and actors. Clifford Leech remained General Editor until 1971, and was succeeded by F. David Hoeniger, who retired in 1985.

Ever since then, the Revels Plays have been under the direction of four or five general editors: initially David Bevington, E. A. J. Honigmann, J. R. Mulryne, and E. M. Waith. E. A. J. Honigmann retired in 2000 and was succeeded by Richard Dutton. E. M. Waith retired in 2003 and was succeeded by Alison Findlay and Helen Ostovich. J. R. Mulryne retired in 2010. Published originally by Methuen, the series is now published by the Manchester University Press, embodying essentially the same format, scholarly character, and high editorial standards of the series as first conceived. The series now concentrates on plays from the period 1558–1642. Some slight changes have been made: for example, starting in 1996 each index lists proper names and topics in the introduction and commentary, whereas earlier indexes focused only on words and phrases for which the commentary provided a gloss. Notes to the introduction are now placed together at the end, not at the foot of, the page. Collation and commentary notes continue, however, to appear on the relevant pages.

The introduction to each Revels play undertakes to offer, among other matters, a critical appraisal of the play's significant themes and images, its poetic and verbal fascinations, its historical context, its characteristics as a piece for the theatre, and its uses of the stage for which it was designed. Stage history is an important part of the story. In addition, the introduction presents as lucidly as possible the criteria for choice of copy-text and the editorial methods employed in presenting the play to a modern reader. The introduction also considers the play's date and, where relevant, its sources, together with its place in the work of the author and in the theatre of its time. If the play is by an author not previously represented in the series, a brief biography is provided.

The text of each Revels play, in accordance with established practice in the series, is edited afresh from the original text of best authority (in a few instances, texts), in modern spelling and punctuation and with speech headings that are consistent throughout. Elisions in the original are also silently regularised, except where metre would be affected by the change. Emendations, as distinguished from modernized spellings and punctuation, are introduced only in instances where error is patent or at least very probable, and where the corrected reading is persuasive. Act divisions are given only if they appear in the original, or if the structure of the play clearly points to them. Those act and scene divisions not in the original are provided in small type. Square brackets are also used for any other additions to, or changes in, the stage directions of the original.

Rather than provide a comprehensive and historical variorum collation, Revels Plays editions focus on those variants which require the critical attention of serious textual students. All departures of substance from the copy-text are listed, including any significant relineation and those changes in punctuation which involve to any degree a decision between alternative interpretations. The collation notes do not include such accidentals as turned letters or changes in the font. Additions to stage directions are not noted in the collations, since those additions are already made clear by the use of brackets. On the other hand, press corrections in the copy-text are duly collated, as based on a careful consultation of as many copies of the original edition or editions as are needed to ensure that the printing history of those originals is accurately reported. Of later emendations of the text by subsequent editors, only those are reported which still deserve attention as alternative readings.

One of the hallmarks of the Revels Plays is the thoroughness of their annotations. Besides explaining the meanings of difficult words and passages, the annotations provide commentary on customs or usage, on the text, on stage business – indeed, on anything that can be pertinent and helpful. On occasion, when long notes are required and are too lengthy to fit comfortably at the foot of the page below the text, they are printed at the end of the complete text.

Appendices are used to present any commendatory poems on the dramatist and play in question, documents about the play's reception and contemporary history, classical sources, casting analyses, music, and any other relevant material.

Each volume contains an index to the commentary, in which particular attention is drawn to meanings for words not listed in the *OED*, and (starting in 1996, as indicated above) an indexing of proper names and topics in the introduction and commentary.

Our hope is that plays edited in this fashion will promote further scholarly and theatrical investigation of one of the richest periods in theatrical history.

DAVID BEVINGTON
RICHARD DUTTON
ALISON FINDLAY
HELEN OSTOVICH
MARTIN WHITE

Acknowledgements

We wish to thank Viscount De L'Isle CVO MBE for authorising this new edition of the Penshurst Manuscript, and for providing access both to the manuscript and to Penshurst Place as a venue for exploring some of the possibilities for performance in the script. Thanks are also due to Maryann Webster for her help in arranging visits to view the manuscript, and to Ben Thomas, Lucy McLeod and all the team at Penshurst for their help in running the workshops and the productions at Penshurst. We are grateful to Globe Education, particularly Patrick Spottiswoode, for support in bringing 'Read not Dead' to Penshurst and to The Urania Company for their efforts in furthering the stage history of the play. We are indebted to Lancaster University and to the Arts and Humanities Research Council for their financial support which enabled the 'Dramatizing Penshurst: Site, Script, Sidneys' project to stage the 2016 and 2018 workshops and production. We offer heartfelt thanks to Dr Imogen Felstead for her excellent work as Academic Assistant on the project, to David Blacow and his team for recording the performance.

We thank Stephanie Hodgson-Wright for her generosity in giving us ready access to the video recording of her 1999 production with Poetic Justice Theatre Company. We would also like to thank Joanna Labon and Andrew Dawson at The Marlowe Theatre in Canterbury for the opportunity to test the script in action in the newly reopened hall at the Marlowe Kit. We are grateful to Eleanor Findlay for her help with preparing the production photographs.

We owe much to those scholars who have preceded us in drawing attention to Lady Mary Wroth's work, from Josephine A. Roberts and Margaret P. Hannay in particular, forward to Sidney scholars who have offered advice while we have been working on the edition. We are especially grateful to Mary Ellen Lamb for sharing her research on William Herbert's poetry, to Gary Waller for allowing us to see the material from his latest book in advance of publication, and to Katherine R. Larson for her advice on the musical aspects of the play. We also thank Helen Hackett, Marion O'Connor, Naomi Miller, Ilona Bell, Steven May, Paul Salzman and Marion Wynne-Davies for responding to our queries with generosity, and to Barbara Ravelhofer and Elaine Hobby for their support during the productions. The support of Gavin Alexander and Alice Kelly has also been invaluable.

We are grateful to colleagues at the Huntington Library, Lancaster University Library, the Brotherton Library, Leeds and the London Library for their assistance in the course of our research. We thank members of our families, without whose loving support we would not have been able to complete the edition.

Finally, our thanks to Richard Dutton for being such a wonderful, wise General Editor, to Matthew Frost of Manchester University Press for supporting the project with generosity and good humour throughout, and to Lianne Slavin and the production team at the Press.

Sir William Sidney (1482–1554) = Anne Pagenham (d. 1543)

Sir Henry Sidney (1529–86) = Mary Dudley (1531–86)

Philip (1554–86)
= Frances Walsingham (1567–1632)

Mary (1561–1621)
= Henry Herbert (c.1538–1601) second Earl of Pembroke

Robert (1563–1626) first Earl of Leicester
= (1) Barbara Gamage (1562–1621)
= (2) Sarah Smythe

Ambrosia (c.1564–75)

Thomas (1569–95)
= Margaret Dakins (1571–1633)

Elizabeth (1585–1612)
= Roger Manners fifth Earl of Rutland

William Herbert (1580–1630) third Earl of Pembroke
= Mary Talbot (1580–1650)

Philip Herbert (1584–1650) first Earl of Montgomery and fourth Earl of Pembroke
= (1) Susan de Vere (1587–1629)
= (2) Anne Clifford (1590–1676)

MARY (1587–1651)
= Robert Wroth (1576–1614)
(1) James (1614–16)
(2) William and Katherine (b. c.1624) by William Herbert, third Earl of Pembroke

Katherine (c.1589–1616)
= Lewis Mansell

William (1590–1612)

Henry (b.d. c.1591)

Elizabeth (1592–1605)

Philippa (1594–1620)
= John Hobart

Robert (1595–1677) second Earl of Leicester
= Dorothy Percy (1598–1659)

Bridget (1597–99)

Alice (1598–99)

Barbara (1599–1643)
= (1) Thomas Smythe

Vere (1602–06)

Barbara

Dorothy

Philip
= (2) Thomas Colepeper

Thomas

Dorothy (1617–84)

Philip (1619–98)

Robert (1620–22)

Henry (1621–22)

Algernon (1623–83)

Lucy (1624–25)

Lucy (b. 1625)

Robert (1626–68)

Anne (b. c1627/8)

Mary (1629–48)

Frances (1630–51)

Isabella (1634–63)

Elizabeth (d. 1650)

Diana (c.1640–1670)

Henry (1641–1704)

Chronology

People and events connected to Lady Mary Wroth (henceforth MSW) are highlighted in **BOLD**.

1551	(29 Mar)	marriage of **MSW's grandparents**, Henry Sidney and Mary Dudley, daughter of John Dudley, Earl of Warwick
	(11 Oct)	Henry Sidney knighted and John Dudley created Duke of Northumberland
1552	(25 Apr)	estate and manor of Penshurst, Kent, granted in perpetuity by King Edward VI to Sir William Sidney, father of Sir Henry
1553	(6 Jul)	death of King Edward VI, in the arms of Sir Henry Sidney; accession of Lady Jane Grey (deposed 19 Jul)
	(19 Jul)	accession of Queen Mary I
	(22 Aug)	execution of John Dudley, Duke of Northumberland
1554	(7/10 Feb)	death of Sir William Sidney at Penshurst
	(12 Feb)	execution of Lady Jane Grey and her husband Guildford Dudley
	(13 Mar)	Sir Henry Sidney accompanies the Earl of Bedford's mission to bring Philip of Spain to England for his marriage (25 Jul) to Queen Mary I
	(30 Nov)	birth of Henry and Mary Sidney's first child, Philip, named in honour of his god-father, Philip of Spain
1556	(16 Jan)	Queen Mary's husband becomes Philip II of Spain, following the abdication of his father Emperor Charles V

1556–59	Sir Henry Sidney serves in Ireland in military and administrative capacities
1558 (17 Nov)	death of Queen Mary I; accession of Queen Elizabeth I
1560 (Jan)	Sir Henry Sidney appointed Lord President of the Council to the Marches of Wales (until his death in 1586)
1561 (27 Oct)	birth of Mary Sidney, later Countess of Pembroke
(26 Dec)	Sir Henry Sidney's brother-in-law, Ambrose Dudley, created Earl of Warwick
1562	Probable date of birth of **MSW's mother**, Barbara Gamage
1563 (19 Nov)	birth of **MSW's father**, Robert Sidney, so named in honour of his uncle Robert Dudley
1564 (26 Apr)	William Shakespeare baptised at Stratford-upon-Avon
(28/9 Sep)	Robert Dudley created Earl of Leicester
1565 (22 Jun)	Sir Henry Sidney appointed Lord Deputy of Ireland (1565–71, 1575–78)
(29 Jul)	marriage of Mary, Queen of Scots, to Henry Stewart, Lord Darnley (d. 1567), father of King James VI of Scotland and I of England
1566 (19 Jun)	birth of Prince James (later James VI of Scotland and James I of England), son of Mary, Queen of Scots
1567 (24 Jul)	abdication of Mary, Queen of Scots; accession of King James VI
1569 (25 Mar)	birth of Thomas Sidney, **uncle of MSW**, youngest son of Sir Henry Sidney and Lady Mary Dudley Sidney

1570 (25 Feb)	Pope Pius V excommunicates Queen Elizabeth I
(17 Mar)	death of William Herbert, first Earl of Pembroke
1572 (May)	Philip Sidney leaves England for travels on the continent, returning in May 1576
1576 (?)	birth of Robert Wroth, later **husband of MSW**
1577 (21 Apr)	marriage of Mary Sidney, **MSW's aunt**, to Henry Herbert, second Earl of Pembroke
1578/79	Philip Sidney's pastoral drama, *The Lady of May* (as first titled in the 1725 edition of his *Works*) written either for Queen Elizabeth's visit to the Earl of Leicester's house at Wanstead (6–16 May 1578) or for her second stay at Wanstead (1–2 May 1579)
1579 (Apr)	**MSW's father**, Robert Sidney, travels on the continent (until summer 1581; he then travels again to the continent before returning to England in spring 1582)
c. 1577 – c. 1582	Philip Sidney probably drafting his *Arcadia* (first published 1590)
1580 (8 Apr)	birth of William Herbert, eldest son of Henry Herbert, second Earl of Pembroke, and Mary Sidney Herbert, Countess of Pembroke. William was later **MSW's lover** and father of her two illegitimate children
1584 (23 Sep)	marriage of **MSW's parents**, Robert Sidney and Barbara Gamage, promoted by Henry Herbert, second Earl of Pembroke
(16 Oct)	birth of Philip Herbert, second son of Henry Herbert, Earl of Pembroke, and Mary Sidney Herbert, Countess of Pembroke

1585 (10 Aug)   Treaty of Nonsuch agrees English aid for the Dutch and the grant to Queen Elizabeth of the cautionary towns of Brill and Flushing (Vlissingen) and Rammekins fort

(18 Nov)   Philip and Robert Sidney sail for Flushing; Philip is appointed Governor of Flushing

(10 Dec)   Earl of Leicester and Thomas Sidney (Philip and Robert's younger brother) arrive at Flushing

1586 (14 Jan)   Earl of Leicester accepts the Governor-Generalship of the Low Countries; Robert Sidney at The Hague and Leiden

(1 or 5 May)   death of **MSW's grandfather** Sir Henry Sidney at Worcester

(9 Aug)   death of **MSW's grandmother** Lady Mary Dudley Sidney at London

(23 Sep)   **MSW's uncle** Sir Philip Sidney wounded during a skirmish at Zutphen

(7 Oct)   **MSW's father** Robert Sidney is knighted by his uncle, Robert Dudley, Earl of Leicester, for valour at Zutphen

(17 Oct)   death of Sir Philip Sidney

1587 (16 Feb)   state funeral of Sir Philip Sidney at St Paul's Cathedral, London

(18 Oct)   **birth of Robert Sidney's daughter, Mary (d. 1651), later MSW; christening held in the Great Hall at Baynard's Castle in London**

1588 (May–Oct?)   **MSW and her mother with Mary Sidney Herbert, Countess of Pembroke, in Wiltshire prior to and during the Spanish Armada crisis**

(16 Jul)   Sir Robert Sidney appointed Governor of Flushing

(Aug)   Spanish Armada crisis; Robert Sidney joins the English forces at Tilbury, led by his uncle, Robert Dudley, Earl of Leicester, and is then dispatched on a mission to

	King James VI of Scotland to ensure Scotland's support for England against Spain
(23 Aug)	The stationer William Ponsonby granted publication rights for the *Arcadia* and Sidney's translation of Du Bartas
(4 Sep)	death of Robert Dudley, Earl of Leicester
(Nov)	Mary Sidney Herbert, Countess of Pembroke, and her children (**and possibly MSW and her mother**), return to London for the celebrations marking 30 years since Queen Elizabeth I's accession

| 1589 (1 Aug) | assassination of King Henri III of France |
| (?) | birth of Katherine Sidney, **sister of MSW** |

| 1589–1616 | Robert Sidney serves as Governor of Flushing |

1590 (21 Feb)	death of Ambrose Dudley, Earl of Warwick
(Jun–Dec?)	**MSW with family at Flushing**
(10/11 Nov)	birth at Flushing of William, **eldest brother of MSW**
(?)	publication of *The Countess of Pembroke's Arcadia*; probable year of marriage of Frances Walsingham Sidney, widow of Sir Philip Sidney, to Robert Devereux (1565–1601), second Earl of Essex

1591 (autumn)	publication and 'taking in' (withdrawal) of *Astrophil and Stella* as an unauthorized edition
(22 Dec)	marriage of **MSW's uncle** Thomas Sidney to Margaret Dakins Devereux
(?)	birth and death of Henry Sidney, **brother of MSW**

1592 (Feb)	christening of Elizabeth Sidney, **sister of MSW**; Queen Elizabeth is godmother
(Apr–Dec)	**MSW with family at Flushing**
(?)	publication of the Countess of Pembroke's translations of Duplessis-Mornay's

A Discourse of Life and Death and Garnier's Antonius

| 1593 (?) | publication of *The Countess of Pembroke's Arcadia*, with Books I–III from 1590 edition and IV–V from manuscript |

1594 (Jan–Apr)	Sir Robert Sidney sent on an embassy to King Henri IV of France
(18 Aug)	**birth of Philip(pa), sister of MSW**
(?)	Probable date of completion of the Sidney Psalter by Philip Sidney and his sister Mary Sidney Herbert, Countess of Pembroke

1595 (26 Jul)	death of Thomas Sidney, **uncle of MSW**
(17 Sep)	beginning of the surviving correspondence of Rowland Whyte (whose grandfather had been in the service of William Herbert, first Earl of Pembroke) to Sir Robert Sidney (until 28 Dec 1602). **This correspondence is the major source of information about Lady Mary's childhood**
(1 Dec)	birth of **MSW's brother** Robert Sidney (d. 1677), later second Earl of Leicester, at Baynard's Castle

| 1595/96 | **MSW resident with family in London at Alderman John Catcher's house** |
| (Oct–spring) | measles epidemic |

1596 (Apr)	Sir Robert Sidney meets with King Henri IV at Boulogne to discuss the retaking of Calais from the Spanish
(19 Aug)	birth of Princess Elizabeth, daughter of James VI of Scotland and later Queen of Bohemia
(?)	**Marcus Geerhaerts II paints portrait of Barbara Gamage Sidney and six of her children, including MSW**

1596/97	**MSW with family at the Savoy, London, home of Countess of Huntingdon, from October 1596 until May 1597**
1597 (23/4 Jan)	Sir Robert Sidney serves with distinction at Siege of Turnhout; he then unsuccessfully seeks the Wardenship of the Cinque Ports (Mar) and, later, a peerage and the post of Vice-Chamberlain (Oct)
(1 Mar)	christening of Bridget Sidney, **sister of MSW**
(Jun)	**MSW and family travel to Flushing**
1598 (5 Mar)	**MSW's cousin** Elizabeth Sidney (daughter of Sir Philip) marries Roger Manners, Earl of Rutland
(Mar)	**MSW and family return from Flushing**
(5 Aug)	death of William Cecil, Lord Burghley
(Oct)	birth of Alice Sidney, **sister of MSW**
(?)	birth of **MSW's sister-in-law** Dorothy Percy Sidney (d. 1659), later wife of Robert Sidney, second Earl of Leicester. Publication of a 'collected works' of Philip Sidney, including *The Countess of Pembroke's Arcadia*, *Defence of Poetry*, *The Lady of May* and *Astrophil and Stella*
1598/99	**MSW with family at Baynard's Castle from Oct until Apr, a pattern that continues for more than twenty years**
1599 (24 Mar)	death of Alice Sidney, **sister of MSW**
(30 Jun)	death of Bridget Sidney, **sister of MSW**
(2 Jul)	William Herbert, **cousin of MSW**, welcomed to court by Queen Elizabeth
(28 Nov)	birth of Barbara Sidney, **sister of MSW**
1600 (19 Nov)	birth of Prince Charles, later King Charles I

1601 (19 Jan)	death of Henry Herbert, second Earl of Pembroke
(Feb)	William Herbert, now third Earl of Pembroke, refuses to marry Mary Fitton who bears him a still-born child (Mar); he is committed to the Fleet Prison and then placed under house arrest
(7/8 Feb)	rebellion led by Robert Devereux, Earl of Essex (executed 25 Feb)
1602 (?)	birth of Vere, **sister of MSW**
(26 Dec)	**MSW dances before Queen Elizabeth**
1603 (24 Mar)	death of Queen Elizabeth and accession of King James VI of Scotland and I of England
(13 May)	Sir Robert Sidney created Baron Sidney of Penshurst; appointed Queen Anne's Chamberlain and Surveyor of Revenues (Nov); sent to Canterbury to welcome the French Ambassador (early Jun)
(29/30 Aug–Dec)	King James visits Wilton House on several occasions
(?)	marriage of Frances Walsingham Sidney, widow of Sir Philip Sidney and Robert Devereux, Earl of Essex, to Richard Burke (1572–1635), fourth Earl of Clanricarde
1604 (Jan)	William and Philip Herbert and Sir Robert Sidney prominent in court entertainments
(27 Sept)	**Mary Sidney (MSW) marries Sir Robert Wroth at Penshurst**
(4 Nov)	William Herbert, third Earl of Pembroke, marries Mary Talbot, daughter of the Earl of Shrewsbury, at Wilton House
(27 Dec)	Philip Herbert marries Susan de Vere, daughter of the Earl of Oxford, at London
1605 (6 Jan)	**MSW in *Masque of Blackness* with Ann Herbert (sister of the Earl of Pembroke) and Susan Vere Herbert**

(4 May)	Robert Sidney (d. 1626) created Viscount Lisle; Philip Herbert created Earl of Montgomery; Star Chamber rejects the claim on the estate of Robert Dudley, Earl of Leicester, made by his illegitimate son, Robert(o) Dudley
(Aug)	Robert Sidney's vessel to Flushing blown off course and forced to moor at Gravelines (then under Spanish control)
(5 Nov)	discovery of the Gunpowder Plot
(?)	probable year of marriage of Katherine Sidney, **sister of MSW**, to Sir Lewis Mansell; she moves to Margam in Wales

1606 (27 Jan)	**death of Robert Wroth, MSW's father-in-law (funeral 3 March)**
(Jun–Jul)	visit to England of Queen Anne's brother, King Christian IV of Denmark
(23 Jul)	burial of Vere Sidney, **sister of MSW**
(Dec?)	death of Anne Herbert, **cousin of MSW**

1608 (6 Jan)	**MSW in audience for *Masque of Beauty*; praised by a Tuscan visitor to the court, Antimo Galli**
(Jan)	Rowland Whyte describes the harsh winter conditions at Baynard's Castle, London
(Sep–Oct)	**Robert Wroth, husband of MSW, is dangerously ill and makes a generous will**
(?)	**MSW appeals to Queen Anne to allow the Wroths to purchase Loughton and add it to her jointure; Robert Wroth petitions King James**

1609 (Sep)	**MSW dangerously ill with pneumonia and sends for her father**

1610 (Jan)	Prince Henry's Barriers, an entertainment involving William and Philip Herbert
(14 May)	assassination of King Henri IV of France and accession of King Louis XIII

(2–5 Jun)	investiture of Prince Henry as Prince of Wales; Robert Sidney (d. 1677) created a Knight of the Bath
1611 (?)	publication of King James Bible
(?)	Ben Jonson resident at Penshurst as tutor to William Sidney, **MSW's brother**
1612 (24 May)	death of Robert Cecil, Earl of Salisbury
(6 Nov)	death of Prince Henry; Sidney family deaths in 1612 include Roger Manners, Earl of Rutland (26 Jun); Elizabeth Sidney Manners, Countess of Rutland (c. 1 Sep), **cousin of MSW**; Sir Henry Sidney of Walsingham (2 Nov); William Sidney (3 Dec), **brother of MSW** and eldest son of Robert Sidney, Viscount Lisle
1613 (14 Feb)	marriage of Princess Elizabeth to Frederick, Elector Palatine
(Apr–Aug)	Robert Sidney, Viscount Lisle, escorts Princess Elizabeth to Germany; travels home with his son Robert (d. 1677) who is then commanding a military company at Flushing
1613	**MSW's poetry is circulating in manuscript by this date and perhaps earlier**
1614 (Feb)	**birth of MSW's only legitimate son, James**
(14 Mar)	**death of MSW's husband Sir Robert Wroth**
(Jun)	Mary Sidney Herbert, Dowager Countess of Pembroke, travels to the continent where she resides for two years; Philip(pa), **sister of MSW**, marries Sir John Hobart and moves to Blickling Hall, Norfolk
1615 (17 Oct)	arrest of Robert Carr, Earl of Somerset, and his wife, Frances Howard, on

suspicion of the murder of Sir Thomas Overbury

(23 Dec)   William Herbert, third Earl of Pembroke, appointed Lord Chamberlain

1616 (early)   Robert Sidney (d. 1677), **brother of MSW**, marries Dorothy Percy (d. 1659), daughter of the Earl of Northumberland; the Sidneys' neighbour, Lady Anne Clifford, notes in her diary (Feb 1616) that their union is 'openly known' to their family circle; it does not become public knowledge until Mar 1617

(23 Apr)   death of William Shakespeare

(6/7 May)   **MSW's father**, Robert Sidney, Viscount Lisle, created a Knight of the Garter

(8 May)   Katherine Sidney Mansell, **sister of MSW**, dies at Baynard's Castle and is buried at Penshurst

(30 May)   Robert Sidney, Viscount Lisle, accompanied by his son Robert, formally hands back Flushing to the Dutch

(1 Jul)   death of Mary Herbert, daughter of Susan de Vere and Philip Herbert, probably **godchild of MSW**

(5 Jul)   **death of James Wroth, son of MSW, aged two years and five months**

(late?)   Mary Sidney Herbert, Dowager Countess of Pembroke, arrives back in England and receives by royal grant a life interest in Houghton Park, Bedfordshire, where she built a new mansion

1617/21   **period of Wroth's major literary activity; probable date of MSW's Huntington and Penshurst manuscripts of *Love's Victory***

1617 (5 Jan)   George Villiers created Earl of Buckingham

(5 Oct)	baptism of Dorothy Sidney (d. 1684), later Countess of Sunderland, the first child of Robert and Dorothy Sidney
(6 Nov)	marriage of Lucy Percy (d. 1660) and James Hay (d. 1636), later Earl of Carlisle
1618 (1 Jan)	George Villiers created Marquis of Buckingham
(13 May)	Defenestration of Prague, leading to initiation of the Thirty Years War
(2 Aug)	Robert Sidney (d. 1626) created first Earl of Leicester in a public ceremony (after a private ceremony on 22 Jul); Robert Sidney (d. 1677) succeeds his father as Viscount Lisle
c. 1618/19	**probable date of holograph Folger MS of *Urania* by MSW**
1619 (10 Jan)	birth of Philip Sidney (d. 1698), son of Robert and Dorothy Sidney, later third Earl of Leicester
(3 Apr)	marriage of **MSW's sister** Barbara Sidney and Thomas Smythe (d. 1635), later Viscount Strangford
(13 May)	Robert Sidney, Earl of Leicester, Mary Sidney Herbert, Dowager Countess of Pembroke, Dorothy Percy Sidney, **MSW** and Philippa Sidney Hobart attend the funeral of Queen Anne (d. 2 March) as do most of their male relatives
(4 Nov)	Frederick, Elector Palatine and Princess Elizabeth crowned King and Queen of Bohemia
1620 (Aug)	Pilgrim Fathers sail in *Mayflower* for America
(Sep)	death of Philip(pa) Sidney Hobart, **sister of MSW**
(8 Nov)	Battle of the White Mountain; Frederick and Elizabeth lose Bohemia

c. 1620/25	**composition of MSW's *Urania II***
1621 (21 Feb)	christening of Philip Herbert (d. 1669), later fifth Earl of Pembroke
(24(?) May)	death of **MSW's mother** Barbara Gamage Sidney, Countess of Leicester; buried at Penshurst (26 May)
(21 Jul)	King James visits Houghton House, the home of Mary Sidney Herbert, Dowager Countess of Pembroke
(25 Sep)	Mary Sidney Herbert dies from smallpox at her house in Aldergate Street, London; funeral at St Paul's and burial at Salisbury Cathedral
(?)	**publication of MSW's *The Countess of Montgomery's Urania* and poems *Pamphilia to Amphilanthus*; denounced by Edward Denny (Feb–Mar)**
1623 (14/15 Jan)	birth of Algernon Sidney (executed 1683), son of Robert and Dorothy Sidney and **nephew of MSW**
(18 May)	George Villiers created Duke of Buckingham
(May)	Robert Sidney, first Earl of Leicester, transfers his entire estate to his eldest son, Robert, later second Earl of Leicester
(?)	First Folio of Shakespeare's plays dedicated to William Herbert, third Earl of Pembroke, and Philip Herbert, Earl of Montgomery
1624? (spring)	**birth of William and Katherine, illegitimate children of MSW and William Herbert, third Earl of Pembroke**
(Nov)	marriage agreed between Prince Charles and the French Princess Henrietta Maria
1625 (27 Mar)	death of King James I and accession of King Charles I; plague begins to spread across London and southern England
(1 May)	King Charles I marries (by proxy) Henrietta Maria, daughter of King Henri IV of France

(Oct)	King Charles I and Queen Henrietta Maria visit Wilton House
(30 Nov)	Treaty of The Hague, under which England, the Palatinate and the United Provinces form an alliance with King Christian IV of Denmark
1626 (2 Feb)	coronation of King Charles I (delayed from January due to plague)
(23 Feb)	impeachment of George Villiers, Duke of Buckingham, begins
(25 Apr)	**MSW's father** Robert Sidney, first Earl of Leicester, marries Sarah Blount Smythe (d. 1655), widow of Sir Thomas Smythe
(15 Jun)	King Charles I dissolves Parliament and refuses to dismiss Buckingham
(13 Jul)	death of **MSW's father** Robert Sidney, first Earl of Leicester, at Baynard's Castle; buried at Penshurst on 16 July, and succeeded by his son, Robert Sidney, second Earl of Leicester
(Aug)	William Herbert, third Earl of Pembroke, appointed Lord Steward; his brother Philip, Earl of Montgomery, appointed Lord Chamberlain
(19 Sep)	christening of Robert Sidney (d. 1668), son of Robert and Dorothy Sidney, **MSW's nephew**
(Oct)	King Charles I visits Wilton House
1627 (Jul)	expedition to La Rochelle and the isle of Rhé under Duke of Buckingham; the remnants of his defeated forces return to England (Oct)
1628 (7 Jun)	King Charles I accepts the Petition of Right, denying him the option of making forced loans and imprisonment at his personal command
(23 Aug)	assassination of Duke of Buckingham
(18 Oct)	fall of La Rochelle to King Louis XIII of France

1629 (Jan)	death of Susan de Vere, wife of Philip Herbert, Earl of Montgomery
(10 Mar)	King Charles I dissolves Parliament and begins eleven years of personal rule
(Apr)	peace with France through the Treaty of Susa
(Nov)	christening of Mary Sidney, daughter of **MSW's brother** Robert and Dorothy Percy Sidney; **probably a godchild of MSW**
1630 (10 Apr)	death of William Herbert, third Earl of Pembroke; his brother Philip Herbert becomes fourth Earl of Pembroke
(29 May)	birth of Prince Charles, later King Charles II (d. 1685)
(3 Jun)	Philip Herbert, fourth Earl of Pembroke, marries Lady Anne Clifford, widow of Richard Sackville, Earl of Dorset, and daughter of George Clifford, Earl of Cumberland; this union effectively breaks down in 1634
(5 Nov)	peace with Spain through the Treaty of Madrid
1631 (17 Feb)	funeral of Frances Walsingham/Sidney/Devereux/Burke, Countess of Essex and Clanricarde, widow of Sir Philip Sidney and Robert Devereux, Earl of Essex
1632 (Jan)	Viscount Wentworth appointed Lord Deputy of Ireland. Robert Sidney, second Earl of Leicester goes to Denmark with his sons, Philip and Algernon
(late?)	Van Dyck commissioned to paint a series of Sidney and related family portraits
1633 (6 Aug)	William Laud appointed Archbishop of Canterbury
(14 Oct)	birth of Prince James, later King James II (d. 1701)
1635 (15 Mar)	Archbishop Laud appointed as First Lord of the Treasury

(9 May)	France declares war on Spain
1636 (Apr)	**MSW's brother** Robert Sidney, second Earl of Leicester, appointed ambassador extraordinary to France; leaves England on 7 May accompanied by his sons, Philip and Algernon; arrives in Jun and serves there until May 1641; his wife, Dorothy Percy Sidney, manages the Penshurst estate and the building of their London residence, Leicester House, during his absences abroad
1637 (Jan)	Barbara Sidney Smythe, **sister of MSW**, marries Thomas Colepeper
1639 (Feb)	**MSW's brother** Robert Sidney, second Earl of Leicester, temporarily recalled from France (returned in Aug and sworn a privy councillor on 5 May). He is accompanied in France by his wife Dorothy Percy Sidney, Countess of Leicester, between Sep 1639 and Oct 1641
(11 Jul)	**MSW's niece** Dorothy Sidney marries at Penshurst Henry Spencer (1620–43), later Earl of Sunderland
(?)	**William Herbert, illegitimate son of MSW and William Herbert, third Earl of Pembroke, appointed captain under Sir Henry Herbert on Scottish campaign**
1640	King Charles I's 'Short Parliament' (13 Apr–5 May) 'Long Parliament' (30 Nov 1640–20 Apr 1653)
(Dec)	**William Herbert, illegitimate son of MSW and William Herbert, third Earl of Pembroke, given a 'brave living in Ireland' by King Charles I**
1641 (May)	**MSW's brother** Robert Sidney, second Earl of Leicester, and his sons, Philip and Algernon, recalled to England

(spring?)	birth of Henry Sidney (d. 1704), son of Robert and Dorothy Sidney and **MSW's nephew**, later Earl of Romney
(14 Jun)	Robert Sidney, second Earl of Leicester, appointed Lord Lieutenant of Ireland (but he never travels there)
(Jul)	Philip Herbert, fourth Earl of Pembroke and Montgomery, resigns as Lord Chamberlain
(Aug)	Robert Sidney, second Earl of Leicester, briefly returns to France until early Oct
(5 Sep)	birth of Robert Spencer (d. 1702), son of Dorothy Sidney Spencer (d. 1684), later second Earl of Sunderland
(Oct onwards)	Munster rebellion in Ireland
1642 (4 Jan)	King Charles I attempts to arrest the 'five members' of Parliament and leaves London; Robert Sidney, second Earl of Leicester, attempts to cross to Ireland but is recalled by the King
(Apr)	Philip and Algernon Sidney arrive in Ireland
(22 Apr)	**MSW wills her property Prouts, at Woodford Bridge (between Chigwell and Leytonstone), to her daughter Katherine, probably as part of her dowry**
(May–Jun)	Robert Sidney, second Earl of Leicester, serves as temporary Speaker of the House of Lords and is appointed Lord Lieutenant of Kent (replaced in Aug)
(22 Aug)	Outbreak of the First Civil War at Nottingham.
1643 (Jan)	Philip Herbert, fourth Earl of Pembroke and Montgomery, is one of the parliamentary commissioners sent to Oxford to offer peace propositions to King Charles I
(14 May)	death of King Louis XIII and accession of King Louis XIV of France
(13 June)	**MSW sells life interest in Chigwell properties for £10,000, probably for**

	equipage (military equipment) for her son William to join Prince Maurice's elite regiment, and for the dowry of her daughter Katherine, who marries John Lovet of Liscombe
(22 Jun)	Philip and Algernon Sidney leave Ireland
(15 Sep)	English royalists agree to a ceasefire in Ireland
(20 Sep)	death of Henry Spencer (b. 1620), first Earl of Sunderland, at the Battle of Newbury (indecisive)
(26 Sep)	Penshurst sequestered by the Kent county committee
(Nov)	Robert Sidney, second Earl of Leicester, replaced as Lord Lieutenant of Ireland by Earl of Ormond; the Scots agree to send an army to assist Parliament
(Dec)	**burial of John Lovet, son-in-law of MSW; Katherine later marries James Parry and has two sons, James and Philip Parry**
(?)	death of Barbara Sidney Smythe Colepeper, **sister of MSW**
1644 (Jan)	royalist parliament summoned at Oxford; Scottish army crosses into England to assist the Long Parliament
(15 Apr)	Algernon Sidney appointed colonel of a parliamentarian regiment of horse
(Jun)	Robert Sidney, second Earl of Leicester, leaves royalist Oxford and retires to Penshurst
(2 Jul)	Algernon Sidney serves as a parliamentarian cavalry officer at the Battle of Marston Moor (parliamentarian victory)
(Aug)	Battle of Lostwithiel (royalist victory)
(Oct)	second Battle of Newbury (indecisive)
1645 (18 Mar)	Algernon Sidney appointed colonel in cavalry regiment of the New Model Army and Governor of Chichester (10 May)

(19 May)	marriage of **MSW's nephew** Philip Sidney (1619–98), Viscount Lisle and later third Earl of Leicester, to Catherine Cecil (d. 1652)
1646 (21 Jan)	Algernon Sidney elected MP for Cardiff
(May)	surrender of King Charles I to Scots
(Jun)	Oxford surrenders to Parliament; end of the First Civil War
(18 Nov)	Philip Sidney, Viscount Lisle, appointed Lieutenant Governor of Ireland; Algernon Sidney appointed Governor of Dublin Castle
1646/48	**MSW pays poor relief assessment to Woodford parish church**
1647 (Jan)	Scots hand King Charles I over to Parliament
(1 Feb)	Philip and Algernon Sidney return to Ireland but both soon lose their posts there
(Jun)	King Charles I seized by the army
(Nov)	King Charles I escapes and flees to the Isle of Wight; Algernon Sidney is involved in the negotiations with the King
1648 (Apr–Aug)	Second Civil War
(Jun)	Algernon Sidney appointed Governor of Dover Castle (until May 1651)
(Jul)	Scottish invasion of England on behalf of King Charles I
(Aug)	Battle of Preston; defeat of the Scots; end of Second Civil War
(Dec)	Colonel Pride's Purge of Parliament Peace of Westphalia (a series of treaties signed during 1648) brings the end of the Thirty Years War
1649 (30 Jan)	execution of King Charles I; described by **MSW's nephew** Algernon Sidney as 'the justest and bravest act ... that ever was

	done in England or anywhere' (BL Add. MS 32680/9–10); watched from a nearby window by Philip Herbert, fourth Earl of Pembroke and Montgomery
(14 Feb)	Council of State set up (dissolved 20 Apr 1653), with Philip Herbert, fourth Earl of Pembroke and Montgomery, as one of its five peers; Charles II declared king in Edinburgh
(14 Mar)	death at Leicester House of Harry Spencer (b. 1643), son of Dorothy Sidney Spencer, Countess of Sunderland
(15 Mar)	Lucy Percy Hay, Countess of Carlisle and sister of Dorothy Percy Sidney, Countess of Leicester, imprisoned in the Tower of London (released 1 Oct 1650)
(16 Mar)	Kingship abolished
(9 Apr)	birth of Prince James (illegitimate, executed 1685), later Duke of Monmouth
(May)	England declared a free commonwealth
(14 Jun)	two of the royal children, Prince Henry, Duke of Gloucester, and Princess Elizabeth, are lodged at Penshurst (until 9 Aug 1650) having previously been in the charge of Algernon Percy, tenth Earl of Northumberland
(Dec)	Robert Sidney, second Earl of Leicester, accepts wardship of his nephew, Philip Smythe, Viscount Strangford
(?)	birth of **MSW's great-nephew** Robert Sidney (d. 1702), later Viscount Lisle and fourth Earl of Leicester
1650 (23 Jan)	death of Philip Herbert, fourth Earl of Pembroke and Montgomery
(22 Aug)	marriage at Penshurst of Isabella Sidney (b. 1634), daughter of Robert and Dorothy Sidney, to her cousin Philip Smythe, Viscount Strangford
1651 (Jan)	Charles II crowned King of Scots at Scone
(late Mar?)	**death of MSW**

(Aug)	Oliver Cromwell captures Perth and Stirling Castle surrenders to the English; Scottish army crosses into England
(3 Sep)	Battle of Worcester; defeat of Charles II leading to his flight to France (Oct)
(1 Dec)	Philip Herbert, fifth Earl of Pembroke, elected to the Council of State

List of Abbreviations of Frequently Referenced Works

ARC   The Ashgate Research Companion to the Sidneys, 2 vols, ed. Margaret P. Hannay, Mary Ellen Lamb and Michael G. Brennan (Farnham: Ashgate, 2015)

Arcadia   Sir Philip Sidney, The Countess of Pembroke's Arcadia, ed. with introduction and notes by Maurice Evans (London: Penguin Books, 1977)

AS   Sir Philip Sidney, Astrophil and Stella, in The Poems of Philip Sidney, ed. William A. Ringler (Oxford: Clarendon Press, 1962), 163–237

BM   Lady Mary Wroth, Pamphilia to Amphilanthus in Manuscript and Print, ed. Ilona Bell and Steven W. May, The Other Voice in Early Modern Europe: The Toronto Series, 59, Medieval and Renaissance Texts and Studies, Vol. 523 (Toronto and Tempe, Arizona: Iter Press, and Arizona Centre for Medieval and Renaissance Studies, 2017)

Cowell   John Cowell, The Interpreter, or, Book Containing the Signification of Words Wherein is Set Forth the True Meaning of All (London: F. Leach, 1607)

CWD   Lady Mary Wroth, 'Love's Victory [c. 1620]', in Renaissance Drama by Women: Texts and Documents, ed. S. P. Cerasano and Marion Wynne-Davies (London and New York: Routledge, 1996), 91–126 and 199–208

Davies   John Davies, The Holy Rood or Christ's Cross (London: Nick Butter, 1609)

Donne   John Donne, ed. John Carey (Oxford: Oxford University Press, 1990)

ELR	*English Literary Renaissance*
EMWW	Mary Wroth, *Love's Victory* [Huntington Manuscript], in *Early Modern Women's Writing: An Anthology 1560–1700*, ed. with introduction and notes by Paul Salzman, Oxford World's Classics (Oxford: Oxford University Press, 2000), 82–133
EMWRN	Lady Mary Wroth, *Love's Victory* [Huntington Manuscript], ed. Paul Salzman, Early Modern Women Research Network (Newcastle University, Australia, 2017), https://c21ch. newcastle.edu.au/emwrn.marywroth
Faerie Queene	Edmund Spenser, *The Faerie Queene*, ed. Thomas P. Roche with the assistance of C. Patrick O'Donnell Jr (London: Penguin, 1987)
Fraunce	Abraham Fraunce, *The Third Part of the Countess of Pembroke's Ivychurch entitled, Amintas Dale* (London: Thomas Orwin for Thomas Woodcocke, 1592)
Galatea	John Lyly, *Galatea* (1592), ed. Leah Scragg, Revels Student Editions (Manchester: Manchester University Press, 2012)
Gascoigne	George Gascoigne, *The Steel Glass: A Satire Compiled by George Gascoigne Esquire* (London: Richard Smith, 1576)
Greene	Robert Greene, *Greene's Never Too Late: or A Powder of Experience* (London: Thomas Orwin for Nicholas Ling and John Bushby, 1590)
Heroical Epistles	Ovid, *The Heroical Epistles of the Learned Poet Publius Ovidius Naso in English Verse, set out and Translated by George Turberville* (London, Henry Denham, 1567)
HLQ	*Huntington Library Quarterly*
HM	Huntington Manuscript
Kingsley-Smith	Jane Kingsley-Smith, *Cupid in Early Modern Literature and Culture* (Cambridge: Cambridge University Press, 2010)
Letters	*Domestic Politics and Family Absence: The Correspondence (1588–1621) of Robert Sidney, First Earl of Leicester, and Barbara Gamage Sidney, Countess of Leicester*, ed. Margaret P.

Hannay, Noel J. Kinnamon and Michael G. Brennan (Aldershot: Ashgate, 2005)

LM   Sir Philip Sidney, *The Lady of May*, in *Renaissance Drama: An Anthology of Plays and Entertainments*, ed. Arthur F. Kinney (Oxford: Blackwell, 1999), 35–44

Malfi   John Webster, *The Duchess of Malfi*, ed. John Russell Brown, Revels Plays, second ed. (Manchester: Manchester University Press, 2009)

Mascall   Leonard Mascall, *The First Book of Cattle, Wherein is Showed the Government of Oxen, Kine, Calves* (London: John Wolfe, 1587)

Menaphon   Robert Greene, *Arcadia or Menaphon* (London, W. Standsby for I. Smethwicke, 1616)

Meta.   *Ovid's Metamorphoses, The Arthur Golding Translation 1567*, ed. with introduction and notes by John Frederick Nims (Philadelphia: Paul Dry Books, 2000)

MSH *Works*   *The Collected Works of Mary Sidney Herbert, Countess of Pembroke*, 2 Vols, ed. Margaret P. Hannay, Noel J. Kinnamon and Michael G. Brennan (Oxford: Clarendon Press, 1998)

MSLW   Margaret Hannay, *Mary Sidney, Lady Wroth* (Farnham and Burlington, VT: Ashgate, 2010)

Old Arcadia   Sir Philip Sidney, *The Old Arcadia*, ed. with introduction and notes by Katherine Duncan Jones (Oxford: Oxford University Press, 1999)

OED   *Oxford English Dictionary* (Oxford: Oxford University Press, current online version: 2015)

PA   Lady Mary Wroth, *Pamphilia to Amphilanthus*, in *The Poems of Lady Mary Wroth*, ed. with introduction and notes by Josephine A. Roberts (Baton Rouge: Louisiana State University Press, 1983), 85–145

Parker   Henry Parker, *The Triumphs of Frances Petrarch* (London: John Cawood, 1555)

Peacham   Henry Peacham, *Minerva Britanna or A Garden of Heroical Devices Furnished and Adorned with Emblems and Impresas of Sundry Natures* (London: Wa. Dwight, 1612)

Phoenix	Margaret Hannay, *Philip's Phoenix: Mary Sidney, Countess of Pembroke* (Oxford: Oxford University Press, 1990)
PM	Penshurst Manuscript
PS *Poems*	*The Poems of Philip Sidney*, ed. William A. Ringler (Oxford: Clarendon Press, 1962)
Psalms	*The Sidney Psalter: The Psalms of Sir Philip and Mary Sidney*, ed. Hannibal Hamlin, Michael G. Brennan, Margaret P. Hannay and Noel J. Kinnamon (Oxford: Oxford University Press, 2009)
R	*Lady Mary Wroth's Love's Victory: The Penshurst Manuscript*, ed. Michael G. Brennan (London: The Roxburghe Club, 1988)
RS *Poems*	*The Poems of Robert Sidney*, edited from the Poet's Autograph Notebook with introduction and commentary by P. J. Croft (Oxford: Clarendon Press, 1984)
SJ	*Sidney Journal*
SM	Mary Wroth, *Loves Victorie*, ed. Marta Straznicky, in *Women's Household Drama*, ed. Marta Straznicky and Sara Mueller, *The Other Voice in Early Modern Europe: The Toronto Series, 66*, Medieval and Renaissance Texts and Studies, Vol. 544 (Toronto and Tempe: Iter Press and Arizona Centre for Medieval and Renaissance Studies, 2017), 15–138
Tilley	Morris Palmer Tilley, *A Dictionary of Proverbs in England in the Sixteenth and Seventeenth Centuries* (Ann Arbor: University of Michigan Press, 1950)
Urania I	Lady Mary Wroth, *The First Part of the Countess of Montgomery's Urania*, ed. Josephine A. Roberts, Renaissance English Text Society, Vol. 140 (Tempe, Arizona: Arizona Center for Medieval and Renaissance Studies, 2005)
Urania II	Lady Mary Wroth, *The Second Part of the Countess of Montgomery's Urania*, ed. Josephine A. Roberts, completed by Suzanne Gossett and Janel Mueller, Medieval and Renaissance Texts and Studies, Vol. 211

	(Tempe, Arizona: Renaissance English Text Society in Conjunction with Arizona Center for Medieval and Renaissance Studies, 1999)
WH *Poems*	William Herbert, *Poems Written by the Right Honourable William, Earl of Pembroke, Lord Steward of His Majesty's Household, whereof many were answered by way of repartee by Sir Benjamin Rudyerd, Knight* (London: Matthew Inman for James Magnes, 1660)
Wroth *Poems*	*The Poems of Lady Mary Wroth*, ed. with introduction and notes by Josephine A. Roberts (Baton Rouge: Louisiana State University Press, 1983)

All references to texts by Ben Jonson are to editions in the online version of *The Cambridge Edition of the Works of Ben Jonson*, ed. David Bevington, Martin Butler and Ian Donaldson (Cambridge: Cambridge University Press, 2012).

References to Shakespeare are to William Shakespeare, *The Complete Works*, ed. Stanley Wells and Gary Taylor (Oxford: Clarendon Press, 1988).

Biblical references are to the King James Bible (1611).

Introduction

I. THE DRAMATIST AND HER WORK

Lady Mary Wroth was born on 18 October 1587, eight months after the magnificent state funeral of her more famous uncle, Sir Philip Sidney (1554–86). As well as following the literary legacy of Sir Philip and the Sidney family, Wroth challenged gender and literary conventions of the time by composing a sonnet sequence, a long prose romance in two parts and, perhaps most surprisingly, an original five-act play. Wroth's decision to write a play might seem remarkable to those who are familiar only with early modern commercial theatre, but is much less so when seen in the context of the Sidney–Herbert coterie and their extensive body of writing. Sir Philip Sidney had composed *The Lady of May*, a dramatic entertainment staged in 1578 or 1579, and Wroth's aunt, Mary Sidney Herbert, published *Antonius*, a translation of Robert Garnier's *Marc Antoine*, in 1592. The family's participation in court and household drama also challenges definitions of *Love's Victory* as a 'closet' drama, intended for reading rather than theatrical performance. Although we have no records of a production of *Love's Victory* in Wroth's time, it is eminently performable, as its relatively recent stage history shows. The text, which was never printed in Wroth's lifetime, suggests that *Love's Victory* was written with performance in mind. It exists in two holograph manuscripts, both written in Wroth's italic hand, as Peter Croft and Josephine Roberts identified.[1] The Huntington Manuscript (*HM*) may have been constructed for a household performance, whilst the Penshurst Manuscript (*PM*) contains more detailed stage directions, perhaps to recall or suggest a performance. Whether Wroth's two manuscripts were written for silent or communal reading with an imagined performance in mind, or to script or record an actual performance, is impossible to determine, but a theatrical imagination is certainly at work in each. The Penshurst Manuscript includes eight more scenes than the shorter Huntington Manuscript, and is privately owned by Viscount De L'Isle, a collateral descendant of Lady Mary Wroth.[2]

I

This edition publishes an authorized version of the Penshurst Manuscript to make it widely available to readers.

Unlike the early printed texts of plays written for the commercial theatres (in which the playing company rather than the playwright owned the intellectual copyright of the scripts), the two manuscripts of *Love's Victory* give a material sense of Wroth's authorial hand controlling the drama. Furthermore, she repeatedly asserts her authorial identity as a Sidney writer by using a signature mark, the *S fermé* (a slashed S), to sign some pages in each of the manuscripts (see Fig. 7 p. 55). As Ilona Bell explains, the *S fermé* was used by Wroth's aunt, Mary Sidney Herbert, Countess of Pembroke (1561–1621) and by the French monarchy and aristocracy as a *signe critique* to mark secret communications.[3] Defining herself thus as a Sidney allies Wroth with her female ancestors – her aunt, and her grandmother Lady Mary Dudley Sidney (1531–86) – rather than with her husband Sir Robert Wroth, whom she married on 27 September 1604. Her Sidney signature may also reflect the fact that, when she wrote *Love's Victory*, she was a widow. Robert Wroth died on 14 March 1614 and the death of their son James Wroth on 5 July 1616, aged only two years and five months, cut off the biological continuation of Mary's 'Wroth' identity, although she retained property given to her by Sir Robert in her marriage jointure, and continued to live in Essex at Loughton, known as 'the Honourable Lady Wroth', until at least 1644, and probably until her death in late March 1651 (*MSLW*, 20–1, 305).[4]

Wroth's family alliances with her Sidney relatives and the powerful Herbert family, Earls of Pembroke, into which her aunt married, remained strong throughout her life. She was the eldest of the eleven children of Sir Robert Sidney, later Earl of Leicester (1563–1626), and Barbara Gamage (1562–1621), the child and sole heir of John Gamage of Coity Castle in Glamorganshire. Henry Herbert, second Earl of Pembroke, the husband of Wroth's aunt, arranged Barbara and Robert's marriage, and the Sidney and Herbert families made regular visits to each other's households: the Sidney home at Penshurst Place in Kent, the Pembroke estates in Wiltshire and their London residence, Baynard's Castle. From London, Wroth's family maintained their important connections with the Elizabethan and Stuart court. Her uncle Sir Philip Sidney and her father Robert Sidney both defended Queen Elizabeth I's Protestant interests in the Netherlands, successively holding appointments as Governor of Flushing. As a result, Wroth grew up spending time with her mother and siblings at Penshurst Place and with her cousins and her aunt and uncle in Wiltshire and in London, with periodic family visits to the Netherlands to see her father. All these places and people influenced her writing.

At Baynard's Castle, Mary and her younger siblings were tutored in courtly accomplishments, as well as reading and writing. In 1600 Robert Sidney's agent at court, Rowland Whyte, reported to Robert that his children 'are kept at their books, they dance, they sing, they play on the lute'. Whyte had already told him, five years before, that Mary was 'very forward in her learning, writing and other exercises she is put to, as dancing and the virginals'.[5] Since the Penshurst portrait (Fig. 1 p. 4) depicts a young woman (often assumed to be Wroth) holding an archlute, it is likely that she was able to play this instrument. Gavin Alexander has pointed out that its thirteen sets of strings 'pronounce quite emphatically the subject's practical musicianship'.[6] In her adult life, some of Wroth's verses were set to music, and songs are an important feature of *Love's Victory*, drawing on the musical training and expertise which were a strong part of the Sidney household.

Wroth's education in dancing proved equally fruitful.[7] In 1602 she danced before Queen Elizabeth, the equivalent of an 'audition' for a role at court and suitability for courtship and marriage (*MSLW*, 84). However, when the Sidney family's court connections faltered from 1601 (due to the death of the second Earl of Pembroke, the fall of Robert Devereux, Earl of Essex, and Robert Sidney's dispute with Henry Brooke, Lord Cobham), so did Mary's chances of an elite aristocratic marriage. A match with Sir Robert Wroth (1576–1614), from a prominent gentry family in Essex, well-known and respected by her parents, was arranged, with negotiations for her dowry probably beginning in 1601 when she was just thirteen (Thomas Nevitt, 'Memorial', British Library MS Add. 12066, cited by Hannay, *MSLW*, 99). Arrangements for the wedding accelerated in the summer of 1604, and on 27 September Mary was married to Wroth at Penshurst Place, with her mother, her siblings, her aunt the dowager Countess of Pembroke, and her cousins William Herbert (1580–1630), now third Earl of Pembroke, Anne Herbert (1583–1606) and Philip Herbert (1584–1650) all present.

The Sidneys' court position grew stronger under the influence of King James I and his Queen, Anne of Denmark. In 1603 Robert Sidney was appointed Lord Chamberlain of Queen Anne's household, a role which involved supervising court entertainments. On

1 John de Critz, Portrait of Lady Mary Wroth (1587–1651), daughter of Robert Sidney, first Earl of Leicester, and wife of Sir Robert Wroth. Penshurst portrait. Full-length, holding an archlute. Oil on canvas. 80 in by 44 in. By kind permission of Viscount De L'Isle from his private collection.

6 January 1605, the newly married Lady Wroth danced with the Queen in *The Masque of Blackness*, written by Ben Jonson. For this winter season at court, and on numerous other occasions, she stayed with her family at Baynard's Castle, the home of her Pembroke cousins. In 1608 she attended the Queen's next masque, *The Masque of Beauty*, along with her cousins William Herbert, Earl of Pembroke, and Philip Herbert, Earl of Montgomery, and their wives (Susan, Countess of Montgomery, was one of the masquers).

Growing up alongside her Herbert relatives, Wroth developed a lifelong passion for her eldest cousin, William Herbert. However, her constancy was not matched by his. In 1601 he was sent to Fleet Prison for fathering a child with Queen Elizabeth's lady-in-waiting, Mary Fitton, but refusing to marry her (*MSLW*, 80). Wroth's writings are full of troubled romantic relationships which, at one level, rewrite her own frustrated love for her cousin. They exchanged poems and music; significantly, manuscript copies of Herbert's poem 'Elegy' and Wroth's poem 'Penshurst Mount' offer strong evidence that they made clandestine vows of marriage and sexually consummated their relationship before they were both married to other people.[8] Herbert married the wealthy heiress Lady Mary Talbot on 4 November 1604, just a week after Mary's wedding to Robert Wroth.

It seems there were difficulties immediately after the Wroths' wedding, since Robert Wroth told his father-in-law that 'there was somewhat that doth discontent him', though he could not take 'any exceptions to his wife nor her carriage towards him', leading Robert Sidney to fear 'It were very soon for any unkindnesses to begin' between the newlyweds (*Letters*, 123). There has been much speculation that the marriage was not a happy one. However, suggestions that Robert Wroth was a boorish or cruel husband owe more to Wroth's fiction than to documentary evidence, as Margaret Hannay has pointed out (*MSLW*, 159–62). Robert Sidney noted Wroth's 'exceeding kindness' to his wife in thinking about her future when he was ill in 1608 (*Letters*, 140), an impression substantiated by his will, which provided carefully for 'my well-beloved wife, Dame Mary Wroth'. In a codicil of 7 March 1614, he made sure that his 'dear and very loving wife' should have £1000 to help her clear debts, and should retain control of her own library, jewels and clothes (*MSLW*, 170–1). The couple may have lost children through miscarriage in the ten years before the birth of their son James in February 1614, just before Robert Wroth's death.[9] Thanks to his provision for her, she was able to continue living in Essex until her own death, in spite of some financial difficulties due to his debts and disputes with Wroth relatives.

Whatever emotions existed between the couple probably did not extinguish Wroth's feelings for her cousin, William Herbert. Robert Wroth and others inside the family coterie may have been aware that he did not hold first place in her affections, perhaps prompting Ben Jonson's remark to Drummond that Wroth was 'unworthily married on a jealous husband.'[10] During her married life, Lady Mary Wroth continued to see William Herbert and her Sidney–Herbert relations in London and Penshurst, and at her Wroth family homes in Essex, Durance and Loughton Hall. In 1607, for example, Robert Sidney told his wife he was going to Loughton 'to see your daughter and to meet my Lord Pembroke there' (*Letters*, 129).

Wroth and her husband were celebrated for their hospitality, frequently entertaining family, friends and the royal court in aristocratic style – with music, feasting and dancing – at their Essex residences. Robert Wroth's duties as the King's Forester (celebrated in Ben Jonson's poem 'To Sir Robert Wroth')[11] included accommodating James I and the court on his frequent hunting trips to Essex, and he rebuilt Loughton after 1608 for this purpose.[12] In 1609, Robert Sidney noted that Lady Mary Wroth 'must be at home because the King will be in the forest' (*Letters*, 142). Robert Sidney's correspondence gives invaluable evidence of Wroth's extended visits to Baynard's Castle and to Penshurst, through which she maintained strong relationships with her Sidney and Herbert relations during her marriage and especially after she was widowed. We have no documentary evidence of how Wroth's relationship with Herbert developed until 1624, when she had twins, Katherine and William, fathered by him. Herbert had no surviving legitimate children so the naming of their son was significant. Wroth's neighbour Sir Edward Herbert of Cherbury (a relative of William's) congratulated her with 'A merry Rhyme sent to the Lady Wroth upon the birth of My Lord of Pembroke's Child, born in the Spring', which hoped that the summer would 'add a Rose' to the comic muse celebrating the happy moment, and allow the family to 'oppose / The tragic buskins of our foes'. Edward Herbert's references to drama in the comic muse and 'tragic buskins' suggest an awareness of Wroth as a fellow dramatist and his own manuscript play *The Amazon* may be a response to *Love's Victory*, possibly written as an entertainment for Wroth and William Herbert.[13]

Work

Lady Mary Wroth's writing, including her tragicomedy *Love's Victory*, allowed her to reflect on and shape the emotional experiences of her life. Her sonnet sequence *Pamphilia to Amphilanthus* and many of the love stories in her epic two-part prose romance *The Countess of Montgomery's Urania* have been widely regarded as multiple rewritings of Wroth's relationship with William Herbert. The position of the agonized lover from Petrarchan sonnet tradition is deftly appropriated by Wroth in her own sonnets, with clear comparisons to the constancy of Wroth's affections in comparison with Herbert's licentiousness. Many of the poems that she collected in a fair-copy manuscript (held in the Folger Shakespeare Library)[14] were printed in revised form at the end of the first part of *Urania* (referred to hereafter as *Urania I*), which was published in 1621. The protagonist and antagonist of the romance – Princess Pamphilia and her faithless lover Amphilanthus (the 'lover of two'),[15] whose relationship is played out, inconclusively, across the two lengthy narratives – are generally assumed to be avatars of Wroth and Herbert. *Urania* offers numerous avatars for other members of the Sidney–Herbert households in its story of the European adventures of the two great dynasties of Morea and Naples, but it is also a sharp, thinly disguised satire of figures at the Jacobean court. When Wroth published the first part in 1621, Sir Edward Denny accused her of depicting him as the jealous father-in-law of Sirelius, damaging his reputation and that of others at court. Wroth claimed that she had not intended this, and that she had carefully 'caused the sale of [her book] to be forbidden' (though both claims are disputable).[16] She continued a lengthy second part of the *Urania* in manuscript (conventionally referred to as *Urania II*).

It would do Wroth a disservice to suggest that her literary output was focused only on exploring her family connections and her relationship with Herbert. Margaret Hannay rightly points out that, as the author of over 175 poems (including a sonnet sequence), a drama and some thousand pages of a prose romance, surely Lady Mary Wroth 'loved to write as much as she loved her cousin'.[17] We know from accounts of the transmission of Jonson's 'To Penshurst' and her sonnets that Wroth's poetry was circulating in manuscript copies amongst members of the family and their households before she revised some of them for publication.[18] As Michael G. Brennan argues, Ben Jonson's extended stay at Penshurst in 1611 was probably instrumental in shaping Wroth's identity as a writer.[19] Jonson dedicated his play *The Alchemist* (performed 1610; published 1612) to her, arguing that 'it is your value, that remembers where, when and to whom it was kindled', suggesting that she was party to its composition.[20] Perhaps she, in turn, was inspired to write drama.

2. DATE

We cannot be certain when *Love's Victory* was written, although it was probably between 1617 and 1621, during the span of Wroth's major literary activity. *PM* is written on paper whose watermark matches that of the manuscript copy of her poems in the Folger Library (V.a.104), as suggested by Garth Bond; Margaret Hannay adds that the same ruling, at the top and left-hand margins, is found on the final leaves of the Folger manuscript and on *PM*, implying that it was written, or at least transcribed, shortly after the private collection of poems, possibly as a companion piece.[21] We know that the Folger manuscript predates the printing of the *Urania*, but we do not know how long before 1621 the two manuscripts were written. The same watermark also appears on one of Robert Sidney's letters dated 25 October 1617 in London, perhaps suggesting an earlier date for *PM*. Margaret Hannay proposes a date of 1619–20, coinciding with the marriage of Lady Mary Wroth's sister, Barbara. This would match the date at which Sir Edward Dering, who owned the Huntington Manuscript, began purchasing copies of play-books.[22] He did so between 1619 and 1624 and his country house, Surrenden (about 14 miles from Penshurst), was the venue for household performances. The two manuscripts also show revisions to the script, so they may have been transcribed at different times; it is possible that *HM* was prepared for a performance, and the finely bound *PM* may have been intended to serve as a memento for future generations.

3. LITERARY INTERTEXTS

Ben Jonson's assertion in a poem addressed to Wroth that his muses will 'say you are / A Sidney' and readers will 'Know you to be a Sidney, though unnamed',[23] highlights the Sidney–Herbert family writings as an immediate literary context for Wroth. The pastoral setting of *Love's Victory* owes much to her uncle Sir Philip Sidney's pastoral romance *The Countess of Pembroke's Arcadia*, published and popularized by its dedicatee, Mary Sidney Herbert. Wroth's shepherdess Climeana explicitly acknowledges this literary debt, saying she is a stranger by birth to the play's world and 'in Arcadia ever kept my sheep' (3.3.67–8). Rustic in *Love's Victory* draws on Sir Philip's comic shepherd Dametas, whilst the structure of the *Arcadia* (c. 1577 – c. 1582, pr. 1590, 1593, 1598), interspersing the narrative with 'Eclogues' featuring songs and lyrics, is adapted in *Love's Victory*, where the shepherd community meet to sing songs or play games in Acts 1, 2 and 4. Pastoral as a leisurely retreat by courtly figures was a literary convention going back to Virgil's *Eclogues* and, more recently, to Spenser's *The Shepheardes Calendar* (1579), which all the Sidney writers imitated. Peter Croft has drawn attention to the verbal similarities between the words of Wroth's shepherds in *Love's Victory* and the pastoral poems of her father Robert Sidney.[24] Mary Sidney Herbert's 'Dialogue Between Two Shepherds, Thenot and Piers' (c. 1599) appropriates pastoral to praise Queen Elizabeth I (as Sir Philip Sidney had done in *The Lady of May*), and William Herbert's lyric 'Dear, leave thy home and come with me' replies to Christopher Marlowe's pastoral poem 'Come live with me and be my love',[25] as had two members of the wider Sidney–Herbert coterie: Walter Raleigh (a cousin of Barbara Gamage) and John Donne.[26] Wroth's *Urania II* refers obliquely back to that family tradition of pastoral in the figure of Lamprino, who admits he has presented his beloved with 'many several copies' of his poems 'and small romances' since 'she did delight in those harmless pretty expressions of wit' (210). Wroth rewrites pastoral romance from a woman's perspective; in *Urania II*, for example, Pamphilia's feelings are written in a 'little book of gold' and handed to her from a magical fountain (307), while *Love's Victory* reimagines female agency in romance through pastoral games, songs and music.

Wroth follows pastoral and family tradition in drawing on the pantheon of classical gods – an alternative to the Sidneys' Protestant Christian orthodoxy – to preside over the action of *Love's Victory*. For example, Sir Philip Sidney's portrayal of Prince Pyrocles in disguise as Zelmane, an Amazon who follows Diana, influences Wroth's depictions of Diana's followers in *Urania*; these intertexts inform the character of Silvesta in *Love's Victory*, who dedicates herself to Diana and to a life of chastity. The gods of love, Venus and Cupid, who are the controlling deities of *Love's Victory*, feature frequently in early modern sonnet sequences, including those of the Sidney–Herbert writers. They are especially prominent in Sir Philip Sidney's sonnet sequence *Astrophil and Stella* (c. 1582/3, pr. 1591,

1598), which was largely responsible for popularising the Petrarchan courtly love tradition in English. These sonnets were certainly known to Wroth. A manuscript of miscellaneous Sidney writings from Penshurst includes a selection of sonnets from *Astrophil and Stella* copied out in an immature hand, possibly by Katherine (Mary's sister) as Peter Croft has noted, or maybe by Lady Mary Wroth herself, whose own formal italic hand can be seen in both manuscripts of *Love's Victory*.[27] Mary Sidney Herbert also participated in the Sidneian dialogue with Petrarch, translating 'The Triumph of Death' from his *Trionfi* sequence, which also included 'The Triumph of Love' and 'The Triumph of Chastity'.[28] From this context Wroth learned many of the literary conventions of courtly love: the distinction between bodily desire and transcendent love as a form of worship; the paradoxical experience of love as a painful pleasure, or a burning frost; desire as unfulfilled, imaged as a never-ending journey or labour, or a confusing labyrinth of twists and turns. Wroth's appropriation of Petrarchan conventions in her own sonnet sequence, *Pamphilia to Amphilanthus*, carries over into *Love's Victory*, especially in the male lovers' worship of their mistresses. As well as adopting the typical tropes of the courtly lover in occasional phrases, these characters often express themselves in partial or complete sonnets which are embedded in their speeches.

Wroth's play was influenced by another literary mode of worship in the form of the Sidney Psalter, a remarkably deft poetic versification of the Psalms of David begun by Sir Philip Sidney and Mary Sidney Herbert which she completed after Sidney's death, by 1594. The songs of the priests and the appeals to Venus and Cupid in *Love's Victory* develop the tradition of singing the psalms which Sir Philip Sidney had referred to in his *Defence of Poetry* (also known as *Apology for Poetry*, both published in 1595), noting that 'the name Psalms being interpreted, is nothing but songs', while John Donne wrote that the Sidneys' verse translations 'teach us *how* to sing'.[29]

Wroth's choice to write drama, even though it was extraordinary in the context of professional theatre, had important precedents in her family. Sir Philip Sidney's *Defence of Poetry* included praise of plays as 'excelling parts of Poetry' when they obeyed the classical unities of time and place, and he had written a short entertainment, *The Lady of May*, for one of Queen Elizabeth I's two visits (6–16 May 1578 and 1–2 May 1579) to Wanstead, the house of his uncle, Robert Dudley, Earl of Leicester.[30] The highly political nature of Sidney's entertainment, commenting obliquely on the potential

suitors for the Queen's hand, provided a precedent which Lady
Mary Wroth may have had in mind when addressing an imagined
audience of 'princes' in *Love's Victory*.[31] Even more important in this
regard was the influence of her aunt, Mary Sidney Herbert. *Antonius*,
her 1590 English translation of Robert Garnier's *Marc Antonie*,
showed Wroth that women could write plays.[32] The lovers' self-
sacrifices leading to 'love's tragedy' in 5.4.71–2 may have been
influenced by the tragic suicides of Antony and Cleopatra in her
aunt's drama. Both Mary Sidney Herbert and Mary Wroth may
possibly have been aware of an earlier family pioneer: Lady Jane
Lumley, the cousin of their mother and grandmother respectively.
Her prose translation of Euripides's tragedy *Iphigenia at Aulis* into
English in c. 1557 was the first of its kind, and the first play by an
English woman. It too dramatized heroic female self-sacrifice.[33]
Both parts of Wroth's *Urania* make frequent references to theatrical
spaces and performances, such as the enchanted 'round building
like a Theater, carved curiously' where Pamphilia and Urania are
trapped (*Urania I*, 372–4), the pastoral or 'very pretty show' presented to Pamphilia (*Urania II*, 113–15) or Rodomandro's entertainment for the Morean Court (*Urania II*, 46–9), which demonstrates
a detailed knowledge of the practical details of staging a masque.[34]
Court drama, a fundamental part of the Sidney–Herbert cousins'
experience, gives emotional resonance to these theatrical metaphors,
as Gary Waller has pointed out.[35] The fate of Lindamira, another
avatar for Wroth, suggests that she was keenly aware of the power
of performance and also its ephemeral nature. Lindamira, rejected
from 'Love's Court', is 'like one in a gay masque', who, the following
morning, finds herself in her 'old clothes again, and no appearance
of what was' (*Urania I*, 500).

4. *LOVE'S VICTORY* AND ITS DRAMATIC INTERTEXTS

Many aspects of *Love's Victory* draw on Wroth's experiences of
theatre at court, both as a performer – in *The Masque of Blackness*
(1605) – and as a spectator, the latter probably enhanced by her
father Robert Sidney's supervision of entertainments in Queen
Anne's court. Immediately after *Blackness* on 6 January 1605, the
season of Christmas Revels continued with productions of *Henry V*
and Jonson's *Every Man Out of His Humour* on subsequent days,
both performed by members of Shakespeare's company, the King's
Men.[36] We do not know whether Wroth saw other plays of that

season – which included Shakespeare's *Othello*, *The Merry Wives of Windsor*, *Measure for Measure*, *The Comedy of Errors* and *The Merchant of Venice* as well as Jonson's *Every Man In His Humour*,[37] Chapman's *All Fools* and Heywood's *How to Learn of a Woman to Woo* (performed by the Queen's Men) – or, later, such as the performances of *The Winter's Tale*, *The Alchemist* (which Jonson dedicated to her), *The Tempest* and *Much Ado About Nothing* in the seasons of 1611–13.[38] As well as possibly seeing these court performances, Wroth would have had access to all Jonson's texts in print by 1616 with the publication of his *Works*, and probably to some of Shakespeare's too; her cousins William and Philip Herbert were the dedicatees of the First Folio of Shakespeare's plays (1623). The commentary notes in this edition record some of the play's striking verbal parallels with Shakespeare's work, and broader connections are drawn in Paul Salzman and Marion Wynne-Davies's collection *Mary Wroth and Shakespeare*.[39]

Venus and Cupid

Wroth's attendance at *The Masque of Beauty* (1608) and familiarity with Ben Jonson's masques – including *The Haddington Masque* (9 February 1608) in which William and Philip Herbert appeared, *Love Freed from Ignorance and Folly* (3 February 1611) in which her sister Philippa performed and *Love Restored* (6 January 1612) – would all have given her ideas for the characters of Venus and Cupid, the overarching deities of her play who vow revenge on the mortals. In addition John Fletcher's play *Cupid's Revenge* was presented at court on 5 January 1612, the night before *Love Restored*, with repeat performances on 1 and 9 January 1613,[40] and Wroth may also have seen Robert White's masque *Cupid's Banishment* (1617) with female performers.[41] White's Cupid complains ('What, are we gods and bear no greater sway? / Is Cupid dead and Venus quite forgot?') like the deities of *Love's Victory*, but he takes no revenge.[42] Fletcher's and Wroth's Cupids both take revenge but with different consequences: in Fletcher's tragedy, the Duke's family desecrate Cupid's temples only to be shown that '*Cupid's* revenge is mighty' (C1) by all dying for love.[43] Wroth's *Love's Victory* is less bloody, imitating the structure of the court masque, in which a threatening anti-masque is followed by a masque sequence that restores order. Unlike Fletcher's play, *Love's Victory* features both Venus and Cupid.

Wroth depicts Venus and Cupid in a relationship of mutual dependency and competition, as do *Astrophil and Stella* and her own

Pamphilia to Amphilanthus.[44] The shifting power dynamic between Venus and Cupid is highlighted in choric prologues to each of the five acts in *PM* (two of which are missing from *HM*). Venus is a commanding maternal figure in 1.1 and 1.4, though she acknowledges she that has been wounded by Cupid's arrow herself and relies on him to reform the mortals. A similar relationship opens *The Haddington Masque*, where Venus complains she is 'undone' and seeks to bring Cupid back under her command.[45] A further, hitherto unnoticed influence on Wroth's Venus and Cupid, is a long poem by the Italian visitor Antimo Galli, dedicated to Elizabeth Talbot (the sister of William Herbert's wife Mary), describing his experience of attending a masque. Scholars have noted that Galli praises Lady Mary Wroth in stanza 70 (B2v), but not the similarities between the poem's opening and that of her play. *Love's Victory* opens with Venus's complaint: 'Cupid, methinks we have too long been still, / And that these people grow to scorn our will' (1.1.1–2). Having commanded him to remove his blindfold and use his bow and arrow on the mortals, she is not satisfied by the end of the act: 'Fie, this is nothing! What? Is this your care?' (1.4.1). Similar details feature in the opening stanza of Galli's poem (which more closely describes the opening of *The Haddington Masque* than *The Masque of Beauty*):[46]

> Amor [Cupid] has been sleeping more than usual on his mother's bosom, so she threatens him, and shouts: 'Lazy child, you make your mother utterly unhappy, she who relies on you. Take your darts and quiver, and make sure that there are more sighs and cries as a result of your shots. Look, wretched child, I foresee that you will be shamed and mocked for your contrariness.'[47]

As in *Love's Victory*, Cupid takes 'the blindfold from his eyes' in stanza 4 of Galli's poem before descending to earth.

The relationship between Venus and Cupid changes at different points in the two manuscripts of *Love's Victory*. After Venus's maternal chastisements in 1.4, there is a brief interlude celebrating Cupid's triumph alongside Venus's glory in 2.3 (introducing Act 3). *PM*'s stage direction 'VENUS'S PRIESTS *to Love or his praise*' suggests that the priests are the speakers for the 32 lines which follow, so this edition inserts a speech heading for them at this point; *HM* lacks a stage direction or any mention of the priests in this scene, and attributes the lines praising Cupid to Venus, thus clearly marking a shift in status between mother and son. Their scene concluding Act

3 and looking forward to Act 4 (missing from *HM*, which instead has a blank page with only a speech heading for Venus) depicts Venus as still firmly in control, protesting that the Cupid's torture of the mortals is 'not enough' and insisting on the infliction of more pain (3.4.7). The dialogue at the end of Act 4 exists in both manuscripts, but lines for both Venus and Cupid have been added and then deleted in *HM*. This may indicate that 3.4 was deliberately omitted to create a different dramatic effect. Marta Straznicky has suggested that the Huntington script may have been designed like a court entertainment for an imagined aristocratic audience, including the 'princes' mentioned by Venus and her priests at 1.4.31, 2.3.6 and 4.2.37–8.[48] In both manuscripts, Cupid has become the controlling deity by the end of Act 4: Venus and her priests appeal to him to 'hold thy hand' and show mercy to the pitiful, suffering mortals rather than continue his tyrannical rule over their hearts (4.2.3). He ignores this and determines to inflict 'more pain' (4.2.14), steering the play towards tragedy before Venus intervenes to create love's victory at the end of Act 5 of *PM*.

Quite what constitutes love's victory, and how it is achieved, is left open to interpretation, literally so in the truncated Huntington Manuscript, which ends after 5.1.105. Indeed, what or who the term 'love' refers to is often unclear in Wroth's text: both Venus and Cupid were referred to as 'Love' in Wroth's time, and the characters' frequent appeals to 'love' in the play – as well as Wroth's inconsistent capitalisation – often make it difficult to ascertain whether characters are referring to 'love' as a concept or addressing Venus and/or Cupid as love's avatars. In terms of Venus's revenge plot, the characters' determination to sacrifice their lives for love certainly demonstrates love's 'sacred power' (3.4.6) over life and death. In the first four acts the lovers' complaints that they will die for love are a courtly convention, reaching a climax when the newly reconciled lovers Simeana and Lissius protest, in turn, that 'thou shalt see me die / For having wronged thee with my jealousy' and 'Alas, I die for thee. / What pleasure can thy death then bring to me?' (4.1.299–302). The resolution to their quarrel functions dramatically to purge the play of flamboyant Petrarchan flourishes, and in Act 5 the idea of dying for love shifts from a metaphor into a material reality for Musella, Philisses, Silvesta and the Forester. The courtly convention of burning with zealous love is translated into a vision of martyrdom in the Forester's dream of Silvesta being 'tied / Fast to a stake' where 'fire' will 'kiss with heat those most unmatchèd limbs' and she will 'to those flames a sacred offering be' (5.6.5–7, 10). The Forester's pledge to take Silvesta's place so that his 'faith to honour' Venus will 'shine bright' (5.7.44), suggests he will enact the physical sacrifice imagined in his dream.

The declaration of love's victory in 5.7 also marks the conclusion of Venus and Cupid's efforts to influence the emotional journeys of characters over the course of the play: their first awakening to love, their learning to balance the expression and control of passion, and, finally, the achievement of an ideal love combining desire, chastity and constancy. Wroth drew on the model of court entertainments like *The Haddington Masque* (1608), *Love Freed from Ignorance and Folly* (1611), *Love Restored* (1612) and *Cupid's Banishment* (1617),[49] in which Cupid's desires are conquered to establish a socially and spiritually acceptable form of love. Chastity is a key facet of this conception of love: contrary to the connotations of this term in modern usage, chastity in the early modern period referred not only to abstention from sex but also to sexual continence within marriage (hence Silvesta bidding Philisses and Musella to live in 'chaste love' at the end of the play – 5.7.97). After Wroth's marriage, Nathaniel Baxter wrote a poem referring to her as a personification of *'Agape'*, the Greek term for the highest form of chaste, spiritual love:

> *Agape* shows thy composition:
> Love it is called in our dialect,
> Eros is venery; but this dilection [spiritual love],
> Chaste, holy, modest, divine and perfect.[50]

Chastity is celebrated as a pure form of love in marriage in *Cupid's Banishment*, where the goddess Diana and all the young 'ladies' banish Cupid and usher in Hymen, the god of marriage.[51] Wroth imagined a dramatic pattern of just this type in *Urania II*, in her detailed description of a court masque presented by Rodomandro, Duke of Tartaria. Here, Cupid pursues the 'stragglers' and 'runaways' from love and must then surrender his arrows and his 'wanton fire' to Honour who is the 'Monarch of Love'. The concluding song states unequivocally: 'Desire should not be styled love / But with honour's wings to move, / Bright love tells us this.'[52] A harmonious blending of love and chastity is achieved by the end of *Love's Victory*, most obviously when Silvesta, dedicated to Diana and chastity, becomes the 'instrument ordained' by which Venus engineers the plot's conclusion (5.7.71–2). The thwarting of Rustic's match with Musella in Act 5 also demonstrates love's victory over

the practice of arranged marriage and particularly matches arranged
for financial gain, echoing the key principle of Jonson's masque *Love
Restored*, where Cupid triumphs over Plutus 'the god of money who
has stolen Love's ensigns'.[53]

In *Love's Victory* the presentation of Venus and Cupid '*appearing in glory*' (2.3.0.SD) on stage is an opportunity for dramatic
spectacle, following in the tradition of court entertainments. The
stage spectacle is a material means of restoring the gods' 'ancient
glory' (1.1.33) in the eyes of spectators. Stage directions place Venus
and Cupid in the Temple in 1.1, 2.3, 5.4 and 5.7, and '*appearing in
the clouds*' (1.4.0SD), the latter reminiscent of court masques like
Blackness where Wroth appeared as one of the Queen's masquers 'in
the upper part of the house' amidst 'clouds' and 'blue silk set with
stars'.[54] Anyone staging *Love's Victory* or imagining a performance
needs to consider whether Venus and Cupid oversee all the action,
watching the scenes from above or possibly from an elevated position amongst elite spectators on a dais at one end of the hall. Wroth
offers some suggestions for staging the Temple through her description of a Palace of Love in *Urania I*, a picture of which is on the
title page.[55] In line with the three stages of love through which the
characters in *Love's Victory* journey under the supervision of Venus
and Cupid, the palace in *Urania I* has three towers. The first has
'the image of Cupid, curiously carved with his bow bent, and quiver'
pointing towards the next, 'on which was a statue of white marble,
representing Venus', who is 'holding a flaming heart'. This statue, in
turn, points to a third tower with 'the figure of Constancy, holding
in her hand the keys of the Palace'. The lovers' progress through the
five acts of *Love's Victory* dramatizes the three stages of love indicated
by the pointing figures and explained by a Priest of Venus:

> Those that are false, may enter this tower, which is Cupid's Tower, or the
> Tower of Desire: but therein once enclosed, they endure torments fit for
> such a fault. Into the second any lover may enter, which is the Tower of
> Love: but there they suffer unexpressable tortures, in several kinds as their
> affections are most incident to; as Jealousy, Despair, Fear, Hope, Longings,
> and such like. The third, which is guarded by Constancy, can be entered
> by none, till the valiantest knight, with the loyalest lady come together,
> and open that gate, when all these charms shall have conclusion.[56]

In *Urania* the 'valiantest knight' and 'loyalest lady' refer to
Amphilanthus and Pamphilia, avatars for William Herbert and
Wroth, who never open the gate together. *Love's Victory* enacts a

more fulfilling conclusion, at least in *PM*. Once their hearts are inflamed, the play's lovers are struck by jealousy, despair, fear, hope and longing, through which their constancy is tested, and achieved in Act 5.

The Temple is also glorified by the presence of the priests, whose seven-syllable lines have an air of ritual, especially when spoken aloud, as do those of Philisses and Musella in 5.4.1–38. John Fletcher used the same verse form for the priest of Venus in *Cupid's Revenge* (B4v). The stage direction '*The music or song of the* PRIESTS' clearly indicates that their lines 4.2.17–38 are sung, but whether those in 2.3 are spoken, chanted or sung like psalms is open to interpretation in performance. In Fletcher's *Cupid's Revenge* the priest's lines are followed by a song and then by '*The Measure*' (B4), a dance of the lovers, whilst Cupid's descents to the stage are announced by '*Cornets*' (C1 and D1). The entrances of Cupid and Venus in *Love's Victory* may also be heralded by triumphal music, as suggested by the diacritical mark of a flourish which is found in *PM* before and after each of their appearances, other than the opening scene (see Fig. 6 p. 53).

Pastoral tragicomedy
The pastoral settings of *Love's Victory* may also owe something to Wroth's experience of court masques, since these often presented idealized, Arcadian rural scenes. *The Masque of Beauty*, for example, featured 'curious and elegant arbours', a 'grove of grown trees laden with golden fruit' and a floor like 'an indented maze' cornered by fountains.[57] Wroth was apparently cast in Jonson's lost pastoral play *The May Lord*, possibly written for performance at Belvoir Castle (home of Wroth's cousin Elizabeth Sidney Manners, Countess of Rutland) or one of the other Sidney–Herbert households.[58] Jonson's *Epigram* 105 described her costumed in the 'wheaten hat' to represent Ceres, goddess of the harvest; and in 'shepherd's 'tire' (or dress) to play Oenone, a pastoral nymph, or the figures of Flora or May, referring possibly to her performance in his own play.

> He that but saw you wear the wheaten hat
> Would call you more than Ceres, if not that:
> And, dressed in shepherd's 'tire, who would not say
> You were the bright Oenone, Flora, or May?[59]

Wroth may also have attended Samuel Daniel's *The Queen's Arcadia*, staged in August 1605 for a court visit to Oxford and published in

1606. This five-act play was an example of English 'pastoral tragi-comedy', a dramatic genre derived from the structure of the court masque, in which an anti-masque threatens to disrupt the established order but is overcome in a restorative masque sequence. Pastoral tragicomedy originated in Italy with the performance of Torquato Tasso's *Aminta* in 1573 (published 1581) and Battista Guarini's *Il Pastor Fido* (1590), reprinted together in England in 1591 by John Wolfe. Wolfe was mentioned as a servant of Sir Philip Sidney in the late 1570s and remained in professional contact with the Sidneys' printers (if not the Sidneys themselves) through the late 1580s and 1590s.[60] That said, Sidney's *Defence of Poetry* did not endorse this fashion in drama, denouncing 'mongrel tragi-comedy' as a genre that violated Aristotle's definition of the unities by being neither 'right tragedies, nor right comedies', and by 'mingling kings and clowns'.[61] Rather, as Barbara K. Lewalski points out, '*Love's Victory* is much more usefully contextualized' in relation to the popularity of tragicomedy in the courts of Italy, France and England.[62] An English translation *Il Pastor Fido: or The Faithful Shepherd*, published in 1602, popularized the play amongst English dramatists, and productions like John Fletcher's *The Faithful Shepherdess* (1610) were staged in the Blackfriars Theatre.[63] Marion Wynne-Davies has argued that Wroth adopted later developments of the genre, such as the introduction of a female helper and a potion, from William Browne's long poem *Britannia's Pastorals* (1613) and Samuel Daniel's *Hymen's Triumph* (1614).[64]

The Italian origins of tragicomedy also included a female author: the celebrated actress and poet Isabella Andreini (1562–1604), who wrote and published *La Mirtilla* – modelled on Tasso's play – in 1588.[65] Andreini was a friend of Tasso and her play was immediately popular, with reprints in Italy and in Paris up to 1616. Although we do not know whether Wroth knew, or knew of, Andreini's play, her celebrity status and the many publications of the work after her death in 1604 are suggestive. Julie D. Campbell notes that 'Like Wroth's opinionated and analytical shepherdesses, Andreini's female characters evoke complex images of Renaissance women that belie the stereotypes'; in addition, Campbell shows how Wroth adapts the dramatic stereotype of the assertive, wooing woman in Tasso's *Aminta* and Daniel's *The Queen's Arcadia*.[66]

The pastoral tragicomic world of *Love's Victory* is governed by an emotional and symbolic geography. Each character experiences the landscape according to his or her fortunes in love.[67] Sunshine and open meadows are associated with happiness, whilst the shady woods are spaces of melancholy and secrecy to which the characters retreat. The action of the mortals opens with the jealous, love-stricken shepherd Philisses bidding farewell to the meadows: '*I shun you for the dark*', he sings, because '*love makes me you leave*' (1.2.1–22). He is followed by Silvesta, another unrequited lover, who bids farewell to the sunny, flower-decked meadows 'free from the check / Of fortune's frown' (1.2.80–1) in order to 'range' in the woods. For Silvesta, the woods represent independence because, in actively choosing a life of chastity, she is no longer a slave to love's torments (1.2.84–124). The shadowy presence of Diana, goddess of chastity and hunting, makes the woods a space of freedom from other people and from conventional values. Indeed, the natural environment becomes a landscape for the characters' romantic and emotional explorations, as the shepherdess Climeana sings:

> *O mine eyes, why do you lead*
> *My poor heart thus forth to range*
> *From the wonted course to strange*
> *Unknown ways and paths to tread?*

> (1.3.31–4)

Given Wroth's own account of ranging from the 'wonted course' at Penshurst Mount, it is not hard to see how the play's pastoral land-scape might allude, at one level, to the estate at Penshurst. Don E. Wayne has shown how Jonson's poem 'To Penshurst' (1611) maps the real landscape of Penshurst Place,[68] and in 1591–2 Abraham Fraunce had relocated Tasso's pastoral tragicomedy *Aminta* to Ivychurch, the favourite home of the Countess of Pembroke. The Countess is portrayed as participating in the performance, 'with her own person' giving 'grace and life to the pastime'.[69] Perhaps Wroth's own pastoral tragicomedy allowed her the authorial power to re-present emotionally significant locations and encounters in the home where she grew up and was married. William Burgess's ret-rospective map 'A Survey of Penshurst' (c. 1740) depicts such fea-tures as 'Lady Gamage's Bower', a wooded walk with a kissing beech, and white-domed structures that resemble the towers on the Palace of Love in *Urania*.[70]

Love's Victory adopts more earthy elements of pastoral convention in the depiction of its clown, Rustic, who is distanced from the shepherds and shepherdesses by his lack of courtly wit. His attempts to use the aristocratic blazon form to sing Musella's praises are made ridiculous by his comparing each of her body parts to livestock and agricultural produce. Her skin is 'whiter than lamb's wool'; her eyes play like goats and kids; and his song culminates with comparisons for her cheeks and breasts:

> *Thy cheeks are red*
> *Like ochre spread*
> *On a fatted sheep's back;*
> *Thy paps are found*
> *Like apples round;*
> *No praises shall lack.*

(1.4.67–72)

Although this is comic, the song also shows Wroth's distaste for the materialistic evaluation of women. It is echoed in *Urania I* in Lisia's arranged marriage to a rich Duke: he is 'a Clown' who 'no more esteeming her, nor indeed understanding her worth more than a beast, or one of his goats' (556:21–3), demonstrates his unsuitability as a husband.[71] Wroth's comic depiction of the wealthy Rustic is more sympathetic but it implicitly critiques the conventional, elevated courtly blazon which uses imagery of jewels to glorify a beloved. Whilst some critics have suggested that Rustic may be a representation of Wroth's husband, this is unlikely; given Robert Wroth's status and reputation, his closest dramatic avatar is the Forester, whose unrequited love for Silvesta strengthens through the course of the romantic plot.

Dramatizing romance

Friendship and love are interwoven in the romantic plot of *Love's Victory*, which stages intimate same-sex dialogues followed by private scenes where the protagonists venture into the unknown territory of heterosexual romance. In two scenes at the heart of the play (2.2 and 3.1) Wroth dramatizes parallel exchanges between Philisses and his best friend Lissius, and between Musella and Silvesta, both of which drive the love plot between Philisses and Musella forward (a similar dramatic technique to Shakespeare's in *Much Ado*, although Beatrice and Benedick are *tricked* into declaring their love in separate scenes). In 2.2, Wroth draws on the classical celebration of male friendship by Cicero, who asks if any man can be 'living in this life, that liveth not in mutual love with some friend? What sweeter thing can there be, than to have one, with whom thou darest so boldly talk all matters, as with thine own self?'[72] Philisses's failure to confide his passion for Musella to his friend, because he believes she loves Lissius, threatens to break the 'band of friendship of our long-held love' (2.2.5); Lissius is hurt by Philisses's mistrust, protesting 'My love hath been / Still firm to you' (2.2.1–2). Philisses and Lissius resolve their misunderstanding with relative ease once Lissius reveals he is in love with Philisses's sister Simeana and not Musella. It is notable that their homosocial bond is strengthened at the expense of female agency: given the shepherdesses' difficulties in pursuing their loves, the breezily transactional tone of Philisses pledging 'the gift' of Simeana's love (2.2.52–5) with a handshake seems ironic.

Unlike the shepherds, Silvesta and Musella have been rivals in love but in 3.1 Silvesta first counsels her friend to turn away from love in favour of chastity, and then suggests a practical plan for Musella to respond modestly to Philisses's protestations of love, and declare her own. Wroth adds to the female-centred focus in 3.3, where the other four shepherdesses (Dalina, Fillis, Simeana and Climeana) confide their experiences and hopes in love. This intimate, all-female gathering encourages Fillis to open up and deliver her longest speech in the play (3.3.43–56), although the mood of sisterly solidarity is disrupted by Simeana and Climeana's rivalry for the love of Lissius. Dalina, who claims to 'know the world' (3.3.143), intervenes and offers 'counsel' on romance (3.3.135). As a shepherdess with a history, she is also a figure who perpetuates pastoral tradition, initiating the shepherdesses' 'sport' (3.3.4) and leading the amusements of the wider shepherd community.[73] Dalina's love of witty 'play' (2.1.1) and 'pretty pastime[s]' like riddling (4.1.352) identify her as a courtly figure, like the so-called 'merry marquess' in *Urania II*, even though her ultimate goal is to find a husband rather than continue witty flirtation.[74] The communal scenes create a public framework for the expressions of romantic love and provide a social context for the varying responses of the protagonists.

Gary Waller has argued that 'one interwoven pattern of labyrinthine fiction-making is Wroth's own participation in her fiction – not just writing versions of the same story over and over, but specifically fragmenting and elaborating particular aspects of her own life into multiple characters and events'.[75] *Love's Victory* extends that process of fragmentation. Rather than assigning a cast of real-life figures to specific *dramatis personae*, it is more profitable to read the romantic plot as a prism through which real-life moments and feelings can be glimpsed, reviewed and reworked under the controlling hand of the playwright. This allows for sympathetic identifications and recognitions which shift across genders and change from moment to moment in the play: for Wroth as playwright, for her contemporaries who read or performed it, and for modern readers, performers and spectators.

Unrequited love is a major feature of Wroth's prose and poetry, which *Love's Victory* allows her to explore differently by dramatizing it. Fillis, whose longest speech is a sonnet, shows how the Petrarchan trope of helpless despair is acutely appropriate for a modest woman. She confesses that she has 'loved, and loved but only one' (3.3.45) and will continue loving Philisses; words which illuminate the quiet masochism of her silent, observant presence on stage in the rest of the play. The agony of repeated disappointment and public exposure is keenly felt when she joins in the riddle game to tell of her fortune:

> A spring I hoped for, but that died.
> Then on the next my hopes relied,
> But summer past, the latter spring
> Could me but former losses bring;
> I died with them, yet still I live,
> While autumn can no comfort give.

> (4.1.425–30)

This is a simple statement of despair, the only riddle being the name of her beloved, which remains perpetually concealed by the conventions of modesty. Fillis's fate demonstrates what might have happened to Musella, whose expression of her feelings for Philisses may be doubly constrained by modesty and by her awareness that she is betrothed to Rustic, though she never states this explicitly. The announcement of their wedding is a shock to spectators and readers in 5.1, just as it appears to be for Musella and may have been for Wroth herself in the summer of 1604 when the date of her marriage to Robert Wroth was confirmed. In a biographical reading Fillis's endurance in the face of unkindness could be interpreted as a portrayal of Wroth's constancy to William Herbert. Simeana's long-suffering experience of Lissius's scorn and alleged infidelity, and his harsh rejection of the more outspoken Climeana, give actors, spectators and readers further focal points of identification with female experiences of unrequited love.

In contrast to Fillis's reticence, the male lovers make full use of Petrarchan tropes to express the pain they feel as unrequited lovers.

Lissius's hyperbolic despair may sound ridiculous given his former disdain for love, perhaps critiquing the superficiality of much male complaint. Philisses's hesitancy in declaring his feelings is met with a simple but telling question by Musella: 'why did you thus hide your love?' His unforced error has made it 'almost too late' for them to be happy (4.1.85–7). Perhaps surprisingly, the most extended picture of the courtly lover, the 'ever wailing' (2.1.19) Forester, is treated sympathetically, even though Silvesta is anxious to escape his attentions. His first speech (1.2.147–60) and his soliloquy in 5.6 are both complete sonnets, and he adopts the conventional pose of the abject lover in kneeling to plead for Silvesta's pity. Whilst Lissius makes 'sport' of the Forester's wooing (2.1.3), Musella reprimands him, offering the pity the Forester seeks. The Forester's love is such that he can identify with Silvesta's pain in loving Philisses – 'still she constant loved / And more she loved, more cruel still he grew' (1.2.187–8) – and her growing passion 'which did firmly burn / So hot as nothing could those flames remove' (1.2.197–8). Since the multilayered folding of heightened emotions in the Forester's speeches crosses gender boundaries in identifying with both male and female experiences of hopeless love, we can perhaps read these passages as representing not only Wroth's re-articulation of her own frustrated love for William Herbert, but also an imaginative reconstruction of her husband's feelings of despair that his love would never be requited. The Forester's hate of the 'Accursèd shepherd' Philisses (1.2.163), the sense of waste he feels at Silvesta's dedication of herself to chastity and his wish to merely see her, even if he cannot enjoy her love, could all have functioned powerfully as a romantic fictional recreation of Robert Wroth's feelings in an early performance or reading. Perhaps a sense of loss and waste would also have been recreated anew for William Herbert as a performer, spectator or reader. The emotional pull of such lines, and the Forester's determination to lay down his life to save Silvesta, would have been all the more resonant in the light of Robert Wroth's death in 1614.

Wroth's depiction of unrequited love in the play is therefore not a straightforward critique of Petrarchan conventions. Through the expressions of the lovers, particularly Simeana, Fillis and the Forester, the play gives voice to multiple viewpoints, and thus elicits complex emotional responses from those listening, on and off stage. It evokes nostalgia, provokes and expresses guilt, and creates empathy in unexpected places.

Lady Mary Wroth uses her power as playwright to plot love's victory over pain and loss, within the play and perhaps beyond it. Her commitment to the value of love is evident in an intervention into the narrative of *Urania II* which is uncharacteristically personal. Wroth breaks off the triumphant love story of Parismeria (an anagram of 'Praise mari') and his lady to assert:

> what is riches, what is fortunes of estate, what indeed is anything (no, not honour itself, though the rarest of earthly treasures), without that inesti-mable jewel, Love? Love is the glory of the world. If without love, the world had not been; the world had had no light; no thing had been if the creator for love had not made man and an associate to him, who must love too. So as Love is the all, by which all is, so without Love nothing can be.[76]

Wroth celebrates Parismeria and his lady as 'love's master-piece' and, equally forcefully, argues that 'it had been an extreme blindness and wickedness in fortune, if she stored not them with all blessedness of her fates and destinies'. She promises that 'some other time will and shall bring forth a longer and continued story of their fortunes, beyond expectation happy' (*Urania II*, 317).[77] Although this may refer to the *Urania* that she did not complete, the tragicomedy she *did* write was an ideal form for bringing forth good fortunes, 'beyond expectation happy'. In *Love's Victory*, Wroth's authorial power to direct the plot and feelings of the characters, the actors who play them and those who watch them, is advertised through the Book of Fortunes and the presiding figure of Venus. In 2.1 Wroth's script tells us that the goddess Fortune 'will direct to Love', while remind-ing us that she is blind and fickle, and the characters draw lots from the Book of Fortunes in a game of romantic horoscopes. In Wroth's campaign to bring about love's victory, neither the possessive Rustic, the villain Arcas, Venus nor Cupid ultimately shapes the destinies of the characters in the play; the *deus ex machina* or goddess who writes their fortunes is Wroth. The Book of Fortunes is the script of *Love's Victory*, perhaps represented on stage in the Penshurst Manuscript, neatly copied and bound, the cover decorated with a cipher which intertwines the initials M S W, W H, P A, P M and L V, thus linking, among others, the identities of Mary Sidney Wroth, William Herbert and their fictional personae Pamphilia, Amphilanthus and Philisses and Musella, as well as invoking the title of the play itself (Fig. 2).[78]

At one level, the play can thus be read as a love riddle presented to William Herbert by Lady Mary Wroth which affords opportuni-

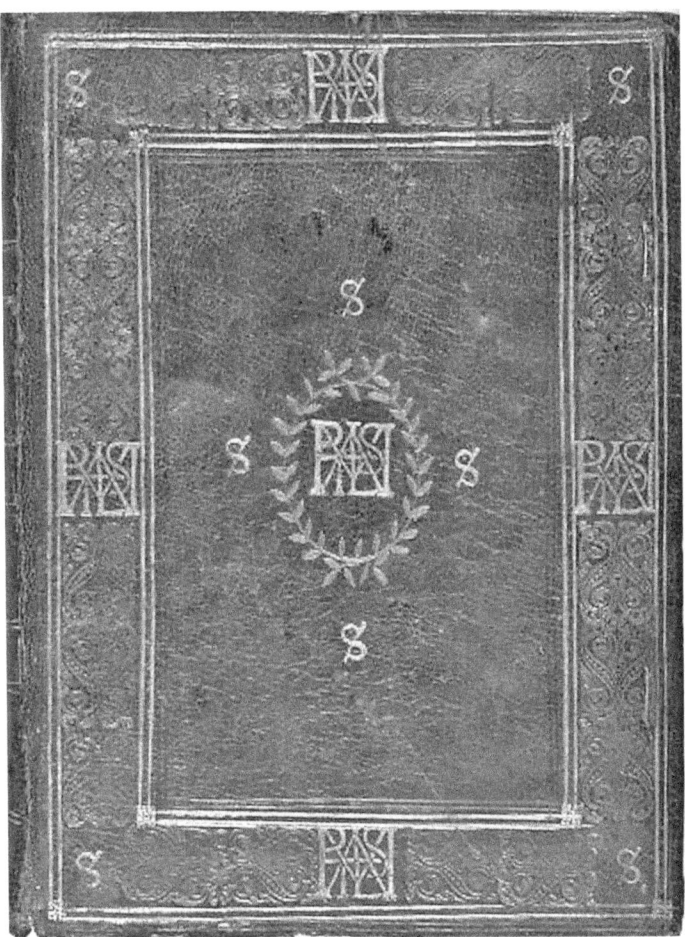

2 Binding of *Love's Victory* by Lady Mary Wroth, Penshurst Manuscript. By kind permission of Viscount De L'Isle from his private collection.

ties to review their relationship through the prismatic reflections offered by the romantic protagonists, Musella and Philisses, Lissius and Simeana and Silvesta and the Forester. Wroth's poetry and prose romance also do this but, as a play, *Love's Victory* requires embodied enactment of those romantic scenarios. For example,

Philisses's line 'Then know, for your dear sake my sorrow is' (4.1.74) obliges the actor to utter admissions of love which Wroth might have longed to hear from William Herbert. When Philisses reads out Dalina's fortune, Wroth may be putting prescriptive words into the actor's mouth, forcing him to deliver a sentence on male inconstancy, including, possibly, his own behaviour:

> They that cannot steady be
> To themselves, the like must see.
> Fickle people fickly choose,
> Slightly like, and so refuse.
> This your fortune, who can say
> Herein justice bears not sway?

(2.1.193–8)

Likewise the script offers the pleasure of revenge when Lissius is obliged to repent for his railing against love and his indifference to the devoted Simeana. When Musella and Philisses declare their love in the wooded grove in 4.1 their performative speech re-enacts and so revivifies vows taken in offstage contexts. In the context of Wroth's own history, the vows spoken by Philisses and Musella (whether in an actual or imagined performance) could function as a renewal of the pledges taken between the lovers at Penshurst Mount, revivifying Wroth's romantic connection with Herbert in spite of their enforced separation through arranged marriages. Whether Philisses's vow 'to die / When I prove false, or show unconstancy' (4.1.105–6) was spoken by William Herbert or not, the script uses the fictional world, governed by Wroth's 'Book of Fortunes' (her play), to plant her ideology into the embodied consciousness of men, for spectators to witness. Such vows are given a concrete, material reality in performance which is hard to simply dismiss as hollow once it has been embodied by an actor.[79]

In the Forester and Silvesta, Wroth perhaps refracts and reflects on her married life including her lost virginity and her rejection by Herbert. Silvesta's heartfelt complaint that 'love is idle, happiness there's none / When freedom's lost, and chastity is gone' (1.2.91–2) would resonate strongly if Robert Wroth had indeed discovered Wroth was not a virgin when he married her, as Hannay suggests he did (*MSLW*, 107–8). Silvesta's dedication of herself to the goddess Diana and chaste independence is a forceful piece of self-assertion that may replay Wroth's attempt to distance herself, physically and emotionally, from Herbert or even, perversely, her commitment to him. If, as Hannay suggests, Wroth believed she had a *de praesenti* marriage to Herbert (that is, based on a simple verbal expression of spousal contract without an ecclesiastical or civil ceremony) before she married Robert Wroth, this would explain her constancy to Herbert and her refusal to remarry after she was widowed, remaining chaste instead (*MSLW*, 107–8). Silvesta promotes her highest value – 'a chaste desire' (1.2.100) – by saving Musella and Philisses. She is prepared to sacrifice her life for this.

Thus, Wroth's ideal of the constant lover, and dream of a reciprocated romantic love that endures the crisis of enforced marriage and the threat of death, is validated and given concrete form through its enactment in her script. Whatever kind of performance Wroth's two manuscripts were written for – silent or communal reading with an imagined performance in mind, or to script or record an actual performance – the play obliges readers, actors and spectators to reiterate, in some form, and so legitimize the triumph of, love's victory over inconstancy and arranged marriage. Whereas the second, unpublished part of the *Urania* breaks off without the fulfilment of Pamphilia's dreams, *Love's Victory* realizes the possibility of romantic fulfilment by making it materially present – scripted to be enunciated and embodied – by virtue of its genre as drama.

5. PERFORMANCE HISTORY

There is no record of a seventeenth-century performance of *Love's Victory*, or indeed of any performance until the very end of the twentieth century. However, as noted, the play is eminently stageworthy. The two manuscripts of Wroth's text, and records of other country-house performances – including exceptional cases of scripts written or directed by women – provide evidence that *Love's Victory* may have been staged in Wroth's lifetime, and open up multiple possibilities for where that might have happened.[80] Both manuscripts start scenes or sections of dialogue with a list of the characters involved in the action, and mark exits at appropriate points for the most part, suggesting an awareness of stage business (notable uncertainties are the point at which Climeana enters in 1.3 and where Rustic enters in 4.1). Both scripts have a cue for music and the play makes frequent use of song, not only as a feature conforming with pastoral style but also to create a freeze-frame effect in the action, shining a spotlight on the characters' emotions. *PM* has more elaborate directions at several points; *HM*, whose pages have been stitched together on at least five occasions, looks like a working copy of the script assembled for, or from, a performance, as discussed below. This manuscript was owned by Sir Edward Dering, who collected and edited playtexts for performances at his house at Surrenden in Kent; Marta Straznicky has argued that *HM* was deliberately fashioned as a two-part entertainment in the style of a masque. Other than his purchase of Jonson's *Works* (1616) – which contained his masques – Dering's interest seems to have been in drama from the commercial playhouses rather than the court so, if we accept Straznicky's thesis about *HM's* masque structure, Surrenden does not seem a likely venue for a masque-like performance. *HM* may, however, be an incomplete version of a text adapted for performance and staged at Surrenden in or after 1619.

Beverley M. Van Note suggests Baynard's Castle or Penshurst as playing spaces for *Love's Victory*, following Margaret Hannay's suggestion that the play may have been performed to celebrate the wedding of Wroth's sister Barbara Sidney, which had taken place relatively privately on 3 April 1619. Van Note proposes that, in addition to providing a belated wedding celebration, such a performance would have helped to 'assuage the lingering disappointment over Barbara's failed court masque', referring to her proposed participation in a masque which was cancelled because of the illness of the King and Queen in 1617–18.[81] Baynard's Castle in London, where Barbara had been christened and where Wroth and her sisters and cousins had rehearsed for their participation in court masques, would have provided a resonant place for the spectacular, masque-like qualities of the play. Van Note argues, however, that staging a celebration in April, shortly after the wedding, would have been both 'politically inexpedient' in the light of Queen Anne's death and the King's serious illness, and practically difficult since the male family members 'most likely to perform it', including William Herbert, would have been unavailable. 'A more likely possibility', she argues, is that it was staged in the summer at Penshurst Place.[82]

Extant records of performances in country houses give grounds for conjecture that there could have been a production of *Love's Victory* at one of the family's residences, either at Wroth's home, Loughton Hall, where she had entertained her family on numerous occasions, or at one of the Sidney–Herbert households. It is not clear from either script whether Wroth envisaged an outdoor setting and venue in a country-house estate, as in Sir Philip Sidney's *The Lady of May*, or a pastoral setting staged indoors, such as those in

Daniel's *The Queen's Arcadia* (1606), in Fletcher's *The Faithful Shepherdess* or in Ben Jonson's play *The Sad Shepherd* (printed 1641), which features 'a landscape of forest, hills, valleys, cottages, a castle, a river, pastures, herds, flocks, all full of country simplicity'.[83] Wilton or Ivychurch would have been an ideal venue to emphasize the play's pastoral theme: Wilton was the Herberts' family home, where Sir Philip Sidney had written much of *The Countess of Pembroke's Arcadia*, while Ivychurch was where Mary Sidney took an active part in Abraham Fraunce's local retelling of *Aminta*, and where her play *Antonius* was completed.

Penshurst Place is probably the most likely country-house venue for a performance of *PM*, for a combination of reasons. Firstly, Penshurst's status as the Sidney family's ancestral home, its great hall roofed with chestnut beams and surrounded by an estate of meadows, fields and woodland, made it a natural meeting point for members of the extended family to watch or take part in a pastoral drama that celebrated the family's regeneration through 'children, and their children's children' (5.7.82). Secondly, it was Wroth's home: the place where she grew up; where she may have had her first sexual encounter; where she was married; and to which she seems to have returned for extended periods after she was widowed.

Carolyn Ruth Swift first proposed that Penshurst's Baron's Hall, with its minstrels' gallery, could readily accommodate Wroth's gods, Venus and Cupid. The gallery, at the east end of the hall, faces a raised dais on which the elite members of the household would sit to eat, though more recent research into great-hall performances has shown that such elite spectators conventionally sat amongst the performers, as part of the spectacle. Whatever the precise venue, an early performance of *Love's Victory* in a great hall would probably have followed this pattern. Cupid and Venus could thus have pre-sided over the actions of the shepherd community from the dais, just as the head of the household did over the estate. They may have remained there throughout the play, or perhaps have moved mid-act, to reappear briefly 'in the clouds' from an elevated position like the minstrels' gallery at Penshurst, or just possibly from the 'squint' or small window looking down from the West Solar above. This is a small opening, probably allowing space only for one actor to appear and speak down to those on the dais: Venus could have addressed Cupid below from this position. If, as seems likely, members of the household took part as actors, then those seated on or near the dais could have moved easily between their seats and the performance space in front, dissolving any barrier between actors and spectators even more effectively than the thrust stage and daylight conditions at the public theatres of the time. The fluid shifting of identities, back and forth, between actor and character in the familiar household space would have enhanced the network of associations between fictional *dramatis personae* and performers. Staging of this kind would have required the participants to play 'in the round' if a larger audience filled the space further down the hall.

For centuries the lack of performance records for *Love's Victory* encouraged critics to view it as a 'closet' drama, unperformable, and not intended for performance, so curtailing its theatre history. Once this premise was challenged, however, the same blank space has given directors and performers freedom to explore the play's theatrical potential from different starting points.

In 1999 Stephanie Hodgson-Wright directed the Poetic Justice Theatre Company in a production at Bede Tower Studio at the University of Sunderland.[84] Half the space was occupied by spectators, in slightly arced rows, facing the acting area. This was dressed to resemble a forest with a brown floor, dappled with light, two green 'banks', one at either side of the stage, for actors to sit on, and a white, moveable screen decorated with ivy leaves as a hiding space. The back of the performance area was hung full length with brown curtains, mottled to suggest tree trunks. These drew back to discover an inner space (about 3 m by 3m) for the Temple, flanked by two white pillars with greenery atop, and with three broad steps backed by a white curtain. The predominance of white made a visual connection with Silvesta's white costume, suggesting the combination of love and chastity celebrated in *Love's Victory*. In this production, Silvesta (Jordana Chapman) was drawn upstage towards the Temple at the end of 5.3 by Venus's outstretched hand, which passed the potion to her 'instrument' (5.7.71). The detail of pearls (a symbol of purity) round Venus's neck at the beginning of the play implied her commitment to chastity from the outset.

The production interpreted pastoral retreat in contemporary terms, opening with a group of young socialites in modern dress entering in a pre-show sequence to pick out dressing-up clothes from a basket. Their actions and greetings were accompanied by the first verse of Robert van Leeuwen's popular song 'Venus', recorded by the English girl-group Bananarama, who thus served as off-stage priests of Venus.[85] In spite of the lyrics praising Venus as 'Goddess on a mountain top / Burning like a silver flame / A summit of beauty

and love', the actors hurried off, taking no notice of the figures of
Venus and Cupid in the Temple behind them. Although Bananarama
proclaimed in chorus 'She's got it; yeah, baby she's got it', it was
obvious that this Venus certainly did *not* have the mortals' love or
respect; her opening address was shouted in anger to Cupid. She
descended from the Temple into the forest world and sat, having
her long red hair brushed (reminiscent of Rubens's painting *The
Toilet of Venus*, 1612–15)[86] while she issued her commands to Cupid.
The white backcloth of the Temple served an additional purpose as
'clouds' through which Venus thrust her head in 1.4, her disembodi-
ment showing a lack of power rather than supernatural superiority
and betraying her reliance on Cupid. The actors playing Arcas and
Simeana doubled as priests of Venus, drawing the curtains of the
Temple for each choric interlude and closing them afterwards.
Cupid reached through a gap in the curtains at the end of 2.1 to
touch Lissius with an arrow and thereby strike him with love.
Opening the curtains for longer scenes in 5.4 and 5.7 effectively
signalled the mortals' increased openness to love, and the four
couples were welcomed on to the steps of the Temple at the conclusion of the play, Silvesta and the Forester sitting appropriately at
the feet of Venus (representing chaste love) rather than Cupid
(representing desire).

The lovers were played by young actors who lent authenticity to
Wroth's depictions of the giddiness of love. Colin Reid's Lissius, a
tall gangly figure, used his Scottish accent to good effect to convey
his scorn for love, and read a newspaper rather than joining the
others in the singing game in 1.3. His transformation into a helpless victim of love in 3.3, prostrating himself on the floor to deliver
his complaint, produced a comic effect. Climeana was portrayed
as flirtatious, beginning her song in 1.3 by crossing the stage and
caressing first Philisses, then Rustic, to show how her poor heart
was set to '*range*' in '*gadding thought*' (1.3.32–6). In the final stanza,
she sang '*let it home return again*' (1.3.35) to an extremely uncomfort-
able Lissius, placing her arm round his neck from behind so that
the only way he could break away was to ask others to sing (1.3.43).
Dalina was cast as a maternal figure, slightly older than her peers,
so able to speak with authority to Climeana and Simeana to break
up their quarrel over Lissius. This production cut the role of Fillis.
In the portrayal of Musella and Philisses, Musella was the dominant
figure, in spite of her concerns about modesty. She took a lead in
the couple's sacrificing their lives for love; in a surprising move, she

raised the dagger to plunge it into Philisses's breast rather than her own, and was prevented only by Silvesta's entrance. The Forester's love for Silvesta was presented sympathetically in the production by casting a diminutive female actor, Helen Walden, with a musical north-eastern accent which gave a lively lyric energy to the Forester's protestations of love. His pursuit of Silvesta was never threatening and her pity for him was expressed tenderly. Silvesta was portrayed as having a feistier relationship with the assertive Climeana, who challenged her choice of independent lifestyle 'alone to range' (5.3.26).

In the 1999 production the courtly games of Wroth's text were accompanied by picnics and Lissius reading his newspaper, which gave an immediate sense of the young elite of the 1980s taking a leisurely break from their work in the city. All the actors played in bare feet, except for Rustic who retained his heavy boots throughout to mark his difference from the others. In the pre-show sequence where they put on pastoral fancy dress, he lagged behind and so remained in his working dungarees. Scott Wilson, a much taller actor than the others, played Rustic in the style of John Steinbeck's Lennie from *Of Mice and Men*, moving slowly, mentally and physically, but with no real sense of malice. His attempts to join in the game of fortunes and the songs were clumsy but not offensive to the shepherds and shepherdesses. In 5.7, he stood by Musella's mother, his physical presence quietly comforting her grief at Musella's death.

In addition to the recorded 'Venus' song which bookended the performance, the 1999 production used the opening line of Nina Simone's 'I Put a Spell on You'[87] in a dumbshow following 3.4 in which Arcas whisked Simeana stage right, away from Lissius, while Climeana took Lissius's arm and exited with him stage left. The rest of the shepherds' music was of a simple folk style, unaccompanied, or accompanied by guitar in the case of Philisses. The director creatively interpreted the debate between Musella and Silvesta on chastity and love (3.1) as a musical exchange in which the stanzas of each character's lyrics were alternated. The two performers entered together, each playing the flute, and Silvesta sang the first verse of her defence of chastity accompanied by Musella on her flute. Musella then replied by singing her first verse on love, accompanied by Silvesta. The process was then repeated for the second verses of each of their lyrics. The play's intertwining of love and chastity was thus echoed musically to suggest the interdependence of the two. Musella and Philisses's lines on entering the Temple in 5.4 were sung in harmony rather than in unison to show their love and united, but differing, intentions (5.4.1–38). Their individual addresses to Venus and to Cupid, marked in the script, were sung as solos directed across each other and towards the respective gods standing on the top steps, creating a chiasmic pattern to highlight their independent approaches. They ended by singing the final two lines 'Fame hereafter swell with pride / Never love thus lived, thus died' (37–8) in harmony (Fig. 3). For the Temple in 2.3 and 4.2, the 1999 production set the priests' words to the popular tune of 'Staines Morris', to retain a rural tone. The tune was published in John Playford's *The Dancing Master* but it is found much earlier, for instance in William Ballet's lute book, dating from 1590–1603.[88] Overall, this non-professional production, working with a small budget, was a lively and sensitive interpretation, with many detailed touches that responded intelligently to Wroth's text.

Two further public performances of *Love's Victory* followed in the Baron's Hall at Penshurst Place in 2014 and 2018, both directed by

3 The sacrifice of Musella and Philisses to Venus and Cupid at the Temple (5.4), Poetic Justice Theatre Company, dir. Stephanie Hodgson-Wright (1999).

Martin Hodgson. The first was a staged reading as part of the Globe Education Team's 'Read Not Dead' series, in which the actors received their scripts in the morning, rehearsed through the day and performed to a full house of seated spectators at 5 pm on 8 June 2014. The reading demonstrated how appropriate the Baron's Hall could be as a playing space. With only very minimal decoration (a few bundles of wheat placed against the wooden screen), the production made use of the existing features of the hall to set the scene for the performance, with the attendance of members of the Sidney family adding a sense of historical continuity. The magnificent high-beamed ceiling and the view of the gardens and estate beyond, through the large windows to the south, brought the woods and meadows into the medieval hall.[89] The minstrels' gallery served as the Temple throughout, emphasizing the significance of Venus's descent to the main playing level in 5.7 to create love's victory. In her Temple, Venus led the actors through improvised performances of the songs using the tunes of Christmas carols.[90]

The 2018 professional production, funded by the Arts and Humanities Research Council, was rehearsed in the gardens of Penshurst Place to explore how the house and its cultivated and rural surroundings might influence a performance of the play. Full performances were staged in the Baron's Hall on 16 September.[91] The roles of Venus and Fillis were doubled, as were those of Cupid and Arcas, the latter serving as an earthly manifestation of Cupid's mischievous and malicious power. Venus remained ascendant and resplendent in 5.7, wearing a gold hat and gently lit from behind on the minstrels' gallery. Her white costume with a red sash visually suggested the ideal blending of desire and chastity. Cupid's arrows were physical props, fletched with labels reading 'love', 'jealousy', 'malice', 'fear' and 'mistrust', which he showed Venus in 1.4. The 2018 production did not show Lissius being struck with the love arrow some time during or after 2.1 (as the 1999 production had done), so his confession of his love for Simeana in 2.2 was a surprise to spectators who did not know the script; members of a coterie audience who read or performed the script may not have needed such stage business as a prompt. Cupid descended from the minstrels' gallery in his own person to watch the effects of his arrows on the mortals as the priests sang in 2.3, and again in 3.4. Here Cupid (Zak Douglas) marked the end of the first half of the performance by scampering across the playing area with mischievous delight to confide to spectators his plots for the second half, singing the final six lines of the scene to bring the action to a close.

Incidental music and accompaniment for the songs were provided by a trio of cornetto, played by musical director Sam Ogle, theorbo (Robin Jeffrey) and lute (Lynda Sayce). Although the accompaniments for the songs did not use early modern music, the tunes in Robert Jones's books *The First Book of Songs and Airs* (1600) and *The Muses' Garden For Delights* (1610), dedicated to Wroth and to her father, offer exciting possibilities to be explored in future productions.[92] The instrumentation and the use of theorbo (a larger version of the archlute) were successful in evoking the musical sounds and styles that would have been familiar to Wroth and her family, the theorbo recalling the archlute which the figure in the Penshurst portrait is holding (Fig. 1 p. 4). As the Sidneys were accomplished musical performers and patrons of musicians, there would be value in considering how the songs in *Love's Victory* might be accompanied by tunes associated with the family.

The action involving the shepherds, played in front of the wooden screen at the east end of the Baron's Hall, made use of the screen's two archways for entrances and exits. A two-tier rostrum covered in green created a raised area for the shepherds to sit on or speak from. This was necessary since the Baron's Hall had no raked seating for spectators. The use of long brown drapes hung from the minstrels' gallery with further green swathes to suggest trees was, arguably, less helpful because it obscured much of the wooden screen that was part of the organic fabric of the Baron's Hall, though the Hall's stone walls would have been decorated with 'boskage work' and 'forest work' in Wroth's time.[93] While Venus and Cupid spoke the play's opening lines from the minstrels' gallery, all the mortal characters entered below and stood arranged in rows like pieces on a chess board facing the screen, and remained like this for 1.1 and 1.2, turning round to face spectators when their names were mentioned or when they entered the action, and then turning back. This was intended to introduce and clarify the relationships between the shepherds for a modern audience, though it did little to suggest the pastoral atmosphere evoked in Philisses's opening song. In contrast to the bustle of the pre-show sequence in the 1999 production, this arrangement established a formal division between spectators and performers, setting the actors apart from those seated on the three sides of the performance space.

When the performers moved out of this static frame, however, excellent use was made of opportunities to engage members of the audience. Philisses (Robert Heard) showed that he had been love-struck by handing one of Cupid's arrows to a spectator, before resuming his position in the square of actors and bidding farewell to the walks, meadows, paths, grass and flowers of the pastoral landscape (1.2.1–24). Lissius (Jonny McPherson) broke away from his position in the square, moving forward, centre front, to ask spectators 'Alas, what means this? Surely it is love' (1.2.65) and to challenge Cupid, effectively presenting the essence of his character before returning to his position. As the action unfolded, the per-formers exploited further opportunities for addressing members of the audience. For instance, in 4.1 Philisses gave out copies of his love poems to individual spectators, whilst Musella concealed herself amongst them to overhear his words. Two wooden tree stumps, set level with the front row of spectators, were used by Musella and Philisses to sit on in 1.3, and helped to incorporate spectators as members of the shepherd community in judging the singing. A large central aisle running to the dais at the back of the hall allowed for effective long entrances for Silvesta arriving with the potion in 5.4, and for the Mother in 5.5, her slow entrance building up tension for Simeana's revelation.

The production featured some very skilful acting, within a severely limited rehearsal period, by all the professional performers, creating the mixture of comedy, suspense, poignancy and tragedy that the play demands. Comic moments like Rustic's song were enhanced by business between him and the three musicians as he prepared to perform. Rustic's arrogance in his flamboyant green satin wedding costume was offset by an underlying insecurity in Dylan Frankland's rendition of the role: casting Frankland, a slight and young actor, made Rustic more sympathetic. Although Wroth's script clearly identifies Rustic as the 'clownish part' (5.7.103), the chance to maximize the comic potential of the role was compromised by the portrayal of the Forester as a second comic figure. At times this production choice created an eccentric effect when set against the character's more heartfelt declarations of love. In 2.1 the production followed Lissius's cue to 'mock at love' (reproved by Musella in 2.1.7) and presented the Forester's pleas to Silvesta as 'sport' (2.1.3), making him a figure of fun for all the shepherds. Silvesta's dismissal of him was applauded by all. In 5.7 the Forester offered to sacrifice his life for Silvesta with a joyful enthusiasm that cut across the seriousness of the scene. Andrew Hodges re-emphasized the strength of the Forester's devotion in terms that encouraged sympathy and laughter from spectators.

Silvesta's determination to pursue independence and chastity was signalled by her attire: a firmly laced white Jacobean period costume, with one sleeve detached to allude to her role as a huntress of Diana. Anne-Marie Piazza's strong performance as Silvesta realized the possibilities of this role as a dramatic avatar for Wroth. Piazza's excellent singing voice made her a natural leader for the group songs and she emphasized Silvesta's support and care for Musella in the musical duet on chastity and love which begins 3.1.

Rachel Winters illuminated the role of Dalina with vivacious enthusiasm as the instigator of 'sport' (3.3.4) or entertainments, very much in the spirit of the merry marquess of the *Urania* whose company is so welcomed by Pamphilia.[94] As well as conveying Dalina's keen wit and eagerness to direct events, Winters showed the vulnerable side of the character in 2.1, where her fickle behaviour is criticized via the sheet she draws from the Book of Fortunes. The Book is a difficult prop to manage in performance as actors have to select the appropriate leaves with the fortunes of their characters from the book, supposedly without looking. In the 2018 production, a prop was specially made by a local calligraphy expert, Els Van Den Steen, which allowed actors to 'draw' their fortunes correctly (see Fig. 4 p. 38). To recreate the metagraphic significance of the Book of Fortunes as a dramatic avatar of (or perhaps physical representation of) Wroth's own controlling script, the Book's cover was modelled on the cover of the Penshurst Manuscript, tooled with decorations which included the letters LV for *Love's Victory*.

The play's unexpected twists and turns of fortune in love were deftly portrayed by the actors. Jonny McPherson's performance highlighted the contrast between Lissius's misogynistic comments and indifference to love, and his surprise at his 'joy' (4.1.309). These provoked disapproving 'tuts' and laughter respectively from spectators. The production emphasized Philisses and Musella's struggles to express their love for each other. Robert Heard subtly conveyed Philisses's gradual recognition from 2.1 that his love for Musella was reciprocated, drawing in spectators to enjoy his surprise. Likewise, in 2.1 Nichole Bird's acting made tangible the emotional cost of Musella's modesty and her regret that Philisses could not name her as the object of his affection, hardly moving a muscle in her seated position on the rostrum. The sympathy created by both actors

4 Musella chooses a leaf from the Book of Fortunes, held by Rustic (right) watched by (left to right) Philisses, Arcas, Lacon, Dalina, Climeana, Simeana, Lissius and Silvesta, in the Baron's Hall, Penshurst Place, dir. Martin Hodgson (2018), funded by the Arts and Humanities Research Council.

allowed the performance to turn movingly from joy to 'love's tragedy' (5.4.72). The affectionate bond between Philisses and his sister was brought into focus by Laura Soper, who played Simeana. Soper's rendition of Simeana's speech in 5.5, giving an account of Philisses and Simeana's 'hapless end' (5.5.82), was especially moving, ending with Simeana breaking down and unable to continue the story. Serendipity in casting meant that the actors playing Philisses and Simeana both had the red hair typical of the Sidney family. In performance, the tragedy of loss registered in Simeana's lines evoked memories of Mary Sidney Herbert's mourning for her brother.

Careful attention to detail in the production also illuminated moments of poignancy embedded in the script's stories of love. For example, during the priests' song of 2.3 the director inserted a dumbshow in which Philisses mimed to Simeana the news that Lissius was in love with her (following the promise made in 2.2.53–5). Climeana, played by Nadia Shash, watched this from a comparatively lonely position, standing on the podium with her shepherdess's staff, thus emphasizing her status as a stranger by birth to the world of the play. In 3.3, when Lissius rejected Climeana's love,

Shash showed that Climeana was visibly shaken at being considered 'Unfit and shameful' (3.3.169). Her powerful portrayal of Climeana as an unrequited lover made her naturally sympathetic to Lacon, giving a logical through-line to their entrance together in 5.3 where she comforted him. Charlie Mulliner gave a wonderful cameo performance of Fillis's unrequited love for Philisses, silently watching him whenever they were on stage together. The sadness of her situation was brought out fully in 4.1 when Lissius asked her to partner him in the riddles game (the riddles were performed in pairs from the rostrum in the production). Fillis bravely recounted her constant, hopeless love but was totally ignored by Philisses, who gazed past her, and concentrated his rapt attention on Musella at the other side of the stage as she read the letter she had just received. After completing her riddle, Fillis hurried off stage. Mulliner's exit needed to be quick since she had to appear as Venus on the upper balcony 15 lines later, but this necessity of staging helped to demonstrate how upset Fillis was.

Many other smaller details of interpretation offered by these productions are mentioned in the commentary notes; we refer to characters rather than actors here, but readers can find full details of the company for the 1999 and 2018 productions in Appendices I and II. Many possibilities in the text remain to be explored in future performances.[95] These could be seated readings giving emphasis to oral performance and gesture, or staged readings which test the spatial dimensions of the script, such as that which took place in May 2018 at the Marlowe Kit, a medieval hall which forms the outreach centre of the Marlowe Theatre in Canterbury. Full stagings require a cast of at least thirteen performers (if the roles of Venus, Cupid and the priests are doubled by those playing minor shepherd or shepherdess parts) for the seventeen roles; the cast could be expanded to involve more priests (with lines), and a larger community of silent shepherds, perhaps doubling as musicians. It is hoped that this edition will open up at least some of those possibilities to readers, actors and directors, amateur and professional, so that the stage history of *Love's Victory* will grow in future years. As Musella says, 'who will begin this play?' (1.3.52).

6. CRITICAL RECEPTION

In the opening line of *Love's Victory* Venus proclaims to Cupid that that they have 'too long been still' (1.1.1), and the body of criticism

around the play shares this sense of belated emergence. No sign of
Love's Victory has yet been found in any seventeenth-century source:
it is unmentioned in any extant letters or diaries, there is no record
of a performance and it went ignored or unnoticed by literary critics
until the nineteenth century.

Indeed, for much of the nineteenth century the play was barely
considered a literary text at all. Tracing the movements of the
Huntington and Penshurst Manuscripts through the Victorian era,
comment on the quality of the writing is minimal, and at best
equivocal: Bernard Quaritch's catalogue of 1899 ventured that *HM*
(designated as 'Anonymous') was 'full of musical lines and does not
deserve to be lost'.[96] Excerpts from *HM* had been published by
James Orchard Halliwell in an anthology of historic manuscripts in
1853, but he wrote that the play was 'not found to be of sufficient
interest for [full] publication'.[97] The extracts he printed were based
on a transcription of *HM* by his wife Henrietta, whose contribution
to the revival of interest in the play 'at a time when Wroth herself
was at her least visible' is significant, as Paul Salzman remarks; the
choice of extracts, including 3.3, 'opens up the possibility of a mid-
nineteenth century reading of the play as a quite radical interroga-
tion of Victorian norms'.[98] This truncated incarnation of *Love's
Victory* was the basis of a brief critical account of the play by W. W.
Greg in 1906: although he noted the originality of the shepherdesses'
sharing their adventures in love (3.3.1–146), he concluded that 'on
the whole the poetic merit is small'.[99]

With the exception of C. H. J. Maxwell's edition of *HM* for a
Master of Arts thesis at Stanford in 1933, critical interest in *Love's
Victory* was almost non-existent until the closing decades of the
twentieth century.[100] The critical history of Wroth's drama has,
broadly speaking, consisted of a process of contextualization and
complication of this still comparatively 'new' text, and this process
is still ongoing, with Joyce Green MacDonald stating in 2011 –
nearly a quarter of a century after the text of the Penshurst
Manuscript was first published – that 'we are still in the very early
stages of deciding what to say about it'.[101]

It is arguable that interest in *Love's Victory* as an object of literary
inquiry was first sparked by the identification of Lady Mary Wroth
as its author, firstly by Peter Croft (probably in the 1970s) and
subsequently by Josephine Roberts in 1983.[102] This discovery
enabled critics to create a meaningful position for the play within
early modern literature: hitherto unaccommodated, it could now be

contrasted with Wroth's other works (themselves being rediscovered around that time). Arthur Freeman points out that, before Roberts's edition of Wroth's poems in 1983, 'we had virtually nothing to look at', but subsequently Wroth's work could be considered within a tradition of early modern female authorship that was being established as critical interest in women writers increased in the 1980s.[103] Most saliently, Wroth's membership of the Sidney circle – the web of familial, marital, literary and political ties centred on her uncle Sir Philip Sidney, her aunt Mary Sidney Herbert and her father Robert Sidney – provided a useful biographical and literary context for interpreting the play.

The wealth of historical material available about the Sidney coterie, combined with the volume of their literary output and willingness to allude to themselves, or versions of themselves, in their work, readily lends itself to biographical readings. Wroth's identity as a Sidney was very important to her; Margaret Hannay writes that she 'position[ed] herself as a Sidney first and woman second', and an awareness of Wroth's self-consciousness as a Sidney has often led critics to read her work through the lens of her family history, the more so because – through her relationship with her cousin William Herbert – her family history was intimately linked with her romantic history. Karen L. Nelson stated in 2015 that, up to that date, '*Love's Victory* has garnered attention from contemporary readers largely because of Wroth's biography'.[104] A dominant strand of *Love's Victory* criticism has therefore focused on the play as an exemplar of what Gary Waller has influentially termed 'the Sidney family romance'.[105]

Interpreting Wroth's plot as a reimagination of events in the family history of the Sidneys was pioneered by Josephine Roberts's identification of 'an intricate series of personal allusions' in the play, suggesting that Philisses's and Musella's names refer to Sir Philip Sidney and (as an amalgam of 'Muse' and 'Stella') Penelope Devereux, the female muse of Sidney's sonnet sequence *Astrophil and Stella*. On this reading, the threat of Musella's marriage to Rustic for 'base unworthy riches' (5.1.33) is a reference to Penelope's eventual marriage to Robert Rich rather than Sidney himself.[106] Roberts also suggests that Philisses's sister Simeana is a portrayal of Sir Philip Sidney's sister Mary Sidney Herbert, and ventures that Lissius may be a representation of Matthew Lister, the doctor who was rumoured to have become her lover after the death of her husband.[107] Subsequent critics – most prominently Marion Wynne-

Davies – have developed and extended this set of familial allusions to chart correspondences between the play's characters and
Sidney–Herbert coterie members of Wroth's own generation as well
as her uncle and aunt's, with Musella and Philisses proposed as
representations of Wroth herself and William Herbert, and the buffoonish Rustic seen as a satirical portrait of her deceased husband
Sir Robert.[108]

The identification of Rustic as Robert Wroth has met with resist-
ance, however, particularly following Hannay's re-examination of
his and Mary Wroth's relationship;[109] as noted above, his position
as the King's Forester may make him a more plausible model for
the Forester in the play, with Mary Wroth as a possible model for
Silvesta. Equally, Marion O'Connor convincingly identifies Edward
Russell, third Earl of Bedford – a keen huntsman until he was rendered impotent by a hunting accident in 1613 – as a dramatic avatar
for the Forester in terms of the character's commitment to celibate
chaste love, and she also suggests that the matchmaking activities
of his wife Lucy Harington Russell, Countess of Bedford, provide
a basis for Silvesta's efforts to aid Philisses and Musella.[110] Wroth's
close friend Susan de Vere, Countess of Montgomery – to whom
she dedicated *Urania* – has been proposed as a model for Simeana,
an identification that reinforces the play's braiding of familial, social
and romantic ties given that she was married to Wroth's cousin (and
William Herbert's brother) Philip Herbert, Earl of Montgomery.[111]

In presenting 'an overlapping series of shadowings of figures from
the Sidney-Herbert families', it has been argued that *Love's Victory*
enacts a form of romantic 'wish fulfilment' that rewrites, and rights,
the Sidney family's romantic history: the portrayal of Philisses and
Musella overcoming parental opposition and finding married happiness with each other is read as an idealized allegorical resolution
to the forbidden romances between Sir Philip Sidney and Penelope
Devereux on the one hand, and between William Herbert and
Wroth herself on the other.[112]

As noted above, this plot takes on additional resonance if the play
was performed to a family coterie audience, and critics have raised
the possibility of Wroth and her fellow participants playing versions
of themselves, or of their contemporaries.[113] In the context of such
a performance, the play has been interpreted as a celebration of
Sidney family bonds and literary production – Alison Findlay, for
example, has suggested that *Love's Victory* 'follows a Sidney tradition of using pastoral romance as family recreation', an 'active

refashioning' of Sidney literary tradition that allows Wroth to take forward the family's story on stage through a plot that celebrates 'romantic passion over economic, paternally sanctioned matches', playing out 'a family celebration of new-found freedom after Robert Wroth's death'.[114]

Other critics have conjectured that a contemporaneous performance of the play may have had a more oppositional edge: *Love's Victory* has been figured as a protest against the institution of arranged marriage, and it is possible that it was intended to resist, or even rebuke, the Sidney family's treatment of its members.[115] Ilona Bell posits that Arcas's false reports of Lissius and of Musella – leading Simeana to angrily reject Lissius, and Musella's mother to compel her to marry Rustic – were veiled references to the actions of William Herbert's steward Hugh Sanford, whose communications with Herbert and Mary Wroth's mother, Barbara Gamage Sidney, appear to have precipitated a break in the relationship between Wroth and Herbert, and expedited her mother's efforts to marry her to Sir Robert Wroth.[116]

The Sidney family context has led some critics to ascribe directly instrumental motives to the writing and possible performance of the play. For Louise Schleiner the widowed Wroth intended through *Love's Victory* – especially the character of Silvesta – to encourage 'a wooer for her hand' with whom she could enjoy a 'chaste friendship'; in particular Schleiner suggests that she intended Henry de Vere, Earl of Oxford (with whom her family was in negotiations in 1619 for a possible match with Wroth), to 'recognise himself in the Forester and be duly urged on'.[117] Likewise Beverly M. Van Note raises the possibility of Wroth taking the role of Silvesta in a performance of the play in order to 'portray the purity of her feelings for [William Herbert], and perhaps to entice [him] further'.[118]

Clearly readers of *Love's Victory* should resist the temptation to be too prescriptive in drawing parallels between the play's characters and members of the Sidney–Herbert coterie; as well as the complexity and elusiveness of her allusions to two generations of the Sidney circle, the nuances and ambiguities in Wroth's drama as a whole prohibit a simple 'who's who' interpretation of the play. Hannay's argument that Rustic is 'the standard rustic clown of pastoral' alerts readers to the need to look beyond the bounds of the Sidney–Herbert coterie in interpreting *Love's Victory*, to the literary, social, political and material contexts that informed Wroth's authorship of the play.[119]

In particular, a great deal of criticism has focused on the ways in which *Love's Victory* deals with the position of women in Wroth's time, and how Wroth's play examines female experience in general, rather than necessarily dwelling on the fortunes of those within the Sidney family: indeed, Naomi J. Miller suggests that reading *Love's Victory* primarily in the context of *roman à clef* allusions 'tends to obscure the significance of gendered differences of representation and interpretation'.[120] The rediscovery of Wroth's play coincided with a flourishing of feminist literary criticism in the last decades of the twentieth century, and *Love's Victory*'s emphasis on women's agency and relationships has yielded a substantial body of criticism focusing on the play's treatment of gender.[121] As the early critic Carolyn Ruth Swift notes, the play emphasizes 'the power of women to shape destiny as well as to endure it', and its exploration of female autonomy, both on the specific question of choosing whom to marry and in terms of freedom of action more generally, has consistently attracted critical attention.[122] In Miller's influential formulation, *Love's Victory* 'changes the subject' of Jacobean gender discourse by directing its focus towards female subjectivities and relationships, showing women as actors rather than acted-upon.[123] The shepherd-esses in the play are not defined only by their romantic relationships with men but instead cultivate friendship with one another, sharing advice in a collective 'womanspace not ruled by men' where 'None can accuse us, none can us betray' (3.3.5).[124] On this reading Wroth's drama shows a world of 'female friendships, female agency, and female control', with women able and willing to pursue their own destiny, and willing to help others to do the same. Silvesta, in particular, has been seen as a totemic example of female self-determi-nation in the play – even a 'prototype feminist' – in her wish to remain 'Free' (1.1.124) and unmarried while aiding the union of Musella and Philisses.[125]

That said, recent studies have argued that the play cannot solely be understood as a 'triumphalist feminist fable of women's roman-tic empowerment'.[126] Paul Salzman's characterization of *Love's Victory* as 'a narrative of female solidarity and also female competi-tion' is a salutary reminder that some of the female characters in Wroth's drama find fulfilment at the expense of others: Musella's and Simeana's marriages to Philisses and Lissius mean that Fillis and Climeana are left without partners at the end of the play.[127] Whilst it lacks the vehemence of Lissius's condemnation of women taking the initiative in love (3.3.167–8), Silvesta's comment that 'a woman to make love is ill' (3.1.79) at the very least emphasizes the social norms under which the female characters in the play are compelled to operate, and scholars have productively explored how *Love's Victory* shows women not escaping patriarchal structures but rather, in Alexandra G. Bennett's phrase, 'acquiescing to the strictures of codified conduct in order to deviate from them as subtly as possible'.[128]

As Bennett notes, this process is 'strikingly akin to Wroth's own game-playing as a dramatist', and the ways in which *Love's Victory* engages with and repurposes genres and literary forms, particularly in adapting them to female perspectives, have been a common theme in criticism of the play; Margaret Anne McLaren has observed that the play rewards approaches that acknowledge its status as 'an intersection of discourses, an example of give and take between social and literary structures'.[129] Wroth's adoption of pastoral as a form (discussed above) has been a fertile line of inquiry for critics: Barbara K. Lewalski suggests that 'pastoral is adapted to the concerns of a feminist politics' in *Love's Victory*, and Josephine Roberts traces Wroth's deployment of 'the coded language of pastoral' in order to create a landscape 'in which the political and social relationships of women might be questioned, challenged, and refashioned'.[130] In an important essay Joyce Green MacDonald argues that Wroth's version of pastoral is admonitory rather than triumphant, an 'attempt to engage with and defuse the sexual and emotional danger that the pastoral mode could pose for women'.[131] In particular *Love's Victory*'s significance as an example of pastoral tragicomedy has led critics to explore the play's parallels with other examples of the genre (see above).[132]

Whilst there are of course many links, discussed above, between *Love's Victory* and the writings of other members of the Sidney–Herbert coterie, Heather Dubrow highlights the risk of 'barking up the wrong family tree' in connecting Wroth's work only with that of her relatives.[133] The play has been productively compared with Shakespeare's dramatic output, and work to establish 'fuller understanding of Wroth as a dramatist rather than as a poet' is ongoing, with readings exploring *Love's Victory*'s relation to dramatic forms such as closet drama, court masque and even revenge tragedy.[134] Beyond conventional literary forms Katherine R. Larson has drawn attention to the ways in which the structure of Wroth's drama reflects the conversational games popular in the Jacobean court, arguing that the riddles and verbal contests engaged in by the shepherds and shepherdesses carve out a 'ludic framework' that enables Wroth 'to imagine and cultivate authorising rhetorical spaces for women'. She has also commented on how the play's use of song forms part of the games and serves to amplify the emotions of characters.[135]

The courtly context of *Love's Victory*, and the potential political resonances of the play arising therefrom, has also been a productive critical avenue. The Sidney–Herbert coterie's active participation in court politics gives additional weight to the relationships and social structures at work in the play; as Van Note writes, *Love's Victory* 'blurs the line between domestic and political spectacle', and a number of critics have outlined the ways in which Wroth uses the private (or, in Salzman's useful formulation, 'less public') forum of household drama to comment on the wider political scene.[136] It has been ventured that Wroth's contemporaries could have read the play as 'a potential attack on a lax court', or, alternatively, that the witty, riddling shepherds and shepherdesses in Wroth's drama are an approving representation of the Stuart court's sophisticated culture, in contrast to the wealthy but uncultivated Rustic.[137] More directly, some scholars have suggested that the events in *Love's Victory* make reference to specific issues of factional and international politics.[138]

Consideration has also been given to the wider hierarchies of power in the play, and critics have taken particular interest in the roles of, and relationship between, Venus and Cupid in this regard, with one critic proposing that they are '[t]he most important characters in the play's scheme'.[139] McLaren suggests that the 'victory' in the play's title refers to 'the power of Venus and Cupid to humble everyone in the play', and Wroth's representation of the gods 'asserting absolute power' clearly has political implications, although, as noted above, the divine hierarchy is complicated by the challenge posed to Venus by Cupid's insistence in 4.2 that 'some yet must try / More pain'.[140] Marta Straznicky has drawn attention to the 'concentration of political references' in 2.3 and 4.2, where gestures to Venus and Cupid's authority conflate obedience to love with subservience to the crown ('Love the king is of the mind' – 2.3.21).[141] Here statecraft merges with stagecraft, with the audience (addressed as 'princes' in 2.3.6 and 4.2.37) urged to accept love's supremacy, and Venus's priests proclaiming that 'Rebels' against love are now 'subjects' (4.2.19) – a triumphant affirmation that may nevertheless carry coercive undertones.

The context in which such lines might be delivered or received adds considerably to the range of interpretations that might be attributed to them, and in the past twenty years increasing focus has been directed towards the implications of considering *Love's Victory* as a performance text. Accounts exploring the musical, choreographic and other theatrical practices that may have informed Wroth's writing of the play and accompanied any potential performance (Van Note pictures a 'prominent display of female bodies – splendidly costumed and jewelled, buxom and fully voiced') have added valuable colour to critical perceptions of the play.[142]

A prominent strand of criticism has centred on the interpretative possibilities of Penshurst Place as a venue for a production of *Love's Victory* in Wroth's lifetime (discussed above).[143] Some critics have sought to ground *Love's Victory* in Penshurst's wider topography, mapping its pastoral landscape on to the gardens and rural estate surrounding the Sidney family's ancestral home, and the productions in 2014 and 2018 furnished further opportunity for exploring Penshurst as a setting for the play.[144]

Given the lack of concrete evidence that *Love's Victory* was produced at Penshurst – or indeed at any location – in Wroth's time, there is clearly value in maintaining, as Straznicky recommends, 'a continued inquisitiveness and openness about its possible places of writing, reading, and performance'.[145] Bearing this in mind, ongoing reflection on how the play might have been and may still be performed, and the testing of theories in performance, will doubtless shed more light on the nuances of Wroth's drama.

The two manuscripts of *Love's Victory* have also driven critical discussions around the dating, structure and potential performability of the play. Whilst critical consensus has typically maintained that the Penshurst Manuscript – written in fair copy, finely bound, and containing scenes that do not feature in the Huntington Manuscript – is a later, more fully realized version, recent accounts have challenged this view, promoting a reading of *HM* as the more dynamic text, or even as a working script for a possible performance.[146] For Paul Salzman, *HM* 'might represent Wroth's second thoughts on the perfection of the Penshurst manuscript', with Huntington as 'a radically and ... *consciously* unfinished text'; Marta Straznicky's forensic analysis of *HM* as a material text has drawn attention to the interpretative possibilities raised by the manuscript's 'patchwork' nature, whilst Ilona Bell argues that *HM* could be a 'revised and expurgated' version of *PM*, edited for performance outside the Sidney family circle, much as Wroth omitted parts of her sonnet sequence *Pamphilia to Amphilanthus* from the published version.[147] The relationship between the two manuscripts – including their differences both as material objects and literary texts – promises to yield further insights in future as scholars continue to explore how *Love's Victory* was perceived (and, perhaps, performed) in Wroth's time, regardless of the chronological order in which they were produced: as Straznicky concludes, the two manuscripts 'have different stories to tell'.[148]

The volume of stories told by and about *Love's Victory* since it first came into public view is testament to its appeal, and its suggestiveness as a dramatic artefact. It is to be hoped that, as the play takes its place in the canon of early modern drama, further critical and theatrical interpretations will allow readers and spectators alike to explore the intricate, beguiling and at times surprising pathways of Wroth's pastoral tragicomedy to their fullest extent.

7. THE TEXT

There is no early modern printed text of *Love's Victory*. As noted above, the play exists only in two, different, holograph versions: HM600, which is in the Huntington Library, California, and has become known as the Huntington Manuscript (*HM*), and the Penshurst Manuscript (*PM*), privately owned by Viscount De L'Isle at Penshurst Place. Wroth's handwriting and her use of diacritical marks like slashes, flourishes, and the *S fermé* all show that here we have, as Barbara K. Lewalski puts it, 'the thing itself, the bare, unaccommodated text'[149] – or rather two texts or 'things', because the manuscripts are very different. *HM* is what might be described, in the most positive sense of the word, as a working copy: it shows Wroth as a dramatist at work. *PM*, by contrast, is written in a neat autograph hand and bound as a presentation copy, possibly as a gift for William Herbert or as a family copy.

The Huntington Manuscript

HM has been identified as the manuscript transcribed by James Orchard Halliwell, who published extracts from it in *A Brief Description of the Ancient & Modern Manuscripts Preserved in the Library, Plymouth* (1852), and listed it as 'Love's Victorie, a play, copied from the original MS in the possession of Sir E. Dering, Bart. 4to.'. The only quarto manuscript of the play that has come to light so far is *PM*, and *HM* is a folio. Dering may have been in possession of *PM* as well as *HM*, or a third quarto copy of the play which has been lost. *HM* somehow made its way from Dering's estate to the Proprietary Library at Plymouth, referenced as MS No. 102, whence Halliwell took possession of it with a view to publishing it. Since over eighty of the substantive variants in the 538 lines printed by Halliwell correspond exactly – including spelling and punctuation – to the text in *HM*, it has been assumed that *HM* is the 'Plymouth' manuscript from which he was working and that he made a mistake in describing it as a quarto. Halliwell selected extracts from the play and printed them for private circulation in 1853.[150] *HM* was sold by Quaritch in December 1899 and was later owned by the American banker and collector W. A. White, and it was acquired by the Huntington Library from the bookseller and scholar A. S. W. Rosenbach in 1923 (a note on the manuscript's flyleaf states that it was 'acquired from the Rosenbach Company in 1923').[151] It was subsequently edited by C. H. J. Maxwell as her Master of Arts thesis at Stanford University,[152] and then by Paul Salzman in his anthology *Early Modern Women's Writing*, followed by an electronic edition with high-quality digital photographs of *HM* provided by the Huntington Library as part of the Early Modern Women Writers Network.[153] Marta Straznicky edited a print edition of *HM* in the anthology *Women's Household Drama* in 2018.[154]

HM contains twenty-one leaves, two of which (folios 9 and 10), are smaller sheets which are stitched and glued (or 'tipped') to the spine of the manuscript.[155] The manuscript looks as though it has been stitched five times, and evidence along the spine suggests that pages have been removed at the beginning and at the end.[156] This might explain why *HM* has no title page, and why it breaks off so suddenly on folio 21v. The title 'Loves Victorie' that occurs at the top of the first page of *HM* also appears in the same juncture – the beginning of 1.2 – in the Penshurst Manuscript, at the top of folio 2r. The abrupt ending of *HM* on a speech heading ('Phi.') may also be the result of pages being removed from the end of the manuscript, although critics have pointed out that the abrupt ending might also be an artistic choice on Wroth's part: she leaves readers waiting for more by ending the printed text of *Urania I* with the word 'And' (661), and breaks off the manuscript of *Urania II* with the intriguing words 'Amphilanthas wa[s] extremely' (418).

The possibility of removed pages at either end of *HM* does not explain the omission of Cupid and Venus's dialogue at 3.4.1–38,

the blank page (5v) after 1.4, the insertion of the smaller leaves –
including Cupid and Venus's interlude at 2.3 – or the insertions,
corrections and small differences in wording in the manuscript.
These features, along with the physical features of *HM* – its com-
piled leaves and stitching – all suggest that Wroth prepared each
manuscript with different literary and dramatic intentions in mind.
In 2.3 for example, the lines praising Cupid are assigned to Venus,
dispensing with the priests who are specifically included in a stage
direction in *PM*, and Straznicky notes that the presence of a semicolon and slash after Cupid's line 28 in *HM* suggests that the last four
lines, which could be seen as a direct address to the audience, may
be an addition to the script. After 3.3 *HM* has a new page (fol. 15v)
headed with 'The 4 Act;/' and a speech heading for Musella, which
are both erased. Other than a speech heading for Venus, the rest
of the page is blank. The omission may have been because Wroth
mistakenly started, and did not finish, writing or copying dialogue
for the scene at the end of Act 3, or because she chose to omit it –
we do not know. As noted above, the assignment to Venus of the
song praising Cupid in 2.3 and the omission here do create a shift
in power from Venus to Cupid in *HM*. The most obvious revisions
in *HM* are in the dialogue between Venus and Cupid at the end of
Act 4 (4.2 in this edition). The two deleted lines and a word spoken
or sung by Venus before the word '*musique*', and a deleted reply
by Cupid after the song lyric 'Love, thy powerful hand withdraw'
in *HM* make a significant variation to the scene here. Straznicky
argues that this scene is an interlude that concluded a performance
of the play in the style of a court masque.[157] It is plausible that such
a performance took place, given the play's theatrical and compo-
sitional context. Whilst *HM* continues after this scene (and may
have included additional pages beyond its current conclusion), the
script may well have been adapted to fit a particular occasion or set
of circumstances. Overall, the evidence suggests that *HM* is a compilation of pieces of script that may have been written at different
times, possibly distributed to or collected from other players around
a production at Surrenden. *HM* has fewer rather than more stage
directions than *PM* but, as well as being a working copy, it offers
the intriguing suggestion that Wroth may have been writing for a
company of performers.

The Penshurst Manuscript

The Penshurst Manuscript, which forms the copy text for this
edition, is a formal, presentation or personal copy, consisting of

49 quarto leaves, which are foliated. The collation is 1^2 + 2–6^4 + 7^4 (minus 3rd leaf) + 8–13^4. It is written throughout in Wroth's formal, italic hand. At the end of the manuscript, on 49v, a list of 'Men's Names' and 'Wemen Names' has been added in another hand, possibly later. The binding is of dark red turkey leather, tooled in gold, over paste-boards with marbled endpapers. The quarto measures 19.5 cm by 14.5 cm. The decoration on the cover consists of a frame of two double lines in gilt, which is decorated at each corner with an *S fermé*, also in gilt (see Fig. 2 p. 25). A complex gilt monogram, intertwining 9 or more letters (P, H, I, L, M, A, S and *S fermé*, V, W) in the centre is surrounded by a circle of vine leaves and four more *S fermés*, also in gilt, proclaiming the Sidney identity (see Fig. 5 p. 52). Four further copies of the monogram appear at the midpoint of each side of the cover. The intertwined letters form a hieroglyph or cipher which suggest, firstly, the multiple fictional identities which are overlaid as avatars for Wroth and her cousin William Herbert. As Josephine Roberts first noticed, Philisses and Musella and Pamphilia and Amphilanthus are easy to identify; in addition, one can pick out LV for *Love's Victory*, and, in addition to the P for Pembroke and S for Sidney, the strongest upright strokes which border the right and left, and the diagonals and central horizontal bar, also create the personal signatures WH (William Herbert, third Earl of Pembroke), MSW (Mary Sidney Wroth), MSH (Mary Sidney Herbert), PS (Philip Sidney), PH (Philip Herbert, Earl of Montgomery) and SVH, his wife Susan Vere Herbert, Countess of Montgomery, thus symbolizing the multilayered interfolding of real-life identities across time.[158] The absence of any R (for Robert Sidney), B for Barbara or K for Katherine may suggest that the monogram and the presentation copy are intended to incorporate Wroth into the Herbert side of the family through an alliance with William.

Although *PM* is a presentation or personal copy, it is not strictly speaking a complete text of *Love's Victory*, because a space has been left blank for the song of celebration that Venus calls for towards the end of the play (5.7.134.1SD). Other lyrics are, for the most part, clearly lineated and indented in the manuscript to distinguish them from the rest of the text, which is all written in decasyllabic rhyming verse (mostly couplets). The manuscript is divided into acts but not into scenes. Character names are usually listed at the beginning of acts/scenes but their entrances are not given; instead, Wroth writes the full name of a character who newly appears in the scene. Many – though not all – exits are marked. Significantly, exits

5 Detail of central monogram from the binding of *Love's Victory*
by Lady Mary Wroth, Penshurst Manuscript. By kind permission
of Viscount De L'Isle from his private collection.

are never marked for Venus or Cupid, perhaps suggesting that they
remain on stage throughout the play. Their entrances and exits are
heralded graphically with elaborate flourishes following the lines
of the previous speaker, and again following their lines (see Fig.
6). These flourishes appear to be stage directions, used instead of
the word 'flourish', a stage direction 'used over 500 times in early

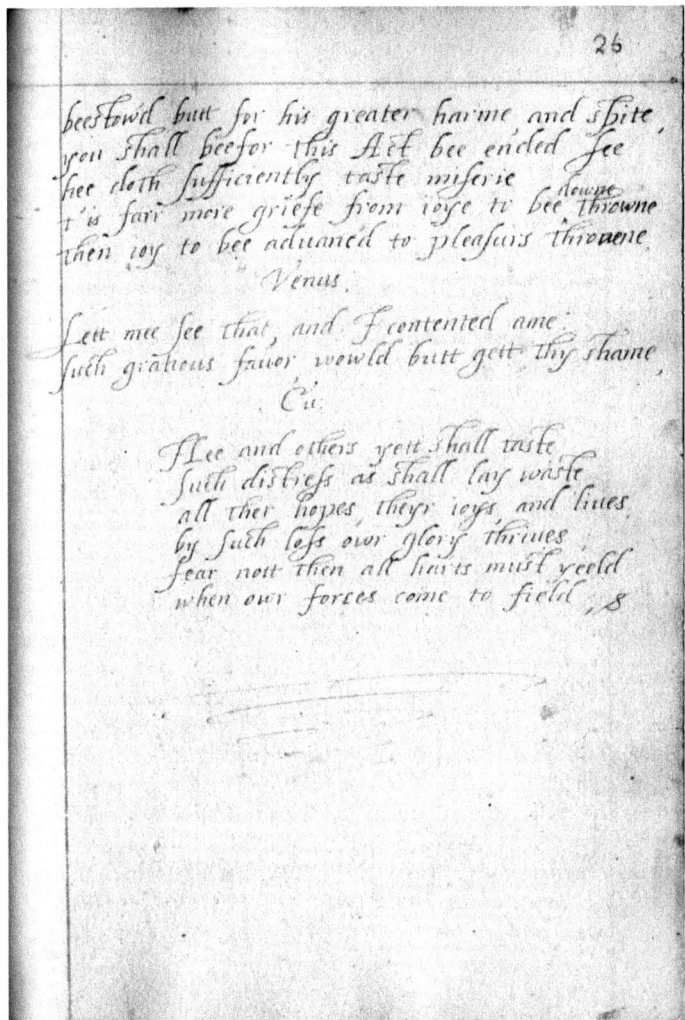

6 Folio 26r of the Penshurst Manuscript of *Love's Victory*, showing examples of overwriting (throane), insertion (downe), and capitalisation (Act). By kind permission of Viscount De L'Isle from his private collection.

modern drama for a fanfare, usually played within on a trumpet or cornet, primarily when important figures enter and exit'.[159] *PM* concludes with a truncated flourish marking the end of the play (see Fig. 7 p. 55). In line with normal Revels practice, this edition interpolates stage directions, enclosed by square brackets, in order to make more immediate sense of the action for readers, actors and directors. All such interpolations, if debatable, are discussed in commentary notes.

Whilst it has often been assumed that *PM* has always been in the possession of the Sidney family, its provenance remains unclear. The manuscript was auctioned by Puttick and Simpson on 25 September 1850 and sold to the book dealer Thomas Thorpe (1791–1851) for £3 7s 6d, before making its way to Penshurst some time thereafter.[160] *PM* was first published in 1988 by William Sidney, first Viscount De L'Isle, for the Roxburghe Club, a society of book collectors and scholars founded in 1812. This folio edition combines black and white photographs of each page of the manuscript and diplomatic transcriptions on the opposite pages by the editor, Michael G. Brennan. The Roxburghe edition (*R*) contains an introduction, brief commentary notes and a collation that compares readings in *HM* and *PM*. Roxburghe is now out of print so the present edition draws on it, making corrections and offering a new, fuller introduction and much-expanded annotation, in order to succeed it as the fully authorized edition of the Penshurst Manuscript. S. P. Cerasano and Marion Wynne-Davies's groundbreaking *Renaissance Drama by Women: Texts and Documents* also uses *PM* as a copy text, though the edition places the text from folios 42v, 43r and 43v in the wrong order, making the action hard to follow in 5.5. We make reference to useful notes provided by these editors in our own commentary, using the abbreviation *CWD*, page numbers and note number. Variant readings of the text in *CWD* are also included in the collation.

This edition

This edition interpolates likely settings as well as entrances and exits for each of the scenes, since only those of the Temple and '*the clouds*' are specified in *PM*. As outlined above, the contrast between meadows and woods is an important part of the play's emotional geography, so the conjectured rural settings make explicit for readers what is often embedded in the dialogue. Commentary notes explain our choices in each case. We have silently modernized typography

7 Folio 49r of the Penshurst Manuscript of *Love's Victory*, showing Lady Mary Wroth's formal italic hand, with capitalisation, slash mark / and signature mark of the *S fermé*. By kind permission of Viscount De L'Isle from his private collection.

and spelling throughout. Wroth's use of long s forms and contractions like w^{ch} (which) or w^t (with) and overlinings like suñ or duñ have been silently expanded. Her use of the additional 'e' as in 'cheere' or her use of 'y' and 'i' as in 'wayling' or 'chastitie' are all common in early modern English. Such markers of the period and Wroth's own peculiarities such as the reversal of 'ie' in 'freinds' are therefore invisible to the modern reader and are not included in the collations, though we have collated her use of 'Ô' and 'ô' in both *PM* and *HM,* as these may be markers of emphasis for exclamations. We have also silently modernized spellings for the lemmas for commentary notes and for references to *PM* in the collation notes unless there are good reasons to do otherwise. Forms such as 'my self' or 'her self' have been silently contracted to single words ('myself' or 'herself'). We have, however, retained Wroth's use of two distinct forms 'can not' or 'cannot' as they appear to be used to give different emphases in her text: 'can not' (Wroth's preferred form in *PM*) is used to give emphasis to both syllables even when this breaks the iambic metre in cases like 'can **not** miss' (2.1.149 and 223), 'I can **not** blame you' (2.1.181) and 'and can **not** say you're true?' (3.3.114). By contrast, 'cannot' puts stronger emphasis on the first syllable and its resonances of agency (or lack of it), as in '**Can**not refuse, and but this I require' (2.1.38) or 'But oh, she may not, **can**not, will not take' (1.2.135). Wroth is not absolutely consistent in this pattern, but it does seem to create specific effects in most cases.

Modernizing punctuation has been a priority for the edition in order to make the text as clear as possible for the modern reader; Wroth abides by many of the conventions of early modern punctuation, which read strangely to modern eyes and ears. For example, a semicolon is commonly used instead of a full stop, so we have silently replaced these to denote the end of a sentence. In addition Wroth sometimes uses a comma or occasionally a colon instead of a full stop. We have silently inserted modern punctuation in such cases. We have also silently used an initial capital for the opening word of each line of verse. Exclamation marks and question marks are often marked by the same symbol in Wroth's texts and those of her contemporaries. Our edition distinguishes between the two, making judgements in ambiguous cases. Much of *PM* (and *HM*) is characterized by light punctuation which predominantly uses commas. In 2.3, for example, the first 20 lines of the priests' praise of Cupid have only six punctuation marks, and two of these are serial commas which appear before the word 'and': 'Words against yourselves, and lines / Where his good, and your ill shines' (2.3.15–16). Use of punctuation mid-line rather than at the end of lines is a typical feature of Wroth's writing, often to point up a balance of opposites as in the example 'his good, and your ill' above. When inserting additional punctuation, as in the speech above, we have endeavoured to be sensitive to the rhythm of Wroth's writing, making cross-reference to *HM* wherever possible, in order to insert additional punctuation marks that clarify meaning.

Although Wroth's vocabulary is relatively simple to understand, her sentences can at times be long and somewhat labyrinthine. In cases such as the Forester's speech in 1.2.191–202 or Silvesta's dense lines in 1.2.99–108 we have broken up the speeches with additional punctuation to clarify meaning, recording any alternative readings in commentary notes. Both *PM* and *HM* make occasional use of emphatic capitals (see Fig. 7 p. 55). For the sake of consistency, we have limited our use of non-standard capitalization to personifications. Where words such as 'love', 'death', 'echo' or 'chastity' refer to the thing or concept we have represented these in lower case and collated Wroth's use of capitals; where they refer to embodied manifestations of those concepts in examples like the goddess Fortune, or Love, or Reason, we have used capitals, even when Wroth does not do so. The collations in the edition focus on differences between our copy text and *HM*, citing this alone unless there are subsequent different readings from previous editors. As stated above, we have collated diacritical marks in the manuscripts that may add to readers' understanding or appreciation of Wroth's text. For instance, *PM* ends emphatically with a flourish that is truncated by the bottom of the page (see Fig. 7); Wroth also marks the ending with her signature mark, the *S fermé*, and the word 'Finis', concluding her manuscript by celebrating both the Sidney family identity and her own achievement in perpetuating its literary legacy in dramatic form.

NOTES

1 Josephine A. Roberts, 'The Huntington Manuscript of Lady Mary Wroth's Play *Loves Victorie*', *HLQ*, 46:2 (1983), 156–74, 160, 172 n.6.
2 Scenes in the Penshurst Manuscript which are not in the Huntington Manuscript are 1.1, 3.4, 5.2, 5.3, 5.4, 5.5, 5.6 and 5.7. For further details of the manuscripts see pp. 48–54.
3 Ilona Bell, 'The Circulation of Writings by Lady Mary Wroth', in *ARC*, Vol. 2, 77–85, 79.

4 This summary of Wroth's life relies on Margaret P. Hannay's biography *Mary Sidney, Lady Wroth* (hereafter *MSLW*), which has been an invaluable source of inspiration and information throughout our work on the edition.

5 *The Letters (1595–1608) of Rowland Whyte*, ed. Michael G. Brennan, Noel J. Kinnamon and Margaret P. Hannay (Philadelphia: American Philosophical Society, 2013), 421, 67.

6 Gavin Alexander, 'The Musical Sidneys', *John Donne Journal*, 25 (2006), 64–105, 92. Roberts, in *The Poems of Lady Mary Wroth*, points out that John Davies of Hereford addressed a sonnet 'To the Lady Wroth, 'In deserved praise of the heavenly Music: resembling it to God Himself' (Wroth *Poems*, 18).

7 Andrew Sabol, ed., *Four Hundred Songs and Dances* (Providence: Brown University Press, 1982), notes two dance tunes of the period which seem to be named after Wroth: the 'Durance Masque' no. 119, 219, referring to her married home and 'My Lady Wroth's Mascharanda' no. 40, 510.

8 See *BM*, 38–44.

9 See *MSLW*, 146, and Miller's idea that Wroth's writing 'suggests personal experience of the physical and emotional loss of miscarriage'. Naomi J. Miller, *Changing the Subject: Mary Wroth and Figurations of Gender in Early Modern England* (Lexington: University of Kentucky Press, 1996), 84–5.

10 *Informations to William Drummond of Hawthornden*, ed. Ian Donaldson, in Ben Jonson, *Works*, ll. 275–6.

11 Ben Jonson, *The Forest*, 3 (1616), ed. Colin Burrow in Jonson, *Works*.

12 *MSLW*, 137–45.

13 Edward Herbert, *Occasional Verses of Edward Lord Herbert, Baron of Cherbury, Deceased in August 1648* (London: Thomas Dring, 1665), 42. The singular 'child' here suggests that Edward Herbert is thinking primarily of the birth of William, as perpetuating his father's name. See *The Amazon* by Lord Herbert of Cherbury, ed. Christina Malcolmson, Matteo Pangallo and Eugene Hill in *Collections* XVII (Oxford: Malone Society, 2016), 207.

14 The manuscript collection of poems is MS V.a.104, Folger Shakespeare Library, Washington, DC.

15 *Urania I*, 300.22.

16 Roberts, *The Poems of Lady Mary Wroth*, 236.

17 *MSLW*, 181, 306.

18 Roberts notes Joshua Sylvester's praise of Wroth as one 'in whom her Uncle's noble vein renews' (H2) in his 1613 poem *Lachrimae Lachrimorum* (Wroth *Poems*, 18–19), and Hannay says 'she was known to have been circulating poems by 1613 but probably began earlier' (*MSLW*, 181). Ilona Bell and Steven W. May have shown that Wroth's manuscript collection of poems V.a.104, including *Pamphilia to Amphilanthus*, differs considerably from the versions printed at the end of the printed *Urania* of 1621, suggesting revision for the public. See *BM*.

19 Michael G. Brennan, 'Creating Female Authorship in the Early Seventeenth Century: Ben Jonson and Lady Mary Wroth', in *Women's*

Writing and the Circulation of Ideas: Manuscript Publication in England 1550–1800, ed. George L. Justice and Nathan Tinker (Cambridge: Cambridge University Press, 2002), 73–93.

20 *The Alchemist*, ed. Peter Holland and William Sherman, in Jonson, *Works*, Dedication, ll. 7–8. The play was in performance by October 1610, suggesting that the connection between Jonson and Wroth predates his visit to Penshurst.

21 *MSLW*, 218. Folios 55r–65r have the same ruling as *PM*.

22 Bell, 'The Circulation of Writings by Lady Mary Wroth', 80. See 48–50.

23 *Epigrams*, ed. Colin Burrow, in Jonson, *Works*, 103, ll. 4, 9–10, 12.

24 P. J. Croft, ed. *The Poems of Robert Sidney* (Oxford: Oxford University Press, 1984), 342–5.

25 See MSH *Works*, Vol. 1, 81–91; *LM*, 35–44; William Herbert, *Poems* (1660), 38–9. See Mary Ellen Lamb, 'The Poetry of William Herbert, Third Earl of Pembroke', in *ARC*, Vol. 2, 269–82.

26 Christopher Marlowe, 'The Passionate Shepherd to his Love' and Sir Walter Raleigh, 'The Nymph's Reply to the Shepherd', in *Elizabethan Lyrics*, edited by Norman Ault (London: Faber and Faber, 1986), 134–6, and John Donne, 'The Bait', in *John Donne*, ed. John Carey (Oxford: Oxford University Press, 1990), 117–18.

27 See Sir Philip Sidney, 'A volume of poetry written in various hands', British Library Add MS 15232. For an example of apprentice penmanship see, for example, folio 29r. Peter Croft points out in *The Poems of Robert Sidney* that the manuscript passed to the Montagu family, descendants of Katherine, and suggests the anonymous poems in it could be hers (5–6).

28 For Mary Sidney Herbert's translation of Petrarch's 'The Triumph of Death' see MSH *Works*, Vol. 1, 255–82. Henry Parker's translation was *The Triumphs of Frances Petrarch* (London: John Cawood, 1555).

29 *The Sidney Psalter: The Psalms of Sir Philip and Mary Sidney*, ed. Hannibal Hamlin, Michael G. Brennan, Margaret P. Hannay and Noel J. Kinnamon (Oxford: Oxford University Press, 2009), 22.

30 Sir Philip Sidney, *Apology for Poetry (or the Defence of Poesy)*, ed. R. W. Maslen (Manchester: Manchester University Press, 2002), 113, and *LM*.

31 See 2.3.6 and 4.2.37–8.

32 See MSH *Works*, Vol. 2, 139–207.

33 Lady Jane Lumley, 'The Tragedy of Iphigenia', in *Three Tragedies by Renaissance Women*, ed. Diane Purkiss (Harmondsworth: Penguin, 1988), 1–35.

34 Marion Wynne-Davies, 'The Queen's Masque: Renaissance Women and the Seventeenth-Century Court Masque', in *Gloriana's Face: Women, Public and Private in the English Renaissance*, ed. S. P. Cerasano and Marion Wynne-Davies (Detroit: Wayne State University Press, 1992), 79–104, 96.

35 Gary Waller, *The Sidney Family Romance: Mary Wroth, William Herbert, and the Early Modern Construction of Gender* (Detroit: Wayne State University Press, 1993), 232.

36 See John H. Astington, *English Court Theatre 1558–1642* (Cambridge: Cambridge University Press, 1999), 229–30, and Richard Dutton, *Shakespeare, Court Dramatist* (Oxford: Oxford University Press, 2016).

37 Shakespeare is the first of the 'principal comedians' who played in *Every Man In His Humour* in 1598, so Wroth probably knew him as an actor as well as a writer. See *Every Man In His Humour*, ed. David Bevington, in Jonson, *Works*, 5.4.85.

38 Astington, *English Court Theatre*, 244–7.

39 Paul Salzman and Marion Wynne-Davies, eds, *Mary Wroth and Shakespeare* (London and New York: Routledge, 2015).

40 Astington, *English Court Theatre*, 247.

41 Rebecca Lemon notes a similarity between the overthrow of Cupid in *Pamphilia to Amphilanthus* and *Cupid's Banishment* in 'Indecent Exposure in Mary Wroth', in *Women and Culture at the Courts of the Stuart Queens*, ed. Clare McManus (Houndmills: Palgrave Macmillan, 2003), 140–60, 141.

42 Robert White, *Cupid's Banishment*, in *Renaissance Drama by Women: Texts and Documents*, ed. S. P. Cerasano and Marion Wynne-Davies (London and New York: Routledge, 1996), 83–9, ll. 81–2.

43 John Fletcher, *Cupid's Revenge as it hath Been Diverse Times Acted by the Children of Her Majesty's Revels* (London: T. Creede for J. Harrison, 1615), C1v.

44 Sonnet 17 of *Astrophil and Stella* (one of those copied out in a junior hand in BL, MS Add 15232), for example, describes how 'His mother dear *Cupid* offended late' because of his slackness, so she scolded him, pushed him from her lap and broke his bow and arrows. In Sonnets 19 and 20, however, Cupid is triumphant, a 'Tyran[t]', over the sonneteer (PS *Poems*, 273, 174–5). Wroth's *Pamphilia to Amphilanthus* emphasizes their hierarchical relationship as mother and childlike but often cruel son. The opening sonnet presents 'bright Venus, Queen of love, / And at her feet her son still adding fire / To burning hearts which she did hold above'. Wroth *Poems*, 85.

45 *The Haddington Masque*, ed. David Lindley, in Jonson, *Works*, l. 38.

46 There may be some confusion about which dramatic event is described here, as Galli's friend Lotti seems to have mixed up the two masques in his discussion. See John Orrell, 'The London Stage in the Florentine Correspondence, 1604–18', *Theatre Research International*, 3:3 (1978), 157–76.

47 Antimo Galli, *Rime di Antimo Galli all' Illustrissima Signora Elizabetta Talbot-Grey* (Londini: M. Bradwood, 1609). Elizabeth Talbot Grey (1582–1651) was the sister of William Herbert's wife Mary Talbot. In 1601 she married Henry Grey, the Earl of Kent. The stanza praising Wroth is on B2v. The translation is by Orietta da Rold and Guyda Armstrong and is taken from the Masque Records section of Jonson, *Works*, *Masque of Beauty*, 26.

48 Marta Straznicky, *SM*, 39–41. It should be noted, however, that such a reference would have been very ill-judged in the Jacobean court in the years following the death of Prince Henry, whose memory continued to haunt King James I. See Catriona Murray, '"Great Britaine, all in Blacke": The Commemoration of Henry, Prince of Wales in a Portrait of his Father, King James I', *The British Art Journal*, 12:3 (2012), 20–5, 21.

49 See *The Haddington Masque, Love Freed from Ignorance and Folly* and *Love Restored*, all ed. David Lindley, in Jonson, *Works*. There are strong verbal parallels between *The Haddington Masque*, where Cupid is called 'Venus runaway' (68) and 'straggler' (145) and the masque described in *Urania II*, and between the complaints against Cupid in Jonson's masques and in *Love's Victory* (e.g. 1.2.97–108).

50 Nathaniel Baxter, *Sir Philip Sidney's Ourania, that is Endymion's Song and Tragedy* (London: E. Allde for Edward White, 1606), A4r. 'Venery' is 'the practice of pursuit of sexual pleasure, indulgence of sexual desire' (*OED*, n. 2).

51 White, *Cupid's Banishment*, ll. 69–126.

52 *Urania II*, 46–8.

53 Jonson, *Love Restored* (1611), l. 162.

54 *The Masque of Blackness*, ed. David Lindley, in Jonson, *Works*, ll. 186–92.

55 On the significance of the image see Mary Ellen Lamb, 'Selling Mary Wroth's *Urania:* The Frontispiece and the Connoisseurship of Romance', *SJ*, 34:1 (2016), 33–48.

56 *Urania I*, 48–9.

57 See *The Masque of Beauty* (1608), ed. David Lindley, in Jonson, *Works*, ll. 188–93.

58 Jonson, *The May Lord* (c. 1611). This lost play was described by Jonson to Drummond in 1618, naming the Countess of Rutland, the Countess of Montgomery, William Herbert and Wroth as performers. See Ian Donaldson's Introduction to *The May Lord* in Jonson, *Works*.

59 *Epigrams* (1616), ed. Colin Burrow, in Jonson, *Works*, 105.7–10.

60 *Il Pastor Fido, Tragicomedia Pastorale Di Battista Guarini* (London: per Giovanni Volseo, 1591), *Aminta Favola* follows on 227 (sig. L3). See Michael G. Brennan, 'Philip Sidney's Book-Buying at Venice and Padua, Giovannni Varisco's Venetian Editions of Jacopo Sannazaro's *Arcadia* (1571 and 1578) and Edmund Spenser's *The Shepheardes Calendar* (1579)', *SJ*, 36:1 (2018), 19–40, 24–5.

61 Sidney, *Apology for Poetry*, 112.

62 Barbara K. Lewalski, 'Mary Wroth's *Love's Victory* and Pastoral Tragicomedy', in *Reading Mary Wroth: Representing Alternatives in Early Modern England*, ed. Naomi J. Miller and Gary Waller (Knoxville: University of Tennessee Press, 1991), 88–108, 89.

63 *Il Pastor Fido or The Faithful Shepherd*, translated out of Italian into English (London: Simon Waterson, 1602); John Fletcher, *The Faithful Shepherdess* (London: Edward Allde, 1610).

64 Marion Wynne-Davies, *Women Writers and Familial Discourse in the English Renaissance: Relative Values* (Houndmills: Palgrave Macmillan, 2007), 96.

65 Julie D. Campbell, '*Love's Victory* and *La Mirtilla* in the Canon of Renaissance Tragicomedy: an Examination of the Influence of Salon and Social Debates', *Women's Writing*, 4:1 (1997), 103–25. For more on Andreini see Anne MacNeil, *Music and Women of the Commedia dell'Arte* (Oxford: Oxford University Press, 2003).

66 Campbell, '*Love's Victory* and *La Mirtilla*', 118, 108.

67 For a reading of the play's emotional geography see Alison Findlay, *Playing Spaces in Early Women's Drama* (Cambridge: Cambridge University Press, 2006), 83–6.

68 Don E. Wayne, *Penshurst: The Semiotics of Place and the Poetics of History* (London: Methuen, 1984).

69 *The Third Part of the Countess of Pembroke's Ivychurch, entitled, Amintas Dale* (London, 1592), B2v.

70 For more on Penshurst as setting and venue see Findlay, *Playing Spaces*, 90–4.

71 See Akiko Kusunoki, *Gender and Representations of the Female Subject in Early Modern England* (Houndmills: Palgrave, 2015), 105, who notes this similarity.

72 Marcus Tullius Cicero, *Laelius De Amiticia* (44 BCE), translated by John Harrington as *The Book of Friendship of Marcus Tullie Cicero* (London, 1550), 15r–v.

73 See 1.3.21–2 and 2.1.1–2.

74 The Marquise of Gargardia, or 'merry Marquess', as she is usually called, is one whom 'no accident could befall' to make her sad 'or lose so much good time (as she called it) so as not to use her wit and merry jesting' (*Urania II*, 280). Her ideas on wifely behaviour are proto-feminist (281–2), and she is a source of comfort to Pamphilia in *Urania II* (307–9).

75 Gary Waller, *The Female Baroque in Early Modern English Literary Culture from Mary Sidney to Aphra Behn* (Amsterdam: Amsterdam University Press, 2020), 209.

76 *Urania II*, 316.33–317.5.

77 *Urania II*, 317.25–36.

78 Josephine A. Roberts first noticed the monogram's links between Wroth (MSW) and Herbert (WH) and their fictional personae in 'Deciphering Women's Pastoral: Coded Language in Wroth's *Love's Victory*', in *Representing Women in Renaissance England*, ed. Claude J. Summers and Ted-Larry Pebworth (Columbia: University of Missouri Press, 1997), 163–74. The monogram contains many possible links to members of the Sidney–Herbert coterie (see p. 51).

79 See Findlay, '*Love's Victory* in Production at Penshurst', *SJ*, 34:1 (2016), 107–21, 118–19, for more on how these effects may have worked.

80 On the practice of touring to great houses, the most detailed records are collected in the Records of Early English Drama series. For scripts composed and directed by women see Findlay, *Playing Spaces*.

81 Beverly M. Van Note, 'Performing "fitter means": Marriage and Authorship in *Love's Victory*', in *Re-Reading Mary Wroth*, ed. Katherine R. Larson and Naomi J. Miller with Andrew Strycharski (Basingstoke and New York: Palgrave Macmillan, 2015), 69–81, 72.

82 Robert Sidney was preoccupied with arrangements for Queen Anne's funeral and William Herbert was at the bedside of the King – Van Note, 'Performing "fitter means"', 71.

83 *The Sad Shepherd*, ed. Anne Barton and Eugene Giddens, in Jonson, *Works*, 'The Persons of the Play', 29–30.

84 For details see Appendix I.

85 Bananarama, 'Venus' (London: London Records, 1986), written by Robert van Leeuwen in 1969 and originally recorded by Shocking Blue in 1970.

86 Rubens made copies of Titian's painting of c. 1555. See, for example, that in the Museo Nacional Thyssen-Bornemisza, Madrid, dated 1612–15.

87 Nina Simone, 'I Put a Spell on You' (Philips Records, 1965), written by Jalacy 'Screamin' Jay' Hawkins.

88 John Playford, *The Dancing Master, or, Plain and Easy Rules for the Dancing of Country Dances, with the Tune to Each Dance* (London: Printed by Thomas Harper and are to be sold by John Playford in his shop in the Inner Temple, 1651), 87; William Ballet's Lute Book. Trinity College Dublin, Library, MS 408 (1590–1603), 91.

89 See Findlay, '*Love's Victory* in Production', 120–1.

90 See accounts by Katherine R. Larson, 'Playing at Penshurst: The Songs and Musical Games of Mary Wroth's *Love's Victory*', *SJ*, 34:1 (2016), 93–106, and Marion Wynne-Davies, 'Performance of Lady Mary Wroth's *Love's Victory*: A Review', *SJ*, 34:1 (2016), 123–6.

91 For details see Appendix II.

92 *The First Book of Songs and Airs of Four Parts with Tablature for the Lute* (London: Peter Short, 1600) was dedicated to Robert Sidney, and *The Muses' Garden For Delights, or The First Book of Airs, Only for the Lute, the Bass-Viol, and the Voice* (London: William Barley, 1610) was dedicated to Wroth.

93 See Findlay, *Playing Spaces*, 92.

94 See note 74.

95 For details on performance rights for this edition of *Love's Victory* please see the note under Acknowledgements.

96 Quoted in Roberts, 'Huntington', 162; for accounts of the manuscripts' movements in the nineteenth century see 'THE TEXT' 48–57.

97 James Orchard Halliwell, ed., *A Brief Description of the Ancient & Modern Manuscripts Preserved in the Public Library, Plymouth: To Which Are Added Some Fragments of Early Literature Hitherto Unpublished* (London: Printed by C. and J. Adlard for Private Circulation only, 1853), 212.

98 Paul Salzman, 'Henrietta's Version: Mary Wroth's *Love's Victory* in the Nineteenth Century', in *Material Cultures of Early Modern Women's Writing*, ed. Patricia Pender and Rosalind Smith (Houndmills: Palgrave Macmillan, 2014), 159–73, 165, 170.

99 W. W. Greg, *Pastoral Poetry and Pastoral Drama: A Literary Inquiry with Special Reference to the Pre-Restoration Stage in England* (London: A. H. Bullen, 1906), 368.

100 C. H. J. Maxwell, ed., *Loves Victorie*, Master's thesis, Stanford University, 1933.

101 Joyce Green MacDonald, 'Ovid and Women's Pastoral in Lady Mary Wroth's *Love's Victory*', *Studies in English Literature 1500–1900*, 51:2 (Spring 2011), 447–63, 459.

102 Arthur Freeman, '*Love's Victory*: A Supplementary Note', *The Library*, 19 (1997), 252–54, 253; Roberts, 'Huntington', 156–60.

103 Arthur Freeman, 'Review of Michael G. Brennan (ed.), *Lady Mary Wroth's Love's Victory: The Penshurst Manuscript*', *The Library*, 6:13 (1991), 168–73, 170.

104 Karen L. Nelson, '"Change Partners and Dance": Pastoral Virtuosity in Wroth's *Love's Victory*', in *Re-Reading Mary Wroth*, ed. Katherine R. Larson and Naomi Miller with Andrew Strycharski (New York: Palgrave Macmillan, 2015), 137–56, 139.

105 *MSLW*, 1; Waller, *The Sidney Family Romance*.

106 Roberts, 'Huntington', 166.

107 Roberts, 'Huntington', 167.

108 Marion Wynne-Davies, '"So Much Worth": Autobiographical Narratives in the Work of Lady Mary Wroth', in *Betraying Our Selves: Forms of Self-Representation in Early Modern English Texts*, ed. Henk Dragstra, Sheila Ottway and Helen Wilcox (Houndmills and New York: Macmillan Press and St Martin's Press, 2000), 76–93, 81–3; see also Louise Schleiner, *Tudor and Stuart Women Writers* (Bloomington and Indianapolis: Indiana University Press, 1993), 135–8.

109 *MSLW*, 214. Schleiner, *Tudor and Stuart Women Writers*, 136. For other identifications of Rustic as Sir Robert Wroth see Waller, *Sidney Family Romance*, 240, and *CWD*, 92.

110 Marion O'Connor, '"Silvesta Was My Instrument Ordained"?: Lucy Harington Russell, Third Countess of Bedford, as Family Marriage Broker', *SJ*, 34:1 (2016), 49–66; for Lucy Russell as Silvesta see also Wynne-Davies, *Women Writers*, 100–3.

111 Paul Salzman, '*Love's Victory*, Pastoral, Gender, and *As You Like It*', in *Mary Wroth and Shakespeare*, ed. P. Salzman and M. Wynne-Davies (London and New York: Routledge, 2014) 125–36, 126.

112 Salzman, '*Love's Victory*', 127; Schleiner, *Tudor and Stuart Women Writers*, 143.

113 See for example *MSLW*, 221, or Wynne-Davies, *Women Writers*, 103.

114 Findlay, *Playing Spaces*, 89, 90.

115 Campbell, '*Love's Victory* and *La Mirtilla*', 116; Heide Towers, 'Politics and Female Agency in Lady Mary Wroth's *Love's Victorie*', *Women's Writing*, 13:3 (2006), 432–47, 444.

116 *BM*, 54–5. Clare Dawkins suggests that Arcas is a composite of Sanford and Lord Denny, who attacked Wroth in verse following the publication of *Urania I* ('Victorious Service in Lady Mary Wroth's *Love's Victory*', *SJ*, 31:1 (2013), 131–49, 149.

117 Schleiner, *Tudor and Stuart Women Writers*, 140–1.

118 Van Note, 'Performing "fitter means"', 77.

119 *MSLW*, 214.

120 Miller, *Changing the Subject*, 167.

121 Roberts's attribution of *HM* to Wroth was published shortly before the first edition of the *Norton Anthology of Literature by Women*, ed. Sandra Gilbert and Susan Gubar (New York: W. W. Norton and Company, 1985).

122 Carolyn Ruth Swift, 'Feminine Self-Definition in Lady Mary Wroth's *Love's Victorie* (c. 1621)', *ELR*, 19:2 (Spring 1989), 171–88, 177.

123 Miller, *Changing the Subject*, 4 and 217.

124 Waller, *Female Baroque*, 181.

125 Barbara K. Lewalski, *Writing Women in Jacobean England* (London and Cambridge, MA: Harvard University Press, 1993), 7; Wynne-Davies, 'Absent Fathers: Mary Wroth's *Love's Victory* and William Shakespeare's

King Lear', in *Mary Wroth and Shakespeare*, ed. P. Salzman and M. Wynne-Davies (London and New York: Routledge, 2015), 61–72, 66.

126 MacDonald, 'Ovid and Women's Pastoral', 455.

127 Salzman, 'Henrietta's Version', 171.

128 Alexandra G. Bennett, 'Playing by and with the Rules: Genre, Politics, and Perception in Mary Wroth's *Love's Victorie*', in *Women and Culture at the Courts of the Stuart Queens*, ed. Clare McManus (Houndmills: Palgrave Macmillan, 2003), 122–39, 131; see also Dawkins, 'Victorious Service', 141.

129 Margaret Anne McLaren, 'An Unknown Continent: Lady Mary Wroth's Forgotten Pastoral Drama, "Loves Victorie"', in *The Renaissance Englishwoman in Print: Counterbalancing the Canon*, ed. Anne M. Haselkorn and Betty S. Travitsky (Amherst: University of Massachusetts Press, 1990), 276–94, 279.

130 Lewalski, 'Pastoral Tragicomedy', 91; Roberts, 'Deciphering', 173.

131 MacDonald, 'Ovid and Women's Pastoral', 449.

132 See for example Lewalski, 'Pastoral Tragicomedy', Campbell, '*Love's Victory* and *La Mirtilla*', and M. Wynne-Davies, 'The Liminal Woman in Mary Wroth's *Love's Victory*', *SJ*, 26:2 (2008), 65–81.

133 Heather Dubrow, *Echoes of Desire: English Petrarchism and Its Counterdiscourses* (Ithaca and London: Cornell University Press, 1995), 145.

134 Findlay, 'Lady Mary Wroth: *Love's Victory*', in *ARC*, Vol. 2, 211–21, 216. For *Love's Victory* and Shakespeare see Findlay's, Kusunoki's, Miller's, Salzman's and Wynne-Davies's essays in *Mary Wroth and Shakespeare*, ed. P. Salzman and M. Wynne-Davies (London and New York: Routledge, 2015), as well as Katherine R. Larson, 'Conversational Games and the Articulation of Desire in Shakespeare's *Love's Labour's Lost* and Mary Wroth's *Love's Victory*', *ELR*, 40:2 (Spring 2010), 165–90. For *Love's Victory* as closet drama, see Helen Hackett, *A Short History of English Renaissance Drama* (London: I. B. Tauris, 2013), 187–8; Bennett explores the play's interaction with masque culture in 'Playing by and with the Rules', whilst Sidney L. Sondergard points out its affinity with aspects of revenge tragedy in *Sharpening Her Pen: Strategies of Rhetorical Violence by Early Modern English Women Writers* (Selinsgrove: Susquehanna University Press, 2002), 109.

135 Katherine R. Larson, *Early Modern Women in Conversation* (Houndmills: Palgrave Macmillan, 2011), 107, and *The Matter of Song in Early Modern England: Texts In and Of the Air* (Oxford: Oxford University Press, 2020), 169–78.

136 Salzman, '*Love's Victory*', 133; Van Note, 'Performing "fitter means"', 72.

137 P. Salzman, *Reading Early Modern Women's Writing* (Oxford: Oxford University Press, 2006), 79; Lewalski, 'Pastoral Tragicomedy', 104.

138 For a reading of the play as a document of factional conflict in the Jacobean court, see Schleiner, *Tudor and Stuart Women Writers*, 134–6; for *Love's Victory* in the context of international diplomacy and dynastic marriage, see Towers, 'Politics and Female Agency', 439–43, and Wynne-Davies, *Women Writers*, 100–3.

139 Waller, *Female Baroque*, 180; Jane Kingsley-Smith gives an account of Venus and Cupid in *Love's Victory* in *Cupid in Early Modern Literature and Culture* (Cambridge: Cambridge University Press, 2010), 128–32.

140 McLaren, 'An Unknown Continent', 283; Roberts, 'Deciphering', 168; Stephanie Hodgson-Wright, 'Beauty, Chastity and Wit: Feminising the Centre-Stage', in Alison Findlay and Stephanie Hodgson-Wright with Gweno Williams, *Women and Dramatic Production 1550–1700* (Harlow: Pearson Education, 2000), 42–67, 64.

141 Straznicky, *SM*, 35.

142 Van Note, 'Performing "fitter means"', 79; for musical and choreographic influences on the play see Nelson, '"Change Partners and Dance"', and Larson, 'Playing at Penshurst'.

143 For explorations of possible performances see *MSLW*, 221, and Alison Findlay, 'Four Weddings, Two Funerals, and Tragicomic Resurrection: *Love's Victory* and *Much Ado About Nothing*', in *Mary Wroth and Shakespeare*, ed. P. Salzman and M. Wynne-Davies (London and New York: Routledge, 2015), 84–94, 92.

144 See Findlay, *Playing Spaces*, 83–94, and '*Love's Victory* in Production'; Wynne-Davies, '"So Much Worth"', 86–8.

145 Marta Straznicky, 'Review of *Love's Victory*, Performance at Penshurst Place, 8 June 2014', *Early Modern Women's Journal*, 9:2 (2015), 166–70, 170.

146 For *HM* as an earlier draft version see, for example, *R*, 14.

147 Salzman, *Reading*, 84; Straznicky, *SM*, 24–32 (see also 'Lady Mary Wroth's Patchwork Play: The Huntington Manuscript of *Love's Victory*', *SJ*, 34:1 (2016), 81–92); *BM*, 56.

148 Straznicky, *SM*, 32.

149 Lewalski, 'Pastoral Tragicomedy', 88.

150 Halliwell, *A Brief Description*, 212.

151 See *Catalogue of English Literary Manuscripts* (https://celm-ms.org.uk/authors/wrothladymary.html).

152 Maxwell, ed., *Loves Victorie*.

153 See *EMWW* and EMWRN in List of Abbreviations.

154 See *SM* in List of Abbreviations.

155 See Salzman's electronic edition – https://c21ch.newcastle.edu.au/emwrn/wrothhistory.

156 Personal discussion with Sara S. Hodson and Vanessa Wilkie, Curators of Medieval Manuscripts and British History, at The Huntington Library, 10 May 2017.

157 Straznicky, *SM*, 39–40.

158 Michael G. Brennan begins this process, identifying further family names (*R*, 16). There is probably still more to unravel from the monogram, in a continuation of the courtly games played by the shepherds. For example, if the monogram is turned 90° one can also see an E, allowing for the spelling out of the whole of Musella and Philisses's names, as well as those of Pamphilia and Amphilanthus, if letters are repeated and the conventions of treating 'u' and 'v' as the same letter are observed. The significance of monograms can be seen in *Urania I* where Pamphilia takes a knife to carve 'a cipher, which contained the letters or rather the anagram of his name she most and only loved' (325).

159 Alan C. Dessen and Leslie Thomson, *A Dictionary of Stage Directions in English Drama, 1580–1642* (Cambridge: Cambridge University Press, 1994), 94. We have not yet found any other examples of a flourish used as a stage direction in this way, although Thomas Dekker's *A Strange Horse-Race at the End of Which, Comes in the Catch-Poles Masque* (London, 1613), says 'Give me leave therefore, first to make a flourish with my pen, and clear the way (as a Fencer doth in a May-game) for more room, until the Masquers come in' (B1). Thanks to Reanna Esmail from Cornell University Library for assistance with searching for the term in Thomas Blount's *Glossographica* (London: Thomas Newcomb, 1661).

160 See Freeman, *'Love's Victory'*, 254.

LOVE'S VICTORY

Dramatis Personae

Men's Names

PHILISSES in love with MUSELLA and beloved by her
LISSIUS in love with SIMEANA and beloved by her
FORESTER in love with SILVESTA

---

1. Men's Names] *PM;* Shepherds *CWD.*   2. PHILISSES] *CWD;* Phillises
PM. love] Love *PM. This word is capitalized throughout the Dramatis Personae.*

Dramatis Personae] This list of names is recorded at the end of *PM* (fol. 49v) in a different hand to Wroth's; its authorship is unclear, as are the reasons for its being bound alongside Wroth's text (though the sloping capital L in the cast list could be seen to resemble that used in the shelf mark L6,27 on the first page of *HM* and in Dering's cast list for *The Spanish Curate* and manuscript compilation of *Henry IV* by Shakespeare, Folger Shakespeare Library V.b.34). There is no cast list included in *HM*.

2. PHILISSES] The faithful lover's name, deriving from the ancient Greek word *philia* or love, recalls Astrophil in Sir Philip Sidney's *Astrophil and Stella* (*c.* 1582/3; pr. 1591 and 1595), Philisides in Sidney's *Arcadia* (*c.* 1577 – *c.* 1582; pr. 1590, 1593) and Amphilanthus ('lover of two' *Urania I,* 300.22) the unfaithful hero of Wroth's sonnet sequence and *Urania,* as well as nodding to Sir Philip Sidney himself. Plato's *Symposium* defines *philia* as friendship or goodwill between lovers, which transforms lust for physical possession (*eros*) into a shared desire for a higher understanding of the self, each other and the world.

3. LISSIUS] a name not found in other pastorals or published writing of the Sidney–Herbert circle, or in *Urania II.* It may be a *nom à clef* for Sir Matthew Lister, the physician and companion of Mary Sidney Herbert who helped her construct Houghton House 'to the design of Sir Philip Sidney in his *Arcadia,* a house of pleasure' (see *Phoenix,* 201, and *MSLW,* 204). Cf. Thomas Cooper's *Thesaurus Linguae Romanae & Britannicae* (London: H. Denham, 1578) which lists 'Lysius' as 'A river of Arcady called also *Lusius*'. It could also be an allusion to the classical orator Lysias (*c.* 445 – *c.* 380 BCE) either in his own right as a historical figure or, more likely, as represented in Plato's *Phaedrus,* in which he gives a speech denouncing love and lovers as irrational (trans. Robin Waterfield (Oxford University Press, 2009), 8–14).

4. FORESTER] a gentleman rather than a commoner, following in the tradition in which the nobility and gentlemen were 'appointed by the King's letters patents' to govern royal forests and parks (Cowell, sig. Gg3). No mention of a 'forest' is made in the script, which prefers the term 'woods',

LACON in love with MUSELLA   5
RUSTIC in love with MUSELLA, marries DALINA
ARCAS a villain

6. RUSTIC] *CWD;* Rustick *PM.*

---

perhaps hinting that the Forester is slightly out of place in this setting. Sir
Robert Wroth was the King's Forester, and, when James I visited to hunt,
Lady Mary was expected to host the King's household (*MSLW*, 136). The
character's relatively passive role contrasts with that of the Forester in
Sidney's *Lady of May*, who personifies the active life. Marion O'Connor
('"Silvesta was my instrument ordained": Lucy Harington Russell, Third
Countess of Bedford, as Family Marriage Broker', *SJ*, 34:1 (2016), 49–65),
convincingly identifies Edward Russell, third Earl of Bedford, as a dramatic
avatar for the Forester in respect of the character's commitment to celibate
chaste love; Russell was a keen huntsman until he was maimed and rendered
impotent by a hunting accident in summer 1613. See Introduction (42) and
SILVESTA below.
    5. *LACON*] a possible pun on 'laconic', given the character only has
sixteen spoken lines in the play. The term derives from Laconia, a mountain-
ous limestone region, south of Arcadia in the Peloponnese, whose main city
is Sparta. Francis Meres's *Palladis Tamia* (London: P. Short, 1598) draws a
typical association between the spartan, classical landscape and 'the Laconic
speech [which] is made more piercing by taking away that which is superflu-
ous' (257v).
    6. *RUSTIC*] as his name implies, a comic rural type. *Urania II* contains a
prose version of Rustic, a black, Morean knight (Follietto) who is retitled
'Rustic' when he becomes a shepherd and is mocked for his 'natural rude-
ness' in pursuing his beloved Magdalaine with 'coarse verses and tedious
songs' which are 'uneven, tattered rhymes of better stuff'. His insistence to
'have his mistress love him whether she will or not' even though his 'lady is
another's by vow' (219–21) parallels Rustic's pursuit of Musella in *Love's
Victory*. See also Sir Philip Sidney's Dametas (*Arcadia*) and Ben Jonson's
'Lorel, the rude, a swineherd' in *The Sad Shepherd*.
    7. *ARCAS*] In mythology, the son of Jupiter and Calisto, who tried to kill
his mother because she was raped and shamed, but was tamed and made
King of Arcadia, which is named after him. See Ovid, *Meta.* (II.580),
and William Biddulph, *The Travels of Certain Englishmen* (London: T.
Haveland for W. Aspley, 1609, 185). Arcas the shepherd is the identity
adopted by Amicles in Wroth's *Urania II*, 214–15. Arcas's role as a melancholic malcontented lover may have been suggested by the young shepherd
Arcas in Nicolas de Montreux's pastoral *Honour's Academy, or the Famous
Pastoral of the Fair Shepherdess Julietta* (London: Thomas Creede, 1610), who
is exiled from Arcadia; far from proving villainous, like Wroth's Arcas,
Montreux's Arcas sympathizes with his rival Phillistes and the other disap-
pointed lovers.

Women's Names

MUSELLA in love with PHILISSES

SIMEANA sister to PHILISSES, and in love with LISSIUS   10

SILVESTA in love with FORESTER, but has vowed chastity

---

8. Women's   Names] Wemen   Names   *PM;*   Shepherdesses   *CWD.*
10. SIMEANA] *CWD;* Semeana *PM.*

---

9. *MUSELLA*] perhaps an amalgamation of 'Muse' and 'Stella' (star), the name of Sir Philip Sidney's muse in *AS,* reputedly modelled on Penelope Devereux. The character is also often seen as an avatar of Wroth herself – see Introduction, 42; she inspires the songs of Rustic and Lacon in 1.3, and Philisses's poetry in 4.1. Philisses (3.2.10 and 4.1.381) and Lacon (5.3.12–13) refer to Musella as a star.

10. *SIMEANA*] possibly a fictional avatar of Susan de Vere, Countess of Montgomery, Wroth's great friend and dedicatee of her fictional romance *Urania.* Susan de Vere was married to Wroth's cousin Philip Herbert, Earl of Montgomery. See Introduction, 42, 51. In order to scan, the name should be trisyllabic (i.e. Sim-ean-a).

11. *SILVESTA*] Her name combines 'sylvan', one who inhabits a wood or forest (*OED*), and the vestal virgins who guarded the temple of Vesta, the Roman goddess of the hearth and household. The character may owe something to the story of Alarina, who dedicates herself to Diana and changes her name to Silviana in *Urania I* (216–25), and the episode in *Arcadia* where Philoclea writes her passion for Zelmane on a white stone 'dedicated in ancient time to the Sylvan gods' (II.240–4) and appeals to Diana. In the play Silvesta is a devoted friend to both Musella and Philisses. In the final scene, she promises to give the Forester her 'chaste love' (5.7.99), a strong feature of Sidney family politics (cf. 'To Penshurst', 90–2), but this does not necessarily mean they end betrothed like the other couples. Marion Wynne-Davies (*Women Writers and Familial Discourse in the English Renaissance* (New York: Palgrave Macmillan, 2007), 100–3), and Marion O'Connor ('"Silvesta was my instrument ordained"') both argue that Silvesta is a dramatic avatar of Wroth's relation Lucy Harrington Russell, Countess of Bedford, whose miscarriage in 1611 probably rendered her sterile (O'Connor, 63). See Introduction, 42.

CLIMEANA in love with LISSIUS
DALINA a fickle lady, marries RUSTIC
FILLIS in love with PHILISSES
MOTHER to MUSELLA   15

12. CLIMEANA] *CWD;* Clemeana *PM.*   13. DALINA] *CWD;* Delina *PM.*
14. FILLIS] *PM; Phillis CWD.*   15.] *CWD adds* Temple of Love *after this
line.*

---

12. *CLIMEANA*] a shepherdess who has relocated from Arcadia, and
having been 'deceived' (3.3.75) by one lover, is now in love with Lissius
(3.3.81–116). No character of this name appears in Philip Sidney's *Arcadia*
or any text by Wroth or her family, though Limeana, the heiress, later Queen,
of Sicily features in both parts of Wroth's *Urania*. The rhyming of her and
Simeana's names may pair them together as rivals for Lissius's affections;
like Simeana, her name should be read trisyllabically (i.e. Cli-mea-na).

13. *DALINA*] Two similar names occur in Wroth's *Urania II.* Roberts
(Wroth *Poems*, 38) suggests that Dalina may be an abbreviation of Magdalaine,
who is wooed by Follietto as Rustick in *Urania II* (see above). However,
unlike the shepherdess in the play, Magdalaine is of noble birth, daughter
to the Duchess of Corona. Dalinea, Queen of Achaya, in *Urania II* is likewise
high born and constant, whereas the Dalina of *Love's Victory* has been fickle
in the past. To that end, the name potentially contains implications of dal-
lying or dalliance.

14. *FILLIS*] a conventional name in pastoral literature for a pretty country
girl or a female sweetheart (*OED*). Wroth's shepherdess is the epitome of
devoted, silent, unrequited love in the play, deriving from Phyllis the figure
in classical myth who was deserted by the Greek hero Demophoon and 'sore
did moan / His absence, whereby that she died', as recalled in Petrarch's
Triumph of Love (Parker, B4) and Ovid, *Heroical Epistles* (5v–11r). However,
in Abraham Fraunce's *Countess of Pembroke's Ivychurch*, 1591 (Fraunce, F1),
a rewriting of Tasso's *Amynta Favola Boscareccia* (Venice: Aldo Manuzio,
1581), Phyllis is a 'pitiless' and 'stony' shepherdess. The spelling Fillis in
both written scripts (*PM* and *HM*) distinguishes the character from Philisses
in stage directions and speech prefixes.

VENUS
CUPID
PRIESTS

17. CUPID] *CWD;* Cuipt *PM.*

---

16. *VENUS*] the Roman goddess of love in her many guises. For early modern significance see Vincentio Catari, *The Fountain of Ancient Fiction* (London: Adam Islip, 1599). For Wroth's depiction of Venus here, in her poems and in *Urania I* see Introduction, 12–17. See also *AS,* Sonnets 13, 33, 42–3, 72, 77, 79, 102, and Songs 1 and 5 and RS *Poems,* Elegy 16. For depictions of Venus see also Catherine Belsey, 'The Myth of Venus in Early Modern Culture', *ELR,* 42:2 (2012), 179–202, Josephine A. Roberts, 'Deciphering Women's Pastoral: Coded Language in Wroth's *Love's Victory*', in *Representing Women in Renaissance England,* ed. Claude J. Summers and Ted-Larry Pebworth (Columbia: University of Missouri Press, 1997), 163–74 and Nora Clark, *Aphrodite and Venus in Myth and Mimesis* (Newcastle-upon-Tyne: Cambridge Scholars Publishing, 2015).

17. *CUPID*] In Roman mythology the son of Venus and Mars, Cupid is god of desire, the erotic and transient aspects of love, and is typically depicted as blind and armed with a bow and arrows to strike his victims. On Wroth's representations of Cupid see Introduction, 12–14, *PA,* Sonnet 43, and Song 2. See also *AS,* Sonnets 5, 9, 12–13, 17, 19, 35, 43, 53–4, 61, 72, 103, and Songs 1, 4, 5 and 8. See also Kingsley-Smith, 1–23, 32–5 and 128–33. On the power dynamic between Cupid and his mother see Introduction, 12–14.

18. *PRIESTS*] The priests appear with Venus and Cupid in her Temple in 1.1, chant or sing as a chorus to Cupid (2.3) and to 'Love' (4.2), and give judgement (5.7). In *Urania I* the Priest of Venus who greets the lovers at the Temple of Love is 'an aged man' (48.26). The priests in the play may be female, since Hero is described as Venus's priest in Nashe's *Lenten Stuff* (London: Thomas Judson and Valentine Simmes for Nicholas Ling and Cuthbert Burby, 1599), 42, and in George Chapman's translation of the Hero and Leander story begun by Christopher Marlowe. See *The Divine Poem of Museus* (London: Isaac Jaggard, 1616), C5. Philemon Holland's translation of *The Roman History* (London: Adam Islip, 1609), bk XIX ch. 1, refers to 'women priests and worshippers of *Venus*' (123).

Act I

VENUS, *and* CUPID *with her in her Temple, her*
PRIESTS *attending her.*

0.0. [ACT I SCENE I]] *CWD.*   0.1-2. SD.] *PM. Scene missing from HM.*

0.1. SD.] The opening scene in Venus's Temple is found only in *PM* (see Introduction, 13, 49). Early modern texts commonly follow Ovid's *Metamorphoses* in locating the Temple of Venus in Cyprus, where she was supposedly born from the foam of the sea, though the English translation of *The Famous History of Herodotus Containing the Discourse of Diverse Countries* (London: Thomas Marshe, 1584) claimed that the 'most ancient temple of Venus and antiquity, amongst all the temples that were ever erected to that goddess' was the 'chapel of Venus Urania' in Syria (fol. 33v, FIv). Wroth's *Urania I* provides a literary model for the Temple, where Venus's priest describes three towers dedicated to Love (48-9). For details of the towers and those on the title page of *Urania* see Introduction, 16. The Temple of Venus reappears later in *Urania I* (168.70), but, when Pamphilia and Urania and their companions reach the rock at Cyprus and enter 'as magnificent a Theatre, as Art could frame', they are enchanted by 'sweetest music' (373.17-25) and imprisoned because Amphilanthus is not there to release Pamphilia, according to the terms set up for the Temple of Constancy (48.41-49.2). Venus's temple in all the Sidney writings may be derived from Petrarch's *Triumph of Love*, which they would have known in Italian, though it had been translated, first by Henry Parker as *The Triumphs of Frances Petrarch*, published in 1555 (A4r-B4v) and subsequently in manuscript by William Fowler in 1587 (see MSH *Works*, Vol. I, 262). For staging the Temple of Venus, Inigo Jones's sets for Jonson's *Masque of Beauty* (1608), including a pastoral garden filled with Cupids, the Temple of Fame for the *Masque of Queens* (1609) or the set for *The Haddington Masque* (1608) may have formed a model for Wroth's staging (see *R*, 232). Carolyn Ruth Swift ('Feminine Self-Definition in Lady Mary Wroth's Love's Victorie (c.1621)', *ELR*, 19:2 (Spring 1989), 171-88, 173), suggests that the minstrels' gallery in the great hall at Penshurst would have been an appropriate setting for the Temple scenes given Cupid's and Venus's supernatural character and choric function, watching and commenting on the action, and it was used in this way for the 2014 staged reading and the 2018 production at Penshurst. However, Richard Dutton, Alan Nelson and Sally-Beth Maclean have argued that such an arrangement would have been unlikely since performances in colleges, guildhalls, private houses and the court would have been presented immediately in front of the noble hosts of the occasion, seated at

75

Venus. Cupid, methinks we have too long been still,
And that these people grow to scorn our will.
Mercy to those ungrateful breeds neglect;
Then let us grow our greatness to respect.
Make them acknowledge that our heavenly power   5
Can not their strength but even themselves devour.
Let them not smile and laugh because thine eyes
Are covered as if blind, or love despise:
No, thou that scarf shalt from thine eyes take off
Which gave them cause on thee to make this scoff.   10

Take mask off eyes

---

1. SP. *Venus.*] Venus / *PM.* 9. scarf] *PM;* scarse *R;* scarce *CWD.*
10.1. SD.] *This ed.*

---

the high table at the other end of the hall. For a full discussion of a conjectured early performance of *Love's Victory*, in which members of the noble
family were also the performers, see Introduction, 28–30.
    1–2. *Cupid ... will*] A dream vision of Venus and Cupid opens Wroth's
sonnet sequence *Pamphilia to Amphilanthus*: 'When night's black mantle
could most darkness prove' (Wroth *Poems*, 85). In this opening speech Venus
feels underworshipped by the mortals, as in *Urania I* where she thinks herself
'in these latter times, not so much, or much less honoured than in ages past'
(*Urania I*, 40.32–3). Cf. 'Venus is undone' in Jonson's *Haddington Masque*
(1608, l. 35). The 1999 production established Venus's desire to dominate
the mortals by opening with Robert van Leeuwen's popular song 'Venus'
(see Introduction, 30).
    3. *Mercy ... neglect*] Showing mercy to ungrateful people causes further
neglect.
    4. *let ... respect*] possibly 'let us demonstrate our greatness so that we are
given fitting respect'.
    5. *Make ... power*] Cf. 'Command that wayward child your son to grant
your right', Wroth *Poems*, 116. '[P]ower' is elided as a single syllable to make
the line scan, a technique often used by Wroth.
    6. *Can ... devour*] Can not only weaken them but totally consume them.
    9. *scarf ... off*] Cupid's unmasking may symbolize a shift from a sensual
form of love to a more sublimated one; 'the addition or removal of a bandage
from Cupid's eyes' continued a medieval tradition of marking 'the difference
between ideal Love and the irrationality of sensual passions', in cultivated
or scholarly circles (C. D. Gilbert, 'Blind Cupid', *Journal of the Warburg and
Courtauld Institutes*, 33 (1970), 304–5, 305). Cf. Wroth's 'Love shall lose all
his darts, have sight, and see / His shame and wishings hinder happy hours'
(*Poems*, 37). The removal of the scarf (10.1.SD) may also cue his entry into
the mortal world, which creates a possibility of the role being doubled with
that of Arcas, as in the 2018 production at Penshurst Place. See Introduction,
34.
    10. *scoff*] a derisive jest or expression of mockery (*OED*, n.1).

[CUPID takes off his blindfold.]

Thou shalt discern their hearts, and make them know
That humble homage unto thee they owe;
Take thou the shaft which headed is with steel
And make them bow whose thoughts did lately reel.
Make them thine own, thou who didst me once harm;   15
Can not forget the fury of that charm.
Wound them but kill them not, so may they live
To honour thee, and thankfulness to give.

Wound but don't kill so they will honour + be thankful to them

---

11. *discern*] perceive, see into.

13. *steel*] Traditionally Cupid's arrows were said to be headed with different metals (e.g. gold meaning the lover would be rewarded, lead that his or
her desires would be unfulfilled). Steel, the hardest, was said to provoke
sparks in those whose 'hearts were flints entire' (Richard Brome, *A Jovial
Crew, or, The Merry Beggars* (1641), ed. H. Ostovich, Richard Brome Online
(www.hrionline.ac.uk/brome), 4.2.157–62, speech 773). In the pastoral
entertainment in *Urania II* Cupid has wounded a young lad 'with his sharpest
and killingst-steeled darts' (113.26–7).

14. *bow*] possibly with a visual pun as Cupid takes the bow and arrows;
these make him a visual counterpart to Diana's huntress, Silvesta.

lately reel] recently whirl. The meanings of 'reel' include 'to be emotionally
or psychologically shaken by an event, experience, etc.; to feel disorientated,
bewildered, overwhelmed, or intoxicated as a result of an occurrence, a
powerful emotion, etc.' (reel, v.1, *OED*, 5a), 'to shake, rock, or swing vio-
lently; to totter, tremble' (reel, v.1, *OED*, 6) or 'to be in a whirl, to spin; to
be or become giddy or confused' (reel, v.1, *OED*, 7b). Wroth uses the word
to describe the wheel of Fortune 'Whose favours, fickle, and unconstant,
reel; / Drunk with delight of change, and sudden pain' (*Poems*, 119), and
Amphilanthus's defeat of the King of Cicilia in battle where 'reelingly he ran
with his last fury upon him' (*Urania I*, 567.28).

15. *me ... harm*] Venus refers to her own experience of being pierced by
one of Cupid's darts. In a song to Venus in *PA* Wroth makes the same point:
'you your self a wound he gave', probably an allusion to Venus being struck
with love for Mars, as Roberts (Wroth *Poems*, 117) and *CWD* (200n.5) point
out. In Ovid's *Metamorphoses* the two lovers are entrapped in a net by her
husband Vulcan (cf. 1.1.38n.); Golding's translation of the story (IV.206–36)
tells that Venus suffers from a 'wound of raging love' (232). The line may
also be a reference to Venus's being struck with unrequited love for Adonis,
who was then killed hunting a boar, also told by Ovid, *Meta.* (X.602ff.), and
Shakespeare's bestselling poem *Venus and Adonis* (1594). Both stories would
have been widely familiar; they are depicted, for example, in Acts 2 and 4
of Thomas Heywood's *The Brazen Age* (London: Nicholas Okes, 1613), with
Homer as the chorus linking the two affairs (II2).

16. *Can not ... charm*] Venus refers to herself being unable to forget the
violence of her passion when she was under Cupid's spell.

Shun no great cross which may their crosses breed
But yet let blessed enjoying them succeed;   20
Grief is sufficient to declare thy might,
And in thy mercy glory will shine bright.

Cupid. Mother, I will no cross, no harm forbear
Of jealousy, for loss, of grief, or fear
Which may my honour touched again repair,   25
But with their sorrows will my glory rear.
Friends shall mistrust their friends, lovers mistake,
And all shall for their folly woes partake.
Some shall love much yet shall no love enjoy,
Others obtain when lost is all their joy.   30
This will I do your will and mind to serve,

---

23. forbear] forbeare *catchword* 'of =' *PM*.

---

19. *Shun ... breed*] Omit no trouble that will increase their sufferings.
Here and in 23 'cross' is meant in the sense of a trouble, vexation or annoyance; in its verbal form 'to cross' means 'to thwart'. The verb and noun
occur frequently (24 times), as at 1.1.23, 1.3.26 and when the lovers draw
fortunes (2.1.159–61 and 177), carrying Christian resonances of suffering in
addition to the obstructions typical of new comedy and courtly love tradition. In *Urania II* Wroth creates an chiasmic pattern of crossed or unrequited
love where Drusio loves Cordelia who loves his best friend Flavio; Flavio
loves Isabella who, in turn, loves Drusio who reports that 'never so strange
an[d] unhappy crosses fell out' under Cupid's influence (293). Crosses take
on a spatial dimension in the first of Wroth's crown of sonnets sequence,
where Pamphilia is trapped at a crossroads in a labyrinth yet is determined
to go forward 'though crosses with my fortune kiss' (*Poems*, 128).
20. *them succeed*] follow them. Venus directs and advertises the tragicomic plot.
21. *Grief ... might*] Making them feel grief (i.e. suffering in love and
repentance for their former disdain of love's power) will be enough to prove
your strength.
25. *touched*] hurt, damaged. Cupid's reputation has been injured; his
arrows will repair the dishonour.
26. *rear*] rise up (*OED*, v.6a) i.e. like a rearing horse. Cf. Wroth, *P4*,
Sonnets 36 and 47 (107, 114).
29–30. *enjoy ... joy*] As well as appearing five times in this opening scene
(cf. 20, 37) the word 'joy' and its cognates feature 91 times through the
script, often carrying religious overtones of perfect bliss or a state of paradise
(*OED*, n.2). The quest for it, and its absence or presence, are key to the
emotional dynamics and landscape that drive the tragicomic plot. 'Grief',
by contrast, appears 26 times and 'woe(s)' 20 times.
31. *mind*] desire, intention. Cf. Silvesta's setting of Philisses's 'will' and
'mind' against each other in 3.1.39.

And to your triumph will these rites preserve.
Venus. Then shall we have again our ancient glory,
       And let this callèd be love's victory.
       Triumphs upon their travails shall ascend,   35
       And yet most happy ere they come to end.
Cupid. Joy and enjoying on some shall be set,
       Sorrow on others caught by Cupid's net.   [*Exeunt.*]

---

34. love's victory] *PM;* 'Love's Victory' *CWD.*   35. travails] *EMWW;*
travells *PM;* travels *CWD.*   38. net.] nett; / *PM.*   SD.] *CWD.*

---

32. *triumph*] Cf. Petrarch, *The Triumph of Love,* trans. Henry Parker
(1555), and Ben Jonson, *The Haddington Masque* (1608), in which Venus
descends to earth to see 'so much honour won / Unto Venus and her son'
(141–2) by the actions of 'all-triumphing' Cupid (168).

34. *this*] the play itself. Venus speaks as a prologue to the performance.
See Introduction, 13 and note to 1.2.0.0.

love's victory] *PM* shows unequivocally that this is the spelling Wroth
intended for the title of her play. The rhyme 'glory/victory' here and at the
end of the play (5.7.160) seems strange to modern ears; Wroth may be
choosing to prioritize eye-rhyme here. Cf. 1.4.25 and 5.7.56 and Otto van
Veen, emblem 'Love is the cause of virtue': 'Love's victory hath made more
victories be won', *Emblemata Amoratia* (Antwerp: n.p., 1608, 32, https://
emblems.hum.uu.nl/v1608017.html#folio_pb32_LEI.); for other examples
of this phrasing in Wroth see Lemnia's song 'Love grown proud with victory',
Urania I, 650, and Emelina's lament 'From victory in love I now am come'
(*Urania I,* 299.18, *Poems,* 162). James Shirley's tragicomedy *The Doubtful
Heir* (London: William Wilson and Thomas Warren, 1652) was licensed in
1640 under the title *Rosania* or *Love's Victory.* Another *Love's Victory: A
Tragicomedy* (London: E. Cotes), by William Chamberlaine, appeared in
1658. It is unclear whether Venus is referring to the victory of 'love' as a
concept, or to her and Cupid's own victory as the personifications of love;
PM's use of a lower-case 'l' here implies the former. See Introduction, 14.

35. *travails*] labours or sufferings, but also evoking 'travels' or journeys
(*CWD,* 200n.11). Wroth uses the term in this sense in *Urania II,* where
Amphilanthus asks to 'travail alone in his sadness (as sadness most requires
loneliness)' (190.27).

36. *most happy*] 'most will be happy'; alternatively, 'they will be most
happy'.

ere] before (*OED,* adv.2).

38. *net*] Cf. *AS,* 'thy day-nets', Sonnet 12, line 2 (*Poems,* 170), and
George Whetstone, *The Rock of Regard* (London: H. Middleton for Robert
Waley, 1576), 'Be warned by wisdom's law / So shalt thou scape blind
Cupid's net' (103). Cupid is armed with nets in Francis Quarles's *Emblems*
(London: G. Miller for J. Marriot, 1608): 'Go save the Nets for that rebel-
lious heart / That scornes thy pow'r', 72–3.

[ACT I SCENE 2]

[*The meadows*]

[*Enter* PHILISSES, *alone.*]

Philisses. [*Sings.*]
            You pleasant flowery mead
            Which I did once well love,

0.0. *top margin*] Loves Victory; *PM;* Loves Victorie [*S fermé*] *HM.*   0.0. [ACT
I   SCENE   2]] *CWD.*   0.1. SD.] *This ed.*   0.2. SD.] *R.*   I. SD.] *This
ed.   flowery*] flowrie *PM;* floury *HM.*

0.0.] The placing of the play's title here in *PM* suggests this may originally
have been the opening of the play proper, as it is in *HM* where it heads the
first page. The repetition of the title in *PM* positions Venus and Cupid's
opening dialogue in 1.1 as a prologue framing the action (such as in the
opening scene of Shakespeare's *Taming of the Shrew*). The 2018 production
brought on all the shepherds and shepherdesses to stand like chess pieces in
a grid, with their backs to the audience, each turning as they were introduced. While this created a somewhat static opening, it helped to define the
characters and their relationships to a modern audience.
    0.1. SD.] Neither surviving manuscript of *Love's Victory* provides any
details of the setting for the play. Wroth perhaps envisaged an outdoor setting
and venue in a country house estate, as in Sir Philip Sidney's *The Lady of
May*, or an indoor pastoral setting such as those in Daniel's *The Queen's
Arcadia* (London: Simon Waterson, 1606), in Fletcher's *The Faithful
Shepherdess* (London: Edward Allde, 1610) or in Ben Jonson's play *The Sad
Shepherd* (printed 1641) which features 'a landscape of forest, hills, valleys,
cottages, a castle, a river, pastures, herds, flocks, all full of country simplicity'
('The Persons of the Play', 29–30). See Introduction, 17–18, 28–9. The script
indicates that the setting is outside in spring, in sunny, flowery meadows
crossed with pathways. Philisses's opening song sets the scene by bidding
farewell to the meadows and streams and embracing '*the dark*', whilst Silvesta
(73–80) describes the valleys and meadows which she will leave to range in
the woods.
    1. Sings] No score for this lyric has yet been discovered. Its structure,
however, would fit to simple 8- or 16-bar rural folk tunes. Wroth had received
musical training and may have been a competent performer on the virginals
and archlute. See *MSLW*, 157–8. See Gavin Alexander, 'The Musical Sidneys',
John Donne Journal, 25 (2006), 65–105; Katherine R. Larson, *The Matter of
Song in Early Modern England: Texts In and Of the Air* (Oxford: Oxford
University Press, 2020), 112–13 and 168–73, and Introduction, 3–4, 35. In the
2018 production Philisses sang accompanied by lutes and cornett, whilst in
the 1999 production he accompanied himself on an acoustic guitar, a simple
contrast to the opening recorded number 'Venus' (see 1.1.1–2n).
    mead] meadow. Cf. the opening of *Urania I* in which Urania comes 'into
the mead' where 'she usually drove her flocks to feed' followed by other
shepherds who 'come into the mead with their flocks' (1.6–7, 31).

Your paths no more I'll tread,
Your pleasures no more prove,
Your beauty more admire,   5
Your colours more adore,
Nor grass with daintiest store
Of sweets to breed desire.

Walks, once so sought for, now
I shun you for the dark.   10
Birds to whose song did bow
Mine ears, your notes ne'er mark.
Brook which so pleasing was,
Upon whose bank I lay,
And on my pipe did play   15
Now unregarded pass.

Meadows, paths, grass, flowers,
Walks, birds, brook, truly find

---

5. *more*] more ~~more~~ HM.   8. *desire*] ~~desiyre~~ desire [*inserted above*] HM.
12. *Mine*] *PM;* my *HM.*   14. *bank*] *PM;* banks *HM.*

---

4. *prove*] experience (*OED*, 2) or demonstrate, establish (*OED*, 4). An important word in *Love's Victory*, not least as a convenient rhyme for 'love'; it occurs 42 times in the text, taking on a number of meanings including (in this instance) 'experience, taste', or 'demonstrate, show oneself to be' (as in 19).

7. *daintiest*] elided to two syllables dain-tiest in order to scan.

8. *sweets ... desire*] the 'sweets' stored by the grass are flowers whose scent inflames desire. Cf. Parselius in *Urania I* who imagines the earth sending forth 'soft and tender grass, mixt with sweet flowers' where his beloved has stepped (*Urania I*, 27.4–6) and RS *Poems*, Pastoral 2 (167).

11–12. *did ... ears*] I listened (i.e. 'mine ears did bow'), a variant of bending the ears to listen as in Psalm 71 (*Psalms*, 130). Thomas Wilcox's *Right Godly and Learned Exposition Upon the Whole Book of Psalms* (London: Thomas Dawson, 1586) remarked that 'men, if they mind to be familiar and yield to suits, will easily bow their ears to such as sue to them' (fol. 193r).

15. *pipe ... play*] playing on the pipe and singing are conventional activities for shepherds in pastoral tradition going back to Virgil's *Eclogues*. The Sidneys pick up on this tradition, for example shepherds 'being accorded to the pipe' in *Arcadia* (I.182), and Amphilanthus hearing 'a lad pipe merrily, on a pipe he had made of one of the stalks of oats' in *Urania I* (497.16–17).

17–18. *Meadows ... brook*] Cf. Robert Sidney, Song 3: 'Meadows, fields, forests, hills' (RS *Poems*, 152–3), and Urania's first song, where she complains 'To rocks, to hills, to meadows and to springs' in Wroth's *Urania I* (2.37, *Poems*, 146).

> All prove but as vain showers:
> Wished welcome, else unkind.   20
> You once I lovèd best
> But love makes me you leave;
> By love I love deceive:
> Joy's lost for life's unrest.

Joy's lost for life's unrest, indeed I see.   25
Alas poor shepherd, miserable me!
Yet, fair Musella, love, and worthy be;
I blame thee not but mine own misery.
Live you still happy, and enjoy your love,
And let love pains in me distressèd move,   30
For since it is my friend thou dost affect,
Than wrong him once, myself I will neglect;
And thus in secret will my passions hide
Till time or fortune doth my fear decide,

---

24. *Joy's*] *PM, HM;* Joys *CWD.* *life's*] *CWD;* lives *PM, HM.*   25. Joy's]
PM, HM; Joys *CWD.* life's] *CWD;* lives *PM, HM.* unrest, indeed I
see.] unrest indeed I see. *PM;* unrest indeed I see *HM.*   30. love pains] *PM;*
loves paine *HM.*   31. dost] *PM;* doest [*overwritten orig.* 'dost'] *HM.*
32. Than] *This ed.;* then *PM, HM.*

19–20. *vain ... unkind*] futile showers, welcome when they are wished for
but otherwise unpleasant. Philisses comments on the lack of sympathy
between the features of the landscape and his own feelings.
   21. The metre of this line could be stressed differently, i.e. '*You* once *I*
loved *best*'.
   23. *By ... deceive*] Philisses feels that his love for Musella has led him to
betray his love for the pastoral landscape by abandoning it.
   28. *I ... misery*] I do not blame you (i.e. Musella) for my unhappiness,
but my own misery. Philisses follows the Petrarchan model of the helpless
lover. See Introduction, 7, 9–10, 14.
   30. *move*] (in this sense) stir. Another important verb in Wroth's text,
deployed in multiple senses, from 'cause' (66) to 'affect' (148).
   31. *my friend*] i.e. Lissius.
   affect] (in this context) show affection for, incline towards or love (*OED*,
v.4 cites Shakespeare, *TN* 2.5.23, 'Maria once told me she did affect me').
   32. *Than*] rather than.
   33–6. *And ... born*] Philisses decides to conceal his love until his fear (i.e.
that Musella loves Lissius) is confirmed or refuted, after which his love will
be as clear as the dawn. Cf. *TN* 2.2.40–1. Philisses's reluctance to declare
his love, and his delay in doing so, have serious consequences in the play.
Cf. 1.3.6 and 4.1.85–8.

Making my love appear as the bright morn   35
Without or mist, or cloud, but truly born.

[*Enter* LISSIUS.]

Lissius. [*Sings.*]
   Joyful pleasant spring
   Which comforts to us bring,
     Flourish in your pride.
   Never let decay   40
   Your delights allay,
     Since joy is to you tied.

Philisses. [*Aside*] No, joy is tied to you, you 'tis do prove
   The pleasure of your friend's unhappy love.
   'Tis you enjoy the comfort of my pain,   45
   'Tis I that love, and you that love obtain.

Lissius. [*Sings.*]
   Let no frost nor wind
   Your daintiest colours blind
     But rather cherish.
   Your most pleasant sight   50
   Let never winter bite
     Nor season perish.

Philisses. [*Aside*] I can not perish more than now I do
   Unless my death my miseries undo.
   Lissius is happy but Philisses cursed,   55

36. born] *CWD;* borne *PM, HM.* 36.1 SD.] *R.* 37. SD.] *This ed.*
39. *Flourish] HM;* flowrish *PM.* 43. SD.] *CWD.* tied] ty'de *PM;* tide
HM. 47. SD.] *This ed.* 48. *daintiest] PM;* dainty *HM.* 50. *pleasant] PM;* pleasing *HM.*

36. *or ... cloud]* either mist or cloud.
40–1. *Never ... allay]* allay means subdue or destroy. Lissius's carefree celebration of springtime flourishing, and his wish for it to last for ever, contrast starkly with his song in 4.1.53–8.
43–4. *you ... love]* i.e. it is you who is experiencing the pleasure of your friend's (i.e. Philisses's) unhappy love.
48. *blind]* used here in the sense of 'to put out of sight', i.e. destroy. Cf. John Leo's *A Geographical History of Africa*, trans. John Pory (London: Elliot's Court Press, 1600): 'the southeast wind doth so often blind them, that they can not live here without great peril' (282).

Love seeks to him, on me he doth his worst.
And do thy worst on me still, froward boy;
More ill thou canst not, but poor life destroy.
Which do, and glory in thy conquest got.
All men must die, and Love drew my ill lot.   60
Lissius. My dear Philisses, what, alone and sad?
Philisses. Neither, but musing why the best is bad.
But you were merry, I'll not mar your song;
My thoughts are tedious, and for you too long.   *Exit.*
Lissius. Alas, what means this? Surely it is love   65
That doth in him this alteration move.
This is the humour makes our shepherds rave.
I'll none of this, I'll rather seek my grave. → Humorous
Love, by your favour, I will none of you.
I rather you should miss, than I should sue. → Humour   70

---

56. Love] love *PM, HM.*   60. Love] love *PM, HM.*   60.] *CWD adds* SD
[*He sees* PHILISSES] *after this line.*   64. SD.] *CWD;* ex. *PM, HM.*   66. doth]
PM; makes *HM.*   68. rather] *PM;* souner *HM.*   69. Love] *PM;* love *HM.*

---

56. *seeks to him*] seeks him out.

57. *froward boy*] perverse, naughty boy (i.e. Cupid).

58. *More ... destroy*] You cannot do worse to me except by killing me.

60. *Love ... lot*] Philisses feels that Love has chosen a token of ill-luck for him, and that it is his fate to die for love. Scene 2.1 continues the metaphor of lot-taking with the Book of Fortunes.

62. *the ... bad*] even the best things are bad. The phrase is found in satires by Gascoigne, *The Steel Glass* (Q3r), and Thomas Middleton, *Microcynicon* (London, Thomas Creede for Thomas Bushell, 1599, C6r).

63. *mar*] spoil.

67. *humour*] a mood or temperament, drawing on early modern beliefs of the physiological balance of four humours in the human body: melancholic (sad), choleric (angry), sanguine (enthusiastic), phlegmatic (apathetic). Lissius feels that the imbalance of humours in love is what makes the shepherds 'rave' or speak irrationally (*OED*, v.1a).

69. *Love ... you*] In the 2018 production Lissius raised his hands to the minstrels' gallery above, a gesture which dramatized the imprecise nature of his address to 'Love', including both Venus and Cupid. His following lines 70–1 indicate that he is addressing Cupid with his bow and arrows. For further discussion of Venus and Cupid as personifications of love see Introduction, 14.

70. *I ... sue*] I had rather you [Cupid] should miss [in shooting your arrow at me] than be a lover, with 'sue' here used in the sense of being a suitor. Lissius would rather miss out on love instead of being subject to it. His rejection of love resembles that of Benjamin Rudyerd, speaking for Reason

Yet, Cupid, poor Philisses back restore
To his first wits, and I'll affect thee more.

[LISSIUS *retires so he is not seen. Enter*] SILVESTA.

Silvesta. Fair shining day, and thou Apollo bright
    Which to these valleys giv'st thy pleasant sight,
    And with sweet showers mixed with golden beams   75
    Enrich these meadows and these gliding streams
    Wherein thou seest thy face like mirror fair,
    Dressing in them thy curling, shining hair.
    This place with sweetest flowers still doth deck
    Whose colours show their pride, free from the check   80
    Of fortune's frown so long as spring doth last,

72.] *HM adds* ex:. 72.1. SD.] *This ed.*; Silvesta. *PM, HM;* [LISSIUS *retires backstage. Enter* SILVESTA] *CWD.* 73. bright] bright *catchword* 'Which =' *PM.* 74. Which ... sight] *PM;* W^{ch} to these pleasant vallys gives thy light *HM.*

---

in the poetic dialogue with William Herbert, who warns him 'For not to love, than scorn in love is worse' (WH *Poems*, 13, B7r). Lissius's indifference to love and his subsequent fall parallel that of the shepherdess Lemnia, who falls in love with the Prince of Venice in *Urania I* (650–1, *Poems*, 194–5), and the Lady of Cyprus in *Urania II* (411–15).

72. *affect ... more*] think better of you.

73–8. Silvesta's address to Apollo broadens out to survey the landscape, perhaps explaining why the sentence lacks a main verb ('Enrich' could be read as a request to Apollo and the shining day, although the phrasing is still problematic for a modern reader). In the 2018 production Silvesta delivered the lines from a rostrum at the rear of the performance space, emphasizing the speech's panoramic perspective.

Apollo] classical Greek god of the sun, poetry and music; son of Zeus and twin brother to the chaste Diana (Artemis). Cf. *Arcadia*, Basilius's hymn to 'Apollo great, whose beams the greater world do light' (II. 396).

78. *curling, shining hair*] Apollo was also thought of as the most beautiful god: see 'fair Apollo' whose 'golden Hair did hang about his eyes' in Damiano of Odemira, *Ludus Sacchiae, Chess-Play* (London: Valentine Simmes for H. Jackson, 1597, 10). In *The Third Part of the Countess of Pembroke's Ivychurch* (1592), Abraham Fraunce writes that 'Apollo hath long yellow hair: noting his rays and beams, which heat and hit, like darts, a far off' (32v).

79. *flowers ... deck*] 'flowers [you, i.e. Apollo] still doth deck'. Cf. Lodowick Bryskett's 'Pastoral Eclogue' in which nymphs will always 'deck with fresh and sweetest flowers' the tomb of Sir Philip Sidney. See Edmund Spenser, *Colin Clout's Come Home Again* (London: Thomas Creede for William Ponsonby, 1595), H4v.

81. *fortune's frown*] 'The frown of the goddess Fortune signified ill luck' (*CWD*, 201n.31).

But then feel change whereof all others taste.
As I for one, who thus my habits change:
Once shepherdess, but now in woods must range,
And after the chaste goddess bear her bow,   85
Though service once to Venus I did owe
Whose servant then I was, and of her band.
But farewell folly, I with Dian stand
Against love's changing and blind foolery
To hold with happy and blessed chastity.   90
For love is idle, happiness there's none

---

85. goddess] *This ed.;* Goddess *PM, HM.*   89. changing] *PM;* changings
HM.   foolery] foulerie *PM;* foulery *HM.*

---

82. *change ... taste*] Seasonal changes are linked to changes in mood here
and throughout the play. Unlike Lissius, who hopes for a never-ending
spring (40–1, 47–52), Silvesta acknowledges that the season cannot last for
ever. In 2018 Silvesta broke the spell of eternal sunshine by changing her
tone of voice on 'so long as spring doth last', and pausing before continuing
the speech and descending from the rostrum to address spectators.

83. *habits*] Silvesta punningly refers to both the change of dress and
change of behaviour that she has undergone in becoming a follower of Diana.
Equipped with a bow, Silvesta acts as a dramatic counterpart to Cupid in
the play, albeit she also acts as Venus's 'instrument' (5.7.71). Cf. Silviana in
Urania I, who has 'put on these habits, hoping by pureness and vowed
chastity, to win Diana's favour' (224.7–10), and also carries a bow: 'hard by
her on the bank her quiver lay, her bow by that' (216.27–8). Leonius dis-
guises himself with 'the apparel of colour and fashion like Diana, buskins
[boots] upon her legs of white, her hair tied up' and crowned with 'roses
and hyacinths' (*Urania I*, 433.4–6).

85. *chaste goddess*] Diana, goddess of hunting and chastity, often depicted
wearing white and carrying a bow and arrow. Diana is a figure celebrated – in
association with Elizabeth I as the Virgin Queen – in characters such as
Britomart in *The Faerie Queene*, renowned for 'glory and great valiance / As
for pure chastity and virtue rare' (III.IV.3) and Hesperus's Hymn in Jonson's
masque *Cynthia's Revels*, which praises her as 'Queen and huntress, chaste
and fair' (5.1.1). As goddess of the Amazons, Diana is an icon of female
independence. See 92n. below.

86–7. *Though ... band*] Silvesta's characterization of herself as a former
servant of Venus is presumably a reference to her since-renounced love of
Philisses. The text is unclear on the degree to which this allegiance is formal
or figurative; Lissius's reference to 'Love's band' (161) implies the latter. In
contrast, Silvesta's 'vow' (111) to Diana seems to be a formal religious pro-
fession – she is later described as a 'priest' in 5.4.65 and 5.5.31.

88. *Dian*] Diana. On the opposition of Diana to love see Wroth's lyric
'Pray thee Diana tell me, is it ill / As some do say, thou thinkst it is, to love?'
sung by Steriamus (*Urania I*, 180–1, *Poems*, 157).

When freedom's lost, and chastity is gone.
And where on earth most blessedness there is
Love's fond desires never fail to miss,
And this, believe me, you will truly find.   95
Let not repentance therefore change your mind,
But change before; your glory will be most
Whenas the waggish boy can least him boast.
For he doth seek to kindle flames of fire
But never thinks to heal; a chaste desire   100
He calls his foe, he hates none more than those
Who strive his law to shun, and this life chose.

93. where on] where on *PM;* wher,on *HM.*   97. But ... glory] butt
change beefor your glory *PM;* butt chang before, yor glory *HM.*   100. heal]
PM; quench *HM.*   101. than] then *PM, HM.*   102. strive] *PM;* strives
HM.   life chose] *PM;* have chose = [*end of page*] *HM.*

---

92. *freedom ... gone*] Service to the all-female followers of Diana is typically associated with freedom from marriage and from male company, as in
Greene's *Never Too Late* (1590): '*Mirimida* singing that there was no Goddess
to *Diana*, no life to liberty, nor no love to chastity' (K3). Silviana in *Urania
I* says she is 'free from bond of vain affection' in dedicating herself to Diana
(225.2–3). See 120n. below.
   94. *Love's ... miss*] Love's foolish desires never fail to miscarry.
   96–8. *Let ... boast*] Silvesta argues that mortals should change to a life of
chastity before they are struck with desire by Cupid, the 'waggish' or mischievous boy, and suffer regret or 'repentance' for unrequited love. Vowing
chastity before experiencing love means that one's glory will be greater, and
Cupid's credit will be less.
   99. *flames ... fire*] Cupid kindling fire in lovers' hearts is a common idea
in courtly love poetry. See 140n. below.
   100. *thinks ... heal*] Cupid can spark but does not satisfy desires, as
Silvesta has found in her unrequited love for Philisses.
   chaste desire] a desire for chastity or chastity in love.
   101–2. *he ... chose*] i.e. he (Cupid) hates none more than those who
attempt to evade his rule and have chosen chastity as a way of life. The past
tense 'chose' contrasts with the present tense of 'strive' and of other verbs
in the preceding lines, but such shifting of tense is not unusual in early
modern writing. As well as making a perfect rhyme with 'those', Silvesta's
words 'this life chose' signal the personal choice she has made (*HM* reads
'this have chose'), to join a community of 'those' who have already chosen
to be Diana's followers. In other dramas of the period Cupid is depicted
attacking the followers of Diana (e.g. in Lyly's *Galatea*), and is banished by
the chaste young female performers in Robert White's masque *Cupid's
Banishment*. See Kingsley-Smith (121 32) for how Wroth draws on these
traditions. In *P4* Wroth writes of Cupid captured as Diana's prisoner 'in
chains, and fetters like a thief' (Wroth *Poems*, 123) and Philip Sidney's
Sonnet 35 similarly asks 'what hope, that hope should once see day, / Where
Cupid is sworn page to Chastity?' (PS *Poems*, 182). Cf. also 1.2.88–90.

All virtue hates, his kingdom's wantonness,
His crown desires, his sceptre idleness.
His wounds hot fires are, his help's like frost,   105
Glad to hurt but never heals; thinks time lost
If any gain their long-sought joy with bliss,
And this the government of folly is.
But here Philisses comes, poor shepherd lad,
With love's hot fires, and his own, made mad.   110
I must away, my vow allows no sight
Of men, yet must I pity him, poor wight:
Though he rejecting me this change hath wrought,
He shall be no less worthy in my thought.
Yet wish I do he were as free as I;   115
Then were he happy now feels misery.

---

104. crown] *HM;* Crowne *PM.* idleness] idlenes *HM;* Idlenes *PM.*
105. fires are] *PM;* fires *HM.*   113. hath] *PM;* have *HM.*

---

103. *All ... hates*] i.e. Cupid hates all virtue, the particular virtue here
being chastity. In 1603 the Roman Catholic priest Matthew Kellison
described chastity as 'a virtue which always hath been priced at an high rate'
and 'valued as one of the most precious jewels of moral virtues' in all reli-
gions, 'even the heathens' (*A Survey of the New Religion* (Douay and Rheims:
Laurence Kellam, 1603), 609).

103–8. *his ... is*] Silvesta's imagery details Cupid's maleficent authority
over mortals. Her criticisms of Cupid echo Petrarch's *Triumph of Love*, which
describes how Cupid 'hath his first birth of idleness / Nourished with man-
kind's folly and wantonness' (Parker, B2r). Cf. Alarina's sufferings before
she vows chastity as Silviana (*Urania I*, 220–3).

105. *His ... frost*] The paradox of love as a 'freezing fire' is a characteristic
trope of Petrarchan poetry. Cf. *AS*, Sonnet 6 'freezing fires' (PS *Poems*, 167)
and Robert Sidney, 'Pastoral 2' (RS *Poems*, 147) and 'Pastoral 7' (RS *Poems*,
198–201).

109. *here ... comes*] Philisses's entrance is not marked in either *PM* or *HM*
but Silvesta's cue, 15 lines before he speaks, allows the actor ample time to
make a slow entrance that displays Philisses's affliction in love.

111–12. *my ... men*] Diana's nymphs were required to forsake the company
of men, like nuns of most orders, although Silvesta's vows do not prevent
her from being in the presence of men in 2.1, or in Act 5. Cf. *Urania I*, where
Silviana claims 'these habits keep me from discourse with men, my vow from
yielding' (224.15–16).

112. *wight*] an archaic term for a person or creature. Philip Sidney's
translation of Philippe De Mornay's *A Work Concerning the Trueness of the
Christian Religion* (London: John Charlewood and George Robinson for
Thomas Cadman, 1587) explained 'We reduce ... all men under the term of
wight' (15).

For thanks to heaven, and to the gods above
I have won chastity, in place of love.
Now love's as far from me as never known:
Then basely tied, now freely am mine own.   120
Slavery and bondage with mourning care
Were then my living, sighs and tears my fare,
But all these gone, now live I joyfully,
Free, and untouched of thought but chastity.   *Exit.*

[*Enter* PHILISSES.]

Philisses. Love, being missed in heaven, at last was found   125
    Lodged in Musella's fair though cruel breast.
    Cruel, alas, yet whereon I must ground
    All hopes of joy, though tired with unrest.
    O dearest dear, let plaints which true-felt are
    Gain pity once, do not delight to prove   130
    So merciless, still killing with despair;
    Nor pleasure take so much to try my love.
    Yet if your trial will you milder make,
    Try, but not long, lest pity come too late.

---

117. gods] *PM;* Gods *HM.* 118. love] *HM;* Love *PM.* 124. SD.] *CWD;*
not in PM; ex: HM, R. 124.1. SD.] *CWD.* 125. Love] Love *PM, HM.*
129. dearest] Deerest *PM;* deerest *HM;* hearest *CWD.* true-felt] true felt
PM, HM. 131. So merciless, still killing] *HM;* soe merciless still killing
PM. despair;] despair; *catchword* 'nor =' *PM.* 133. trial ... milder] *PM;*
triall, you will milder *HM.* 134. lest] *PM;* least *HM.*

  119. *as never known*] as though I had never known it.

  120. *basely*] unhappily, dishonourably.

  mine own] Cf. Silviana, 'I now live free and uncontrolled of Fortune's self'
and 'I was indeed only his, now am I free myself' (*Urania I*, 224.16–17 and
30–1).

  121. *Slavery ... care*] Slavery is trisyllabic to make the line scan, meaning
slavery and imprisonment [to love], along with grief at unrequited love.

  123–4. *joyfully ... chastity*] Cf. Silviana, 'so are now mine eyes and
thoughts as far from touch of love ... love I not aught [anything] but fair
chastity' (*Urania I*, 224.27 and 225.6).

  127. *ground*] base, build.

  129. *plaints*] complaints, lamentations (*OED*, n.1). In the following lines
Philisses depicts himself as the typically helpless courtly lover, following the
tradition of Petrarch and reworked by Philip Sidney in *AS.* Cf. Forester in
182 below and Philisses and Lissius in 4.1.21 and 187 respectively.

  132. *try*] test.

But oh, she may not, cannot, will not take   135
Pity on me; she loves, and lends me hate.
Lissius. Fie, my Philisses, will you ever fly
    My sight that loves you, and your good desires?
Philisses. Fly you, dear Lissius? No, but still a cry
    I hear that says I burn in scorner's fires.   140
    Farewell, good Lissius, I will soon return,
    But not to you a rival like to burn.   [*Exit.*]
Lissius. Ah, poor Philisses, would I knew thy pain,
    That as I now lament, might help obtain.
    But yet in love they say none should be used   145
    But self-deserts, lest trust might be abused.

---

135. But oh,] butt o *PM;* butt O. *HM.*   may ... not] may nott, cannott,
will nott *PM;* can nott, may nott, will nott *HM.*   138. loves] *PM;* loves
HM.   140. scorner's] scorners *PM, HM.*   142. burn. [*Exit.*]] burne, *PM;*
burne; ex: *HM.*   143. poor Philisses] *PM;* poore Phi: *HM.*   146. self-
deserts] *CWD;* self deserts *PM;* self desarts *HM.*   lest] *CWD;* least *PM,
HM.*   abused] abusde. / *PM;* abus'd; *HM.*   146.1. SD.] *R;* A Forester
PM, HM.

135–6. *she ... hate*] Philisses believes Musella loves elsewhere (i.e. Lissius)
and hates him. Cf. the jealous Antissia who loves Amphilanthus and tells
Pamphilia, 'I cannot, nor may not blame thee for loving him' (*Urania I,*
113.25), and *AS,* Sonnet 47, 'I may, I must, I can, I will' (188).

137–8. *fly ... you*] Cf. *AS,* Sonnet 27, 12–13, where Astrophil admits
that his desire for Stella 'makes me oft my best friends overpass / Unseen,
unheard' (178).

140. *burn ... fires*] This phrase may be spoken aside to spectators, as in
the 2018 production. Burning in desire is another feature typical of the
Petrarchan lover, adopted by all the Sidney writers. See, for example, *AS,*
Sonnets 1, 8, 25, 28, 47, 59, 76; RS *Poems,* Song 1, 35–6; William Herbert's
poem 'Can you suspect a change in me?' which claims 'the resistless flames
of my desire / Make an Aetna of my heart' (WH *Poems,* 2–3). For Wroth's
reworking of the trope see *P4,* Sonnets 1, 2, 3, 17, 25, Songs 2, 5, 'Crown
of Sonnets' 1, 4, 5 and 14 (*Poems,* 127–30, 134) and *Urania II,* where
Amphilanthus's grief over losing Pamphilia 'outflamed all triumphant fires,
and burnt his noblest heart in hotter fires' (294.6–7). On love and martyrdom see Introduction, 14–15.

142. *But ... burn*] possibly 'But not burning in scorner's fires as your
unsuccessful rival for Musella's affections'. This line could conceivably be
spoken as an aside.

145–6. *in ... abused*] Self-deserts mean what the lover himself or herself
deserves. Lissius argues that lovers should press their suit themselves, as
their trust may be abused if another party pleads for them. See *Urania I*
where Pamphilia tells Antissia that even one's own 'conceit of mine own
deserts (which it may be are seen but by my own eyes)' may not be enough
to 'gain' her desires (94.28).

[*Enter*] *A* FORESTER.

Forester. [*To himself*] Did cruelty itself thus ever show?
    Did ever heaven our mildness thus far move?
    All sweetness, and all beauty to o'erthrow,
    All joy deface, and crop in springtime love?   150
    Could any mortal breast invent such harm?
    Could living creature think on such a loss?
    No, no, alas it was the Furies' charm
    Who sought by this our best delights to cross,
    And now in triumph glory in their gain.   155
    Where was true beauty found if not in thee,
    O dear Silvesta? But accursèd swain
    That caused this change; O miserable me,
    Who live to see this day, and day's bright light
    To shine when pleasure's turned into despite.   160
Lissius. [*Aside*] Another of Love's band? O mighty Love
    That can thy folly make in most to move.

147. SD.] *CWD.* Did ... show?] *PM;* Did ever cruelty itt self thus showe?
HM. 148. move?] move? *catchword* 'all =' *HM.* 152. creature] *HM;*
Creature *PM.* 153. alas] *PM;* (alas) *HM.* Furies'] furies *PM, HM.*
159. Who] *PM;* that *HM.* 160. pleasure's] *HM;* pleasures *PM.* 161. SD.]
This ed. 161. Love's ... Love] *PM;* loves ... love *HM.* O] *PM;* ô *HM.*

---

150. *deface*] spoil.
crop ... love] cut down love in springtime (i.e. prematurely). The Forester
likes love to the green shoots of spring, an appropriate metaphor given the
pastoral setting.
153–5. *Furies' ... gain*] In classical mythology the three Furies, from the
underworld, were associated with vengeance and punishment. In both *PM*
and *HM* 'furies' is lower-case.
154. *cross*] See 1.1.19n.
157. *accursèd swain*] i.e. Philisses, whose rejection of Silvesta's love made
her vow chastity. Swain is a conventional term in pastoral poetry for a (male)
lover or suitor. To clarify the reference, in the 2018 production Philisses
turned to face the audience here.
158. *miserable me*] Cf. Philisses in 26 above.
159–60. *Who ... despite*] This couplet concludes the Forester's speech,
making a complete sonnet of fourteen lines. His resentment of the day's
bright light in the meadows echoes Philisses's embrace of '*the dark*' (10).
The pattern of thwarted courtly love exemplified by the Forester is also
found in Dolorindus's lament 'Sweet solitariness, joy to those hearts' in
Wroth's *Urania I* (133–4, *Poems*, 151–3).
160. *despite*] in this sense, indignation, anger or evil feeling (*OED*, 4).
161. *band*] Cf. Silvesta's former membership of Venus's 'band' in 87.
162. *most ... move*] an opportunity for Lissius to address spectators or
readers; the Forester's speech builds on that of Philisses, in confirming his

Forester. [*To himself*] Accursèd shepherd, why wert thou e'er
    born
    Unless it were to be true virtue's scorn?
    Cursed be thy days, unlucky ever be,   165
    Nor ever live least happiness to see;
    But where thou lov'st, let her as cruel prove
    As thou wert to Silvesta, and my love.
Lissius. If one may ask, what is th'offence is done?
Forester. That cursed Philisses hath me quite undone.   170
Lissius. Undone as how?
Forester.   Sit down and you shall know,
    For glad I am that I my grief may tell,
    Since 'tis some ease my sorrow's cause to show,
    Disburd'ning my poor heart which grief doth swell.
    Then know I loved, alas, and ever must   175
    Silvesta fair, sole mistress of my joy,
    Whose dear affections were in surest trust
    Laid up in flames, my hopes clean to destroy.
    For as I truly loved, and only she,
    She for Philisses sighed, who did reject   180

---

163. e'er] *This ed.;* ere *PM, HM.* born] borne *PM, HM.* 174.
disburd'ning] disburding *PM;* disburdning *HM.* 175. alas] *PM;* (alas)
HM. 176. Silvesta fair, sole] *HM;* Silvesta fair sole *PM.* mistress] m^rs
PM, HM. 178. destroy] destroy, *catchword* 'For' *PM.*

---

thesis that love is a kind of madness. His use of 'most', however, implies
that he still considers himself as separate from those affected by Love's folly.
    163. *To himself*] The Forester makes a further apostrophe to Philisses,
the 'accursèd' shepherd.
    171. *Sit ... know*] The Forester's direction warns that this is going to be
a lengthy tale of woe. Lissius's reaction may give this exchange a comic tone,
as in the 1999 production where he reluctantly sat down beside the Forester
and restlessly crossed and uncrossed his legs, yawned and scratched himself
through the Forester's account, drawing laughter from spectators. In 2018
Lissius sat on a tree stump in the middle of the front row of spectators,
allowing the Forester to perform his passionate declaration of love to the
audience as well as to Lissius.
    174. *Disburd'ning*] unburdening; elided to three syllables to make the
line scan.
    177–8. *Whose ... flames*] The Forester protests that Philisses has destroyed
or burned up the affections that Silvesta invested exclusively in him, the
imagery of martyrdom by fire looking forward to 5.7.15–18.
    178. *clean*] entirely.

Her love and pains, nor would she, cruel, see
My plaints, nor tears, but followed his neglect
With greater passion; I her followed still.
She flew from me, he ran from her as fast,
I after both did hie, though for my ill   185
Who thus do live all wretchedness to taste.
Long time this lasted, still she constant loved
And more she loved, more cruel still he grew
Till at the length thus tyrant-like he proved,
Forcing that change which makes my poor heart rue.   190
For she, perceiving hate so far to guide
His settled heart to nothing but disdain,
Having all manners, and all fashions tried
That might give comfort to her endless pain,
But seeing nothing would his favour turn   195
From fondly flying of her truest love,
Led by those passions which did firmly burn
So hot as nothing could those flames remove
But still increase, she for the last resolved
To kill this heat, this hopeless course to take: 200
Making a vow which can not be dissolved,
As not obtaining love, will love forsake.
For she hath vowed unto Diana's life

181. she, cruel, see] she cruell see *PM*; (she cruell) see *HM*.   184. She
... fast] *PM;* she rann from mee, hee flew from her as fast *HM*.   186. all
wretchedness] all a̶l̶l̶ wrechednes *PM*.   189. length] *PM;* last *HM*.   tyrant-
like] *CWD;* tiran like *PM, HM*.   193. Having ... fashions] *PM;* having all
fashions, and all manners *HM*.   202. As] as *PM;* As [*overwritten, orig.*
'*an*'] *HM*.

185. *hie*] hasten.
188. *more she loved*] the more she loved.
189. Brennan (*R*, 233) notes a comparison with Philip Sidney: 'So Tyrant
he no fitter place could spy' (PS *Poems*, 175).
190. *rue*] grieve, with a secondary meaning of sink, from the Latin *ruere*;
possibly also an allusion to rue, a bitter herb often used for medicinal pur-
poses in the period.
196. *fondly*] foolishly.
197–99. *Led ... increase*] Led by the escalating and irrepressible power of
desire. These lines climax with the subject 'she', Silvesta, but they also
describe the power of unrequited passion over Philisses and the Forester
himself. On imagery of flames see 140 and n. above.
199. *for the last*] at last.
203. *Diana's life*] Cf. 111–12n. above.

Her pure virginity, as she who could
No more than once love, nor another's wife   205
Consent to be, nor his now if he would.
This hath he done by his ungratefulness;
Would it might turn to his own wretchedness.
Lissius. O curse him not, alas it is his ill
To feel so much as doth his senses kill;   210
And yet indeed this cruelty and course
Is somewhat strange for shepherds here to use.
Yet see I not how this can prove the worse
For you, whose love she ever did refuse,
But much the better, since your suffered pain   215
Can be no glory to another's gain.
Forester. Would it could be to any's gain the most
Of glory, honour, fortune, and what more
Can added be, though I had ever lost
And he obtained the chief of beauty's store.   220
For then I might have her sometimes beheld,
But now am barred, for my love placèd was
In truest kind, wherein I all excelled,
Not seeking gain, but losing did surpass
Those that obtain, for my thoughts did ascend   225

---

209. O] *PM;* Ô *HM.*   211. course] cource *['o' overwritten or blotted in PM]*;
course *HM.*   212. strange] *PM;* hard *HM.*   214. ever] *PM;* always *HM.*
220. obtained] *PM;* had gain'd *HM.* beauty's] beauties *PM, HM;*
Beauty's *CWD.*   222. barred] *CWD;* bar'd *PM, HM.*

---

205. *No … love*] not love more than once.
211. *course*] behaviour, way of proceeding (*OED*, n.22a), frequently used
by Wroth e.g. *Urania I,* 'this cruel course' (13.12); 'this solitary course'
(16.37); or *PA,* 'guide your course by art' (119). In *PM* the o is blotted in
'cource'. Wroth does not use the spellings 'cource' or 'curce' elsewhere. If
the blotted o in *PM* is a deliberate erasure, 'curse' would refer to the 'hate'
and 'disdain' shown to Silvesta by Philisses, 191-2. In *HM* the word is clearly
'course'.
212. *strange … use*] Not knowing of Philisses's love for Musella, Lissius
ascribes his rejection of Silvesta to unusual cruelty.
217-20.] The Forester claims that he would have preferred any other
suitor to have gained the glory, honour and good fortune of winning
Silvesta's love.
220. *store*] treasure.
224-5. *losing … obtain*] losing her love, I surpassed those who win love.
The Forester declares a Platonic form of chaste, courtly adoration to be a
higher kind of love than physical consummation.

No higher than to look; that was my end.
Lissius. What strange effects doth Fancy 'mong us prove
      Who still brings forth new images of love?
      But this of all is strangest, to affect
      Only the sight, and not the joys respect   230
      Nor ends of whining love, since sight we gain
      With small ado, the other with much pain,
      Doubling the pleasure having left despair,
      And favour won, which kills all former care;
      And sure if ever I should chance to love   235
      The fruitful ends of love I first would move.

---

226. end.] end. / *PM;* end; *HM.*   227. Fancy] *This ed.;* Phant'sy *PM;*
phant'sie *HM;* fancy *CWD.*   231. ends] *PM;* end *HM.*   whining] *PM,*
HM; winning EMWRN.   232. pain] pain *catchword* 'dubbling =' *PM;* care
HM.   234. And ... care] *PM; line omitted from HM.*   236. fruitful] *PM;*
fruictfull *HM.*

---

226. *end*] goal.
227. *Fancy*] Phant'sy in *PM* and Phant'sie in *HM*, though the two senses
of the original Greek word *phantasia*, denoting (1) the appearance of a spec-
tral apparition and (2) the faculty of imagination or fanciful invention, are
combined in early modern English.
230. *the ... respect*] respect the joys. Cf. 3.4.14. In contrast to the Forester's
prizing of the sight of the beloved, Lissius focuses on its more tangible
aspects, seemingly with sexual overtones (see 236).
231. *whining*] complaining, used of both animals and humans (*OED*, v.1).
The whining lover, deriving from Petrarchan tradition, is regarded disparag-
ingly by Sidney's Astrophil, who notes they 'whine' like 'babes' with 'Love's
pain' (PS *Poems*, 173). The lover who looks 'as if he would whine for an ill
look of his mistress' is caricatured in Nicholas Breton's *Choice, Chance and*
Change: or, Conceits in their Colours (London, R. Bradock for Nathaniel
Fosbrook, 1606), sig. D4v. The word may also be read as 'winning';
Straznicky (*SM,* 55) feels this is more likely, though we have retained the
word as written by Wroth in *PM.* She spells 'winning' in the conventional
way at 3.3.87 in *PM,* but with one 'n' in *HM.*
232. *ado*] trouble, effort.
the other] i.e. the 'joys' and 'ends' of love.
233–4. *Doubling ... won*] Lissius argues that the contrast between despair
and success in love makes winning favour doubly pleasurable, an idea
pursued by Venus and Cupid in 3.4. Cf. Floristello in *Urania II,* who declares
'the sharper your pains are at first, the sweeter will be your enjoying afterwards' (95.39–40).
236. *fruitful ... love*] the consummation of love (rather than chaste absti-
nence), with the connotation of reproduction.

Forester. I wish you may obtain your heart's desire,
    And I but sight, who waste in chastest fire.   *Exit.*
Lissius. These two to meet in one I ne'er did find,
    Love and chastity linked in one man's mind.   240
    But now I see Love hath as many ways
    To win as to destroy when he delays.   [*Exit.*]

[ACT I SCENE 3]

[*Under the trees*]

[*Enter*] PHILISSES, DALINA, RUSTIC, LACON,
and LISSIUS.

Dalina. The sun grows hot, 'twere best we did retire.
Lissius. There's a good shade—
Philisses.   But here's a burning fire.

---

240. Love and chastity] Love, and Chastity *PM;* love, and chastity
HM.   linked … one] *PM;* link'd [*inserted above*] in ones *HM.*   man's] *HM;*
Mans *PM.*   241. Love] love *PM, HM.*   242. SD.] *CWD.*

0.0. [ACT I SCENE 3]] *CWD.*   0.1. SD.] *This ed.*   0.2. SD.] Philisses,
Dalina, Rustick, Lacon, and Lissius *PM, HM;* [*Enter*] PHILISSES, DALINA,
RUSTIC, LACON, LISSIUS [*and* CLIMEANA] *CWD.*   1. retire] retire = [*end
of page* followed by SP Li: *HM.*   2. shade—] *This ed.   CWD adds* SD
[*Aside*] *after this line.*

---

238. *but*] only.
241–2. *Love … delays*] i.e. 'Love has as many ways to win humans by
delaying fulfilment as he does to destroy them by the same tactic'. Lissius's
speech may be addressed directly to spectators (as in the 1999 and 2018
productions) to cover the entrance of the shepherd group for the following
scene.

  0.1. SD.] The shady retreat referred to in 1–2 may be at the edge of the
woods abutting the pasture where the shepherds' flocks are grazing, or possibly a bower, 'a place closed in or overarched with branches of trees, shrubs,
or other plants; a shady recess' (*OED*, n.3) in the midst of the meadows.
  1. *retire*] Dalina's line proposing that the shepherds retire from the hot
sun into the shade suggests that this scene takes place at a midday break.
Towards the end of the scene Musella says they should 'tend our flocks who
all this while do burn' (99), indicating they return to work in the pasture.
  2. *burning fire*] again, a metaphorical fire of passion; Philisses pays more
attention to his internal turmoil than to his surroundings. Cf. 100–1, 1.2.140
and n. and Introduction, 14–15.

Lacon. Never did I see man so changed as he.
Dalina. Truly nor I, what can the reason be?
Philisses. Love, love it is, which you in time may know,   5
    But happy they can keep their love from show.

[Enter MUSELLA.]

Dalina. Musella welcome to our meeting is;
    Of all our fellows you did only miss.
Musella. Small miss of me, for oft'nest when I'm here
    I am as if I were another where.   10
    But where is Fillis? Seldom do I find
    Her or Simeana missing, yet the blind
    God Cupid late hath struck her yielding breast,
    And makes her lonely walk to seek for rest.
Philisses. Yet when the pain is greatest, 'tis some ease   15
    To let a friend partake his friend's disease.
Musella. That were no friendly part, in this you miss;
    Impart unto your friend no harm, but bliss.

---

5. Love, love] *HM;* Love, Love *PM.*   6.1 SD.] *R.*   9. miss] *PM;* loss
HM.   11. Fillis] *HM;* Phillis *PM.*   12. Simeana] *HM;* Simena *PM.*   13.
God Cupid] God Cupid *PM;* god Cupid *HM.*

3–6.] Lacon begins a conversation with the others as they observe
Philisses, which suggests he wanders away from the rest of the group,
although he can hear them since he answers Dalina's question in 5.

6. *happy ... show*] happy are they who can conceal their love. In the 2018
production Philisses delivered this line with impatience at being the object
of scrutiny.

8. *you ... miss*] only you were missing.

9. *Small miss of me*] You will not have missed me much.

10. *I ... where*] I am as if I were somewhere else. Musella characterizes
herself as being distracted – possibly due to her feelings for Philisses.

11. *Fillis*] This character's name is spelt Phillis in *PM*, clearly associating
her with Philisses (see note to *Dramatis Personae*). However, all subsequent
references to her in *PM* are spelt Fillis. This avoids confusion with Philisses
in stage directions and speech prefixes, the alteration perhaps offering evidence that *PM* served as a performance text.

16. *partake ... disease*] share his friend's pain (i.e. 'dis-ease'). While
Philisses's hypothetical confidant is male, he may be covertly suggesting that
he wishes to confide in Musella.

17–18. *That ... bliss*] In a witty continuation of the flirtation, Musella
counters that Philisses should share pleasure with his friend rather than pain.

Philisses. Some friend will ready be to ease one's smart.
Musella. So to befriend yourself they should bear part.   20
Dalina. Now we are met, what sport shall we invent
    While the sun's fury somewhat more be spent?
Lacon. Let each one here their fortunes past relate,
    Their loves, their froward chance, or their good fate.
Musella. And so discourse the secrets of the mind: 25
    I like not this, thus sport may crosses find.
Philisses. Let one begin a tale.
Dalina.   Nor that I like.
Lacon. What then will please? We see what doth dislike.
Philisses. Dislike is quickly known, pleasure is scant.
Musella. And where joys seem to flow (alas) there's want.   30

---

20. befriend ... part] *PM;* beefreind your self, you'l make them smart *HM.*
23. fortunes] *PM;* fortune *HM.* 24. fate] *HM;* fat [*hole in page*]
PM. 26. sport] *PM;* mirth *HM.* find.] find: / *PM;* find, *HM.* 28. What
then] *PM;* then what *HM.* 30. (alas)] *PM;* alas *HM.* 30.1. SD.] *This ed.;*
SP Climeana: – [*end of page*] *PM;* Climena s / ~~Climena~~ *HM.*

19. *smart*] pain (in literal and in figurative contexts, *OED,* n.1). As a
convenient rhyme for heart, it is used frequently by Wroth to indicate physical and mental pain – there are ten examples in *Love's Victory,* and fifteen
in *Pamphilia to Amphilanthus.*
  20. *So ... part*] i.e. 'So to befriend you, they should take on the role'. In
2018 this was played in an argumentative tone, with Dalina intervening to
break up the disagreement.
  21. *sport*] amusement or game. The tradition of shepherds singing, recit-
ing verse, playing on pipes and conversing to pass the time derives from
pastoral literature dating back to Virgil's *Eclogues* and revived in Spenser's
The Shepheardes Calendar (London: Hugh Singleton, 1579). It is found in
the Eclogues of Philip Sidney's *Arcadia* and also features in RS *Poems,* and
Wroth's *Urania I* and *II.* The word appears ten times in Wroth's script. For
its early modern resonance, see notes at 2.1.3 and 2.1.134 for King James I's
licensing of public entertainments in 1617–18.
  22. *while*] until.
  24. *froward chance*] bad luck.
  26. *crosses find*] encounter troubles. Musella is reluctant to reveal her
thoughts and feelings (see note to 1.1.19).
  30. *joys ... want*] Musella is (perhaps deliberately) obscure in building on
Philisses's previous line. She suggests that where there appears to be joy,
there is actually lack or yearning; reluctant to reveal her own feelings, she
may be referring obliquely to her own unhappiness.

[*Enter* CLIMEANA.]

Climeana. [*Sings.*]
  O mine eyes, why do you lead
  My poor heart thus forth to range
  From the wonted course to strange
  Unknown ways and paths to tread?

  Let it home return again,   35
  Free, untouched of gadding thought,

---

31. SD.] *CWD.*   31. *O ... lead*] Ô mine eyes why doe you lead *PM;* O my
eyes how do you lead *HM.*

---

31. SP. Climeana] Wroth gives no stage direction for Climeana's entrance
in either *PM* or *HM.* She could appear with the other shepherds at the
beginning of the scene, or enter when her song begins. Wroth's use of
Climeana's full name in both *PM* and *HM* to cue the song reflects a convention used to mark entrances throughout the play, so may indicate the latter.
In *HM* after writing the SP 'Climeana' Wroth has written an S with a slash
mark / closely afterwards, followed by a second 'Climena' which has been
crossed through. The S / may be a hurriedly written *S fermé* signature mark
(see Introduction, 2) or possibly even the first letter of a transcription of the
word 'song' from a separate sheet of paper on which Climeana's lyric was
written. In the 1999 production Climeana entered with the others and Lacon
prompted her to sing, while in the 2018 production she entered singing.
31. SD.] Again, no score is extant for this or for the other songs in this
scene. Like Philisses, Climeana uses the landscape to chart her feelings (see
Introduction, 18–19); her lyric about her heart ranging forth into unknown
territory may refer to her journey from her previous home, Arcadia, to the
world of the play (3.3.67–70). The ranging of Climeana's affections (something which Simeana criticizes as inconstancy in 3.3.99–106) was demonstrated to spectators in the 1999 production when Climeana moved between
the male shepherds caressing Philisses, Rustic and finally a very reluctant
Lissius as she sang.
31. eyes] Wroth makes frequent use of the convention of eyes leading
lovers astray. Cf. 'Can pleasing sight, misfortune ever bring?' and 'You happy
blessed eyes' (Wroth *Poems*, 87, 108).
32. range] Cf. *PA,* Song 'in horrid darkness will I range' (116).
33. wonted] accustomed, familiar.
34. Unknown ... paths] Climeana may be referring literally to her move
from Arcadia (3.3.67–8) and metaphorically to her unconventionally assertive behaviour (for a woman of the period), in pursuing Lissius, the object
of her love, that we see in 3.3.84ff. Cf. Webster's Duchess of Malfi: 'I am
going into a wilderness / Where I shall find nor path nor friendly clew / To
be my guide' (*Malfi* 1.1.359–61).
36. gadding] roving, wandering.

And your forces back be brought
To the ridding of my pain.

But mine eyes, if you deny
This small favour to my heart,   40
And will force my thoughts to fly,
Know yet you govern but your part.

Lissius. Climeana hath begun a pretty sport;
   Let each one sing, and so the game is short.
Rustic. Indeed, well said, and I will first begin.
Dalina. And whosoever's out, you'll not be in.   45
Philisses. Sing they who have glad hearts or voice to sing,
   I can but patience to this pleasure bring.
Musella. Then you and I will sit, and judges be.
Philisses. Would fair Musella first would judge of me.   50
Musella. Will you then sing?
Philisses.   No, I would only say—
Musella. Choose some time else— who will begin this play?
Rustic. Why that will I, and I will sing of thee.

[handwritten margin note: He's reluctant to show his feelings, he thinks Musella is in love w/ Lissius]

---

46. whosoever's] *PM;* who=so=evers *HM.*   51. say—] say [...] *R.*

42. govern ... part] Climeana acknowledges that her eyes are leading her heart astray. On the importance of thoughts in maintaining independence and hope in Wroth's work, see Song 3 in *Pamphilia to Amphilanthus*: 'Stay my thoughts' and 'Still maintain thy force in me / Let me thinking still be free' (97).

46. *whosoever's ... in*] Dalina's hostile reaction implies that Rustic is not in tune, literally or metaphorically, with the rest of the witty lovers.

48. *I ... bring*] i.e. 'I can only endure others playing this game (rather than bringing a glad heart or voice)'. Cf. Wroth's song beginning 'Fairest, and still truest eyes' which counsels 'patient be / Till faithless jealousy gives leave' to clearer sight (*Poems*, 119).

49. *judges be*] judges of the shepherds' singing. In the 2018 performance, Musella invited him to sit with her to judge by occupying the two tree stumps on the front row of the audience.

51. *only say—*] In performance Musella may interrupt Philisses from declaring his affection with 'Choose some time else', or he may simply be unable to find the words to do so. In the 2018 production, she held her hands up to stop him from speaking.

Musella. Sorry I am I should your subject be.

Rustic. [*Sings.*] ⟶ *Comparing Musella's beauty*
⟶ *to that of his animal farm(?)*

    When I do see   55
      Thee, whitest thee,
    Yea whiter than lamb's wool,
      How do I joy;
    That thee enjoy
      I shall with my heart full.   60

    Thy eyes do play
      Like goats with hay,
    And skip like kids flying
      From the sly fox;
    So eyelid's box   65
      Shuts up thy sight's prying.

55. SP. *Rustic*] *not in HM.*   SD.] *CWD.*   61. *eyes*] *HM;* Eyes *PM.*   62.
goats] *HM;* Goats *PM.*   64. *fox*] *PM;* Fox *HM.*

---

54. *Sorry ... be*] Musella may speak with sorrow from a knowledge of her
arranged match with Rustic (5.1.69–74) as well as, more immediately, that
she is the subject of – and subjected to – his inelegant and unwelcome song.

55–72. *When ... lack*] Rustic's song adapts the tradition of the courtly
blazon (where the beloved's body parts are each singled out for praise, with
comparison to jewels, gold or flowers) to the rustic context of his own farm;
he assesses Musella's features in relation to his stock and crops of apples, to
comic effect. His use of verse to do so may owe something to Leonard
Mascall's poem 'A Praise of the Sheep' in *The First Book of Cattle* (1587,
Aa1v). Rustic's style also resembles that of Dametas in Sidney's *Arcadia*
(III. 643–4), or Lorel, the 'rude swineherd' in Ben Jonson's *The Sad Shepherd*,
who woos Earnine with the words: 'Deft mistress, whiter than the cheese
new pressed, / Smoother than cream, and softer than the curds: / Why start
ye from me ere ye hear me tell / My wooing errand and what rents I have,
/ Large herds and pastures, swine and kye [cattle], mine own?' (2.2.2–6). In
the 1999 production Rustic sang to the tune of 'Greensleeves' to emphasize
the song's status as a parody of a conventional romantic ballad.

58–60. *How ... full*] 'How I rejoice; I shall wish you joy with all my
heart'. Rustic's song has an overbearing tone, particularly if Rustic is read
as the subject of 'that thee enjoy' – the phrase may have a sexual undertone,
as one possible meaning of 'enjoy' is 'to have one's will of (a woman)'
(*OED*, 4b).

65–6. *eyelid's ... prying*] Rustic likens Musella's eyelids to a pen or enclo-
sure for animals that closes over her eyes to protect them. His lyrics cast him
as the 'sly fox' attempting to catch her eye, although they may also imply
that she is trying to escape his gaze.

> *Thy cheeks are red*
>   *Like ochre spread*
> *On a fatted sheep's back;*
>   *Thy paps are found*   boobs   70
> *Like apples round;*
>   *No praises shall lack.*

Musella. Well, you have praises given enough, now let
   Another come some other to commend.
Rustic. I had much more to say but thus I'm met,   75
   And stayed; now will I harken, and attend.

---

67. *are*] *PM;* as *HM.*   68. *Like ochre*] like Okar *PM;* as okar *HM.*   70. *are*]
PM; as are [*overwritten*] *HM.*   71. *Like*] *PM;* as *HM.*   74. other] *PM;*
others *HM.*   76. will I] *PM;* I will ['*will*' *inserted above*] *HM.*

68. ochre] pigment, varying from light yellow to brown or red, used to
mark sheep. Wroth's reference to red ochre draws on a long tradition of
protection going back to the Jewish Passover custom of killing a lamb
'without spot of blemish' and 'with the blood thereof coloured the post and
lintern of the doors', as described in Walter Raleigh's *History of the World*
(London: William Stansby for Walter Burre, 1617). Raleigh notes that the
Egyptians imitated this ritual, 'ascribing an exceeding virtue to the red
colour: and therefore they did not only mark their sheep and cattle, but their
trees bearing fruit, to preserve them from lightning and other harms' (253).
In Sidney's *Arcadia* the shepherd Claius protects his young sheep '(Lest
greedy eyes to them might challenge lay) / Busy with oker did their shoulders
mark / (His mark a pillar was ...' (I.199). The husbandman Rustic, perhaps
suspicious of Philisses's interest in Musella, uses the song to mark her protectively as his property and it may offer a comment on Musella's propensity
for blushing (see 4.1.132–4).
70. paps ... apples] paps are breasts. Cf. the poems collected in Robert
Allott's *England's Parnassus or The Choicest Flowers of our Modern Poets*
(London, for N. Ling, C. Burby and T. Hayes, 1600) ascribed to Robert
Greene – 'Her paps are like fair apples in the prime / As round as orient
pearls as soft as down' (398) – and to Sir John Harington: 'large her breast
/ Two ivory apples seemed there to grow' (404). In the 2018 performance,
Musella showed her offence at Rustic's crude praise by getting to her feet
and slapping him on the shoulders during the last three lines of the song
(70–2), finally pushing him away from her with both hands.
73. *Well ... enough*] Lines 75–6 imply that Musella interrupts Rustic's
song here; in the 2018 performance she raised her voice to admonish Rustic
at this point.
76. *stayed*] stopped.

Lacon. [*Sings.*]
  By a pleasant river's side,
  Heart and hopes on pleasure's tide,
  Might I see within a bower,
  Proudly dressed with every flower   80
  Which the spring doth to us lend,
  Venus and her loving friend.
  I upon her beauty gazed;
  They me seeing were amazed
  Till at last up stepped a child,   85
  In his face not actions mild.
  'Fly away,' said he, 'for sight

---

77. SD.] *CWD.*   80. *Proudly*] *PM;* proudly [*'u' inserted above*] *HM.*   81. *doth*] can *HM.*   82. *friend*] freind *PM;* freind *catchword* 'I upon =' *HM.* 85. *up stepped*] *HM;* upstept *PM.*

---

77. Sings.] Lacon is listed as being in love with Musella (*Dramatis Personae* 5; see also 5.3.5–12), so his song is probably addressed to her. *CWD* notes that Lacon's song echoes the lover's vision in Petrarch's *The Triumph of Love* (*CWD*, 202n.8). See Parker, *Triumphs* (1555, sigs A4v–E4v). In the 2018 performance Joel Sams combined a beautiful singing voice with jittery, nervous gestures and a hesitant approach to his beloved Musella. His vulnerability produced laughter and sympathy from onstage and offstage spectators. See 93n. below.
78. tide] with a pun on being 'tied to pleasures, as well as carried on a tide of pleasure' (*CWD*, 202n.9).
79. bower] a recess or arbour enclosed by tree boughs and leaves and often decorated with flowers (*OED*, n.3), but also a specifically feminine private apartment or boudoir (*OED*, n.2b). In Robert Greene's *Never Too Late* Isabel sings of a riverside bower on a bank decked with flowers 'As if Venus there had made / By Flora's hand / A curious bower / To dally with her paramours' (1590, 28). Royal entertainments featured such pastoral scenes with bowers. *The King of Denmark's Welcome to London* [31 July 1606] (London: Edward Allde, 1606), which Wroth may have witnessed with her father (*Letters*, 126), included an 'artificial summer bower of green boughs divided with curtains of crimson taffeta' in which a 'fair shepherd courting a coy shepherdess' could be seen (24–5). In *Urania II* Claramundo, the Knight of Love and newly crowned King of Cicilia, who mourns the death of his father alongside celebrating a victory over rebel forces, walks in his palace gardens with his royal guests and encounters 'a curious arbour' of cypress 'which showed funeral sadness' but where 'pleasant Jasmine and wanton woodbine' wind around 'in amorous manner' to present 'their beauties and sweetness' (245.34–9).
82. loving friend] *CWD* (202n.81) identifies this as Mars, Venus's most famous supernatural lover and father of the 'child' Cupid (18). See 1.1.15n.

Shall both breed and kill delight.
Fly away, and follow me,
I will let thee beauties see.'   90
I obeyed him when he stayed
Hard beside a heavenly maid,
When he threw a flaming dart,
And unkindly struck my heart.

Musella. But what became then of the cruel boy?   95
Lacon. When he had done his worst he fled away.
Musella. And so let us, 'tis time we do return,
    To tend our flocks who all this while do burn.
Philisses. [*Aside*] Burn, and must burn, this suddenly is said,
    But heat not quenched alas, but hopes decayed.   100
Dalina. What, have you done, and must I lose my song?
Musella. Not lose it, though awhile we it prolong.
Dalina. I am content, and now let's all retire.

---

89. *Fly*] *PM;* Come *HM.* 91. *when*] *PM;* then *HM.* 95. cruel] *PM;*
subtile *HM.* 97. 'tis time we do] *PM;* 't'is time that wee *HM.* 98.
while] *PM;* time *HM.* 100. decayed] *PM;* decaid / *HM.* 103. let's] *PM;*
lett *HM.*

   91. when] until.
   92. Hard] close.
   93. When] whereupon.
   dart ... heart] Cupid's treachery and unkindness was a common theme
of love poetry of the period. See, for example, Wroth *Poems*, 139, and *AS*,
Sonnet 20, and Introduction, 12–13. In the 2018 performance Lacon finished
his song with 'my heart' on a high, suspended note, very close to Musella,
with his hand on her heart, and waited for a response. After an embarrassed
pause, she used her question to break away from his rapt attentions. In the
1999 production Lacon (who doubled with Cupid) ended the song sitting
at Musella's feet with his head on her knee, until she extracted herself by
getting up swiftly on 'and so let us' (97).
   98–100. *burn ... quenched*] Musella follows Virgil's counsel, reproduced
in Mascall's husbandry book, to find shade for the sheep, where shepherds
should 'as heat and time do last / Then let them quench their thirst' (Mascall
(1587), 214). However, Philisses laments that his burning desire for Musella
has not been quenched.
   101. *What, have you*] Musella appears to be bringing the singing to a
premature end, perhaps in order to escape further unwanted male
attention.
   102. *prolong*] postpone (*OED*, v.2).

Philisses. [*Aside*] And soon return, sent by love's quickest
　　fire.　　　　　　　　　　　　　　　　　　　　[*Exeunt.*]

[ACT I SCENE 4]

VENUS *and* CUPID *appearing in the clouds.*

Venus. Fie, this is nothing! What? Is this your care?
　　That among ten the half of them you spare?
　　I would have all to wail, and all to weep!
　　Will you at such a time as this go sleep?

104. SP. *Philisses.*] PM; Phi: *PM;* Phi: *inserted HM.*　SD.] *CWD.*　fire.] fire; /
[*flourish below*] PM, HM.　SD.] *CWD.*

0.0. [ACT I SCENE 4]] *CWD.*　0.1. SD.] *PM;* Venus and Cupid. *HM;*
[*Enter*] VENUS *and* CUPID *appearing in the clouds. CWD.*

104. Aside] Philisses may confide his wish for Musella's return to spectators, while or after the others exit.

0.1. SD.] The setting 'in the clouds' rather than in the Temple distinguishes Venus and Cupid as supernatural characters, existing above the
mortal shepherds and shepherdesses. Wroth here draws on the tradition of
court masques such as Jonson's *The Masque of Blackness* (1605) in which she
performed, where the moon is discovered 'in the upper part of the house,
triumphant' and crowned by light 'which striking on the clouds, and heightened with silver, reflected as natural clouds do by the splendour of the moon'
(171–4). The 1999 production evoked the 'clouds' by having Venus address
Cupid (who was on the main stage) through a small opening in a shining
silver curtain stretching across the back of the stage, which was elevated
by three steps. Neither the 2014 staged reading nor the 2018 performance
used anything other than the raised minstrels' gallery to suggest the 'clouds',
although that elevated position would equate to the 'heavens' in professional
theatres such as the Globe.

2. *ten ... half*] Eleven mortals have been mentioned at this point: Philisses,
Lissius, Silvesta, Forester, Musella, Dalina, Lacon, Rustic, Climeana,
Simeana and Fillis (the latter two have not appeared on stage but are mentioned in 1.3.12); of these Philisses, Forester, Climeana and Fillis are explicitly said to be in love in the text, although Musella's words in 1.3.30 imply
that she too is love-struck, as may the songs of Rustic and Lacon in 1.3.

4. *sleep*] Cupid is chastised by Diana's nymphs for nodding off in Lyly's
Galatea (4.2.80), and Antimo Galli's poem describing his experience of a
masque, *Rime di Antimo Galli all' Illustrissima Signora Elizabetta Talbot-Grey*
(Londini: M. Bradwood, 1609), opens with Venus being angry with Cupid
for sleeping rather than acting. In Sidney's *AS*, Sonnet 17, Venus is offended
with Cupid's lack of activity and shoves him from her lap (PS *Poems*, 173).
See Introduction, 13.

Awake your forces, and make Lissius find   5
Cupid can cruel be as well as kind.
Shall he go scorning thee, and all thy train?
And pleasure take he can thy force disdain?
Strike him, and tell him thou his lord wilt prove,
And he a vassal unto mighty Love;   10
And all the rest that scorners be of thee
Make, with their grief, of thy might feelers be.
Cupid. 'Tis true that Lissius, and some others yet,
Are free and lively, but they shall be met
With care sufficient, for 'tis not their time   15
As yet into my pleasing pain to climb.
Let them alone, and let themselves beguile;
They shall have torment when they think to smile.

---

10. Love] love *PM, HM*.   12. Make] *PM*; makes *HM*.   of thy might
feelers be] *PM;* thy powre a feeler bee *HM*.   15. With ... for] *PM;* butt
... y butt *HM*.   16. pleasing] *PM*; [*illegible deletion*] pleasing *HM*.   18.
torment] *PM;* torments *HM*.

---

7. *train*] body of attendants (*OED*, II, a). Cf. John Taylor's sonnet in *The
Nipping and Snipping of Abuses* (London: E. Griffin, 1614): 'No longer I love's
vassal will remain, / I'll be no more of *Cupid's* witless train' (C4v).

8. *And ... disdain*] And take pleasure that he can disdain your power.

9. *thou ... prove*] i.e. you will show yourself to be his master.

10. *vassal*] humble servant, from the feudal system in which a vassal holds
lands for a lord on conditions of homage and allegiance (*OED*, 2b and 1a).
Cf. *Urania I*, where the Lady of Cephalonia and the young nobleman with
whom she is in love are 'faithful vassals of Venus' (42.39–40) and Philistella
confesses she is 'the humblest vassal Cupid cherisheth' (333.37). Pamphilia
too confesses she must 'fall down vassal in despair' to love and 'his babish
[babyish] tricks' (224.15–17).

12. *feelers*] an unusual choice of noun by Wroth. The sense is that Cupid
will make all those who scorn him feel his power through their suffering or
'grief' in love. John Davies of Hereford uses it in a religious context, writing
that God makes rivers, rocks and hills 'True feelers of his [Christ's] pains',
The Holy Rood or Christ's Cross (Davies, G4v).

15. *care sufficient*] appropriate trouble. Cf. *P4*: 'I am by care sufficiently
distressed' (121).

16. *pleasing pain*] Another common trope of Petrarchan love poetry. Cf.
Venus's request that Lissius be allowed to reach bliss 'by love's sweet pleasing pain', 3.4.24.

17. *themselves beguile*] trap themselves (i.e. with their own desires and
misapprehensions).

They are not yet in pride of all their scorn,
But ere they have their pleasures half-way worn   20
They shall both cry and sigh, and wail and weep,
And for our mercy shall most humbly creep.
Love hath most glory whenas greatest sprites
He downward throws unto his own delights.
Then take no care, love's victory shall shine   25
Whenas your honour shall be raised by mine.
Venus. Thanks, Cupid. If thou do perform thine oath –
As needs you must, for gods must want no troth –
Let mortals never think it odd, or vain

---

21. cry and sigh, and wail and weep] cry, and sigh, and wayle, and weepe *PM;* cry, and waile, and weepe *HM.*   23. Love] *PM;* love *HM.*   whenas] when as *PM, HM.*   26. Whenas] *PM;* when as *HM.*   27. thine] *PM;* thy *HM.* 28. As] *PM;* and *HM.*

19. *in ... scorn*] Wroth's syntax is obscure; the phrase may mean either that they are not yet at the peak of their scorn for love (cf. Lissius's outright challenge to Cupid, 2.1.79–84) or that they are not yet in full possession of it and so remain scornful of love.

20. *worn*] experienced, carrying the sense both of 'worn' as in a garment, and 'worn' as in 'worn out'. On pleasure as a garment cf. *MAdo* 3.2.5–7. Wroth does not use the verb 'wear' but does refer to 'stage-play-like disguised pleasures' (*Poems*, 141).

21. *cry ... weep*] Such exaggerated expressions of grief in love are a commonplace of sonnets, combining most extravagantly in the opening lines of Sonnet 60 (LX) of Bartholomew Griffith's *Fidessa, more chaste than true* (London: Orwin for Matthew Lownes, 1596): 'Oh let me sigh, weep, wail, and cry no more, / Or let me sigh, weep, wail, cry more and more: / Yea let me sigh, weep, wail, cry ever-more' (E6v).

22. *mercy ... creep*] Cf. Venus's command, 1.1.14. The phrase has associations of humility and contrition in the Christian phrase 'creep to the cross' (*OED*, v.1c) and is adapted to indicate reverence, e.g. 'To come as humbly as they use to creep / To hold altars' (*T&C* 3.3.67–8). John Evans, *The Sacrifice of a Contrite Heart* (1630), tells God 'unto thy grace I creep' (85).

23–4. *Love ... delights*] Love has the most glory when he throws down the greatest spirits into the pleasures of love.

25. *take ... care*] do not worry.

love's victory] another reference to the play's title. See 1.1.34n.

26. *Whenas*] when that. Cupid assures Venus that love's triumph will shine out once her honour or reputation has been restored through his power. In the 2018 production he offered a small bow of the head and gesture of the hand to show his respect to her.

28. *gods ... troth*] gods must not lack loyalty; Venus emphasizes Cupid's duty to her.

To hear that love can in all spirits reign.   30
Princes are not exempted from our mights,
Much less should shepherds scorn us and our rites;
Though they as well can love, and like affect,
They must not therefore our commands neglect.
Cupid. Nor shall, and mark but what my vengeance is.   35
I'll miss my force, or they shall want their bliss,
And arrows here I have of purpose framed
Which as their qualities, so are they named:
Love, jealousy, malice, fear, and mistrust.

↳ this type of arrows)

30. hear] *PM;* ~~knowe~~ heere [*inserted above*] *HM.* love] *PM;* Love *HM.*
32. Much] *PM;* ~~much are~~ much [*inserted above*] *HM.* rites] rights *PM,*
HM. 34. neglect] *PM;* reject *HM.* 35. Nor] *PM;* [*deleted letter*] Nor
HM. 38. their] *PM;* they *HM.*

---

31. *Princes … mights*] Cf. Amicles in Wroth's *Urania II*, who tells
Amphilanthus that Cupid's power 'spares none, nor his deadly shafts excepts
none, not the highest princes, but rules and master[s] them, as we poor
swains' (215.21–3). Straznicky (*SM*, 37) suggests that the play's reference to
princes here and at 2.3.6 may indicate that Wroth composed the play
imagining a courtly audience that included princes. See Introduction,
14, 46 and 60n48.

32. *rites*] This word is spelled 'rights' in both *PM* and *HM* (as it is in
Philisses and Musella's offering to Venus and Cupid in 5.4.3), though 'rites'
seems the appropriate rendering given the religious context. That said,
Wroth's orthography here calls attention to Venus and Cupid's guarding of
their 'right' to be worshipped by mortals.

33. *Though … affect*] although they [shepherds] can both love and likewise
show affection for others [i.e. just as princes can].

36. *I'll … bliss*] Unclear; possibly 'unless I lose my strength, their happiness will be thwarted'.

37–9. *arrows … mistrust*] Cupid's arrows are made by Vulcan, and the
different feelings aroused by each are listed in popular literature. As Brennan
notes (*R*, 236), *England's Parnassus* (1600) included lines from Peele's lost
play *The Hunting of Cupid* listing the arrows: 'The first is Love, as here you
may behold, / His feathers head and body are of gold. / The second shaft is
Hate, a foe to love'. The third arrow is Hope, whose 'feathers are pulled
from Fortune's wings' and the 'Fourth, Jealousy in basest minds doth dwell'
(177). Robert Greene's *Alcida, Greene's Metamorphosis* (London: George
Purslowe, 1617) notes that as 'Venus hath her frowns, as she hath smiles',
so 'Cupid hath arrows headed with lead to procure disdain, as well as with
gold to increase love' (D2). In the 2018 production Cupid produced the
arrows, with labels on each, to show Venus, handing her the 'love' arrow.
The names of the arrows prefigure the action of the succeeding scenes; it is
unclear whether the intention is for each arrow to refer to the fate of a specific
character, though possibly it is significant that five arrows are named, given
Venus's suggestion in 2 that five characters have yet to be struck by Cupid.

Yet all these shall at last encounter just;   40
Harm shall be none, yet all shall harm endure
For some small season, then of joy be sure.
Like you this, mother?
Venus.   Son, I like this well,
And fail not now in least part of thy spell.   [*Exeunt.*]

---

39. Love] *PM, HM.* fear] ~~hate~~ feare [*inserted above*] *HM.*   41. yet all
shall] *PM;* yet shall they *HM.*   44. thy spell] thy spell; [*flourish below*] *PM;*
this spell [*two S fermés*] *HM.*   SD.] *CWD.*

---

40. *just*] justice, i.e. 'yet all these characters shall see justice in the end'.
43–4. *Son … spell*] In the 2018 performance Venus showed her pleasure
by caressing Cupid on the cheek, but then returned the arrow as a firm
gesture of command not to fail her.

Act 2

[ACT 2 SCENE 1]

[*Under the trees*]

[*Enter*] MUSELLA, DALINA, SIMEANA, PHILISSES,
LISSIUS, LACON, [*and* RUSTIC, *and separately*]
SILVESTA, [*and*] *a* FORESTER.

Dalina. Methinks we now too silent are. Let's play
    At something while we yet have pleasing day.

0.0. [ACT 2 SCENE 1]] *CWD;* The second Act. *PM;* The secound Act:
[*underlined*] *HM.* 0.1. SD.] *This ed.* 0.2–4. SD.] Musella, Dalina,
Simeana, Philissis, Lissius, Lacon, Silvesta, a Forester *PM;* Musella, Dalina,
Simena, Philisses, Lissius, Rustick, Lacon; Silvesta and a forester *HM;*
[*Enter*] MUSELLA, DALINA, SIMEANA, PHILISSES, LISSIUS [*and*] LACON
CWD. 1. Methinks] Mee thinks *PM;* My thinks *HM.* 2. pleasing] *PM;*
[*inserted above*] *HM.* 2.] *CWD adds* [*Enter* SILVESTA *and* FORESTER; *they
do not see the others*] *after this line.*

0.1. SD.] The location of this scene is not specified in *PM* or *HM*, but
seems to echo the retreat to the shade in 1.3. Because it features the Forester's
pursuit of Silvesta it is conceivable that it takes place in the woods, given
her intention to 'range' there (1.2.84); as Straznicky notes (*SM*, 50n.102),
Diana's status as goddess of hunting means that she was regularly associated
with the woods. Cf. *Urania I*, 527.38–9. In the 2018 performance at Penshurst
Place the fine chestnut beams of the roof of the Baron's Hall conjured the
overarching trees, and the wooden screen at the west end of the Hall was
decorated with additional vertical drapes of brown, with green above, hung
from the minstrels' gallery.
    0.4. a FORESTER] In *HM* Wroth added the Forester to the list of char-
acters later. He and Silvesta are the object of the others' sport, so they may
enter afterwards or at a different entrance. *CWD* marks an entrance after 2.
In the 1999 performance, Musella, Simeana, Dalina and Philisses entered
with a picnic and sat on a bank stage left whilst Rustic and Lissius sat to eat
their picnic on a bank stage right, leaving a space centre stage for the Forester
and Silvesta, who entered cued by Lissius's line.
    1. play] Dalina characteristically encourages the other shepherds and
shepherdesses to begin the leisure entertainments – singing, dancing,
games – found in pastoral tradition. Cf. her lines 1.3.21–2, 3.3.1–4 and
4.1.351–2. Rachel Winters brought out this dimension of the character in the
2018 performance (see Introduction, 21, on comparisons to the 'merry
Marquess' in *Urania II*).

Lissius. [*Observing* SILVESTA *and* FORESTER]
    Here's sport enough; view but her new attire,
    And see her slave who burns in chaste desire.
Dalina. Mark but their meeting.
Lissius.   She I'm sure will fly,   5
    And he poor fool will follow still, and cry.
Musella. What pleasure you do take to mock at Love!
    Are you sure you can not his power prove?
    But look, he kneels, and weeps.
Lissius.   And cries 'ay me',
    Sweet nymph have pity, or he dies for thee.   10

---

3. SD.] *This ed.*   5. meeting] *PM;* greeting *HM.*   6. cry.] cry: / *PM.*   7.
Love!] love *PM, HM.*   8. prove?] *R;* prove *PM, HM.*   9. 'ay me'] ay mee
PM, HM; 'Ah me!' *CWD.*   10. nymph] Nimph *PM, HM.*

---

3. *sport*] entertainment. This may allude to King James I's *Declaration of
Sports* (*The King's Majesty's Declaration to his Subjects, Concerning Lawful
Sports to be Used* (London: Bonham Norton and John Bill, 1618) – see notes
to 1.3.21 and to 134 below). In 2018, Lissius and Dalina gestured offstage
through the two breaks in the screen to cue the entrances of Silvesta (at 5)
followed by the Forester (at 7), and then sat at the back of the acting area
to watch them.
    view … attire] a reference to Silvesta's costume as a follower of Diana. Cf.
1.2.83n.
    8. *Are … prove?*] Musella questions Lissius's certainty that he cannot be
subject to Love's power.
    9. *But look*] In the 2018 performance Musella gestured to the Forester,
kneeling, and to Silvesta who held out her hand at arm's length to keep
him away.
    'ay me'] Cf. Wroth's Song 2 in *P4*: 'All night I weep, all day I cry, ay me'
(93). Pamphilia also exclaims 'Ay me, sad night' when grieving for the death
of Leandrus (*Urania I*, 466.11).
    10. *nymph*] in mythology a semi-divine spirit taking the form of a maiden
inhabiting a natural environment (e.g. the woods or trees) and often portrayed as attendant on a particular god (*OED*, 1). In pastoral poetry it signifies a beautiful maiden (as in Robert Sidney's dialogue poems between a
shepherd and nymph, *Poems*, 140–7). By addressing Silvesta as 'Nymph',
which is capitalized in *PM*, Lissius and the Forester emphasize her identity
as a follower of Diana.
    dies] This is the first mention of dying for love, a typical trope (deriving
from Petrarch and courtly love tradition) which often carries sexual connotations in early modern poetry, drama and fiction. Lissius mocks the convention
here, as does Phoebe in Shakespeare's *As You Like It* (3.3.10–26). Wroth uses
it with increasing seriousness in Act 5 of the play. See Introduction, 14–15.

Forester. [*To* SILVESTA] Alas, dear nymph, why fly you still
   my sight?
   Can my true love and firm affection
   So little gain me, as your fairest light
   Must darkened be for my affliction?
   O look on me, and see if in my face   15
   True grief and sorrow show not my disgrace.
   If that despair do not by sighs appear,
   If felt disdain do not with tears make show
   My ever wailing, ever saddest cheer,
   And mourning, which no breath can overblow,   20
   Pity me not, else judge with your fair eyes
   My loving soul which to you captive lies.

---

11. SD.] *CWD.* nymph] *HM*; Nimph *PM.* 15. O] *PM;* Ô *HM.*
16. my] *PM;* my [*overwritten orig.* 'me'] *HM.* 20. overblow] *PM;* e're
o'reblowe *HM.* 22. lies.] lies. / *PM.*

11–22.] The Forester's verse follows the rhyme scheme – often used in
sonnets – of abab cc, repeating this in a second group of six lines. Silvesta
answers with a matching phrase 'Alas, fond Forester' and six lines of verse
following the same rhyme scheme; the rest of their dialogue continues in this
vein until 59, when the Forester returns to speaking in rhyming couplets.
The onstage audience of shepherds groaned when the kneeling Forester
began his appeal 'dear nymph', setting him up as a ridiculous figure in the
2018 production. The pathos of the character was more sympathetically
portrayed in 1999, when the role was performed by a diminutive female actor
(Helen Walden).

   13–14. *fairest ... affliction*] The idea of the beloved as the sun was a
common Petrarchan image (cf. 250). *CWD* (202n.4) notes its use in Robert
Sidney's Sonnet 30 (RS *Poems*, 252–3) and Wroth, *P4*, Sonnet 23 (98). In
the geographical context of the play, it alludes to Silvesta's decision to turn
away from 'Apollo bright' (1.2.73) and retreat to range in the woods (1.2.84)
as Diana's follower.

   16. *disgrace*] i.e. lack of favour in the eyes of Silvesta (*OED*, n.1b), with
the implication of social humiliation – borne out in the mockery the Forester
receives from Lissius.

   17–22.] In these clauses the Forester uses a series of negatives to ask for
Silvesta's pity. He protests that if his grief at being rejected by her is *not* clear
from his sighs, tears, wailings and mournful countenance, then she should
not pity him. Otherwise, she must be able to see and judge (and, implicitly,
reward) his loving soul.

   18. *felt disdain*] i.e. the disdain of Silvesta, felt by the Forester.

   19. *cheer*] mood, demeanour (*OED*, I.1a).

Silvesta. Alas, fond Forester, urge me no more
    To that which now lies not within my might;
    Nor can I grant, or you to joy restore   25
    By any means to yield you least delight.
    For I have vowed, which vows I will obey,
    Unto Diana. What more can I say?
Forester. Oh, this I know, yet give me but this leave,
    To do as birds, and trees, and beasts may do;   30
    Do not, oh do not me of sight bereave,
    For without you I see not. Ah, undo
    Not what is yours, o'erthrow not what's your own,
    Let me, though conquered, not be quite o'erthrown;
    I know you vowèd have, and vows must stand,   35

---

23. Forester] *PM;* forester *HM.*   29. Oh] Ô *PM, HM.*   31. oh] o *PM;* ô
HM.   32. Ah, undo] *PM;* ah! Undoe *HM.*   34. o'erthrown;] or'ethrowne
HM; orethrown [*'n' inserted above*] *PM.*

---

23. *fond*] (in this sense) doting (*OED*, 5a), with implications of foolish-
ness or folly (*OED*, 2).

28. *Unto ... say?*] In the 2018 performance Silvesta indicated the firmness
of her resolve to follow Diana by standing with her hands on her hips, and
was applauded by the other shepherds and shepherdesses, to the disquiet of
the Forester.

30–2. *To ... not*] This image of the lover being deprived of the beloved's
company may be derived from Shakespeare, *RJ* 3.3.29–33 and *TGV*
3.1.174–81.

31. *sight bereave*] deprive me of the sight of you. Brennan (*R*, 234) notes
a parallel in Wroth's *PA*: 'Poor eyes be blind, the light behold no more' (101).
Note also Rodomandro's 'fear of offending and losing that which above all
he esteemed (her sight), though that were all he could ever hope for' (*Urania
II*, 107.12–14).

32–3. *Ah ... own*] The Forester argues that since he has given himself to
Silvesta, she should not destroy her own possession.

32. *undo*] ruin.

33–4.] The page in *PM* may have been trimmed and the ends of words
'owne' and 'orethrown' go beyond the end of the page; Wroth has written
them above the lines. See also below 43, 47 and 49.

35–8. *vows ... refuse*] As Brennan notes (*R*, 234), the purity of the
Forester's love is confirmed by his acknowledgement that the 'strictest band'
of vows to Diana remains inviolable. Wroth uses 'band' rather than 'bond'
for vows and ties in love and friendship (cf. 2.2.5 and 5.7.73 and *Urania I*,
23.16 and 495.11–13); equally, the Forester may be referring to the 'band'
of Diana's followers that Silvesta has joined (cf. 1.2.87). The Forester's wish
to do no more than look at the chaste Silvesta reflects the behaviour of the

Yet though you chaste must be, I may desire
To have your sight, and this the strictest band
Cannot refuse, and but this I require.
Then grant it me, which I on knees do seek,
Be not to nature and yourself unlike.   40
Silvesta. No, no, I ne'er believe your fond-made oath.
I chastity have sworn, then no more move.
I know what 'tis to swear, and break it both,
What to desire, and what it is to love;
Protest you may that there shall nothing be   45
By you imagined 'gainst my chastity,
But this I doubt; your love will make you curse
(If you so much do love) that cursèd day

---

38. cannot] *PM;* can not *HM.*   40. unlike] unleeke *PM;* unlieke *HM.*
41. ne'er] *PM;* ne're [*'r' overwritten*] *HM.*   43. both] *HM;* both [*'h' inserted above*] *PM.*   47. curse] *HM;* ~~cur~~ curse [*inserted above*] *PM.*

Shepherd in Robert Sidney's 'Pastoral 8' towards his scornful nymph: 'My
soul to love and look, naught else affects' (RS *Poems,* 209) and Rodomandro
(31n. above).

40. *Be ... unlike*] Do not be untrue to nature and yourself (i.e. by hiding
yourself from sight). The spelling 'unleeke' in *PM* ('unlieke' in *HM*) suggests
a perfect rhyme with 'seek' and the Forester's use of an archaic style found,
for example, in Bede's *History of the Church of England* (Antwerp: John Laet,
1565) which recounts 'a miracle worthy of perpetuall remembraunce and not
vnleke to the olde auncient miracles of tymes past' in which a faithful wife
sees her husband restored from what seemed like death to declare his future
existence must be 'farr vnleeke to my former life' (fol. 161r–v). Similar
archaic spellings are found in Turberville's chivalric *Tragical Tales translated
by Turberville in time of his Troubles out of Sundry Italians* (London: Abel Jeffs,
1587), 'aleeke' (71), and Spenser's *Faerie Queene,* 'misleeke' (V.II.49). On the
Forester's chivalric style see Introduction, 23.

41. *fond-made*] foolish, ill-conceived.

42. *move*] argue.

43. *swear ... both*] Silvesta may be referring to her previous service to
Venus (1.2.87) which she has now broken to serve Diana. Brennan (*R,* 234)
notes that the end of the word 'both' has been cut off (possibly because the
page has been trimmed) and has been written in above 'perhaps in the hand
of Lady Mary'.

47. *curse*] See note above. This word has also been written in above the
end of the line but the tail of the long s can be clearly seen, possibly suggesting that this letter at least was written and has been cropped.

When this I vowed, attempt it may be worse.
Then follow not thus hopeless your decay,   50
But leave off loving, or some other choose
Whose state or fortune need not you refuse.
Forester. Indeed, sweet nymph, 'tis true that chastity
To one that loves may justly raging move,
Yet loving you, those thoughts shall banished be;   55
Since 'tis in you, I chastity will love,
And now depart, since such is your pleasure.
Depart, O me, from joy, from life, from ease,
Go I must, and leave behind that treasure
Which all contentment gives. Now to displease   60
Myself with liberty I may free go,
And with most liberty, most grief, most woe.

        Exeunt [FORESTER *and* SILVESTA, *severally*].

---

49. worse] ~~wurs~~ wurse [*inserted above*] = [*end of page*] *PM;* wurse *HM.*
53. nymph] *HM;* Nimph *PM.*   58. Depart, O me] *PM;* depart (ô mee)
HM.   from joy, from life] *PM;* from lyfe from ioy *HM.*   60. gives] *PM;*
gave *HM.*   62. grief] *PM;* griev'd *HM.*   woe.] woe; / *PM.*   SD.] *This
ed.;* ex: *PM, HM; Exit. CWD.*

---

   49. *attempt ... worse*] [and to] test ['make a trial of' *OED* v3] your pro-
testation by being in your sight might prove even worse; or perhaps 'attempt
it [i.e. try my chastity] even more strongly'. An implication of aggressive
seduction, or even rape, here may also be present in *Arcadia* (V.811). In *PM*
the word 'wurse' has been written above. See above 43n.
   51. *some ... choose*] In both 1999 and 2018 productions Silvesta's invita-
tion to the Forester to choose another was taken as an opportunity for actors
to indicate members of the audience as potential partners.
   52. *state*] situation, circumstances.
   56–7. *love ... depart*] The 2018 performance made the Forester's final
declaration and departure comic by staging a contrast between Silvesta's
eagerness for him to leave (nodding vigorously) and his long delay (five lines)
in doing so.
   62. *liberty*] The paradox of pleasure and imprisonment suffered by the
courtly lover was a conventional trope. See for example, Philip Sidney's *AS*,
Sonnet 47 (188).
   62. SD.] In this edition, we have interpreted *PM* and *HM*'s 'ex:' as referring to both characters, giving Silvesta an exit because she does not, in this
edition, have any more lines in this scene (see below note on 206). We have
added 'severally' to indicate separate exits, since the Forester says he must

Musella. Lissius, I hope this sight doth something move
    In you to pity so much constant love.
Lissius. Yes, thus it moves: that man should be so fond   65
    As to be tied t'a woman's faithless bond.
    For we should women love but as our sheep,
    Who being kind and gentle gives us ease,
    But cross, or straying, stubborn, and unmeek,
    Shunned as the wolf, which most our flocks disease.   70

---

65. so] *PM;* soe [*inserted above*] *HM.*   66. bond] *HM;* band *PM.*   69. and unmeek] *PM;* or unmeeke *HM.*

'Depart' from Silvesta at her request. Although Alan C. Dessen and Leslie Thomson, *A Dictionary of Stage Directions in English Drama, 1580–1642* (Cambridge: Cambridge University Press, 1994) note that 'severally' commonly signifies characters using different doors to exit or enter the stage (192), Silvesta's exit could be separated from that of the Forester by a delay in time if staging does not allow for two physically separate exit points.

   63–4. *Lissius ... love*] Lissius's indifference to love and its effects was shown to comic effect in the 1999 performance where, throughout the exchange above, he read a newspaper while eating a sandwich.

   66. *t'a*] to a.

   67–70. *sheep ... disease*] women were proverbially described as sheep or shrews, depending on whether they were meek or disobedient (see Pamela Allen Brown, *Better a Shrew than a Sheep: Women, Drama and the Culture of Jest in Early Modern England* (Ithaca: Cornell University Press, 2003), and Tilley, S4r2, S4r s, S414). Brennan suggests that these lines are 'a clumsy and unconvincing attempt to represent Lissius as a provocative male character' (*R*, 67); *CWD* notes the connection between Lissius's misogynistic views and the pamphlet debate on women (202n.11). In a riposte to Joseph Swetnam's *The Arraignment of Lewd, Idle, Froward and Unconstant Women* (London: George Purslowe for Thomas Archer, 1615), Rachel Speght's 1617 defence of women, *A Muzzle for Melastomus, the Cynical Baiter of, and Foul-Mouthed Barker against Evah's Sex* (London: Nicholas Okes for Thomas Archer, 1617), pointed out 'though there are some scabbed sheep in a flock, we must not therefore conclude all the rest to be mangy' (18).

   70. *wolf ... disease*] Wolves dis-ease sheep by troubling or disturbing them with attacks. Wroth gives an example of a female wolf beginning to attack the shepherdess Urania, but then stopping miraculously when Urania pleads to heaven for mercy, the wolf then being needlessly killed by Steriamus and Selarinus, who spring to Urania's rescue (*Urania I*, 16–17). A less attractive allusion to a she-wolf savaging a lamb occurs later in *Urania I*, when a young lady tells her mother that she has been 'bred by your hand like a lamb, till seized by the wolf of love'; it later transpires that she has fallen in love with her half-brother (523–4).

Musella. We little are beholding unto you,
   In kindness less, yet you these words may rue;
   I hope to live to see you wail and weep,
   And deem your grief far sweeter than your sleep.
   Then but remember this, and think on me   75
   Who truly told you could not still live free.
Lissius. I do not know, it may be very well,
   But I believe I shall uncharm love's spell.
     And Cupid, if I needs must love,
     Take your aim, and shoot your worst.   80
     Once more rob your mother's dove.
     All your last shafts sure were burst,

---

72. In] *PM;* ~~and~~ in [*inserted above*] *HM.*   80. Take your aim, and shoot your worst.] *PM; HM adds* ~~all your last shaftes~~ *after this line.*

71–2. *We … less*] Musella appears to object to Lissius's opinion of women in the previous speech by telling him 'we women are little obliged ['beholding'] to you for your estimation and are even less likely to be kind as a result'.

72. *rue*] regret.

73. *wail … weep*] Musella's phrasing echoes that of Venus and Cupid, 1.4.3 and 21, and the Forester's lines 2.1.18–19.

74. *sweeter … sleep*] This line may recall the love-stricken shepherd Menaphon, whose popular 'Song in his bed' features the refrain 'Welcome, sweet grief' (Robert Greene's *Arcadia or Menaphon*, 1616, sig. H3r–v). Wroth's own poems frequently feature night as a companion to grief (e.g. 'Come darkest night, becoming sorrow best', *Poems*, 98).

79. *And Cupid*] The text of lines 79–84 is inset in the manuscripts, suggesting this is a declamation or song to taunt Cupid. In the 2018 performance Lissius opened his arms to deliver the speech to the heavens. In the 1999 performance Cupid watched the whole scene through a gap in the curtains centre back. Lissius's challenge may be a cue for the actor playing Cupid to prepare his bow in order to shoot Lissius at the end of the scene. See below, 248n.

80.] In *HM* after line 80 Wroth has mistranscribed and then erased the beginning of line 82, 'all your last shafts'.

81. *rob … dove*] The dove, a symbol of love, was commonly associated with Venus in early modern culture. Lissius challenges Cupid to fletch his arrows with dove feathers. Paintings such as Guido Reni's *Cupid* (1637–38, oil on canvas, Madrid, Museo Nacional Del Prado, www.museodelprado.es/en/the-collection/art-work/cupid/79460be4–4261–4084-bcb0–369f885a31df), which depicts Cupid with a white-feathered arrow held in a dove's beak, may be based on Cesare Ripa's emblem 16 '*Amor domato*' (Love tamed) in *Iconologia* (Oxford, 1700), which shows Cupid disempowered, in line with Lissius's declaration at 82–3 that Cupid's arrows are broken.

Those you stole, and those you gave;
Shoot not me till new you have.
Philisses. Rustic, faith tell me, hast thou ever loved?   85
Rustic. What call you love? I've been to trouble moved,
    As when my best cloak hath by chance been torn,
    I have lived wishing till it mended were,
    And but so lovers do; nor could forbear
    To cry if I my bag, or bottle lost,   90
    As lovers do who by their loves are crossed,
    And grieve as much for these, as they for scorn.
Philisses. Call you this love? Why, love is no such thing!
    Love is a pain which yet doth pleasure bring,
    A passion which alone in hearts do move,   95
    And they that feel not this, they cannot love.
    'Twill make one joyful, merry, pleasant, sad,
    Cry, weep, sigh, fast, mourn; nay sometimes stark mad,
    If they perceive scorn, hate, or else disdain
    To wrap their woes in store for others' gain.   100

---

84. have] *PM;* have; / *HM.*   85. hast] *PM;* d̶i̶d̶s̶t̶ hast [*inserted above*] *HM.*
92. for scorn] *PM;* for [*inserted above*] scorne *HM.*   94. Love] love *PM,*
HM.   96. cannot] *PM;* can nott *HM.*   98. stark] *HM;* [*inserted above*]
PM.   100. wrap] *R;* wrop *PM;* wrop ['*o*' *blotted*] *HM.*

---

83. *Those ... gave*] It is unclear which arrows Cupid is supposed to have
stolen or given in the context of the play, but Lissius may be referring to the
idea, depicted in an emblem in Henry Peacham's *Minerva Britanna* (1612),
of Death and Cupid stealing one another's arrows (172).

89. *And ... do*] And this is all lovers do, with 'but' used to mean 'only'.
The earthy Rustic does not understand the heightened register of the courtly
lovers.

92. *And ... scorn*] And I grieve as much for these (i.e. a lost bag or bottle)
as they would at the scorn of their beloveds. Again, Rustic shows a very
different, pragmatic view from that of the romantic hero Philisses.

94. *pain ... pleasure*] Philisses uses a conventional Petrarchan trope of
'pleasing pain'. Cf. Venus and Cupid, 1.4.16 and 3.4.24, and Philisses's own
fortune below (180).

98. *stark*] completely, as in 'stark raving mad' in modern and in early
modern usage (*OED*, adv. 8b2b).

99–100. *If ... gain*] If they perceive scorn, love will make them hate, or
otherwise disdain to hold their woes in reserve for others' benefit (i.e. their
rivals in love). In counselling the shepherds and shepherdesses to disclose
their love and to shun jealousy, Philisses is of course concealing the repres-
sion of his own jealous love for Musella.

For that (but jealousy), is sure the worst,
And than be jealous, better be accursed!
But oh, some be, and would it not disclose
They silent love, and loving fear. Ah, those
Deserve most pity, favour, and regard;   105
Yet are they answered but with scorn's reward.
This their misfortune, and the like may fall
To you, or me, who wait misfortune's call.
But if it do, take heed, be ruled by me:
Though you mistrust, mistrust not that she see.   110
For then she'll smiling say, 'alas, poor fool,
This man hath learned all parts of folly's school.'
Be wise, make love, and love, though not obtain,
For to love truly is sufficient gain.
Rustic. Sure you do love, you can so well declare   115
    The joys and pleasures, hope, and his despair.
Philisses. I love indeed.
Rustic.   But who is she you love?
Philisses. She who best thoughts must to affection move;

---

102. than] *This ed.;* then *PM, HM.*   103. oh, some be,] O some bee *PM;*
ô some are *HM.*   104. They] *PM;* though *HM.*   108. or] *PM;* or [*letter
deleted*] *HM.*   114. gain.] gaine. / *PM.*   116. hope ... his] *PM;* hopes ...
theyr his [*inserted above*] *HM.*   117. SP. *Rustic.*] Ru: *PM;* Ru: Phi: *HM.*
118. who] *PM;* whose who [*inserted above*] *HM.*

---

101. *For ... worst*] For that, i.e. suppressed woe, is the worst feeling, apart
from jealousy. In *Urania II* Amicles tells Parselius that the shepherds suffer
'fear, suspicion, doubt, and the worst of all ills, Jealousy', inflicted on them
by Cupid (217.13–14). Brennan notes a parallel with Ben Jonson's 'Against
Jealousy' (Poem 10 of *The Underwood*).

102. *And than*] And rather than.

104. *silent love*] Cf. 4.1.85–7 on the dangers of silent love.

110–12. *Though ... school*] 'Though you mistrust, do not mistrust in a way
that she can see', i.e. keep your suspicions secret; if your beloved sees that
you mistrust, she will know that love has made a complete fool of you. The
phrase 'Folly's school' appears in John Davies of Hereford's *The Holy Rood*
(Davies, C1).

113. *make love*] used in this sense as 'court' or 'woo', rather than with
sexual connotations.

113–14. *love ... gain*] love, even if you are not successful, because to love
truly is sufficient achievement in itself.

118. *She ... move*] Philisses's reluctance to name Musella was marked in
the 2018 performance by Musella's eager look towards him (and the expectation of the other shepherds), but when he turned to face her, he could not
do so.

If any love, none need ask who it is.
Within these plains, none loves that loves not this   120
Delight of shepherds, pride of this fair place;
No beauty is that shines not in her face,
Whose whiteness whitest lilies doth excel,
Matched with a rosy morning to compel
All hearts to serve her, yet doth she affect   125
But only virtue, nor will quite neglect
Those who do serve her in an honest fashion,
Which, sure, doth more increase than decrease passion.

[*Enter* ARCAS *with the Book of Fortunes.*]

Arcas. Here are they met, where beauty only reigns,
Whose presence gives the excellentest light   130

---

122. shines] *PM;* ~~flowes~~ shines [*inserted above*] *HM.*   123. lilies] Lillies
PM; Lillys *HM.*   excel] excell *HM;* ~~disgrace~~ excell *PM.*   124. with] *PM;*
~~like~~ wth [*inserted above*] *HM.*   126. nor] *PM;* ~~yett~~ nor [*inserted above*] *HM.*
127. an honest] *PM;* a modest *HM.*   128.1. SD.] *This ed.;* [*Enter* ARCAS]
CWD.   129. beauty] *PM, HM;* Beauty *CWD.*   130. gives] *PM;* brings
HM.

---

120. *none ... this*] With the exception of Lissius and the Forester (and
Cupid), all the male characters in the play express a romantic interest in
Musella; as well as Philisses, Musella is pursued by Rustic and Lacon, and
we are told in 5.2.25 that Arcas has also offered her his love.

121–5. *Delight ... her*] Brennan (*R*, 235) points out that Philisses's praise
of Musella as beloved of all hearts echoes Ben Jonson's praise of Wroth
herself as 'nature's index', comparing her to a nymph or a goddess: 'dressed
in shepherd's 'tire [clothing], who would not say / You were the bright
Oenone, Flora or May?' (*Epigrams* 1616, 105.20, 9–10). This may be a reference to Wroth's performing in a masque or other entertainment, either at
court or within a private household. See Introduction, 17.

123. *lilies ... excel*] originally Wroth wrote 'Lilies doth disgrace', with an
emphatic capital L, as though completing a rhyming couplet with 'face' in
the line above. She uses the conventional symbolism – 'like a pure lily of
chaste and virtuous love' – again to describe Pamphilia in *Urania I* (363.25).

128.1 SD. Book of Fortunes] See Introduction, 24, 37, on the metagraphic significance of the Book of Fortunes.

129–32. *beauty ... might*] Arcas's words describe the assembled shepherds
in idealistic terms, claiming that their brightness and beauty make the sun
(Phoebus) look dull in comparison. Cf. the idealization of Amphilanthus 'for
whose sake the sun would hide himself, in grief he could not shine so bright
as his glory did' (*Urania I*, 363.4–5) and the chivalric comparison of a

And brightness, dimming Phoebus, who but feigns
To outshine these; it is not in his might.
Fair troop, here is a sport will well befit
This time and place, if you will license it.
Philisses. What is't, good Arcas?
Arcas.   Why stay, and you shall see.   135
Here is a book wherein each one shall draw
A fortune, and thereby their luck shall be
Conjectured. Like you this? You ne'er it saw.
Rustic. It is no matter, 'tis a pretty one.
     Musella, you shall draw.
Musella.   Though choose alone.   140
Philisses. I never saw it, but I like it well.

---

131. dimming] *PM;* ~~moveth~~ dimming [*inserted above*] *HM.*

---

mistress's 'heavenly beauty' which dazzles like the sun in *Arcadia* (I.167).
How the lines are performed is open to interpretation. Given Arcas's romantic interest in Musella (5.2.25), he may be addressing her in particular as the
queen of beauty (cf. Perdita as queen of the sheepshearing feast in *WT*
4.3.3–5). The lines might also be delivered by the actor speaking as a chorus
to describe the tableau of shepherds; or, if Arcas's role as the villain of the
piece is being emphasized, they could be spoken sarcastically.

131. *Phoebus*] god of the sun. Cf. 1.2.73–8.

feigns] pretends (with the implication of deception, possibly prefiguring
Arcas's trickery later in the play).

134. *license*] permit, approve. Cf. 2.1.3n. King James I's *Declaration of
Sports*, licensing celebratory public ales and festivals, was published in 1617
for Lancashire and for the remainder of the country in 1618.

136–7. *draw ... fortune*] The practice of drawing fortunes at random from
a book derives from medieval religious traditions of bibliomancy, where the
books of Homer and Virgil or the Bible were used to divine one's destiny.
The *sortes sanctorum* (lots of the saints) involved letting books of the Bible
open at random and pricking an individual verse with a pin. In secular terms,
telling fortunes was a fashionable game in French courtly salon culture, and
it appears on stage in Ben Jonson's *The Gypsies Metamorphosed* (1621), ed.
James Knowles in Jonson, *Works*, ll. 200–414, though not with a book. In
Wroth's scene the rules of the game are that each player draws a leaf from
the book in turn, alternating by sex (see 2.1.168), and gives it to someone
of the opposite sex to read out for the group. As a stage prop, the 'Book'
which determines each character's fortunes may allude to the physical manuscript of *Love's Victory*, in which Wroth has already decided the destinies of
each. The Book of Fortunes in the 2018 production at Penshurst Place was
modelled to resemble the Penshurst Manuscript.

Lissius. Then he 'chieves best of all must bear the bell.
Rustic. Pray thee, good Arcas, let me hold the book.
Arcas. With all my heart, yet you'll not some lots brook.
Rustic. [*Takes the book.*]

    Fairest, sweetest, bonny lass,   145
    You that love in mirth to pass
    Time delightful, come to me,
    And you shall your fortune see.

Musella. You tell by book, then sure you can not miss,
    But shall I know what shall be, or what is?   150

---

142. 'chieves] *PM;* chiefs *HM.*   must] *HM;* must must *PM.*   143. good]
PM; [*inserted above*] *HM.*   145. SD.] *This ed.;* [*Takes the book and reads.*]
CWD.   147. come to] *PM;* [*written over an indecipherable word*] *HM.*   148.
see.] see; / *PM.*

---

142. *'chieves ... bell*] he who achieves the best fortune must be the leader.
The leading sheep in the flock, the so-called 'bell-wether', was the one which
wore the bell. *OED* cites Spenser's *Prosopopoia*: 'To follow after their bell-
wether'. It is used figuratively (and mostly contemptuously as by Lissius
here) for a chief or leader (*OED*, 1 and 2), perhaps recalling the opening of
Philip Sidney's *Arcadia* which describes 'setting a bell for an ensign of a
sheepish squadron' (I.61).

143. *good Arcas*] As Brennan notes (*R*, 235) Rustic imitates the polite
form of address used by Philisses above, 135.

hold the book] In early modern commercial theatre the 'book' of the play
referred to the copy held by the 'book keeper' or prompter. If the 'book of
fortunes' on stage represents or is itself the 'book' or prompt copy of *Love's
Victory*, then the actor playing Rustic would literally be holding the fortunes
or destinies of all the characters in the play in his hands.

144. *yet ... brook*] although you will not put up with, or profit by (*OED*,
v.1a and 3), some of the 'lots' or fortunes that come to you.

145-8. *Fairest ... see*] Rustic's superlatives in 145 are commonplace in
early modern love poetry. Although there is no stage direction to indicate
how 145-8 are to be delivered, they employ the same verse form as the
fortunes which follow (161-4, 177-80), and are inset in both *PM* and *HM*.
Given that Rustic is now holding the book, in performance his sudden
change to an uncharacteristically more romantic register may be explained
by him reading this rhyme from the book rather than composing it spon-
taneously. See 143n. above. In the 1999 production Rustic's lines were
pasted on to the front cover of the book, at which he glanced as he spoke
to Musella from his knees. In 2018 Rustic took the book from Arcas (while
Musella was covering her eyes), opened it and read the lines from the first
page to Musella.

149. *can ... miss*] cannot make a mistake (*CWD*, 202n.31). If Rustic does
read the verse from the book, Musella's comment may refer to this, expressing her annoyance at his renewed attentions, as in the 2018 performance.

Rustic. What shall be you need not fear,
 Rustic doth thy fortune bear.
 Draw, and when you chosen have,
 Praise me who such fortune gave.
Musella. And so I will if good, or if untrue   155
 I'll blame mine own ill choice, and not blame you.

    [*Draws a page from the book.*]

Philisses. Pray, may I see the fortune you do choose?
Musella. Yes, and if right, I will it not refuse.
Philisses. None can be cross to you, except you will.
Musella. Read it.
Philisses.   I will, although it were my ill. [*Reads.*] 160
 Fortune can not cross your will,
 Though your patience much must be.
 Fear not that your luck is ill,
 You shall your best wishes see.

 Refuse, believe me, no, you have no cause;   165
 Thus hope brings longing, patience passion draws.

---

151. you need not] *PM;* nay never *HM.*   156. own ill] *HM;* owne ill [*inserted above*] *PM.*   156.1. SD.] *This ed.*   157. do] *PM;* did *HM.*   160. SD.] *CWD.*   166. longing] *PM;* lingring *HM.*

151–4. Rustic does not read a fortune from the Book of Fortunes here, but he has modelled his seven-syllable rhyming lines on those in the Book. His attempt to draw Musella to him figuratively as well as literally – by telling her to draw first, then asking Arcas to let him hold the book – gives the opportunity for some stage business. He may also be referring to his own 'fortune' or the material wealth he can offer her through marriage.

159. *None ... will*] None can be vexatious unless you allow them to be (*CWD*, 202n.32–3). Philisses appears to be saying, in response to Musella's pledge not to refuse her fortune, that no one (including, by implication, himself or Fortune) can go against her wishes unless she wills it. He is unaware of any other impediment to their match, although Musella may already know that it is threatened by her betrothal to Rustic. See Introduction, 22.

165. *Refuse ... cause*] Believe me, you have no reason to refuse this fortune. Cf. 158.

166. *hope ... draws*] Philisses's positive interpretation of deferred fulfilment of love, that longing and patience will increase passion, contrasts with the usual Petrarchan image of suffering, and puns on the idea of 'drawing' the fortune as *CWD* notes (202n.35).

Dalina. I'll try what mine shall be, good Rustic hold.
Arcas. A man must follow.
Dalina.   I am still too bold.
Philisses. Then I will try, though sure of cruelty.

[*Draws and reads to himself.*]

And yet this lot doth promise good at last,   170
That, though I now feel greatest misery,
My blessèd days to come are not all past.
Dalina. Come, this fond lover knows not yet the play,
He studies while our fortunes run away.
What have you got? Let's see, do you this love?   175
Philisses. Read it, but heaven grant me the end to prove.
Dalina. [*Reads.*]
          You do live to be much crossed,
          Yet esteem no labour lost,
          Since you shall with bliss obtain
          Pleasure for your suffered pain.   180

169.1. SD.] *This ed.;* [*He draws.*] *CWD.*   170. lot doth promise good] *PM;*
promises some joy *HM.*   172. to come] *PM;* [*inserted above*] *HM.*   177.
SD.] *CWD.*   179. bliss] *PM;* joy *HM.*

---

167. *good Rustic*] Dalina now joins in with the decorous, courtly form of
address.
    168. *man ... follow*] Arcas tells Dalina the rules of the game, namely that
lots are drawn alternately between the sexes. See 136–7n. above.
    still ... bold] possibly a reference back to 1.3.101.
    172. *past*] over.
    173. *knows ... play*] doesn't know how to play the game yet.
    174. *studies ... away*] Philisses reads silently ('studies') rather than giving
his fortune to someone else to read aloud, and so prevents the game moving
forward (Dalina is impatient to know her fortune). *CWD* notes 'there is a
sense that fortune, like time, cannot be halted' (202n.39).
    176. *the ... prove*] to win and experience the [happy] ending. Cf. 180.
    178. *labour lost*] Brennan (*R*, 235) notes that '[i]t is tempting to specu-
late that Wroth may have had Shakespeare's *Love's Labour's Lost* in mind'.
See also William Herbert's lament claiming that the god of love makes
'Lost labour easeful' (*WH Poems*, 6), and the long pastoral ballad narrated
by the Duke of Wertemburg in Wroth's *Urania I*, in which a shepherdess sees the willow branch as a sign of 'labour lost in love' (616.6; *Poems*,
185).

Truly I can not blame you. Like you this?
So I at last might gain, I well could miss.
Musella. After a rain the sweetest flowers do grow,
So shall your hap be, as this book doth show.
Dalina. Now must I draw, sweet Fortune be my guide.   185
Musella. She cannot see, yet must your chance abide.
Dalina. Blind or no, I care not, this I take, and [*Draws.*]
If good, my luck, if not, a luckless hand.
Philisses. If Fortune guide, she will direct to Love;
They can not parted be. How now dost move?   190

185. must I] *PM;* I may *HM.*   Fortune] fortune *PM, HM.*   186. cannot]
PM; can nott *HM.*   187. no] *PM;* nott *HM.*   SD.] *This ed.; She draws*
CWD [at following line].   189. Fortune ... Love] *This ed.;* Fortune ... love
PM, HM.   190. How] *PM;* what *HM.*

182. *So ... miss*] So that I would win in the end, I wouldn't mind not
succeeding at first. Cf. Dalina's past fortunes, detailed in 3.3.11–24.
183. *rain ... grow*] In the *Arcadia* Pamela tells Musidorus that her love
can 'no more be diminished by these showers of evil hap, than flowers are
marred with the timely rains of April' (IV.758). Philoclea's tears are compared to rain 'which seemed to water the sweet and beautiful flowers of her
face' (III.450; cf. III.570). Wroth uses a metaphor of flowers regrowing after
being cropped by sheep to show increased pleasures in *Urania I* (181.38–40).
184. *hap*] chance.
186. *cannot see*] Fortune is traditionally blind. 'Fortune is painted blind,
as if she saw not where she distributed her favours, nor cared not to whom'
explains Thomas Gainsford in *The Rich Cabinet Furnished with Variety of*
Excellent Descriptions, Exquisite Characters, Witty Discourses and Delightful
Histories (London: J. Beale for R. Jackson, 1616), 46v. She is depicted as a
blind though comforting, redeeming figure allied to love in Wroth's Sonnet
31: 'After long trouble in a tedious way' (*Poems*, 105). *CWD* remarks that
Fortune's blindness 'echoes the portrayal of Cupid' (203n.44), something
that Pamphilia observes in *Urania I*: 'O Love, O froward fortune ... both
cruel to me, but both, alas, are blind' (92.11–13). Since the characters are
supposed to select their fortunes 'blindly', their actions parallel those of
Fortune. In the 1999 performance the fortunes were sealed up and decorated
as flowers. In 2018 Musella shielded her eyes as she reached to draw a sheet
out from the Book. See Fig. 4 p. 38.
189. *If ... Love*] In Roman mythology Venus is the mother of Fortuna.
The shepherd in *Urania I* tells Leonius not to be 'displeased with your
fortune, or love, since fortune hath brought you to love one most love-
worthy' (430.29–31).
190. *How ... move?*] Philisses may be asking if Dalina is upset by what
she reads. In this context the word 'move' means 'to become excited or
angry, to be perturbed' (*OED*, vb. II 25b). It also means 'to exhibit motion
or physical activity' (*OED*, 3) so may comment on Dalina moving across the
stage to give the fortune to him to read aloud. Cf. 1.2.30n.

Dalina. Move? Did you ever see the like?

Philisses.   Not I.

Dalina. Nay, read it out, it shows my constancy.

Philisses. [*Reads.*]

> *They that cannot steady be*
> *To themselves, the like must see.*
> *Fickle people fickly choose,*   195
> *Slightly like, and so refuse.*
> *This your fortune, who can say*
> *Herein justice bears not sway?*

In troth, Dalina, Fortune is proved cursed
To you without desert.

Dalina.   This is the worst   200
That she can do; 'tis true I've fickle been,
And so is she, 'tis then the lesser sin.
Let her prove constant, I will her observe,
And then, as she doth mend, I'll good deserve.

Arcas. Who chooseth next?

Lissius.   Not I, lest such I prove.   205

Simeana. Nor I, it is sufficient I could love.

---

193. SD.] *CWD. cannot*] *PM;* can nott *HM.*   199. Fortune] *PM;* fortune
HM.   proved cursed] prov'd curst *HM;* provd curst *PM;* proud curst
R; proud-cursed *CWD.*   202. is] *PM;* [*inserted above*] *HM.*   203. will]
PM; ~~shall~~ will [*written over*] *HM.*   204. she] *PM;* shee [*inserted above*]
HM.   deserve] deserve; / *HM.*   206. SP. *Simeana.*] *This ed.;* Si: *PM,*
HM; Silvesta. R.

---

191. *Move? ... like?*] Dalina's response suggests she hands the fortune to
Philisses; having been eager to select her fortune, she is moved, or upset, by
what she reads.

192. *constancy*] Spoken sarcastically. The fortune says that, because
Dalina has been inconstant, she will experience the same inconstancy in
others.

196. *slightly*] lightly, carelessly (*OED*, 2a).

199. *troth*] truth.

202. *And ... she*] Fortune's fickle, changing nature was symbolized by a
ball or wheel. In *P4* Wroth writes 'Justly on Fortune was bestowed the wheel
/ Whose favours fickle and unconstant reel' (*Poems*, 119).

204. *as ... deserve*] as Fortune reforms, I will deserve good fortune.
Dalina's lines look forward to the mending of fortunes in the resolution of
the play, where Dalina actively pursues a stable, constant relationship in
marriage and is rewarded as part of love's victory.

Arcas. I'll wish for one, but Fortune shall not try
   On me her tricks, whose favours are so dry.
Dalina. None can wish, if they their wishes love not,
   Nor can they love, if that their wishings move not.   210
Philisses. You fain would solve this business.
Dalina.   Who? Would I?
   Nay, my care's past; I Love and his deny.
Philisses. [*Takes the book and reads.*]
   Love and Reason once at war,

---

207. one, but Fortune] *PM;* one but [*inserted above*] fortune *HM.*   208.
whose] *HM;* who *PM.*   210. that their] *PM;* that *HM.*   212. I Love and
his] *This ed.;* I, Love, and his *PM;* I Love, and his *HM;* I, Love, and his,
CWD.   deny.] deny. / *PM.*   212. SD.] *This ed.* *Love and Reason*] *HM;*
Love, and reason *PM.*

---

206. *Nor ... love*] Most editions follow *R* in attributing this line to Silvesta,
though as *PM* and *HM* have the speech heading 'Si:' it could be spoken by
Silvesta or Simeana; Simeana seems more likely given that Silvesta's lines
earlier in the scene are given the speech heading 'Sill:' in *PM* and *HM.*
Significantly, Simeana also speaks after – and possibly in response
to – Lissius, who we find out in 3.3 has disdained her in the past. See also
2.1.62.SDn.

208. *favours ... dry*] gifts are so meagre. Arcas's comment may also have
erotic overtones, suggesting that Fortune's 'offers of intimacy are sterile and
unattractive' (*CWD*, 203n.56).

209–10. *None ... not*] No one can wish, if they don't love what they are
wishing for, nor can they love, if their wishes don't allow it. Dalina's meaning
is obscure; she may be lamenting her past fickleness, in particular her lack
of will in committing to previous lovers (see 3.3.11–24).

211. *solve*] clear up, but the spelling *saulve* in *PM* also invokes the meaning
of to soothe or cure (*OED*, v.2a), used both in a medical sense and possibly
also in an agricultural sense to refer to smearing sheep with tar and butter
(*OED*, v.1e).

212. *Love ... deny*] I deny Love and everything to do with him. Dalina
probably makes this comment rather grumpily in the light of her past experience of losing both her suitors (as revealed in 3.3.11–24 and 29–30).

213–24. *Love ... is*] As above there is no stage direction for the delivery
of these lines, which are indented in *PM* and *HM,* but the debate between
Reason and Love was a familiar feature of Platonist philosophy and the lines
here recall Sidney circle poetry on the topic, especially William Herbert's
poetic dialogue with Benjamin Rudyerd in WH *Poems* (5–23, esp. 20–2), as
Wynne-Davies notes ('"For *Worth*, not Weakness, Makes in Use but One":
Literary Dialogues in an English Renaissance Family', in *This Double Voice*,
ed. Danielle Clarke and Elizabeth Clarke (New York: St Martin's Press,
2000), 164–84, 176). Roberts (Wroth *Poems*, 213) noted a parallel in Sidney's
Arcadia, where the second Eclogues start with a 'skirmish betwixt Reason

Jove came down to end the jar.
Cupid said Love must have place,   215
Reason, that it was his grace.
Jove then brought it to this end:
Reason should on Love attend;
Love takes Reason for his guide,
Reason cannot from Love slide.   220
This agreed, they pleased did part,
Reason ruling Cupid's dart.

---

215. *Cupid ... place*] *This ed.;* Cupid sayd love must have place *PM;* Cupid
said love must have place *HM;* 'Cupid,' said Love, 'must have place' *CWD.*
218. *Reason ... Love*] *CWD;* Reason ... love *PM;* reason ... love *HM.*   219.
Love takes Reason] *CWD;* Love takes reason *PM;* love takes reason *HM.*
220. *Reason ... Love*] *CWD;* Reason ... love *PM;* reason ... love *HM.*   222.
Reason] *PM;* reason *HM.*

---

and Passion', the shepherds forming into two opposing teams to dance and
sing with instruments (II.407–8). The opposition between Reason and
Passion features in *AS*, Sonnets 10 and 18, and in Robert Sidney's Song 20
where the senses have laid the beloved 'In my reason and my heart / Where
since of them each hath part / As in their own temples stayèd' (RS *Poems,*
292–3) and Wroth, *PA*, Sonnet 10: 'Be from the court of Love, and reason
torn / For Love in reason now doth put his trust' (132, 125). It is therefore
possible that, in performance, Philisses's lines are a set reading from the
Book of Fortunes that alludes to an existing Sidney poem, a similar effect
to Pamphilia's performance of William Herbert's poem 'Had I loved but at
that rate' to Amphilanthus in Wroth's *Urania II* (30–1).

   214. Jove] i.e. Jupiter, ruler of gods and men in Roman mythology.
   jar] The term 'jar', meaning a disagreement or conflict of opinions, origi-
nates with music; *OED* (n. 2, 5) cites T. Taylor's *Commentary upon the Epistle
of S Paul written to Titus,* Vol. 1 (Cambridge, 1612): 'Not admitting discord,
and jar in things whereof the one should be as the true exposition of the
other.'
   215. Cupid ... place] 'Have place' means 'take precedence'. The lack of
punctuation in *PM* and *HM* makes it unclear precisely who speaks (Love or
Cupid) and who in turn should 'have place'. *CWD* prioritizes one meaning
by using punctuation marks to specify Love as the speaker: '"Cupid," said
Love, "must have place"'. This seems appropriate given that Love and
Reason are the warring parties, and so logical speakers in the poem, but, as
Love is given a masculine pronoun in 219, it is arguable that 'Love' here is
a synonym for Cupid himself (who is referred to at 222 and 225–35). This
edition has therefore not emended *PM*'s punctuation other than capitalizing
Love as a personification to parallel Reason.
   216. it ... grace] that it was his right (i.e. to have precedence).

So as sure Love can not miss,
Since that Reason ruler is.

Lissius. It seems he missed before he had this guide.   225
Philisses. I'm sure not me, I ne'er my heart could hide
        But he it found, so as I well may say,
        Had he been blind I might have stolen away.
        But so he saw, and ruled with Reason's might,
        As he hath killed in me all my delight.   230
        He wounded me (alas) with double harm,
        And none but he can my distress uncharm.
        Another wound must cure me or I die;
        But stay, this is enough. I hence will fly,
        And seek the boy that struck me. Fare you well –   235
        Yet make not still your pleasures prove my hell.   [*Exit.*]

---

223. *Love*] *CWD;* love *PM, HM.*   224. *Reason*] *PM;* reason *HM.*   *is.*] is. /
PM; is; / *HM.*   229. Reason's] *CWD;* reasons *PM, HM.*   236. SD.] *CWD.*

223. Love ... miss] i.e. his arrow cannot miss. *CWD* reads 'a pun on miss
as in "to cause offence" as well as "to mistake the way"' (203n.65).

226. *I'm ... me*] i.e. I'm sure he didn't miss me.

228–9. *blind ... saw*] Cf. 1.1.10SD.

231. *double harm*] The double injury Philisses has suffered from Cupid
appears to be that of his unrequited love to Musella combined with that of
jealousy, which has injured his loving friendship with Lissius (2.2.1–6). Time
wishes to inflict 'double harm' on humankind in Parker's translation of
Petrarch's *Triumph of Time* (L4v), but it is not a phrase found in Wroth's
writings or those of the Sidney coterie. That said, Sonnet 14 of Wroth's
'Crown of Sonnets' makes reference to multiple harms, the first caused by
the heart's tribute of 'faith untouch'd', followed by 'other mischiefs' including 'Cursed Jealousy' which 'doth all her forces bend / To my undoing, thus
my harms I see' (Wroth *Poems*, 134). The phrase occurs in a romantic context
in John Gower's fourteenth-century poem *Confessio Amantis* (London:
Thomas Berthelette, 1532), which tells how the gods were moved by the
'infortune of double harm' (80) resulting from the suicide of Alcyone after
Ceyx's death at sea.

232. *uncharm*] free from a spell or enchantment.

233. *Another ... die*] presumably caused by another of Cupid's arrows
striking Musella and making her fall in love with Philisses. The Petrarchan
paradox of being healed by a wound looks forward to 5.4.

235. *boy*] Cupid.

236. *Yet ... hell*] Philisses's parting line could be delivered as an aside,
although Lissius's lines 239–42 imply they could be directed towards him.

Lissius. Philisses now hath left us, let's go back
　　And tend our flocks, who now our care do lack.
　　Yet would he had more pleasant parted hence,
　　Or that I could but judge the cause from whence　　240
　　These passions grew; it would give me much ease
　　Since I perceive my sight doth him displease.
　　I'll seek him yet, and of him truly know
　　What in him hath bred this unusual woe.
　　If he deny me, then I'll swear he hates　　245
　　Me, or affects that humour which debates
　　In his kind thought which should the master be;
　　But who the friend is, I will quickly see.　　*Exit.*
Musella. Well, let's away. [*Aside*] And hither soon return
　　That sun to me, whose absence makes me burn.　　250
　　　　　　　　　　　　　　　　　　　　Exeunt.

238. now] *PM;* now [*inserted above*] *HM.*　lack.] lack = [*end of page*] *PM.*
239. *CWD adds* SD [*Aside*].　241. grew] *PM;* grow *HM.*　243-7. *Written down the central margin in HM.*　248. *Missing in HM.*　249. SD.] *CWD.*
250. burn.] *PM;* burne; / [*flourish below*] *HM.*　SD.] *PM; not in HM.*

243-7. As Straznicky points out, these five lines are written vertically down the central margin of *HM.* Lissius's final line (248) is missing and may have been cropped in the process of binding (*SM*, 71n.174).
246-7. *affects ... be*] Unclear; possibly Lissius feels that Philisses is trying to decide whether he loves or hates Lissius, or whether Philisses or Lissius is the 'master'.
248. *who ... see*] Again unclear. Possibly 'I will quickly find out who it is he is in love with'; alternatively, 'I will quickly see which of us is willing to be friendly'. This line is missing from *HM* (see above 243-7n). In the 1999 production Lissius exited quickly and then re-entered walking slowly across the back of the stage searching for Philisses at the end of Musella's aside at 249-50. Cupid stood up behind the gap in the curtains, drew his bow and touched Lissius with an arrowhead as he passed the gap. Lissius rubbed his shoulder, walked slowly downstage and sat on the bank, in position for the beginning of 2.2. This is a neat solution to the problem of explaining Lissius's change in the text from outspoken opponent of love in 2.1 to lover of Simeana in 2.2. The 1999 stage business also enabled Lissius to exit and re-enter within 12 lines in the script. Such speed of exit and re-entrance is uncommon in professional drama, but perhaps less so in a non-commercial performance context.
250. *whose absence*] i.e. that of Philisses.

[ACT 2 SCENE 2]

[*The meadows*]

[*Enter*] PHILISSES [*and*] LISSIUS.

Lissius. O plainly deal with me! My love hath been
    Still firm to you, then let us not begin
    To seem as strangers; if I've wronged you, speak,
    And I'll forgiveness ask, else do not break
    That band of friendship of our long-held love,   5
    Which did these plains to admiration move.

0.0. [ACT 2 SCENE 2]] *CWD.* 0.1. SD.] *This ed.* 0.2. SD.] *CWD;*
Philisses, Lissius *PM.* 1. O] *PM;* Ô *HM.* 3. I've] I'have *PM, HM.* 5.
love] *HM;* loves *PM.* 6. did] *PM;* all did [*inserted above*] *HM.*

___

0.1. SD.] The location of this scene is not indicated by *PM* or *HM*, but
it is probably a part of the meadows to which the shepherd characters return
at the end of 2.1. Although Philisses vowed to leave the meadows in 1.2.1–4,
here Lissius refers to 'these plains' (6).
    0.2. SD.] In *PM* the change of scene is indicated by the listing of the two
speakers' names. In *HM* this scene is written across two smaller sheets
(9r–10r) which are pasted and sewn into the larger manuscript.
    1. *love*] Lissius's lines draw on the classical celebration of love and friend-
ship between men in Cicero, who claimed that none 'liveth not in mutual
love with some friend', and that 'he that beholdeth his friend, doth as it were
behold a certain pattern of himself'. See Cicero, *Laelius De Amiticia* (44
BCE), trans. John Harington as *The Book of Friendship of Marcus Tullie Cicero*
(London, Thomas Berthelette, 1550), 16–17. Erasmus's *Proverbs or Adages*,
trans. Richard Taverner (London: Richard Banks, 1539) echoed Pythagoras's
idea of '*Amicus alter ipse*', the friend as another self: 'my friend is as who
should say an other self' (C5r–v). These ideas were revived through early
modern translations of classical texts. See Laurie Shannon, *Sovereign Amity:
Figures of Friendship in Shakespearean Contexts* (Chicago: University of
Chicago Press, 2002), and Introduction, 20–1, for friendship in the play.
    5. *band*] Wroth uses this term in *Urania* to indicate both physical bonds
and emotional bonds of love and friendship. The man whose wife was
seduced by Dattareus accuses him of 'the breach of hospitality and the
noblest band of friendship' (*Urania I*, 487.8–9) while in *Urania II*
Amphilanthus longs for Pamphilia 'to tie me in the strictest bands, and such
as I pray may never be untied but by death' (272.26–7) and Rosindy is 'tied
in the bands of mutual love to his wife' (*Urania II*, 273.38–9). Cf. 5.7.73.
    6. *plains*] 'flat meadow lands, a suitable setting for a pastoral romance'
(*CWD*, 203n.72). Lissius puns on 'plainly' (see 0.1. SDn. above) and claims
that the enduring love between him and Philisses has become renowned
across the pastoral world of the play. In the 2018 production the actor gestured towards the audience with open arms to invoke the wider community.

Philisses. I can not change but love thee ever will,
　　For no cross shall my first affection kill.
　　But give me leave that sight (once loved) to shun,
　　Since by the sight I see myself undone.   10
Lissius. When this opinion first possessed thy heart
　　Would Death had struck me with his cruel dart.
　　Live I to be mistrusted by my friend?
　　'Tis time for me my wretched days to end.
　　But what began this change in thee?
Philisses.   Mistrust.   15
Lissius. Mistrust of me?
Philisses.   I am not so unjust.
Lissius. What then? Pray tell, my heart doth long to know.
Philisses. Why then, the change and cause of all my woe
　　Proceeds from this: I fear Musella's love
　　Is placed in you; this doth my torments move,   20
　　Since if she do, my friendship bound to you

---

7. can not] *HM*; cannott *PM*. 9. (once loved)] *PM*; once lov'd *HM*.
12. Death] *CWD*; death *PM*; i̶t̶ death *HM*; devils *R*. 13. friend?] *HM*;
freind *PM*. 14. for ... end] *HM*; for mee t̶o̶ ̶e̶n̶d̶ my wreched days to
end *PM*. 17. know] *PM*; ['w' inserted above] *HM*. 20. in] *PM*; on *HM*.
21. Since] *PM*; for *HM*.

---

　　7. *can not*] As discussed (Introduction, 56), this edition argues that
Wroth's use of two words for 'cannot' is designed to give 'not' a stress for
emphasis. Where such emphasis seems appropriate we have preferred use of
the two words (this line is one of the few cases where 'can not' appears in
HM but not in *PM*).

　　8. *cross*] trouble (*CWD*, 203n.73). Cf. 1.1.19n. The 2018 production
emphasized the sense of discord between the friends who spoke crossly to
each other, whereas in 1999 Lissius adopted a jokey, affectionate tone to try
to comfort his friend.

　　10. *undone*] ruined (*OED*, adj.2) i.e. by looking at Lissius, whom he
thinks is beloved by Musella. Cf. the Forester in 1.2.170–1.

　　12. *Death ... dart*] As god of erotic love, Cupid personifies the inextricable
connection between desire and death, Eros and Thanatos, which manifests
in Western Christian culture through the idea of the 'Fall' of humankind,
especially the temptation of Adam and Eve in Genesis. *CWD* observes 'Like
Cupid, Death is often depicted carrying a spear or arrow' (203n.4), and
Henry Peacham's *Minerva Britanna* (1612) includes an emblem where Death
and Cupid steal each other's arrows (172). For another example of Wroth's
deployment of the bond between the two, see *P4*, Sonnet 30.

　　15. *Mistrust*] Cf. 2.1.110; 'mistrust' is also the name of one of Cupid's
arrows in 1.4.39.

Must make me leave for love or joy to sue.
For though I love her more than mine own heart,
If you affect her I will ne'er impart
My love to her; so constant friendship binds   25
My love where truth such faithful biding finds.
Then truly speak, good Lissius, plainly say,
Nor shall a love make me your trust betray.
Lissius. O my Philisses! What? Was this the cause?
Alas, see how misfortune on me draws: 30
I love, but vow 'tis not Musella's face
Could from my heart my freer thoughts displace,
Although I must confess she worthy is,
But she (alas) can bring to me no bliss.
It is your sister who must end my care;   35
Now do you see you need no more despair?

---

22. for] *PM;* my for [*inserted above*] *HM.* to] *PM;* for to [*inserted above*] *HM.* 24. ne'er] ne're *PM;* not *HM.* 26. My] *PM;* mee my [*overwritten*] *HM.* 30. draws] *PM;* drause *HM.* 31. not] *PM;* nott [*inserted above*] *HM.* face] *PM, HM;* love *R.* 32. heart] *PM;* thou hart [*inserted above*] *HM.* displace] *PM;* displ [*end of word cropped from trimmed page*] *HM.* 34. (alas)] *PM;* allas *HM.* 35. It] *PM;* i['t' *blotted*] *HM.* 36. despair] *PM;* despa [*end of word cropped from trimmed page*] *HM.*

22. *leave ... sue*] stop seeking for love and happiness (by wooing her).

24. *affect*] have affection for; like or love (*OED*, v4a).

25–6. *so ... finds*] Philisses appears to tell Lissius that their friendship constrains his love, as their friendship is so true. 'Biding' here is used in the sense of 'home' or 'dwelling' but also with the sense of 'enduring'.

29–52. These lines are on the verso of fol. 9, a smaller sheet inserted into *HM*. See Introduction, 49.

30. *misfortune ... draws*] misfortune falls on me, perhaps with reference back to the drawing of fortunes in 2.1. Lissius may refer here to the unsettling of his relationship with Philisses, or may be referring to being in love as a misfortune in itself (potentially to comic effect in performance).

31. *I love*] At some point during or after Lissius's challenging speech to Cupid in the previous scene (2.1.79–84), Cupid strikes Lissius with an arrow, making him fall in love with Simeana, Philisses's sister. This could happen onstage, as in the 1999 production (see 2.1.248n.) or spectators could be surprised at the beginning of this scene with the appearance of a love-stricken Lissius. The 2018 production did not show the wounding of Lissius by Cupid's arrow.

35. *It ... sister*] Simeana. *CWD* suggests that 'as brother and sister Philisses and Simeana represent Philip and Mary Sidney' (203n.76) though they may also refer to a younger generation of family relationships (see Introduction, 41–2).

care] suffering, sorrow.

Philisses. Yet she may love you, can you that deny?
Lissius. And swear I never yet least show could spy.
    But well assured I am that she doth love,
    And you, I venture dare, doth her heart move;   40
    'Tis true she speaks to me, but for your sake,
    Else for good looks from her I might leave take.
    Her eyes can not dissemble, though her tongue
    To speak it hazards not a greater wrong.
    Her cheeks can not command the blood but still   45
    It must appear, although against her will.
    Thus have I answered and advice do give:
    Tell her your love, if you will happy live.
    She can not, neither will she, you deny;
    And do as much for me, or else I die.   50
Philisses. What may I do that you shall not command?
    Then here I 'gage my word, and give my hand.
    If with my sister I but power have,
    She shall requite you, and your sorrow save

---

45. still] *PM;* sti [*end of word cropped from trimmed page*] *HM.*   46. must]
PM; ~~will~~ must [*inserted above*] *HM.*   47. answered] *HM;* answr'd ~~you~~ *PM.*
54. your sorrow save] *PM;* the love you gave *HM.*

---

38. *I ... spy*] I have never seen the least sign of love [from her].

42. *Else ... take*] Otherwise [i.e. if the conversation wasn't for your sake], I could say goodbye to receiving any fond looks from her.

43. *dissemble*] lie, deceive.

43–4. *though ... wrong*] Although she dare not risk causing a greater wrong by declaring her love [because this would infringe her female modesty]. Cf. 3.1.79 and 3.3.167–8.

45–6. *Her ... will*] She cannot help blushing, even though she doesn't want to. Blushing was seen as both a sign of modesty and a sign of shame.

50. *And ... die*] Lissius adopts the heightened register of the other lovers in the play, having mocked it in the previous scene (2.1.9–10). His embarrassed delivery of this line as a throwaway aside in the 2018 production elicited a laugh from spectators.

52. *'gage ... word*] Give my word, promise. From French military origins, the gauge or glove, meaning 'a pawn of pledge' but also used as a verb where 'the use hath turned the G into W so as it is oftener written (*wage*)'. See Cowell, sigs II$_v$–2$_r$). In Wroth's *Urania I* Amphilanthus cannot 'engage' his word to promote Leandrus's suit to his cousin (and beloved) Pamphilia (263–4).

53–60.] In *HM* these lines are on 10r, a smaller sheet bound in.

With gift of her love. But once more say this,   55
From fair Musella hope you for no bliss?
Lissius. None but her friendship, which I will require
From both, as equal to my best desire.
Philisses. Then thus assured that friendship shall remain,
Or let my soul endure eternal pain.   *Exeunt.*   60

[ACT 2 SCENE 3]

[*The Temple*]

VENUS's PRIESTS *to Love or his praise.*

The goddess [VENUS] *and her son* [CUPID] *appearing
in glory.*

---

55. With gift of her love] *PM;* soe freely to her *HM.*   58. to my] *PM;*
to [*ink blot*] my *HM.*   60. endure eternal] *PM;* indure [*ink blot*] endless
HM.   SD.] Ex: [*flourish below*] *PM;* ex = *HM.*

0.0. [ACT 2 SCENE 3]] *CWD.*   0.1. SD.] *This ed.*   0.2. SD.] *PM; not
in HM;* VENUS' PRIESTS TO LOVE, *or his praise, CWD.*   0.3–4. SD.] *This
ed.;* the Goddess, and her Sonne apeering in glory. / *PM; not in HM;* [and]
the GODDESS *and her* SON, *appearing in glory. CWD.*

---

58. *both*] probably Musella and Philisses (therefore excluding Simeana
from his 'best desire'), but possibly referring to Simeana and Musella.
59. *Then ... assured*] Although both friends end the scene reassured in
their enduring friendship, the direction of this phrase is not very clear.
Philisses seems to say 'be assured' to Lissius but could also be expressing
his own sense of reassurance.

0.1. SD.] This scene clearly takes place in Venus's Temple but the stage
direction in *PM* ('Venus's Priests to Love or his praise' and on two subsequent lines 'The goddess and her son / appearing in glory') is ambiguous. It
may suggest that the Priests sing or chant '*to Love* [i.e. Cupid] *or his praise*',
and the scene was played in this way in 1999, in the 2014 staged reading
and 2018 production at Penshurst Place; alternatively, the SD may simply
identify that they *are* priests 'to Love or his praise'. In *HM* the lines are part
of an inserted half-page beginning with the last eight lines of Act 2 Scene
2 and are headed 'Venus:', possibly a speech heading assigning her these
lines. Straznicky argues that in *HM* Venus appears alone in this scene (*SM*,
37), and that this interlude is a 'fulcrum' of the *HM* script. In *PM* it seems
unlikely for Venus to be speaking these lines, even in combination with the
Priests, given their supplicatory tone; Venus is still in command of Cupid
in 3.4, and takes on a more conciliatory tone only in 4.3. This edition has
therefore assigned the lines to Venus's Priests.

Priests. Cupid, blessèd be thy might,
    Let thy triumph see no night;
    Be thou justly god of love,
    Who thus can thy glory move.
    Hearts, obey to Cupid's sway,   5
    Princes, none of you say nay;
    Eyes, let him direct your way,
    For without him you may stray.
    He your secret thoughts can spy,
    Being hid else from each eye.   10
    Let your songs be still of love,
    Write no satires which may prove

---

1. SP. *Priests.*] *CWD;* Venus *HM*.   3. god of love] *HM;* God of Love *PM*.
6. Princes] *PM;* princes *HM*.   7. Eyes] *PM;* eyes *HM*.   12. satires] *HM;*
Satires *PM*.

1–32.] The seven-syllable rhyming couplets give these lines a ritualistic
tone, invoking the religious setting (cf. 5.4), and *PM* does not specify how
they are to be delivered; the lack of clear written direction possibly points
to Wroth's presence as a director of any performance based on this manuscript. Modern productions may have actors speak the lines or choose a
performance style to echo the singing or chanting of the Psalms, since the
verse form echoes that of Mary and Philip Sidney's translations of the Psalms
(e.g. Psalm 44). The 1999 production set the words to the popular tune of
'Staines Morris' found in William Ballet's lute book (*William Ballet his Book
written William Vince,* Trinity College Dublin Library, MS 408, *c.* 1590s) and
later published in John Playford's *The Dancing Master* (London: Thomas
Harper and John Playford, 1651, 87) to keep a pastoral tone, but cut 13–25
(see Introduction, 33).
    1. *Cupid … might*] In 1999 two priests with gold masks drew back the
curtains and raised their arms in adulation of the figures of Venus and Cupid,
who posed on the top step, brightly lit 'in glory'. Venus also gestured to
Cupid as the priests sang.
    2. *triumph*] Cupid is referred to as Venus's 'all-triumphing son' in Ben
Jonson's *The Haddington Masque* (1608, l. 211), and in *Love Freed from
Ignorance and Folly* (1611) where the Sphinx celebrates her capture of Cupid
and 'All the triumphs [and] all the spoils' he has enjoyed (15). See 1.1.32n.
and 5.4.47–8.
    6. *Princes*] Cf. 4.2.37 and note and Introduction, 14, on princes in an
imagined audience.
    12. *satires*] See for example George Gascoigne's *The Steel Glass: a satire*
(1576), written against the seductive lover 'Vain Delight' at court. The
priests' rejection of satire as antipathetic to love echoes Theseus in *A
Midsummer Night's Dream* who claims satire is 'keen and critical / Not sorting
with a nuptial ceremony' (5.1.54–5).

Least offensive to his name;
If you do you will but frame
Words against yourselves, and lines   15
Where his good, and your ill shines,
Like him who doth set a snare
For a poor betrayèd hare,
And that thing he best doth love
Lucklessly the snare doth prove.   20
Love the king is of the mind,
Please him, and he will be kind.
Cross him, you see what doth come:
Harms which make your pleasures' tomb.
Then take heed, and make your bliss   25
In his favour; and so miss
No content, no joy, nor peace,
But in happiness increase.

---

19. And] *PM; this line and the rest of the scene are on* 10v *of HM.*   21. Love] *PM, HM.*   26. miss] miss = [*end of page*] *PM.*   27. no joy] *PM;* nor joy *HM.* 28. in happiness] *PM;* s̶t̶i̶l̶l̶ [*inserted above*] in a̶l̶l̶ happiness *HM.*   increase] increase *PM;* increase; / *HM.*

14–15. *frame ... yourselves*] These lines seem to respond particularly to Lissius's scorn for love (2.1.65–70) and direct challenge to Cupid (2.1.79–84) which have resulted in the 'misfortune' of his being love-struck in 2.2.30.

17. *Like ... snare*] The 2018 production, in which Venus did not appear in this scene at all, used the line as a cue for Cupid to enter onto the ground-floor performance area and sit to watch a dumbshow in which Philisses imparted news (of Lissius's love) to his sister Simeana while her rival Climeana watched and then exited looking upset.

17–20. *Like ... prove*] This is a more complex metaphor than it first appears. Although the hare was often associated with lechery, Wroth uses the trapped hare to symbolize self-inflicted suffering in *Urania I*: Pelarina, who follows her beloved and her rival out hunting, is 'unmarked, but weary, and dabbled like a hunted hare in winter, tired with my disgrace' (*Urania I*, 532.16–17). The idea of the hunter caught by his own snare appears in Sydelia's story of her beloved, disguised as a huntsman, who is killed by her brother, having no more protection 'than a poor hare hath in the hands of the hounds, who have long hunted to prey on it' (*Urania I*, 275.34–5). The association of the hare and being trapped by 'words against yourselves' (15) may also have been familiar to Wroth from theological debate, as when the Jesuit writer Robert Parsons mocks an aggressive Protestant who finds himself 'as a hare in the net mesheth himself more and more by struggling' (*A Relation of the Trial Made Before the King of France* (Saint-Omer: F. Bellet, 1604), 214–15).

Love command your hearts and eyes,
And enjoy what pleasure tries.   30
Cupid govern, and his care
Guide your hearts from all despair.   [*Exeunt.*]

---

29. Love] Love   *PM, HM.*   32. Guide] *PM;*   guard   *HM.*   despair]
dispaire; / [*flourish below*] *PM;* dispaire; [*two S fermés with flourish below*]
HM.   SD.] *CWD.*

31. *Cupid govern*]   i.e. let Cupid govern.
32. Exeunt.]   See Introduction, 52–3, for discussion of the lack of stage
directions in scenes with Venus and Cupid.

Act 3

[*The woods*]

[*Enter* SILVESTA *and* MUSELLA.]

Silvesta. [*Sings.*]
>*Silent woods with desert's shade*
>>*Giving peace,*
>*Where all pleasures first are made*
>>*To increase,*
>*Give you favour to my moan* 5
>*Now my loving time is gone.*

0.0. [ACT 3 SCENE 1]] *CWD;* The third Act *PM;* The 3 Act; / *HM.*   0.1.
SD.] *This ed.*   0.2. SD.] *CWD.*   1. SD.] *This ed.*   *woods*] *PM;* [*inserted
above*] *HM.*   *desert's*] *CWD;* desarts *PM, HM.*   5. *you*] *PM;* your *HM*

0.1. SD.] This scene takes place in the woods, the same wooded setting
as 4.1, since Silvesta says that Philisses 'Walks in this place' (3.1.83).
    1. SD.] No setting has been found for this exchange between Silvesta
and Musella but however it was performed it is, significantly, the only sung
exchange in the script, highlighting the bonds of female affection. The sym-
biotic relationship between the two characters was emphasized in the 1999
performance by the actors playing flutes together, then alternating to accompany each other's singing, and by alternating verses of their songs (Silvesta
1–6, Musella 13–18, Silvesta 7–12, Musella 19–23). In the 2018 performance
the actors entered and sang from opposite sides of the stage, coming together
only at line 49. On Lady Mary Wroth's musical abilities see Introduction, 3.
    1. desert's shade] i.e. the woods are deserted of people. Cf. *AYLI*, 'Why
should this a desert be? / For it is unpeopled?' (3.2.112–13). Wroth uses it
to mean sparsely populated and uncivilized, for example in *Urania II* where
Amicles tells Amphilanthus 'I did little look to see you in these deserts, and
amongst such rustic creatures' (217.1–2). In *Love's Victory*, Silvesta's
reminder that the woods are relatively uncharted territory also alerts spectators to their potential dangers. *CWD* glosses the term as 'wild' (203n.1). See
Introduction, 19.
    5. Give ... moan] Give your blessing to my lament.

Chastity my pleasure is,
    Folly fled;
From hence now I seek my bliss,
    Cross love dead.   10
In your shadows I repose,
You than love I rather chose.

Musella. [*Sings.*]
    Choice ill-made were better left,
        Being cross;
    Of such choice to be bereft   15
        Were no loss.
    Chastity you thus commend
    Doth proceed but from love's end.

    And if love the fountain was
        Of your fire,   20
    Love must chastity surpass
        In desire.
    Love lost bred your chastest thought,
    Chastity by love is wrought.

Silvesta. O poor Musella, now I pity thee;   25
    I see thou'rt bound, who most have made unfree.
    'Tis true disdain of my love made me turn,
    And happily I think, but you to burn

---

12. than] *CWD;* then *PM, HM.*   *rather*] *PM;* now have *HM.*   13. SD.] *This ed.*   19. *love*] *HM;* Love *PM.*   21. *Love*] *PM;* love *HM.*   22. *desire*] desire = [*end of page*] *PM.*   23. *Love*] *PM;* love *HM.*   25. O] Ô *PM, HM.*

---

8. Folly fled] having fled folly; alternatively, 'with Folly having fled'.

9. From hence] henceforth (*CWD,* 203n.2); 'hence' (in the sense of 'from here') also reinforces Silvesta's attachment to the woods as her abode.

10. Cross ... dead] i.e. 'I reject love by killing it in my heart' or possibly 'my crossed love for Philisses is now dead'.

12. You ... rather] You [i.e. the woods, associated with chastity] rather than love.

13–16. Choice ... loss] A badly made choice is best not made at all, being unfavourable; not to have to make such a choice would be no loss. Musella rejects Silvesta's characterization of love as folly, suggesting that as her vow of chastity proceeded from love, love is therefore more valuable.

26. most ... unfree] who have captivated the most hearts.

In love's false fires yourself – poor soul, take heed:
Be sure, before you too much pine, to speed.   30
You know I loved have, but behold my gain:
This you dislike, I purchased with love's pain
And true-felt sorrow, yet my answer was
From my (then dear) Philisses, 'You must pass
Unloved by me, and for your own good, leave   35
To urge that which, most urged, can but deceive
Your hopes. For know, Musella is my love.'
As then of duty I should no more move.
And this his will he got, but not his mind,
For yet it seems you are no less unkind.   40
Musella. Wrong me not, chaste Silvesta; 'tis my grief
That from poor me he will not take relief.
Silvesta. What, will he lose what he did most desire?
Musella. So is he led away with jealous fire.
And this, Silvesta, but to you I speak,   45
For sooner should my heart with silence break
Than any else should hear me thus much say
But you, who I know will not me betray.

---

30. you too] *PM;* ['*too' inserted above*] *HM.*   31. have, but] *PM;* have *HM.*
33. true-felt] *CWD;* true felt *PM, HM.*   34. my (then dear)] *PM;*
(my then deere) *HM.*   35. own good] *PM;* owne [*inserted above*] good
HM.   39. but] *PM;* yet *HM.*

---

30. *Be ... speed*] make haste. 'Be sure that you achieve your love before
you pine away too much.'

32. *This ... dislike*] i.e. chastity, which Musella dismisses at the start of
her song.

34. *You ... pass*] You must move forward or depart ('pass' *OED*, vII.6).

35–7. *leave ... hopes*] Cease protesting that [your love], which, however
much you protest it, can only deceive your hopes. By quoting Philisses's
rejection of her entreaties, Silvesta reveals to Musella that Philisses loves
her (37).

38. *As ... move*] From then it was my duty not to express my love to him;
another example of counsel against female wooing. Cf. Musella below, 46–8
and 77–80.

39. *will ... mind*] Philisses gets what he wanted (i.e. for Silvesta to cease pursuing him), but not what he wished for, Musella's love; cf. Cupid's distinction
between 'will' and 'mind' in 1.1.31. *CWD* suggests that 'will' here and in
subsequent lines (42–3 and 48–50) may allude to William Herbert (203n.11).

48. *betray*] Musella's trust in Silvesta looks forward to the sharing of
confidences among the female shepherdesses in 3.3, as well as Arcas's
betrayal of Musella later in the play.

Silvesta. Betray Musella? Sooner will I die.
  No, I do love you, nor will help deny   50
  That lies in me to bring your care to end,
  Or service which to your content may tend.
  For when I loved Philisses as my life,
  Perceiving he loved you, I killed the strife
  Which in me was; yet do I wish his good,   55
  And for his sake love you, though I withstood
  Good fortunes. This chaste life well pleaseth me,
  And would joy more if you two happy be.
  Few would say this, but fewer would it do,
  But th'one I loved, and love the other too.   60
Musella. I know you loved him, nor could I the less
  At that time love you; so did he possess
  My heart, as methought all hearts sure must yield
  To love him most, and best. Who in this field
  Doth live, and hath not had some kind of touch 65
  To like him? But oh, you and I too much.
Silvesta. Mine is now past; tell me now what yours is,
  And I'll wish but the means to work your bliss.
Musella. Then know, Silvesta, I Philisses love.
  But he, although (or that because) he loves,   70

---

51. That] [*first* 't' *blotted*] *PM; that HM;* What *R.* 57. life well] *PM;*
lyfe well [*inserted above*] *HM.* 58. would ... more] *PM;* yet ... most *HM.*
62. At that] *PM;* at *HM.* 63. methought] my thought *PM, HM.* 65. hath
... had] *PM;* have ... had [*'had' inserted above*] *HM.* 66. oh] Ô *PM;* ô *HM.*
70. loves] loves = [*end of page*] *PM.*

 49.] Again, Silvesta's line looks forward to her actions in 5.4.
 54. *strife*] 'The action of striving together or contending in opposition'
and also 'distress' (*OED,* n.1a,e). Silvesta may refer to the pain of her unrequited love for Philisses.
 56. *withstood*] was denied, prevented from (*OED,* withstand *v.* 2).
 58. *And would*] And I would.
 59. *but*] (in this context) even.
 it do] i.e. joy in a friend's union with a former beloved.
 62–4. *possess ... best*] He so possessed my heart that I thought all hearts
must yield to me in loving him most and best. Musella's view that Philisses
is the object of everyone's love parallels what Silvesta says of Musella herself
(26), and what Philisses says of her in 2.1. 'Most and best', looks forward to
Simeana and Climeana's competing claims in 3.3.113.
 65–6. *hath ... him*] has not been touched with affection for him.
 68. *work ... bliss*] engineer your happiness.

Doth me mistrust. Ah! Can such mischief move
As to mistrust her who such passion proves?
But so he doth, and thinks I've Lissius made
Master of my affections, which hath stayed
Him ever yet from letting me it know   75
By words, although he hides it not from show.
Sometimes I fain would speak, then straight forbear,
Knowing it most unfit; thus woe I bear.

Silvesta. Indeed a woman to make love is ill,
But hear, and you may all these sorrows kill: 80
He, poor distressèd shepherd, every morn
Before the sun to our eyes new is born,
Walks in this place, and here alone doth cry
Against his life, and your great cruelty.
Now, since you love so much, come here and find   85
Him in these woes, and show yourself but kind.
You soon shall see a heart so truly won
As you would not it miss to be undone.

---

71. mistrust. Ah! Can] mistrust (ah) can *PM, HM*; mistrust. Ah, can *CWD,
EMWW.* 72. proves?] *PM;* proves; *HM.* 73. I've] I have *PM;* I'have
HM. 77. straight] strait *PM;* straite *HM.* 80. all] *PM;* [*inserted above*]
HM.

---

71. *mischief*] misfortune, but with a stronger sense of evil or wickedness
in early modern usage. *OED*, 1, cites Mary Sidney Herbert's translation of
Antonius: 'O breast where death (Oh mischief) comes to choke up vital
breath' (MSH *Works I*, 207).

72. *proves*] demonstrates (cf. 1.2.4n.).

74. *stayed*] prevented.

76. *hides ... show*] Cf. 1.3.6 and 2.1.110–12. Philisses's attempts to conceal
his love are clearly unsuccessful; these lines can provide guidance to actors
in interpreting Musella's reaction to him in earlier scenes.

77. *fain*] gladly (*CWD*, 203n.14).
straight forbear] immediately refrain (in the sense of 'refrain from').

78. *unfit*] inappropriate (i.e. because she is a woman, and telling Philisses
of her love would violate the conventional bounds of female modesty). Cf.
3.3.168. Perhaps surprisingly, Musella and Silvesta, 79, are taking the same
position that Lissius adopts rather more forcefully in 3.3.167–8.

82. *Before ... born*] Before the sunrise.

88. *As ... undone*] Wroth's phrasing is obscure here. At 1.2.170–1ff. the
Forester explains to Lissius that he has been 'undone' (or thwarted) in love
by Philisses; Philisses, in turn, believes he has been 'undone' by Lissius
(2.2.10). Possibly, here, Silvesta means that if Musella shows herself 'but
kind' (86) to Philisses, she will soon see she has won his heart so truly that

Musella. Silvesta, for this love I can but say
    That piece of heart which is not given away   90
    Shall be your own; the rest will you observe
    As saver of two hearts, which too will serve
    You ever with so true and constant love
    Your chastity itself shall it approve.
Silvesta. I do believe it, for in so much worth   95
    As lives in you, virtue must needs break forth.
    And for Philisses, I love him and will
    In chastest service hinder still his ill.
    Then keep your time; alas, let him not die
    For whom so many suffered misery.   100
Musella. Let me no joy receive if I neglect
    This kind advice, or him I so respect.
Silvesta. Farewell Musella, love, and happy be.   *Exit.*
Musella. And be thou blessed that thus dost comfort me.
                                Exit.

---

90. That ... given] *PM;* ~~you have of mee that is nott yet~~ [?] ~~given~~ [*followed by 90*] *HM.*   96. break] *PM;* spring *HM.*   97. and] *PM;* & [*inserted above*] *HM.*   104. me.] mee /. *PM.*

---

she would not wish to 'miss' out on seeing it even at the cost of being undone (i.e. breaking the female convention of modest silence herself). Alternatively, if 'miss' and 'undone' refer to the action 'truly won', Silvesta could be saying 'you would not make the mistake of thinking that it – the winning of his heart – had not been done'.

90. *given away*] i.e. to Philisses.

92. *too*] with a pun on 'two' (the hearts of both Musella and Philisses).

95. *worth*] virtue, but, as *CWD* notes, Wroth is possibly adding to the catalogue of puns on her name, as made by figures like John Davies of Hereford in *The Scourge of Folly* (London: Edward Allde for Richard Redmer, 1611, S1r–v) and George Wither, *Abuses Stripped and Whipped* (London: G. Eld for Francis Burton, 1613, X4), and William Gamage, *Linsi-Woolsie or Two Centuries of Epigrams* (London: A. Matthews for Henry Bell, 1613, D3v). See also Hannay, *MSLW*, 158–9, 233 and 5.1.4–5n.

99. *keep your time*] Be here at the right time. Cf. 4.1.1.

101. *neglect*] (in this sense) ignore.

102. In both 1999 and 2018 productions Musella and Silvesta embraced at this line, contrasting with the handshake between Philisses and Lissius in 2.2.52.

[ACT 3 SCENE 2]

[*The woods*]

[*Enter* PHILISSES.]

Philisses. O wretched man, and thou, all-conquering Love
   Which showst thy power still on hapless me,
   Yet give me leave in these sweet shades to move,
   Rest but to show my killing misery;
   And be once pleased to know my wretched fate,   5
   And something pity my ill, and my state.
   Could ever Nature or the bright heavens frame
   So rare a part so like themselves divine?
   And yet that work be blotted with the blame
   Of cruelty, and dark be who should shine?   10
   To be the brightest star of dearest prize,
   And yet to murder hearts which to her cries
   Cry, and even at the point of death for care,

0.0. [ACT 3 SCENE 2]] *CWD.* 0.1. SD.] *This ed.* 0.2. SD.] *CWD.*
1. Love] *PM;* love *HM.* 7. Nature ... heavens] *PM;* Nature ['*n*' *overwritten as* '*N*'] ore the heavns e're *HM.*

0.1. SD.] This is the same setting from which Silvesta and Musella have just exited. Philisses refers to the 'sweet shades' (3), and his laments over Musella echo Silvesta's characterization of his solitary walking in 3.1.83–4.

1–20.] *CWD* notes a similarity to 'You blessed shades, which give me silent rest', Sonnet 30 in Wroth's *P4* (103–4).

5–6. *be ... state*] Philisses asks Love to note his suffering and have pity for it and his ill fortune.

7–8. *Could ... divine?*] Philisses's typically Petrarchan blazon elevates the beloved, Musella, 'that work' (9) to a heavenly body with radiant, divine qualities, created or 'framed' by Nature or the heavens. In the 2018 production Philisses (Robert Heard) addressed this question to spectators in the front row.

12–13. *And ... care*] Wroth's syntax is unclear here, and the uneven metre of line 13 adds to the sense of confusion. Possibly 'And yet to murder those hearts which cry out [in response to] her calls, even at the point of death for care [from Musella]'. In the first 14 lines, which draw on the sonnet tradition, the subject of Philisses's sentences shifts from 'Love' (1–6) to 'Nature' and the 'bright heavens' (6–10) making Musella 'a part' (8), and 'that work' of Nature, whose cruelty blots her beauty as 'the brightest star of dearest prize'. There may be a suggestion that Musella as 'the brightest star' has become a version of Venus herself. The star invokes the name 'Stella', the beloved in Philip Sidney's sonnet sequence *Astrophil and Stella*, a

Yet have I nothing left me but despair.
Despair, oh but despair? Alas, hath hope   15
No better portion? nor a greater scope?
Well then, despair with my life coupled be,
And for my sudden end do soon agree.
Ay me, unfortunate; would I could die –
But so soon as this company I fly.   *Exit.*   20

[ACT 3 SCENE 3]

[*The woods*]

[*Enter*] DALINA, CLIMEANA, SIMEANA [*and*] FILLIS.

15. oh] ô *HM;* Ô *PM.*   19. Ay me] *PM;* ay! mee *HM.*

0.0. [ACT 3 SCENE 3]] *This ed.*   0.1. SD.] *This ed.*   0.2. SD.] *CWD*;
Dalina. Climeana, Simeana, Fillis *PM;* Dalina. Climena, Simena, Fillis *HM.*

---

metaphor Wroth develops in the love of Selarinus for Philistella: "'Dear
Star," said he, "which only gives me light, how mayest thou darken thy self
from favouring me?'" (*Urania I*, 309.7–8).
    15. *but*] only.
    despair] Despair is a common complaint of the unrequited courtly lover.
Wroth's Pamphilia suffers from 'heart-held despair' and claims 'Despair thus
governs me' for example (*Poems*, 88, 91) and the actor may choose to deliver
these lines as an apostrophe to a personification of despair. Robert Heard
did this in the 2018 performance. In early modern England the word also
retained its theological meaning of despair of God's mercy, so carried connotations of judgement and eternal punishment. See Spenser's *The Faerie
Queene* I.IX.21–54, and Elizabeth Hunter, 'Damned above Ground: Dreadful
Despair in Elizabethan and Stuart Literature', in *Fear in the Medical and
Literary Imagination, Medieval to Modern: Dreadful Passions*, ed. Daniel
McCann and Claire McKechnie-Mason (Basingstoke: Palgrave, 2018),
157–76, as well as 5.1.64 below.
    15–16. *hath ... scope*] does not hope have any better fortune [portion] or
greater influence.
    19. *Ay me*] Cf. Lissius's mockery of the Forester's use of similar language
in 2.1.9.
    20. *soon ... company*] just as quickly as I flee from this company.

0.1. SD.] As shown by Philisses's hurried exit, this scene follows immediately after 3.2, which suggests it is again set in the seclusion of the woods.
In contrast to Philisses's solitary laments, the shepherdesses share their
confidences.

Dalina. Now we're alone, let everyone confess
    Truly to other what our lucks have been,
    How often liked, and loved, and so express
    Our passions past. Shall we this sport begin?
    None can accuse us, none can us betray,   5
    Unless ourselves our own selves will bewray.
Fillis. I like this, but will each one truly tell?
Climeana. Trust me I will; who doth not, doth not well.
Simeana. I'll plainly speak, but who shall be the first?
Dalina. I can say least of all, yet I will speak.   10
    A shepherd once there was, and not the worst
    Of those were most esteemed, who sleep did break
    With love, forsooth, of me. I found it, thought
    I might have him at leisure, liked him not.
    Then was there to our house a farmer brought,   15
    Rich, and lively but those bought not his lot
    For love. Two jolly youths at last there came

---

1. we're] *CWD* w'are *PM;* wee're *HM.*   3. express] ~~exsesess~~ express [*added later*] *PM;* express *HM.*   9. I'll ... first] *PM;* ~~Da: I like this least of all yet~~ [*followed by* 9] *HM.*   10. SP. Dalina] = [*followed by*] = [*at end of page*] *HM.* 12. who] *PM;* whose *HM.*   15. our] *HM;* [*erased letter*] o [*inserted above*] wr *PM.*

---

   1. *Now ... alone*] There is obvious comic irony in this line being delivered in front of a group of spectators in performance. In the 2018 production the four actors looked carefully around the space in silence before taking their seats on the green rostrum at the back of the stage, with Dalina's line producing a laugh.

   6. *Unless ... bewray*] Unless we ourselves will expose ourselves (i.e. by divulging our secrets). Dalina's line serves to position spectators, both male and female, as privileged confidantes to this private, all-female conversation.

   9. In *HM* Wroth appears to have mistakenly transcribed the beginning of Fillis's line 7 'I like this' and the middle of Dalina's line 10 'least of all yet' and then erased it.

   10. *I ... speak*] Dalina once again leads the activity, being eager to speak first.

   11–12. *not ... esteemed*] not the least of those who were most esteemed.

   12. *who ... break*] who did not sleep. *HM* has 'whose'.

   13. *forsooth*] in truth.

   found it] i.e. found out that he was in love with me.

   14. *I ... leisure*] I could have him whenever I wanted. Cf. the story in *Urania II* of the fickle shepherdess who earns her lover's scorn for being scornful herself (36–7).

   16–17. *those ... love*] those qualities did not buy him my love.

Which both methought I very well could love:
When one was absent, t'other had the name;
In my stayed heart, he present did most move.   20
Both at one time in sight, I scarce could say
Which of the two I then would wish away,
But they found how to choose, and as I was
Like changing, like uncertain, let me pass.

Simeana. I would not this believe if other tongue   25
Should this report, but think it had been wrong.
But since you speak this, could not you agree
To choose someone, but thus unchosen be?

Dalina. Truly not I, I plainly tell the truth,
Yet do confess 'twas folly in my youth.   30
The next that comes, this fault I'll mend, and have.
I will no more be foolish, or delay,
Since I do see the lads will labour save.
One answer rids them, I'll no more say nay;
But if he say 'Dalina, will you love?'   35
'And thank you,' I will say, 'if you will prove'.

---

20. stayed] *PM;* staid *HM.*   21. one] *PM;* a *HM.*   24. pass] pass: / *PM;* pass; *HM.*   25. if] *HM;* [*inserted above*] *PM.*   28. thus] *PM;* this *HM.* 31. The ... have] the ... have ['e' *inserted above*] *PM;* wch now I'le mend the next that comes I'le have *HM.*   32. or] *PM;* nor *HM.*   35. he] *PM;* hee [*inserted above*] *HM.*   36. I will] *PM;* I'le *HM.*

---

19. *had ... name*] i.e. was my love.

20. *stayed*] stopped (*OED*, adj.1); Dalina says her heart was most moved by whichever suitor was present at the time. Wroth uses the term to mean a stubborn constancy in *Urania I*, which describes 'stayed creatures' as those who are constant (545.9) and says that Myra's attachment to her lover Alariunus 'won to herself a stayed constancy' (592.14–15).

21–2. *Both ... away*] Dalina's past history recalls that of Sidney's Lady of May, who cannot choose between suitors: 'I like them both but love neither' (*LM*, 40.167)

24. *changing ... pass*] similarly changing and uncertain [in my affections towards both], let me go. Cf. Dalina's reputation for unconstancy in the Book of Fortunes, 2.1.193–200.

31. *The ... have*] i.e. 'The next lover that comes, this fault [of inconstancy] I'll amend, and accept'.

33. *Since ... save*] Since I see that men want to save the effort [of wooing].

34. *One ... nay*] One answer will dispatch them; I won't say no any more.

35–6. *But ... prove*] Dalina's promise that she has reformed, and will accept the next offer of love with thanks if it is genuine, looks forward to 5.7.125–8.

The next go on, and tell what you have done.
Simeana. I am the next, and have but losses won.
　　　Yet still I constant was, though still rejected,
　　　Loved, and not loved I was, liked, and neglected.　　　40
　　　Yet now some hope remains when love thought dead
　　　Proves like the spring's young bud, when leaves are
　　　　fled.
Fillis. Your hap's the better, would mine were as good,
　　　Though I as long as you despisèd stood.
　　　For I have loved, and loved but only one,　　　45
　　　Yet I, disdained, could but receive that moan
　　　Which others do for thousands; so unjust
　　　Is Love to those who in him most do trust.
　　　Nor did I ever let my thoughts be shown
　　　But to Musella, who all else hath known,　　　50
　　　Which was long time I had Philisses loved,
　　　And ever would, though he did me despise;
　　　For then, though he had ever cruel proved,
　　　From him, not me, the fault must needs arise.
　　　And if, Simeana, thus your brother dear　　　55
　　　Should be unkind, my love shall still be clear.

---

39. Yet still] *PM;* butt yet *HM.*　41. hope remains] hopes remains *PM;*
hope revives *HM.*　love] *HM;* [*inserted above*] *PM.*　42. Proves] *PM;*
~~clothed~~ doth [*overwritten*] *HM.*　spring's young] *PM;* spring=young *HM.*
fled] *HM;* ~~fle~~ fled [*inserted above*] = [*end of page*] *PM.*　43. SP. *Fillis*] Fill:
/ *PM;* Fillis *HM.*　48. Love] love *PM, HM.*　53. though he had] *PM;*
although he *HM.*

38–42. Wroth's script includes little indication of Lissius and Simeana's
previous relationship, although Simeana's line at 2.1.206 may hint obliquely
at it; in performance, the interaction between the two in 2.1 could also give
an idea of their romantic history (see 2.1.206 and n.).

42. *spring's*] Cf. Lissius's invocation of spring in his songs in 1.2.37 and
(less happily) 4.1.153. See Introduction, 9.

43. *hap*] fortune.

43–56. This is the longest speech Fillis has in the script and is a complete
sonnet. The 1999 production – which cut Fillis's role entirely – jumped
straight to Simeana's line 63 at this point. *CWD* suggests that Wroth based
Fillis's story on the classical tale of Phyllis, who hangs herself when she
believes she has been deserted by her lover Demophoon (*CWD*, 204n.38;
Ovid, *Heroical Epistles*, 5v–11r).

46–7. *receive … thousands*] Fillis points out that, unlike those who express
grief for thousands of lovers, her lament is for only one person (i.e. Philisses).

56. *clear*] (in this sense) pure and undiminished.

Simeana. 'Tis well resolved, but how liked she your choice?
    Did she or blame, or else your mind commend?
Fillis. Neither she seemed to dislike or rejoice,
    Nor did commend I did this love intend,   60
    But smiling told me 'twere best to be advised,
    Comfort it were to win, but death despised.
Simeana. I do believe her; but Climeana yet
    Hath nothing said, we must not her forget.
Climeana. Why, you have said enough for you and me,   65
    Yet for your sakes, I will the order keep,
    Who though a stranger here by birth I be,
    And in Arcadia ever kept my sheep,
    Yet here it is my fortune with the rest
    Of you to like, and loving be oppressed.   70
    For since I came I did a lover turn,
    And turn I did indeed when I loved here,

---

57. she your choice?] she yor choyce? *PM;* she you yor choyse *HM.*   61. told
me] *PM;* said *HM.*   67. a] *PM;* I *HM.*   be] bee = [*end of page*] *PM.*

---

57. *she*] i.e. Musella.

58. *or ... commend*] either blame or commend your thoughts.

59–62. Musella's noncommittal response to Fillis's confession of love for
Philisses implies that Musella shares Philisses's idea of hiding one's
passion – albeit Fillis's account implies that she is much more successful in
doing so than Philisses is.

61. *told me*] *HM* has 'said' here, which makes the line scan as ten syllables.
Here it is eleven syllables.

65. *you ... me*] Climeana's first line in response to Simeana foreshadows
her declaring her love for the same man.

67. Climeana's song in 1.3 introduces her as a stranger whose love has
made her '*range*' into '*strange / Unknown ways and paths to tread*' (1.3.32–4).
She implies below (75–80) that she is a stranger in the shepherd community,
having left Arcadia where she was deceived by her lover. She was welcomed,
but has now lost her heart again (by falling in love with Lissius). Cf.
Introduction, 9, 19 and *Dramatis Personae* 12n. and 1.3.32–4n.

68. *Arcadia*] Arcadia was the typical name for a pastoral retreat, taken
originally from Greek idealizations of Arcadia, a province in the Peloponnese
with a harsh rocky terrain where shepherds found comfort in a virtuous life,
aided by their songs and pipes. The Greek tradition was taken up in classical
Rome by Virgil and revived in the Renaissance, in England by Philip Sidney's
prose romance *The Countess of Pembroke's Arcadia*, and Wroth's own pastoral
romance *The Countess of Montgomery's Urania*, for example. See Adam
Nicholson, *Arcadia: The Dream of Perfection in Renaissance England* (London:
Harper Collins, 2008), 2–3.

Since for another I in love did burn,
To whom I thought I had been held as dear,
But was deceived. When I for him had left   75
My friends and country, was of him bereft
And all, but that you kindly did embrace
And welcome me into this happy place,
Where for your sakes, I meant to keep some sheep,
Not doubting ever to be more deceived.   80
But now alas, I am anew bereaved
Of heart, now time it is myself to keep,
And let flocks go, unless Simeana please
To give consent, and so give me some ease.
Simeana. Why, what have I to do with whom you love?   85
Climeana. Because 'tis he who doth your passion prove.
Simeana. The lesser need I fear the winning of his love,
Since all my faith could never so much move;
Yet can he not so cruel ever be
But he may live my misery to see.   90
Climeana. And when his eyes to love shall open be,
I trust he will turn pity unto me,
And let me have reward, which is my due.
Simeana. Which is your due? What pity's due to you?
Dream you of hope? Oh, you too high aspire.   95
Think you to gain by kindling an old fire?

---

79. meant ... sheep] *PM;* meant to keep [*'to keep' inserted above*] some sheep
~~to keepe~~ *HM.*   80. Not ... deceived] *PM; this line is inserted later in HM.*
86. prove] *PM;* move *HM.*   87. The lesser need I fear] *PM;* The les I fear
HM.   winning] winning *PM;* wining *HM.*   91. be] bee = [*end of page*]
PM.   93. let me] lett me [*'me' inserted above*] *PM.*   95. Oh, you] ô you
HM; O you *PM.*

---

77. *but that*] i.e. were it not that. Climeana is thankful to the shepherd
community for welcoming her as a stranger into their community, as she
would otherwise have been left with nothing when she was deserted by her
lover.
   80. *Not ... deceived*] Not thinking that I would be deceived in love any
more. In *HM* this line was inserted later.
   87–8. *The ... move*] Simeana protests that she has nothing to fear from
Climeana's affection for Lissius, since Lissius has been totally unmoved even
by her longstanding love.
   96. *Think ... fire*] Simeana suggests Climeana will not be successful in
rekindling her former passion and directing it on to a new lover, Lissius.

Climeana. My love will be the surer, when I know
    Not love alone, but how love to bestow.
Simeana. You make him yet, for all this, but to be
    The second in your choice; so was not he   100
    In mine, but first, and last, of all the chief
    That can to me bring sorrow, or relief.
Climeana. This will not win him; you may talk, and hope,
    But in love's passages there is large scope.
Simeana. 'Tis true, and you have scope to change and
      choose,   105
    To take and dislike, like, and soon refuse.
Climeana. My love as firm is to him as is thine.
Simeana. Yet mine did ever rise, never decline;
    No other moved in me the flames of love,
    Yet you dare hope as much as I to move.   110
    Folly indeed is proud, and only vain,
    And you his servant feeds with hope of gain.
Climeana. I love him most!
Simeana.   I love him best! Can you
    Challenge reward, and can not say you're true?
Climeana. In this you wrong me; false I have not been   115
    But changed on cause.
Simeana.   Well, now you hope to win

---

112. And] *PM;* ~~Wch~~ and *HM.*   servant] servant~~s~~-['e' *overwritten*] *HM.*
113. most!] most, *HM;* most: / *PM.*

---

97. *when*] (in this sense) since.
98. *love ... bestow*] Climeana says she will have learned by her former experience. Her distinction between knowing love, and knowing how to bestow or give it, contrasts with the model of love elsewhere in the play as involuntarily inflicted on mortals by Cupid.
104. *love's passages*] transactions in love (*CWD*, 204n.52), with the oblique suggestion of love as a labyrinth.
large scope] As well as indicating Climeana's agency in pursuing her desires, these words may refer to Venus's and Wroth's own freedom to direct the plot.
113. *I ... best*] In the 2018 performance Simeana and Climeana got to their feet and fired these claims forcefully at each other from opposite ends of the backstage rostrum on which the shepherdesses were seated.
116. *changed ... cause*] Climeana indicates that her change of heart is not due to inconstancy but has been caused (presumably) by her abandonment by her first lover.

This second, yet I, like those, lose no time.
But can you think that you can this way climb
To your desires? This shows you love have tried,
And that you can both choose, and choice divide;　　　120
But take your course, and win him if you can,
And I'll proceed in truth, as I began.
Dalina. Fie, what a life is here about fond love!
Never could it in my heart thus much move.
This is the reason men are grown so coy　　　　　125
When they perceive we make their smiles our joy.
Let them alone, and they will seek, and sue,
But yield to them, and they'll with scorn pursue.
Hold awhile off, they'll kneel, and follow you,
And vow, and swear, yet all their oaths untrue.　　　130
Let them once see you coming, then they fly,
But strangely look, and they'll for pity cry.
And let them cry, there is no evil done,
They gain but that which you might else have won.

---

117. lose] *HM*; loose *PM*.　118. climb] clime [*inserted above*] c̶l̶i̶m̶ *PM*.
120. choose] *PM*; chouse ['*u' inserted above*] *HM*.　122. began.] began; /
PM.　123. fond love] *PM*; fond [*letter erased*] love [*overwritten*] *HM*.　128.
and they'll with] *PM*; they will wᵗ *HM*.　129. awhile off] a while of *PM*;
awhile of *HM*.　and] *PM*; nay *HM*.　131. see] [*inserted above*] *PM*.

---

117. *second*] i.e. Lissius, who is her second choice because her first love
rejected her.

120. *both ... divide*] both choose, and separate [your] choice. Simeana
accuses Climeana of having less than complete love for Lissius, since she
had chosen another man before.

123. As in 2.1.173, Dalina uses 'fond' to mean foolish.

125. *coy*] reticent or evasive, resistant to (romantic) advances. Cf. Andrew
Marvell's 'To His Coy Mistress' (in *The Complete Poems*, ed. Elizabeth Story
Dunno (London: Penguin Classics, 2005), 50).

129–34.] In the 2018 performance Dalina (Rachel Winter) got up from
the rostrum and moved downstage right to deliver her advice to members
of the audience. Her lines recast from a female perspective the contemporaneous proverb claiming that 'Woman, like a shadow, flies one following
and pursues one fleeing' (Tilley L518). Cf. 4.1.437–40n.

132. *strangely*] reservedly, from a distance like a stranger.

134. *They ... won*] 'They [the suitors] only gain what you would otherwise
have won' – i.e. the rejection of a lover.

Simeana. Is this your counsel? Why, but now you said   135
     Your folly had your loves and good betrayed,
     And that hereafter you would wiser be
     Than to disdain such as have left you free.
Dalina. 'Tis true, that was the course I meant to take,
     But this must you do, your own ends to make.   140
     I have my fortunes lost; yours do begin,
     And to cross those could be no greater sin.
     I know the world, and hear me, this I advise:
     Rather than too soon won, be too precise;
     Nothing is lost by being careful still,   145
     Nor nothing so soon won as lover's ill.
     Here Lissius comes, alas, he is love-struck,
     He's even now learning love without the book.

[*Enter* LISSIUS.]

Lissius. Love, pardon me, I know I did amiss
     When I thee scorned, or thought thy blame my bliss.   150
     O pity me, alas I pity crave;
     Do not set trophies on my luckless grave.
     Though I, poor slave and ignorant, did scorn

---

138. Than] then *PM, HM.* such as] *HM;* such as [*blotted*] *PM.* free.] free;
= [*end of page*] *PM.* 140. ends] *PM;* ~~good~~ ends [*inserted above*] *HM.* 143. I
advise] I' advise *PM, HM.* 147. he] *PM;* thee *HM.* love-struck] *CWD;*
love strooke *PM, HM.* 148.1. SD.] *CWD.* 149.] *CWD adds* SD [*To
himself*]. Love] *PM, HM.* 151. O] *PM;* Ò *HM.* 152. trophies] *HM;*
Trophes *PM.*

---

135. *but*] just.
136. *your ... good*] i.e. both your lovers and your own good.
139–40. *that ... make*] *that* course (i.e. being more receptive to lovers),
was what I meant to do, but *this* course (i.e. remaining disdainful) is what
you need to do to achieve your goals.
144. *precise*] strict or exacting, with the implication of modest reserve
appropriate for an early modern woman.
146. *ill*] ill fortune.
148. *learning ... book*] Dalina says that Lissius is learning about love by
feeling it himself, rather than knowing it 'by the book' or according to
convention.
149. *Love ... amiss*] These lines are spoken to Cupid rather than to the
shepherdesses, whose presence Lissius does not seem to notice. The actors
playing Lissius in the 1999 production and 2018 productions both delivered
the lines contritely, addressing an imaginary Cupid.

Thy blessèd name, let not my heart be torn
With thus much torture. O but look on me,   155
Take me a faithful servant unto thee.
Climeana. Dear Lissius, my dear Lissius, fly me not;
Let not both scorn and absence be my lot.
Lissius. Pray let me go, you know I can not love;
Do not thus far my patience strive to move.   160
Climeana. Why, cruel Lissius, wilt thou never mend,
But still increase thy frowns for my sad end?
Lissius. Climeana, 'tis enough that I have said
Be gone, and leave me; is this for a maid
To follow, and to haunt me thus? You blame   165
Me for disdain but see not your own shame.
Fie, I do blush for you – a woman woo?
The most unfitting'st, shamefull'st thing to do.
Climeana. Unfit and shameful, aye indeed 'tis true,
Since suit is made to hard, relentless you.   170

155. thus] *HM;* [*inserted above*] *PM.*   O] *PM;* ô *HM.*   156. unto thee.] unto
thee; / *PM;* now to thee, *HM.*   168. unfitting'st, shamefull'st] *PM;* unfittest, shamfullst *HM.*   169. aye indeed] I indeed *PM, HM;* I? indeed *CWD.*

166–8. *shame ... do*] Lissius's condemnation of female wooing is more
vehement than Silvesta's earlier comments on it being unseemly for women
to take the lead in professing love (3.1.79). Cf. the lady from the court of
Lycia in *Urania II*, who excuses her blindness to convention and 'spirit of
being so bold' to Philarchos as the work of Cupid: 'alas into his false fetters
I fell, and so forgot all modesty a maid should have in speaking my love'
(128.8–14).

168. *unfitting'st*] In *HM* 'unfittest' makes the line scan, but the extra syllable and quirky rhythm in *PM* aptly expresses Lissius's shock that Climeana
is engaging in such transgressive behaviour, and so has been retained in this
edition.

169. *aye*] spelt 'I' in *PM*. This spelling of 'aye' as an affirmative is found
again at 4.1.442 and, for example, in Sonnet 8 of Michael Drayton's *Idea* in
*The Barons' Wars in the Reign of Edward the Second with England's Heroical
Epistles* (London: J. Roberts for N. Ling, 1603): 'Nothing but no and I, and
I and no' (sig. FIV). An alternative punctuation of the line that follows
CWD's reading ('Unfit and shameful, I? Indeed 'tis true') was used in the
1999 and 2018 performances. In the 2018 performance Nadia Shash played
Climeana as deeply upset by Lissius's words, skilfully changing the mood
from spectators' laughs at lines 166–8.

170. *suit ... you*] Climeana's retort here resembles Helena in *A Midsummer
Night's Dream*: 'Your wrongs do set a scandal on my sex / We cannot fight
for love as men may do / We should be wooed and were not made to woo'
(2.1.240–2).

Well, I will leave you, and restore the wrong
I suffer for my loving you so long.
No more shall my words trouble you, nor I
E'er follow more, if not to see me die.   *Exit.*

Lissius. Farewell, you now do right. [*Aside*] This is the way   175
To win my wish, for when I all neglect
That seek me, she must needs something respect
My love the more; and what though she should say
I once denied her, yet my true-felt pain
Must needs from her soft breast some favour gain.   180

Dalina. Lissius is taken; well said, Cupid, now
You partly have performed your taken vow.
Of all our shepherds, I ne'er thought that he
Would of thy foolish troop a follower be,
But this it is a goddess to despise,   185
And thwart a wayward boy that wants his eyes.

---

172. so] *PM;* too *HM.*   175. Farewell] [*blotted but visible*] *PM.*   SD.] *This ed.*   177. something] *PM;* [*inserted above*] *HM.*   179. true-felt] *CWD;* true felt *PM, HM.*   185. goddess] *HM;* Goddess *PM.*   186. that] *PM;* who *HM.*

173–4. *No … die*] Obscure because Climeana (the speaker) changes the subject of the sentence from Lissius to herself and back again. She may mean 'You will not be troubled any more by my words [of love], nor will I trouble you by following you any more, unless you come to see me die.'

177. *she*] i.e. Simeana.

178. *what though*] even if.

181. *taken*] shot or captured by Cupid. Cf. *OED,* v1b: 'to seize or hold a person as a captive or prisoner'.

181–2. *Cupid … vow*] It is unclear how Dalina, worldly wise though she is, knows about Cupid's promise to take care of Lissius's indifference to love (1.4.13–16 and 1.4.27). If the same actor plays the roles of both Venus and Dalina the doubling would add resonance to the lines (although in performance a means would have to be found for the actor to change role between 1.3 and 1.4, and back again for 2.1). Pamphilia tells the 'merry Marquess' (a possible equivalent for Dalina in *Urania II*) that she 'can not but imagine the Goddess of Love is transformed and is your self, else could never such a happiness have arrived here' (280.27–8, 40–2).

185–6. *goddess … boy*] Dalina refers to Venus and Cupid. In production, there is an opportunity to direct spectators' gaze to them and see their satisfaction if they are surveying events from above. Lines 175–88 were cut in the 1999 performance, but in 2018 Dalina raised her eyes to the gallery above to address Venus and Cupid.

186. *wants*] lacks.

Come, let's not trouble him, he is distressed
Enough, he need not be with us oppressed.
Simeana. I'll stay, and ask him who 'tis he doth love.
Dalina. Do not a pensive heart to passion move.   190
Simeana. To passion? Would I could his passion find
   To answer my desire, and grievèd mind.
Dalina. Stay then, and try him, and your fortune try;
   It may be he loves you. [*To* FILLIS] Come, let's go by.
                                       Exeunt.

Lissius. O sweet Simeana, look but on my pain;   195
   I grieve, and curse myself for my disdain.
   Now but have pity, love doth make me serve,
   And for your wrong and you I will reserve
   My life to pay, your love but to deserve,
   And for your sake I do myself preserve.   200
Simeana. Preserve it not for me; I seek not now,
   Nor can I credit this or any vow
   Which you shall make. I was too long despised
   To be deceived. No, I will be advised
   By reason now; my love shall no more blind   205
   Me, nor make me believe more than I find.
Lissius. Believe but that, and I shall have the end
   Of all my pain, and wishes. I pretend
   A virtuous love; then grant me my desire,
   Who now do waste in true and faithful fire.   210

---

188. need] *PM;* neede [*inserted above*] *HM.*   189. SP. *Simeana*] Si: = [*end of page*] *PM.*   192. desire] *PM;* distressed *HM.*   194. SD.] *This ed.*   194.1. SD.] ex: *PM; not in HM; Exeunt* [DALINA *and* PHILLIS.] *CWD.*   195. O] *PM;* Ô *HM.*   200. myself] *CWD;* my self *PM;* my lyfe *HM.*   205. reason ... love] reason now, my love *PM;* my owne reason, love *HM.*   210. fire] fire: / *PM.*

---

187. *him*] i.e. Lissius.

194. *go by*] walk on, from the phrasal verb 'to go by', meaning to move, walk, or travel past.

198-9. *And ... deserve*] i.e. 'And I will give up my life to pay you for the wrong you suffered, just to deserve your love'.

205 6. *blind ... find*] drawing on the conventional image of Cupid (now unmasked in the world of the play), and the common associations between love and blindness (e.g. *PA*, Sonnets 33, 106, and *MND* 1.1.234–5).

208. *pretend*] profess.

Simeana. How can I this believe?
Lissius.   My faith shall tell
    That in true love I will all else excel;
    But then will you love me as I do you?
Simeana. I promise may, for you can not be true.
Lissius. Then you will promise break.
Simeana.   Not if I find   215
    That as your words are, so you'll make your mind.
Lissius. Let me nor speech, nor mind have when that I
    In this or any else do falsify
    My faith, and love to you.
Simeana.   Then be at rest,
    And of my true affection be possessed.   220
Lissius. So, dear Simeana, be of me and mine;
    Now do my hopes and joys together shine.
Simeana. Nor let the least cloud rise to dim this light,
    Which love makes to appear with true delight.
                                        [*Exeunt.*]

                    [ACT 3 SCENE 4]

        [*Enter*] VENUS *and* CUPID [*speaking from the clouds*]

Cupid. Is not this pretty? Who doth free remain
    Of all this flock that waits not in our train?

224. delight. *Exeunt.*] delight; / [*flourish below*] *PM;* delight; / ex [*flourish below*] *HM.*

0.0. [ACT 3 SCENE 4]] *This ed.;* Scene iii *CWD;* ~~The 4 Act~~ SP Venus; / [*blank sheet*] *HM.* 0.1. SD.] *This ed.;* Venus, and Cupid; *PM;* [*Enter*] VENUS *and* CUPID. *CWD.*

---

214. Simeana wittily suggests that she can promise that she will love Lissius as much as he loves her, since she does not believe he loves her at all.

0.1. SD.] It is not clear whether Venus and Cupid are speaking from the Temple (as in 1.1. and 2.3) or from the clouds above (as in 1.4), but, since they are commenting on the action and the Priests are not listed, the latter seems more likely.
    1. *pretty*] Cf. 'The wanton child, how he can fain his fire / So prettily, as none sees his disguise!' (Wroth *Poems*, 120).
    2. *train*] retinue, group of attendants. Cf. 'Love's band' (1.2.161) and Love's 'foolish troop' (3.3.184).

Will you have yet more sorrow? Yet more woe?
Shall I another bitter arrow throw?
Speak if you will, my hand now knows the way
To make all hearts your sacred power obey.
Venus. 'Tis pretty, but 'tis not enough. Some are
　　Too slightly wounded; they had greater share
　　In scorning us. Lissius too soon is blessed,
　　And with too little pain hath got his rest;
　　Scarce had he learned to sigh before he gained,
　　Nor shed a tear ere he his hopes obtained.
　　This easy winning breeds us more neglect;
　　Without much pain, few do Love's joys respect.
　　Then are they sweetest purchased with felt grief,
　　To floods of woe sweet looks gives full relief.
　　A world of sorrow is eased with one smile,
　　And heart-wounds cured when kind words rule, the
　　　　while
　　That foregone wailings in forgotten thought
　　Shall wasted lie, disdained, once dearly bought.
　　One gentle speech more heals a bleeding wound
　　Than balms of pleasure, if from other ground.
　　Strike then to favour him, and let him gain
　　His love and bliss by Love's sweet pleasing pain.

5

10

15

20

---

13. winning] wining *PM*.　14. Love's] *This ed.;* lovs *PM*　19. thought]
thoughts *PM*.　22. balms] baulms *PM;* baulins *R;* bawlings *CWD*.　24.
Love's] *PM*.

---

13. *breeds … neglect*] encourages more mortals to neglect us.

15. *they*] i.e. Love's joys.

18–19. *the … That*] i.e. while.

19. *foregone*] former, with implications of 'forgo', to give up.

22. *balms*] Soothing ointments for healing wounds. Spelt 'baulms' and
somewhat difficult to decipher in *PM* (this scene is missing in *HM*), this
word has been transcribed as 'baulins' (*R*) and 'bawlings' (*CWD*), to indicate
a sound of pleasure. The editors thank Gavin Alexander for the reading used
here. Wroth follows the archaic spelling from Middle English, still common
in early modern use and carrying religious connotations (*OED*, n.1–6). She
uses 'baulmes' in *Urania II*, where wounded knights quickly recover 'having
such Baulmes' as the attentions of noble ladies to cheer them (91.26) and
later in the story of the King of Norway and Queen of Denmark where rescue
by the knight Faire Design is 'the onely pretious baulme' that can heal the
wounds of the prisoners (326.36–8).

Cupid. That shall be done, nor had he this delight 25
 Bestowed but for his greater harm, and spite.
 You shall before this Act be ended see
 He doth sufficiently taste misery.
 'Tis far more grief from joy to be down thrown
 Than joy to be advanced to pleasure's throne. 30
Venus. Let me see that, and I contented am;
 Such gracious favour would but get thy shame.
Cupid. He and others yet shall taste
 Such distress as shall lay waste
 All their hopes, their joys, and lives; 35
 By such loss our glory thrives.
 Fear not then, all hearts must yield
 When our forces come to field. *[Exeunt.]*

25. delight] delight = [*end of page*] *PM.* 29. down thrown] downe [*inserted above*] throwne *PM.* 30. throne] throwane *PM.* 38. field] field; [*S fermé*] [*flourish below*] *PM.* SD.] *CWD*

27. *this Act*] A reference to the forthcoming Act 4, in which Lissius will taste misery as Simeana rejects him. Cupid's labelling of it as '*this* Act' points to the liminal nature of Cupid and Venus as the play's prophetic chorus, whose supernatural commentary prefigures the events on stage as well as demonstrating their control of the future.

32. *Such … shame*] i.e. showing such gracious favour to the lovers (by sparing them pain) would only multiply your shame, 'get' being used in the sense of 'beget'.

35. *All … lives*] Cf. Pamphilia's jealousy over losing Amphilanthus: 'what torments will that prove, when I shall with him see his hopes, his joys, and content come from another?' (*Urania I*, 92.10–11). See also the shepherd's lament in Lycenia's long pastoral poem in *Urania I*: 'For life, and joy, and ease, and all / Alas lies in your hands' (621.25–6, *Poems*, 190).

38. *field*] i.e. the battlefield.

Act 4

[ACT 4 SCENE I]

[*The woods*]

[*Enter* MUSELLA *and* PHILISSES, *who does not see her.*]

Musella. [*Aside*] This is the place Silvesta 'pointed me
To meet my joy, my sole felicity.
And here Philisses is; ay me, this shows
The wounds by Love given are no childish blows.
Philisses. You blessèd woods into whose secret guard   5

0.0. ACT 4 SCENE I]] *CWD;* The Forth Act, *PM;* The 4 Acte; [*underlined*]
HM. 0.1. SD.] *This ed.* 0.2. SD.] *This ed.;* [*Enter* MUSELLA] *CWD.*
I. SD.] This ed. 3. ay me] *PM;* (ay mee) *HM.* 4. Love] *CWD;* love
PM, HM. CWD adds SD [*Enter* PHILISSES, MUSELLA *hides*] *after this line.*

0.0.] In *HM* folio 15r is headed 'The 4 Act' along with the first three
letters of the first speech heading 'Mus'. These are then erased and a speech
heading 'Venus: /' is written but the rest of the page is blank (the interlude
called Act 3 Scene 4 in this edition is missing from *HM*). The heading 'The
4 Acte;' appears on the next page in *HM* (fol. 15v).
    0.1. SD.] This scene is set in the same place as Act 3 Scene I, amidst the
trees to which Philisses addresses his first eighteen lines.
    0.2. SD.] Musella enters and either stands aside or conceals herself to
overhear Philisses, who enters immediately afterwards.
    I. *This ... place*] Musella's opening lines offer an opportunity to engage
spectators as fellow eavesdroppers on Philisses. In the 2014 staged reading
and the 2018 performance she addressed the audience and then concealed
herself amongst them in the Baron's Hall. In 1999 Musella hid behind a
screen decorated with leaves at upper stage left, having spoken the lines.
    'pointed] appointed.
    4. *no ... blows*] i.e. the wounds are serious, even though Cupid is a child.
    5. *You ... woods*] *CWD* (204n.2) points out that Philisses's address resem-
bles that of Dicus to the trees in Philip Sidney's *Arcadia* (IV.775–7) and
Urania's first sonnet (*Urania I*, 1–2). In the 2018 production Philisses
addressed spectators as the trees, springs and echoes, giving individuals
copies of love poems through lines 5–18, and pointing at an individual spectator on 'dear secrets utter' (13).
    guard] keeping, protection.

I venture dare my inward wounding smart,
And to you dare impart the crosses hard
Which harbour in my love-destroyèd heart,
To you, and but to you I durst disclose
These flames, these pains, these griefs which I do find,   10
For your true hearts so constant are to those
Who trust in you, as you'll not change your mind.
No echo shrill shall your dear secrets utter,
Or wrong your silence with a blabbing tongue;
Nor will your springs against your private mutter,   15
Or think that counsel-keeping is a wrong.
Then since woods, springs, echoes, and all are true,

---

13. echo] Echo *PM, HM*.   17. echoes] Echoes *PM;* echoses *HM*.

6. *I ... dare*] I dare to risk.
smart] pain (i.e. of love). Cf. 1.3.19n.
9. *durst*] dare to.
11. *hearts*] Philisses addresses the 'hearts' of the trees, and by extension those of the audience.
13. *echo*] Echo is upper-case in both *PM* and *HM*, suggesting that Wroth alludes here to the mythological figure Echo, who appears in Ovid's *Metamorphoses* (III, 443–500). Echo was a nymph whose lengthy conversations distracted Juno from catching Zeus with his paramours, and whom Juno punished by rendering her unable to speak except in reply to others. More pertinently to Philisses's situation, Echo falls in love with Narcissus but cannot speak her love, which remains unrequited. Cf. Philisides' eclogue to Echo in Sidney's *Arcadia* (II.427–9) and the shepherd's lament (IV.776), and Wroth's Philarchos who recounts hearing a song 'so curiously set and cunningly sung as if Echo her self had borne a part in it' (*Urania II*, 121.33–4).
15. *private*] i.e. privacy. Cf. *TN* 'Let me enjoy my private' (2.5.88).
16. *Or ... wrong*] Or think that it is wrong to keep your secrets. *CWD* identifies an oblique reference to whispering the secret of Midas's asses' ears to the waters of a marsh, found in Ovid's *Metamorphoses* and Chaucer's retelling in the *Wife of Bath's Tale* (*CWD*, 204n.7). In Ovid it is Midas's barber who tells the earth Midas's secret and buries his words, only to be betrayed by the quivering reeds that grow up in the spot and spread the news (*Meta.*, XI, 204–16); Chaucer retells this as Midas's wife confiding her 'conseil' to the waters of the marsh (Chaucer, *Wife of Bath's Tale*, in *The Complete Works of Geoffrey Chaucer*, ed. F.N. Robinson, second Edition (Oxford: Oxford University Press, 1957), 84–9 (965–82).

My long-hid love I'll tell, show, write in you.
Alas, Musella, cruel shepherdess
Who takes no pity on me in distress;   20
For all my passions, plaints, and all my woes,
I am so far from gain, as outward shows
I never had could feed least hope to spring,
Or any while least comfort to me bring.
Yet pardon me, dear mistress of my soul,   25
I do recall my words, my tongue control.
For wronging thee, accuse my poor starved heart,
Which withered is with love's all-killing smart,
Since truly I must say I can not blame
Thee, nor accuse thee with a scorner's name.   30
No, no, alas, my pains thou dost not know,
Nor dare I, wretch, my torments to thee show.

---

18. long-hid love] ·long hid love *PM;* long felt woes *HM.*   you.] you; / *PM,*
HM.   25. mistress] M^rs *PM;* m^rs *HM;* Mistress *R.*   30. accuse] *PM;* con-
demne *HM.*   31. alas] *PM;* (alas) *HM.*   32. my torments to thee] *PM;*
to thee my torments *HM.*

---

18. *write ... you*] Philisses refers to the fashion of carving tributes or
expressions of love into the bark of trees, as Musidorus and Pamela do in
Arcadia (III.650–1), as Pamphilia does in *Urania I* (92–3), or as Orlando
does in *As You Like It* (3.2.240). This could also be an oblique reference to
the Sidney family tradition of writing love poetry, something that Wroth
alludes to in *Urania II*, where Lamprino – troubled 'with the catching disease
of love' – wanders in the forest with 'some and many papers in his hand,
and more appearing at his pockets', and is overheard by Parselius who is
hiding in 'a queach' or thicket 'of bushes' (207.14–20). For further discussion
see Introduction, 9. In the 1999 performance Philisses sat down on the bank
stage right, took out a notebook and pencil, and wrote as he spoke 19–23.
   21. *plaints*] complaints.
   22–4. *I ... bring*] There is no punctuation at the end of 22 in *PM* (or
HM); Philisses's lines could accordingly be glossed 'I never had any outward
sign that would feed the least hope to spring up, or give me the least comfort
at any time'.
   25. Philisses continues to address the absent (as he thinks) Musella in
25–40; this passage was cut in the 1999 production.
   28. *withered*] Philisses's verb identifies him even more closely with the
trees. Cf. Polarchus in *Urania I* who 'stood like a blasted tree, the blossom
of his affection killed and withered' (343.15–16) and 'withered me' in Robert
Sidney's Song 13 (RS *Poems*, 265).

Why did I wrong thee then, who all must serve?
And happy he by thee thought to deserve,
Who heaven hath framed to make us here below   35
Discern they strive all worth in thee to show;
And doth these valleys and these meads disgrace
When thou art present with excelling grace,
As now, who at this time doth show more bright
Than fair Aurora, when she lends best light.   40
Oh, that I might but now have heart to speak,
And say I love, though after heart did break.
Musella. [*Aside*] I fain would comfort him, and yet I do not
    know
Whether from me 'twill comfort be or no,
Since causeless jealousy hath so possessed   45
His heart as no belief of me can rest.
But why stay I? I came to give relief;

---

35. below] *HM;* bolowe *PM.*   36. Discern] deserne *PM, HM;* Deserve *R.*
40. Than] then *PM, HM.*   41. Oh] O *PM, HM.*   43. SD.] *CWD.*   do
not know] *PM;* know *HM.*   44. Whether] *PM;* ~~nott~~ [*indecipherable word
deleted*] nott if [*inserted above*] *HM.*   47. But] *PM;* yett *HM.*

35–6. *Who ... show*] Whom heaven has created to make earthly mortals
perceive divine beauty, and they [i.e. the gods in heaven] strive to show this
in you [i.e. Musella]. Philisses repeats the courtly love trope he used in
3.2.7–8.

37. *doth ... disgrace*] It is somewhat unclear who the subject of this verb
is. Most likely it is Musella, whose beauty outshines that of the valleys and
meads or meadows (cf. 1.2.1) and so disgraces or puts them to shame by
eclipsing their beauty. *OED* (v.2a) quotes Robert Greene's *Arcadia or
Menaphon* (1616): 'Flora seeing her face, bids all her glorious flowers close
themselves, as being by her beauty disgraced' (sig. C4).

40. *Aurora*] the goddess of the dawn in classical myth.

41. *but*] even.

42. *break.*] In the 1999 production at the end of his speech Philisses
scribbled out what he had written. In 2018 Philisses lay down at the back of
the stage, read and crumpled up pages of his verses, and threw them over
his head while Musella spoke to spectators downstage.

43. This is a 12-syllable line in *PM*. In *HM* 'do not' has been omitted to
read 'yett I know' to make the line scan better, and 'nott if' replaces *PM*'s
'whether' in 44.

46. *of me*] in me (i.e. in my love or in what I say).

47. *But ... I*] In performance, Musella's questions (47–9) offer the actor an
opportunity for interaction with spectators, especially if she is sitting amongst
them to watch and listen as Nichole Bird was in the 2018 performance.

Should I then doubt? No, I may ease his grief,
And help will seek. None should one's good neglect,
Much more his bliss who for me joys reject.   50

[MUSELLA *approaches*.]

How now Philisses, why do you thus grieve?
Speak, is there none that can your pains relieve?
Philisses. Yes, fair Musella, but such is my state,
    Relief must come from her who can but hate.
    What hope may I, wretch, have least good to move   55
    Where scorn doth grow for me, for others love?
Musella. But are you sure she doth your love disdain?
    It may be for your love she feels like pain.
Philisses. Like pain for me? I would not crave so much;
    I wish no more but that love might her touch   60
    And that she might discern by love to know
    That kind respect is fit for her to show.
Musella. Sure this she knows.
Philisses.   Prove it, and I may live.
Musella. Tell me who 'tis you love, and I will give
    My word I'll win her if she may be won.   65
Philisses. Ay me, that doubt in me made me first run
    Into this labyrinth of woe and care,

50.1. SD.] *This ed.;* [*She comes forward.*] *CWD.*   55. may] *PM;* can *HM.*
62. respect] *PM;* reguard *HM.*   66. Ay me] *PM;* ây mee *HM.*

---

49. *help ... seek*] i.e. seek to provide help for Philisses; cf. Musella's advice
to Philisses in 1.3.18.

50. *for ... reject*] for [love of] me rejects happiness.

SD.] The actor could emerge from a corner of the stage, as in the 1999
production when she entered from behind a screen, or from amidst the
audience, as in the 2014 staged reading and the 2018 production.

55–6. *What ... love*] i.e. 'What hope might I, wretch, have of doing myself
any good [with Musella], where her scorn for me, and love for others,
grows?'

58. *like*] similar.

67. *labyrinth*] A typical trope for the perplexed courtly lover's emotional
journey, often deployed by Wroth. Roberts (Wroth *Poems*, 128n.) observes
that Petrarch uses this metaphor, and the English poet Thomas Watson
refers to the 'doubtful labyrinth of love' in *The Hekatompathia or Passionate
Century of Love Divided into Two Parts* (London: John Wolfe, 1582), explaining its origin in the myth of Ariadne rescuing Theseus from the Minotaur's

Which makes me thus to wed mine own despair.
Musella. But have you made it known to her you love
    That for her scorn you do these torments prove?   70
Philisses. Yes, now I have, and yet to ease some pain
    I'll plainlier speak, though my own end I gain.
    And so to end, it were to me a bliss;
    Then know, for your dear sake my sorrow is.
    It may be you will hate me, yet I have   75
    By this some ease, though with it come my grave.
    Yet dear Musella, since for you I pine,
    And suffer welcome death, let favour shine
    Thus far, that though my love you do neglect,
    Yet sorry be I died; with this respect   80
    I shall be satisfied, and so content
    As I shall deem my life so lost well spent.
Musella. Sorry! Alas Philisses, can it be
    But I should grieve and mourn, nay die for thee?
    Yet tell me, why did you thus hide your love?   85
    And suffer wrong conceits thus much to move?
    Now 'tis almost too late your wish to gain,
    Yet you shall pity for your love obtain.

---

78. death] *PM;* paine *HM.*   83. Sorry! ... Philisses] Sory, alas Philisses *PM;* Sory (alas Philisses) *HM.*   88. for your] *PM;* ~~and my~~ for your [*inserted above*] *HM.*

---

labyrinth (M4v). Urania and her companions are said to travel 'as in a labyrinth without a thread' towards the palace of Love on Cyprus (*Urania I*, 47.31–2). Wroth uses it to open and close her 'Crown of Sonnets Dedicated to Love' with the line 'In this strange labyrinth how shall I turn?' (*Poems*, 127 and 134), and the Lady of Cyprus, who is subject to the power of both Cupid and Venus in *Urania II*, asks Pamphilia 'In this strange labyrinth, help and aid poor afflicted me' (416.34).

   71. *now ... have*] i.e. by speaking of his love in Musella's presence. In the following line he must 'plainlier speak' directly *to* Musella, to tell her it is she that he loves.

   72–3. *my ... end*] In another convention of courtly love, Philisses imagines his death as a result of Musella's rejection. Cf. 76 below.

   76. *grave*] On Philisses's use of the Petrarchan trope of dying for love here and in 80–2 see Introduction, 14.

   83–4. *can ... thee*] How else could it be, but that I would grieve and mourn, even die for you?

   86. *conceits*] conceptions.

   87. *too late*] Musella's comment here and below in 98–100 may derive from her knowledge of the threat posed to their relationship by Rustic.

Philisses. Pity, when helpless 'tis, is endless given.
    Am I to this unhappy bondage driven?   90
    Yet truly pity, and 'twill be some ease
    Unto my grief, though all things else displease.
    But do not yet, unless you can affect,
    For forcèd pity's worse than is neglect,
    And to be pitied but for pity's sake   95
    And not for love, do never pity take.
Musella. Well then, I love you, and so ever must,
    Though time and fortune should be still unjust:
    For we may love, and both may constant prove
    But not enjoy, unless ordained above.   100
Philisses. Dost thou love me? O dear Musella, say,
    And say it still to kill my late dismay.
Musella. More than myself, or love myself for thee
    The better much; but wilt thou love like me?
Philisses. My only life, here do I vow to die   105
    When I prove false, or show inconstancy.
Musella. All true content may this to both procure.
Philisses. And when I break, may I all shame endure.
Musella. Nor doubt you me, nor my true heart mistrust,
    For die I will before I prove unjust.   110
    But here comes Rustic, whose encumbered brain

---

92. things else] *PM;* els doe *HM.*   94. than] then *PM, HM.*   95. pity's]
PM; pitty *HM.*   sake] sake *catchword* 'and =' *HM.*   97. SP. *Musella*] Mu:
= [*end of page*] *PM.*   98. and] *PM;* or *HM.*   fortune] *PM;* Fortune *HM.*
101. O] *PM;* o *HM.*   106. inconstancy] *HM;* unconstancie *PM.*   108. may
I] *PM;* lett mee *HM.*

91–6.] For pity being allied to love, but distinct from it, see Shakespeare
TN 3.1.114–16.
    98–100. *time ... above*] See 87n. Fortune has a capital letter in *HM,* refer-
ring back to the goddess discussed in 2.1.185–90.
    103–4. *More ... me*] i.e. I love you more than I love myself, or love myself
much better for your sake; but will you likewise love me?
    111. *here ... Rustic*] There is no stage direction for Rustic's entrance in
either manuscript, so precisely when the actor comes on stage and how much
of Philisses and Musella's courtship he sees is open for interpretation in
performance. In the 2014 staged reading Rustic entered stage right, saw
Musella and Philisses and exited quickly; in 2018 he called Musella's name
from offstage. Alternatively, this line could be a cue for the actor to make a
long entrance, watch some or all of Philisses's and Musella's dialogue in the

With love and jealousy must our loss gain,
For since he hopes, nay says that I am his,
I can not absent be but he'll me miss;
But when that is, let day no longer shine,   115
Or I have life, if live not truly thine.
But now, lest that our love should be found out,
Let's seek all means to keep him from this doubt,
And let none know it but your sister dear,
Whose company I keep; so hold all clear.   120
Then let him watch, and keep what he can get;
His plots must want their force our joys to let.
I'll step aside awhile till you do meet
This welcome man, whose absence were more sweet.
For though that he (poor thing) can little find   125
Yet I shall blush with knowing my own mind.

---

120. clear.] clear, = [*end of page*] *PM.*   121. can] h̶a̶t̶h̶ can [*inserted above*]
PM.   123. aside awhile] *PM;* awhile aside *HM.*   125. (poor thing)] *PM;*
pour thing *HM.*

---

intervening thirty lines with suspicion, and then exit hurriedly at line 141
(perhaps to report Musella's conduct to her mother). This would then be
the prompt for the message Musella receives from her mother at the end of
the scene.

    encumbered brain] burdened or obstructed mind (*OED*, adj. 3, 6 and 7).
As well as reflecting the idea of Rustic being troubled or preoccupied with
jealousy, Musella's use of the word may also be a reference to the character's
limited intellect, which extends to his inability to perceive Musella's lack of
love for him, and possibly the sense of being encumbered or entrapped that
she feels.

    112. *our ... gain*] bring about our loss (of each other).

    115. *when ... is*] i.e. the day when Musella is Rustic's.

    116. *I ... thine*] Musella tells Philisses she no longer wants to live if she
cannot be his, a vow which looks forward to 5.1.85–6.

    117. *lest that*] in case, for fear that.

    118. *doubt*] suspicion (i.e. about Musella and Philisses's love).

    120. *hold ... clear*] keep everything free from suspicion.

    122. *let*] stop, prevent.

    124. *welcome man*] probably sarcastic given that Musella completes the
line by saying 'whose absence were more sweet', though such sarcasm seems
uncharacteristic in comparison with Musella's conduct elsewhere in the play.

    126–34.] On the female blush as an ambiguous sign of both innocence
and guilt cf. *Oth.* 1.3.95–6 and *MAdo* 4.1.36–41. See also Danielle Clarke,
'The Iconography of the Blush: Marian Literature of the 1630s', in *Voicing
Women: Gender and Sexuality in Early Modern Writing*, ed. Kate Chegdzoy,
Melanie Hansen and Suzanne Trill (Keele: Keele University Press, 1996),
119–20.

Fear and desire, still to conceal it hid,
Will blushing show it when 'tis most forbid.
Philisses. None can have power against a powerful love,
Nor keep the blood but in the cheeks 'twill move.   130
But not for fear or care it there doth show,
But kind desire makes you blushing know
That joy takes place, and in your face doth climb
With leaping heart like lambkins in the prime.
But sweet Musella, since you will away,   135
Take now my heart, and let yours in me stay.

                                        Exit MUSELLA.

Could I express the joy I now conceive,
I were unworthy such bliss to receive;
But so much am I thine as life and joy
Are in thy hands to nurse, or to destroy.   140

                        [*Enter* RUSTIC.]

How now Rustic? Whither away so fast?
Rustic. To seek Musella.
Philisses.   Now that labour's past.

---

127. conceal] *PM;* keepe *HM.*   128. Will] wᵗʰ will [*inserted above*] *HM.*
129. a] *PM;* [*inserted above*] *HM.*   136. stay.] stay;/ *PM.*   SD.] *CWD;*Mu:
ex: *PM, HM.*   138. such bliss] *PM;* soe much *HM.*   140.1. SD.] *CWD.*

134. *lambkins*] young lambs. A term used frequently in pastoral, and in
the Sidney circle, as in Philip Sidney's *Arcadia* (III.709) or Abraham
Fraunce's *The Third Part of the Countess of Pembroke's Ivychurch* (1592) where
Polyphemus boasts to Galathea 'how many lambkins / And young kids I do
keep' (Fraunce, 19r, F1). *CWD* points out that Philisses's simile is 'a sly
parody of Rustic's clumsy use of pastoral language' (205n.25).
    prime] a word with a number of possible meanings; possibly 'spring', 'the
prime of their lives' or (as *CWD* suggests, 205n.5) 'the morning'.
    140. *nurse*] nurture. Cf. Sonnet 7 of Wroth's 'Crown of Sonnets'
(*Poems*, 131).
    SD.] This is the latest point at which the actor playing Rustic could enter,
though, as noted above, Musella may cue a much earlier entrance at 111. If
so, then Philisses's belated acknowledgement 'How now Rustic?' adds insult
to the injury of vowing love to Musella while Rustic watches. Philisses's line
suggests that Rustic begins to exit immediately until prevented by the next
line announcing Musella's entrance.
    142. *now ... past*] now that task is over.

See where she comes.

> [*Re-enter* MUSELLA.]

Musella.   Rustic, where were you?
 I sought, but could not find you.
Rustic.   Is that true?
 Faith I was but (the truth to you to tell),   145
 Marking some cattle, and asleep I fell.
Musella. And I was seeking of a long-lost lamb,
 Which now I found even as along you came.
Rustic. I'm glad you found it.
Musella.   Truly, so am I.
Rustic. Now let us go to find our company.   150
Philisses. See where some be.
Musella.   It seems too soon, alas,
 That love despised should come to such a pass.

> [*Enter* LISSIUS *and* SIMEANA.]

Lissius. [*Sings.*]
 Love's beginning, like the spring,
 Gives delight in sweetness flowing;

---

143. SD.] *This ed.;* [*Returning*] *CWD.* 144. could ... you] *PM;* could nott
['*nott*' *inserted above*] find: you ['*you*' *inserted above*] *HM.* Is that] is y^t *PM;*
~~and~~ is that *HM.* 145. (the ... tell)] *PM;* the ... tell *HM.* 147. lamb] lambe
= [*end of page*] *PM.* 152. pass] pas. / *PM.* 152.1. SD.] *CWD;* Lissius
[*centred*] Simeana. [*far right of page*] *PM;* Li: [*centred*] : Simeana : [*far right
of page*] *HM.* 153. SD.] *This ed.;* LISSIUS [*and*] SIMEANA [*singing*] *CWD.*

---

146. *Marking*] watching over, but with a second, literal sense of 'marking'
the cattle with red ochre to signify ownership. Cf. 1.3.68n.
 147. *long-lost lamb*] Musella's use of the metaphor of the lost lamb for
Philisses – which is based on the Biblical parable of the lost sheep (Luke
15:1–8) – contrasts strikingly with Rustic's material concern for his animals.
The shepherd of Wroth's narrative song in *Urania I* also falls in love with
a maiden he finds when he is looking for a lost lamb (*Urania I*, 614–15,
Poems, 183).
 152. *despised*] Musella seems to refer to Lissius's current predicament of
being despised by the jealous Simeana. Musella's line cues their entrance,
and foreshadows the discord between them, which may be demonstrated by
movement and gesture, even before Lissius starts to sing.
 153. SP and SD.] In both *PM* and *HM* Lissius's speech heading is
centred above the song with Simeana's speech heading appearing on the
right-hand side, perhaps suggesting that he sings the song alone while she

> Ever pleasant, flourishing,   155
> Pride in her brave colours showing.
> But love ending is at last
> Like the storms of winter's blast.

Musella. Lissius, methinks you are grown sad of late,
And privately with your own thoughts debate.   160
I hope you are not fallen in love; that boy
Can not, I trust, your settled heart enjoy.
Lissius. 'Tis well, you may be merry at my fall;
Rejoice, nay do, for I can lose but all.
Simeana. And so too much.   Exit.
Musella.   Sure, some strange error is.   165

---

165. SD.] *This ed.; ex.* [*mid line*] *PM, HM.*

stands by silently, an idea we have followed in this edition. An alternative
interpretation – that they both sing (following *CWD*'s SD) – was enacted in
the 1999 and 2018 performances. Since Lissius and Simeana have had a
disagreement, the positioning of the speech headings on the page may
suggest a physical distance between them on stage or aid a reader's visualiza-
tion of an imagined performance.

153–8.] Lissius's song demonstrates a marked change of outlook from his
hymning of '*joyful pleasant spring*' in 1.2.37–42 and 47–52. The pattern of
decline in the verse contrasts with Simeana's lines on hope rising like
'spring's young bud' from 'love thought dead' (3.3.41–2). On Wroth's use
of the seasons to reflect changes in romantic fortunes see, for example,
Fillis's fortune (below 425–30) and *Urania I*, where Leandrus's 'spring-time
joy, was turned to winter-grief' because Pamphilia did not return his love
(215.25–6). Pamphilia is transformed with joy 'like spring time in her face'
when she sees Amphilanthus, having been 'pale and Winter-like with sorrow'
beforehand (442.23–4). For Wroth's seasonal imagery as part of a family and
pastoral poetic tradition, see Introduction, 9.

156. brave colours] The colours of the spring leaves and flowers; *CWD*
suggests that this is also a reference to a military or naval ensign (205n.29).

161. *boy*] i.e. Cupid.

162. *settled*] undisturbed, fixed (i.e. against love).

164. *And ... much*] The precise meaning of this line is unclear. It is the
first verbal indication that Simeana has been turned against Lissius by
Arcas's slander, but spectators are as yet unaware of the cause of her distress.
In saying that Lissius has lost 'too much', Simeana may be implying that he
has lost her (cf. 185), or she may be stating that he has said 'too much' in
his last lines, hence her departure from the stage.

Exit.] In both *PM* and *HM* the exit is marked mid-line, perhaps indicating
Simeana's haste.

Philisses. Learn you it out.
Rustic.   We'll leave you.
                    [*Exeunt* PHILISSES *and* RUSTIC.]
Musella.   I'll know this.
    Come Lissius, tell me, whence proceeds this grief?
    Discover it, and you may find relief.
Lissius. No, I'll go seek Philisses; he I'm sure
    Will comfort me who doth the like endure.   170
    Yet fair Musella, do thus much for me:
    Tell fierce Simeana she hath murdered me,
    And gain but this, that she my end will bless
    With some, though smallest, grief for my distress;
    And that she will but grace my hapless tomb   175
    As to behold me dead by her hard doom.
    This is a small request, and 'tis my last,
    Whom to obey to my sad end will haste.
Musella. Nay Lissius, hear me. Tell me ere you go
    What sudden matter moves in you this woe.   180
Lissius. Alas! 'tis love of one I did disdain,
    And now I seek, the like neglect I gain;
    Yet at the first she answered me with love,
    Which made my passions more increase and move.
    But now she scorns me, and tells me I give   185
    My love in equal sort to all, and drive
    My sighs and plaints but from an outward part

---

166. We'll … this] *PM;* wee'll leave you, and bring blis *HM.*   SD.] *CWD.*
172. Tell fierce] *PM;* as tell *HM.*   174. some … grief] some though small-
est grief *PM;* some (though smalest griefe) *HM.*   179. you go] *PM;* Ɨ you
[*inserted above*] goe *HM.*

---

    166. *Learn … out*] Find out what it is.
    I'll … this] In *PM* a clear SP marks these words as Musella's but Wroth's
hand is cramped here, and the words 'know this' look as though they may
have been added later. In *HM* Rustic continues speaking with the words
'and bring bliss'.
    168. *Discover*] reveal.
    172–8.] Lissius now adopts the trope of dying for love. See 76n. above.
    175. *hapless*] unfortunate or unlucky.
    181–4.] The fluctuations between scorn and desire in Lissius and
Simeana's relationship reflect Dalina's observation in 3.3.125–32 that suitors
are keener to pursue lovers who do not show interest in them.
    187. *from … part*] superficially, by playing a false role.

Of feignèd love, and never from my heart;
And when on knees I do her favour crave
She bids me seek Climeana, where I gave   190
As many vows as then to her I did,
And thereupon her sight did me forbid,
Vowing that if I did more move or speak
Of love, she would not only speeches break,
But ever more her sight, and would be blind   195
Rather than in my sight herself to find.
This is the cause, and this must be my end,
Which my sad days to saddest night must lend.
Musella. When grew this change?
Lissius.   Alas too late, today,
And yet too early for my joy's decay.   200
Musella. Have no ill tongues reported false of you?
Lissius. I know not, but my heart was ever true
Since first I vowed, and that my death shall tell,
Which is my last hope that will please her well.
Musella. Soft, I will speak with her, and know her mind,   205
And why on such a sudden she's unkind,
Then truly bring you answer what she says.
Till then be quiet, for it can no praise
Bring to your death when you shall wailing die,
Without so just a cause as to know why.   210
Lissius. But will Musella do thus much for me?
Shall I not of all friends forsaken be?

---

193. did more move or speak] *PM;* ever more did speake *HM.*   196.
find] find = [*end of page*] *PM.*   200. early for] *PM;* soune to bring *HM.*
201. no ill tongues reported false] *PM;* nott some made some false report
HM.   204. will] *PM;* ~~shall~~ will [*overwritten*] *HM.*   207. Then] *PM;* and
HM.

194–5. *not ... sight*] not only stop talking to me, but would never see me
again.
199. *late*] recently.
200. *And ... decay*] and yet too early for my joy (at winning her love) to
have decayed.
201. *false ... you*] Musella instinctively suspects that this may be the result
of malicious gossip, and is proved right when Arcas's false report is mentioned below (4.1.234, 271–8).
205. *Soft*] 'be quiet' cf. 'hush' in modern usage.
208–10. *it ... why*] Musella's common sense undercuts Lissius's vow to
die for love.

Musella. Never of me, and here awhile but stay,
    And I shall comfort bring your care t' allay.   *Exit.*
Lissius. Oh no, I know she will not pity me,   215
    Unfortunate and hapless must I be.
    And now, thou powerful, conquering god of love,
    I do but thus much crave: thy forces prove,
    And cast all storms of thy just-causèd rage
    Upon me, vassal; and no heat assuage   220
    Of greatest fury, since I do deserve
    No favour, or least grace but here to starve,
    Fed with sharp tortures. Let me live to see
    My former sin for so much slighting thee;
    Death yet more welcome, were't not in despite   225
    To punish me who knew not day from night.

        [*Re-enter* SIMEANA *and* MUSELLA.]

Simeana comes, ah, most ungrateful maid,
Who answers love as one would welcome death:
The nearer that it comes, the more flies; stayed
Ne'er but by limbs that tire wanting breath.   230
So hastes she still from me whose love is fixed
In purest flames without all baseness mixed.

---

215. Oh] Ô *PM, HM.*   217. powerful, conquering] *PM;* conquering, pourefull *HM*   222. or] *PM;* nor *HM.*   223. with sharp] *PM;* butt w^th *HM.*   224. for] *PM;* in *HM.*   225. were't not in despite] *PM;* were itt nott soe meete *HM.*   226. To punish me who knew not day from night] *PM;* I oft should dy who knew nott souer from sweet; *HM.*   226.1. SD.] *This ed.*   231. hastes] *PM;* flys *HM.*   232. without ... mixed] *PM;* with justest meaning mixt *HM.*   *CWD adds* SD [LISSIUS *prostrates himself, grief stricken. Enter* SIMEANA *with* MUSELLA] *after this line.*

---

214. *t' allay*] i.e. to allay, alleviate.

218. *thy ... prove*] demonstrate your power. Cf. 1.1.5n.

219. *just-causèd*] justified, because Lissius is guilty of previously 'slighting' or scorning love (224).

220. *vassal*] slave or servant. Lissius hyperbolizes the abjection of the courtly lover.

224. *slighting*] disdaining, treating with disrespect; cf. 219n. above.

229–30.] Cf. Mary Sidney Herbert's translated *Discourse of Life and Death* (MSH *Works*, I. 247:679–81)

230. *Ne'er*] Never.

232. *without ... mixed*] i.e. 'not tainted by any base motivation'. *HM*'s 'with justest meaning mixt' makes Lissius's self-defence more assertive.

Musella. Simeana, this can be no ground to take
    So great dislike, upon one man's report,
    And what may well prove false, as thus to make   235
    An honest, loving heart die in this sort.
    Say that he useth others well, and smiles
    On them, who't may be love of him beguiles,
    Or that he used Climeana well, what then?
    'Tis all, poor soul, she gets, who did contemn   240
    And rail at her.
Simeana.   'Tis true, before my face
    He did revile her with words of disgrace;
    My back but turned, she was his only joy,
    His best, his dearest life, and soon destroy
    Himself he would if she not loved him still,   245
    And just what he had vowed his heart did kill
    For my disdain, he shameless did protest
    Within one hour to her caused his unrest.
    Can I bear this? Who lived so long disdained,
    Now to be mocked? I thought I love had gained   250
    And not more scorn, but since thus much I find,
    I'm glad joy sank no deeper in my mind.
Musella. Fie, fie, Simeana! Leave these doubts, too far
    Already grown, to breed so great a jar.
    'Twas but his duty kindly once to speak   255

---

235. make] [*'ke' inserted above*] *PM.*   238. may be] ~~his~~ may bee [*inserted above*] *HM.* him] *HM;* him [*amended from 'them'*] *PM.*   245. still] still, = [*end of page*] *PM.*   252. joy sank no deeper] *PM;* the joy sunk [*blotted but visible*] nott deepe *HM.*

---

234. *one ... report*] i.e. Arcas's report.

236. *sort*] manner.

238. *who't ... beguiles*] 'who, it may be, are beguiled by love of him' (Lissius) – in *PM* 'him' is an overwriting of 'them'.

240–1. *contemn ... her*] disdainfully reject (*OED*, I.a) and rant at her. Musella refers to Lissius's scornful treatment of Climeana (3.3.164–8).

242. *revile*] (in this sense) insult (*OED*, *v.* Ia).

246–8. *And ... unrest*] i.e. 'And the same love that he vowed was killing him because of my disdain, he shamelessly repeated, within the hour, to Climeana, saying she was causing his suffering'.

253–4. *too ... jar*] which have already grown too far, to cause such a quarrel. Cf. 2.1.214n. and 319 below.

To her, who for him would her poor heart break.
Would you not think it sin quite to undo
A silly maid with scorn? But let these go.
Think you if I did love, and that I saw
He used more well, would I my love withdraw   260
From him for that? Oh, no great cause may be
To move good looks; mistrust not, but be free
From this vile humour of base jealousy,
Which breedeth nothing but self-misery.
For this believe: while you yourself are just,   265
You cannot any way your love mistrust.
Let him discourse, and smile, and what of this?
Is he the likelier in his faith to miss?
No, never fear him for his outward smiles,
'Tis private friendship that our trust beguiles,   270
And therefore let not Arcas' flattering skill
Have power in your breast his deserts to spill.
Lissius is worthy, and a worthy love
He bears to you; then these conceits remove.

---

260. withdraw] *CWD;* withdraw! *R.*   261. Oh] Ô *PM;* Ô! *HM.*   266.
mistrust] *PM;* distrust *HM.*

---

256. *her*] i.e. Climeana.
257. *undo*] See 2.1.32n.
260. *He ... well*] He (my beloved) treated others well.
withdraw] Following this word, there is a mark in *PM* which may possibly
be an exclamation mark or question mark. It may have been included in
error and subsequently erased, perhaps once Wroth wrote the following
half-line, ending with a question mark: 'from him for that?'
261–2. *great ... looks*] there may be no great meaning behind kindly looks.
263. *vile humour*] vile temperament. Cf. 1.2.67n. Jealousy was associated
with the melancholic humour produced by black bile. See Emanuel Stelzer,
'Passionate Writing: The Rhythms of Jealousy in Early Modern English
Texts and Drama', in *Writing Emotions: Theoretical Concepts and Selected Case
Studies in Literature*, ed. Ingebord Jandl, Susanne Knaller, Sabine Schonfellner
and Gudrun Tocker (Bielefeld: Transcript Verlag, 2017), 215–32, 222.
267. *discourse*] make conversation.
268. *in ... miss*] falter in his loyalty.
270. *private*] secret. Cf. 278.
272. *power*] monosyllabic here to make the line scan.
Have ... spill] have power in your heart to deprive him of what he deserves.
274. *conceits*] notions or thoughts (*OED*, 1a).

Simeana. Arcas did see them sit too privately,   275
    And kiss, and then embrace.
Musella.   Well, if he did?
Simeana. And in her ear discourse familiarly,
    When they did think it should from me be hid.
Musella. Lord, how one may conjecture if one fear
    All things they doubt to be the same they fear.   280
    Though private, must it follow he's untrue,
    Or that they whispered must be kept from you?
    Fie, leave these follies, and begin to think
    You have your love brought to death's river brink.
    Repent you have him wronged, and now cherish   285
    The dying lad, who else soon will perish.
    Go ask him pardon.
Simeana.   Pardon, why? That he
    The more may brag he twice hath cozened me?

---

276. Well, if he did?] *CWD;* well if hee did *PM, HM.*   278. from me]
PM; from *HM.*   282. you?] you, *PM.*   285. cherish] cherish – [*end of
page*] *HM.*

---

280. *All ... fear*] all things they doubt to be the same [things] they fear.

284. *death's ... brink*] This may be an allusion to the Styx, the river that
separated the worlds of the living and the dead in Greek mythology. In Philip
Sidney's *Arcadia* Amphialus dreams of binding Venus and Diana 'fast by
Styx' to praise his mistress (480). Musella's line recalls a rather confused
anecdote in *Urania I* (642–4), where Rossalea discovers the body of her
beloved in a river, apparently drowned, and rescues him but 'jealousy
appears in yellow mantles dressed against Rossalea kissing him' (643), and
her friend Celina also falls in love with him. See Rahel Orgis, 'Murder on
the Banks of the Medway: The Deceptive Beauty of Penshurst Place and
England in Lady Mary Wroth's *Urania*', *SJ*, 34:1 (2016), 67–80. Sidney
intertexts frequently make use of rivers to discuss the dangers of jealousy:
see, for example, Robert Sidney's Pastoral 8 (RS *Poems*, 209), where the
shepherd imagines the brooks flooding the fields with hate.

286. *dying lad*] Musella's words here and at 291 refer to the actor's pros-
trate position on stage. In the 1999 performance Lissius lay curled up on the
floor but waved pathetically to Simeana, adding a touch of comedy; in 2018
he sat with his head in his hands.

287–8. *Pardon ... me*] The actors playing Simeana in the 1999 and 2018
performances both expressed incredulity at Musella's idea that Simeana was
to blame for the quarrel. Laura Soper (2018) started to exit after these lines,
until Musella stopped her.

288. *cozened*] tricked.

Musella. Nay, he is past all bragging; mend your fault,
    And sorry be you have his torment wrought.   290
    See where he lies, the truest sign of woe –
    Go, haste and save him; Love's wings are not slow.
Simeana. O dearest Lissius, look but up, and speak
    To me, most wretched, whose heart now must break
    With self-accusing of a cursèd wrong,   295
    Which rashly bred, did win belief too strong.
    Ah, cast but up thine eyes, see my true tears,
    And view but her who now all torment bears.
    Do but look up, and thou shalt see me die
    For having wronged thee with my jealousy.   300
Lissius. To see thee die? Alas, I die for thee.
    What pleasure can thy death then bring to me?
    Yet if love make you say this, then poor I
    Shall much more happy, and more blessèd die.
Simeana. Nay, let me end before thy end I see.   305
    Alas, I love you, and 'twas love in me
    Bred this great ill, which jealousy confused;
    I brought your harm, and my best love abused.
Lissius. Oh joy, which now doth swell as much as grief,
    And pleasing yet doth make me seek relief.   310
    Am I myself? No, I am only joy;

---

290. wrought] *PM;* [*'th' overwritten*] wrought *HM.*   292. Love's] loves *PM,*
HM.   *CWD adds* SD [*She approaches* LISSIUS] *after this line.*   293. O] *PM;*
Ô *HM.*   302. death] *PM;* [*'grief' overwritten*] death *HM.*   307. which ...
confused] *PM;* by ... abus'de *HM.*   309. Oh] O *PM;* Ô *HM.*

    292. *Love's wings*] Cf. *Urania I* where Leonius is speedily 'carried by the
wings of love' to rescue Veralinda from a bear (426.39). *CWD* notes 'a reference to Cupid as a winged god' (205n.59).

    293.] *CWD* inserts a stage direction for Simeana to approach Lissius at
this point, but there are alternative possibilities for performance. In 2018,
for example, Laura Soper continued to play Simeana as angry, delivering
these lines with a raised voice from her seat at some distance from Lissius.
Having also protested 'Alas, I love you' with some irritation, she only ran to
embrace him at ''twas love in me' (306).

    297. *true tears*] Cf. the Forester's pointing to his tears as evidence of the
depth of his feelings in 2.1.18.

    309. *Oh joy*] Given Simeana's mixed emotions in the 2018 performance
(see 293n. above), Lissius's words expressed surprise at his good fortune,
eliciting sympathetic laughter from spectators.

Not Lissius, grief did lately him destroy.
I am Simeana's love, her slave revived,
Late hopeless dead, now have despair survived.
Musella. All care now past, let joy in triumph sit;   315
    This for such lovers ever is most fit.
    This doth become that happy, loving pair
    Who seek to nurse the joys that kill despair.
    Let those fall out, mistrust, wrangle, and jar,
    Who love for fashion, not for love; but war   320
    Not you, the couple Cupid best doth love,
    Whose troubled hearts his godhead's self did move.
Lissius. Musella, you have turned this cloudy day
    To sweet and pleasant light, nor can I say
    So much as in my heart this kindness breeds,   325
    For now delight all form and speech exceeds.
    But let us, happy now, unhappy be
    When in us least unthankfulness you see.

---

313. love] *HM;* Love *PM.*   314. dead] ~~death~~ dead *PM.*   318. despair]
PM; all care *HM.*   322. godhead's] Godhead's *PM, HM.*

---

313. *slave*] Cf. 220n. above.

314. *Late ... survived*] Lissius's metaphorical resurrection points to a
dominant theme of the play.

315. *All ... sit*] Musella returns to the conversation to congratulate
Simeana and Lissius, suggesting that she has remained onstage to oversee
their reconciliation and ensure that it is successful. In the 1999 production,
for example, Musella sat to watch them. This is in keeping with her role as
a protective shepherdess of the human flock, promoting love between them
as an avatar of Venus (see 147n., 349n., 3.2.12–13n.). Alternatively, although
there is no corresponding cue or stage direction in the script, she may leave
the stage at 292 (perhaps taking a seat amongst spectators) to give Simeana
and Lissius space to effect their reconciliation, and then re-enter to speak at
315. In the 2018 production she exited and re-entered accompanied by
music, a device which was designed to create a first 'false' happy ending
heralded by her lines (315–22), even though tragic events are still in store.

318. *nurse*] Cf. 140n. above.

320. *fashion*] outward appearance or false performance, often used pejo-
ratively by Wroth; see, for example, the two wicked knights who, 'with a
good fashion, dissembling their true intent', plan to rape Antissia in *Urania
I* (38.31).

war] fight.

326. *form*] manner of behaviour, but also, more broadly, shape or concept.
Lissius cannot find the form of words to express his feelings.

Simeana. Let me myself, nay, my dear Lissius leave,
    When I in service or in faith deceive   330
    Musella, sole restorer of this joy,
    And jealousy anew strive to destroy
    Our loves, and hopes, if I forgetful be
    Of this increase of lost felicity.
    But now, my Lissius, have you me forgiven   335
    My last offence, by love and fearing driven?
Lissius. Thou lov'st me, 'tis enough, and now enjoy
    All rest, nor bring new doubts to cross our joy.
    I all forget, and only hold thee dear,
    And from thee all faults past my love doth clear.   340
Simeana. So let us ever doubtless live and love,
    And no mistrust in least sort our hearts move.
Lissius. No doubt of thee shall ever stir in mine.
Simeana. Nor breed in me, so wholly I am thine.
Musella. Happy this time, and blessèd be your loves,   345
    And most accursèd they that other moves.
    Live both contented, and live still as one,
    Never divided till your lives be done.

        [*Enter*] FILLIS, DALINA, PHILISSES, ARCAS,
                CLIMEANA, RUSTIC.

Musella. Here comes the flock.
Rustic.   We're all here now.
Musella.   'Tis true

---

338. All ... doubts] *PM;* all blis, bring noe doubts now.   340. thee] *PM;*
you *HM.*   344. thine.] thine: / = [*end of page*] *PM.*   347. live still] *PM;*
still live *HM.*   348. done.] dun; / *PM;* dunn; / *HM.*   348.1–2 SD.] *This
ed.* [*Enter ... and*] *CWD.* Fillis, Dalina, Philisses, Arcas, Climeana, Rustick
PM, HM.

---

332. *jealousy ... strive*] may jealousy once more strive.

334. *felicity*] happiness.

345. *blessèd ... loves*] Cf. Urania's role in restoring love between Pamphilia
and Amphilanthus: 'my fortune will be to serve you to all blessedness again'
(*Urania II*, 139.33–4).

346. *that ... moves*] that intends otherwise (i.e. who doesn't wish you
well).

349. *the flock*] i.e. the group of other shepherds and shepherdesses, a
pastoral metaphor which extends the allusion to Musella as nurturing shepherdess at 147 above.

We are all here, and one too much by you.   350
Dalina. Here be our fellows, now let us begin
    Some pretty pastime, pleasure's sport to win.
    Sweetest Musella, what think you is best?
Musella. That whereunto your fancy is addressed.
Dalina. Mine is to riddling.
Simeana.   And indeed that's good.   355
Climeana. But methinks not, lest they be understood.
Simeana. Understood? Why so shall all be that I make.
Climeana. Tush, you'll say one thing, and another take.
Simeana. You'll still be wrangling.
Dalina.   Aye, and for a man.
    Would I might live till quarrel I began   360
    On such a cause. But pray, now quiet be,
    And fair Musella, first begin with me.
Fillis. But must the riddles be expounded?
Dalina.   No.
Musella. Then I'll begin, though scarce the play I know.

---

352. Some ... to] Some pretty pastime pleasures for to *HM;* Some pretty pastime pleasures sport to *PM.*   354. fancy] phant'sie *PM;* phantsie *HM.*
359. Aye] *CWD;* I *PM, HM.*   361. be,] be, = [*end of page*] *PM.*

---

350. *one ... you*] This may be performed as an aside. If the line is said directly to Rustic, Musella is either being uncharacteristically rude and outspoken, as portrayed in the 1999 performance, or relies on the fact that he will not understand her, as suggested in the 2018 production.

354. *fancy ... addressed*] whatever takes your fancy. *PM* uses the early modern synonym 'phant'sie'. See 1.2.227n.

355. *riddling*] Telling riddles, especially romantic riddles, was a typical game for shepherds in early modern pastorals. John Fletcher's *The Faithful Shepherdess* (London: Edward Allde, 1610), for example, refers to 'a green bank or shade where shepherds use, / To sit and riddle, sweetly pipe or choose / Their valentines' (sig. G4r).

358. *take*] unclear; grant or give oneself, esp. presumptuously (*OED*, v.76) or assume (*CWD*, 206n.70).

360–1. *Would ... cause*] Dalina mocks Climeana and Simeana for their behaviour and implies that she would live a long time if she lived until she started a quarrel over a man.

363. *expounded*] interpreted (i.e. out loud). The meanings of the riddles are not given in the script and are tricky to unravel, but suggestions are made in the notes below.

364. *scarce ... know*] I hardly know how to play.

That I wish, which with most pain   365
    I must gain;
That I shun, which with such ease
    Can not please;
That most easy still I fly,
Barred, I fainest would come by.   370
Dalina. I am the next, mark then what I will say,
    Best is, my lovers can not me betray.
      What I seek can never be
        Found in me,
      Fain I would that try and find,   375
        Which my mind
      Ever yet from my heart kept,
      Till away my luck was stepped.
Philisses. Let them alone, the women still will speak;
    Rustic, come, you and I this course will break.   380
      Late I saw a star to shine
      Whose light methought was only mine,
      Till a cloud came, and did hide
      That light from me where light did bide.

---

368. can not] *PM;* cannot *HM.*   370. Barred] *CWD;* bar'd *PM, HM.*
372. Best] *PM;* 'best *HM.*   382. methought] mee thought ['*t*' *inserted above*] *PM;* my mee [*overwritten*] thought *HM.*   384. did] *PM;* doth *HM.*

365–70.] I wish for that (i.e. Philisses) which I must endure the most pain to gain; I shun that (i.e. marriage to Rustic) which cannot be pleasing because it is so easy. I run away from that which is easiest and I most long for that which is forbidden.

372. *best ... betray*] the best thing is, my lovers cannot betray me. Dalina has no lover at present but recalls her former lovers. See 3.3.17–24.

373–8.] Precisely what Dalina seeks is obscure, but her riddle seems to declare her determination to find in herself the love and constancy which her mind has kept from her heart in the past, as she tells the shepherdesses in 3.3.31–6.

379. *Let ... speak*] i.e. if you let them alone, the women will keep on talking.

380. *course ... break*] we will stop the flow of speech (from the women).

381–6. *Late ... see*] 'Lately I saw a shining star [Musella], whose light I thought was only mine, until a cloud [Rustic] came and obscured the source of the light. Yet tell me how both of these things can be: though the light is dimmed, I still see it.' The riddle alludes obliquely to the pattern of loss and recovery in the play's tragicomic plot.

Yet tell me how can these agree: 385
  That light though dimmed, that light I see.
Lissius. Now Rustic, fortune's falling on your head,
  Bring forth your riddle. Fie, in love, and dead
  To such a sport? Think not upon the day,
  There is no danger in't, I dare well say.   390
Rustic. Truly I can not riddle, I was not taught
  These tricks of wit: my thoughts ne'er higher wrought
  Than how to mark a beast, or drive a cow
  To feed, or else with art to hold a plough;
  Which if you knew, you surely soon would find   395
  A matter more of worth than these odd things
  Which never profit, but some laughter brings.
  These others be of body, and of mind.
Philisses. Spoke like a husband, though you yet are none.
  But come, what, is this sport already done?   400
Rustic. I can not riddle.
Dalina.   Whistle, 'tis as good,
  For you sufficiently are understood.

---

392. ne'er] *PM;* noe *HM.*   396. worth] *PM;* waight *HM.*   398. mind.]
mind: / *PM.*

---

389. *Think ... day*] It is not clear what Lissius means here. Perhaps by
saying there is no 'danger' or harm in playing a leisurely game of riddles, he
is telling Rustic not to worry about losing the day's work time, or that the
animals will be harmed by the heat of the sun. Given his proneness to
superstition (demonstrated in 5.5.9–13), Rustic may be thinking about
whether this is a lucky day. Belief in choosing an 'auspicious day' for important events was common in early modern England, as evidenced by Dr John
Dee being asked by the Earl of Leicester to nominate an auspicious day for
Elizabeth I's coronation (John Nichols, *The Progresses and Public Processions
of Queen Elizabeth I: A New Edition of the Early Modern Sources*, ed. Elizabeth
Goldring, Faith Eales, Elizabeth Clarke and Jayne Elisabeth Archer, 5 Vols
(Oxford: Oxford University Press, 2014), Vol. 5, 256, and Charlotte Fell
Smith, *The Life of Dr John Dee* (London: Constable, 1909), 24. More in line
with Rustic's fears of a 'fatal' day, the astrologer-physician Simon Forman
had predicted the date of his own death in 1611. See Barbara Howard
Traister, *The Notorious Astrological Physician of London: Works and Days of
Simon Forman* (Chicago: University of Chicago Press, 2001), 24–5, and
Lauren Kassell, 'Forman, Simon (1552–1611)', *ODNB*, online edition https://
doi-org.ezproxy.lancs.ac.uk/10.1093/ref:odnb/9884.

402. *For ... understood*] i.e. your speech has no more meaning than whis-
tling. Dalina's comment characterizes Rustic as a country bumpkin, unable
to participate in the witty courtly games of the shepherd community.

Rustic. What mean you?

Dalina.   Naught, but that you are
An honest man, and thrifty, full of care.

Rustic. I thought you had meant worse.

Dalina.   Meant worse, what I?   405
Fie, this doth show your doubt and jealousy.
Why should you take my meaning worse than 'tis?

Rustic. Nay, I but smile to see how all you miss,
But some shall find when I do seem to smile,
And show best pleased, I oft'nest do beguile.   410

Dalina. Yourself you mean, for few else do respect
Your smiles, or frowns; therefore do not neglect
Your pleasant youth. Ill will is too soon got,
And once that rooted, not so soon forgot.

Philisses. You grow too wise, dispute no more. Here be   415
Others who will let us their hearers be,
And give this sport some life again, which you
Almost made dead.

Dalina.   I've done; let joy ensue.

Lissius. Guess you all what this can be:
A snake to suffer fire I see,   420
A fog, and yet a clear bright day,

---

418. I've] *This ed.;* I'have *PM, HM;* I have *CWD.*   ensue] *PM;* insue; /
HM.

409–10. *But ... beguile*] beguile: to fool or outwit. Rustic hints that his
smiles disguise a more sinister intention (perhaps to thwart Musella and
Philisses's romance).

411. *Yourself ... mean*] Dalina attempts to undercut Rustic's implicit
threat, saying that he is only fooling himself. Her tone is ambiguous here,
and could be interpreted in performance as being actively hostile or (looking
forward to their pairing off in 5.7.125–8) flirtatiously chiding.

417. *sport*] game (i.e. of riddling). In Sidney's *Arcadia* 'pastoral sports'
refers to games of wit and poetic performance as well as physical games (e.g.
I.163).

420–6. *A ... dear*] Lissius's riddle is particularly difficult to decipher, but
appears to refer to the romantic problems he has experienced earlier in the
scene.

420. *snake ... see*] Possibly this refers to the treacherous snake in *Aesop's
[F]ables* (London: Humphrey Lownes for Thomas Man, 1617) 5–6. It may
also refer obliquely to the villainous mischief-maker Arcas, whose gossip
endangered Lissius and Simeana's relationship.

421. *fog ... day*] a fog of unhappiness, ignorance and jealousy has clouded
the sun of Lissius's happiness with Simeana. Cf. his imagery above in 323–4.

A light which better were away;
Two suns at once, both shining clear,
And without envy hold each dear.
Fillis. A spring I hoped for, but that died.   425
Then on the next my hopes relied,
But summer past, the latter spring
Could me but former losses bring;
I died with them, yet still I live,
While autumn can no comfort give.   430

[ARCAS gives MUSELLA *a message.*]

---

424. dear.] deere: / *PM.*   426. my] *PM;* ł my *HM.*   430. autumn] *HM;*
Autume *PM.*   give.] give: / *PM;* give; / *HM.*   430.1. SD.] *This ed.*

422. *light ... away*] perhaps an allusion to the unwanted illumination by
Arcas upon Lissius's conversations with Climeana – or possibly a disparaging
reference to Climeana herself, given the 'two suns' in the following lines.
423–4. *Two ... dear*] These lines could possibly be a reference to Musella
and Simeana as models of female friendship; alternatively, Lissius might be
attempting to engineer a reconciliation between Simeana and Climeana,
hoping both will be able to live side by side.
425. Fillis's riddle uses the same seasonal metaphors as the narrative song
in *Urania I*, where a shepherdess who is 'love's bond-slave' declares that 'My
hopes are frozen, my spring dried, / My summer drown'd with pain' (*Urania
I*, 622, *Poems*, 191).
430.1 SD.] It is not made clear in *PM* or *HM* how Musella is summoned
to attend on her mother; the message could be delivered via a written note
or spoken confidentially to her. Neither do we know who delivers the
message. Since Arcas is the villain of the piece, who has spread rumours
about Musella's chastity to hasten the arranged marriage, he may be a logical
person to deliver the summons, as was enacted in the 1999 and 2018 productions. Arcas is listed amongst the characters who enter at 348 but has only
one line in the scene, which he speaks after the message is delivered – significantly commenting that 'some ere long will smart' (442). Providing
Musella with the message would give him a purpose in the scene, and this
edition has given him this role. Alternatively, the message could be delivered
by Rustic, on the basis of his earlier behaviour in the scene: as a possible
witness of Musella and Philisses's vows of love (see 111n. and 140n. above),
he exits with Philisses at 166 (and possibly goes to Musella's mother's house
to warn her). He returns at 348 and, if he is the messenger, this would give
added weight to his hints in lines 408–10. He makes no reference to a
message, though in performance he could be portrayed as attempting to
deliver it but being thwarted by the shepherds' riddling game.

Musella. Unmannerly, I must your presence leave,
      Sent for in haste unto my mother. But
      I hope in this sweet place soon to receive
      Your most loved companies, and so to put
      Good Rustic into better humours. Say,   435
      Will you be merry?   *Exit.*
Rustic.   I'll not after stay.   *Exit.*
Philisses. No, follow, shadows never absent be
      When sun shines, in which blessing you may see
      Your shadowed self, who nothing in truth are
      But the reflection of her too-great care.   440
      What will you further do?
Dalina.   Let us depart.
Arcas. Aye, let's away, but some ere long will smart.

---

432. my mother. But] *PM;* mother, ~~soune~~ butt [*inserted above*] *HM.*   436.
stay.] stay: / ex: = [*end of page*] *PM;* stay; / *HM.*   437. *CWD adds* SD
[*Aside*].   438. in which blessing] *PM;* ~~butt soe~~ in which blessing [*inserted
above*] *HM.*   442. Aye] *CWD;* I *PM;* come *HM.*   but some] *PM, HM;*
[*Aside*] But some *CWD.*

---

431. *Unmannerly*] i.e. impolitely, without properly saying farewell.
435. *better humours*] a better mood. Cf. 1.2.67n. and 263n. above.
437–40. *shadows ... care*] Comparing Musella to the sun, Philisses suggests that Rustic is her shadowy counterpart, stating that the light of
Musella's 'blessing' contrasts with the darkness of the 'care' caused by
Rustic. Philisses's metaphor continues the reference to Rustic as a 'cloud'
in his riddle (383), and Wroth uses this opposition again in *Urania II*, where
an unnamed beloved lady is reported by her friends to be 'like a new risen
sun', while those who would wrong her 'appear like black clouds, full and
foul, and burst before they can come near her or touch the shadow of her'
(211.23–6). By casting Musella as the sun, Wroth neatly inverts Ben Jonson's
Song 'That Women Are But Men's Shadows' (*The Forest*, 1616), which he
apparently composed in response to a dispute on the topic between William
Herbert and 'his lady', probably Wroth herself (Drummond, *Informations*,
282–4), as discussed by Mary Ellen Lamb, 'The Poetry of William Herbert,
Third Earl of Pembroke,' in *ARC*, Vol. 2, 269–82. *CWD* suggests Philisses's
comments are directed aside, but because Rustic has already exited (marked
in the SD in *PM*), and because Philisses's view seems to be shared by the
other shepherds and shepherdesses, the lines could be directed offstage and
shared with onstage and offstage audiences.
440. *reflection ... care*] object of her concern, both in terms of concern for
him and, her great worry caused *by* him.
442. *Aye*] See note for 3.3.169 where Wroth also uses this affirmative 'aye'
(spelt 'I' in *PM*).
      some ... smart] Cf. 1.3.19n. Arcas's line looks forward to the suffering of
Philisses and Musella.

Philisses. When shall we meet again?
Dalina.   When day appears.
Lissius. No, not till sun, who all foul mists still clears.
Philisses. Why then at sun, and who shall then miss here   445
   A punishment by us ordained shall bear.
Dalina. Let it be so.
Fillis.   I'm very well agreed.
Lissius. So are we all, and sun appear with speed.   [*Exeunt.*]

[ACT 4 SCENE 2]

[*The Temple*]

[*Enter*] VENUS *and* CUPID.

[*Enter* PRIESTS.]

Venus. Now have thy torments long enough endured,
   And of thy force they are enough assured.
   O hold thy hand; alas, I pity now

446. shall] *PM;* must *HM.* 447. so.] soe; / *PM.* I'm very] *PM;* for
mee I'me *HM.* 448. appear] *PM;* ~~must show~~ appeere [*inserted above*]
HM. speed.] speed; / [*flourish below*] *PM;* speede [*S fermé, flourish below*]
HM. SD.] *CWD.*

0.0. [ACT 4 SCENE 2]] *CWD.* 0.1. SD.] *This ed.* 0.2. SD.] *CWD;*
Venus, and Cupid *PM;* Venus, Cupid *HM.* 0.3. SD.] *This ed.* 3. hand;
alas] hand, alas *PM;* hande, als *HM;* hands! as *Halliwell.*

447. *so*] An oblique mark / appears after Dalina's half of the line in *PM.*
It may indicate the end of the actor's part for this scene, and perhaps their
exit from the stage.

0.0.] There are significant variations to this scene in *HM* due to the
deletion of the first lines of a song sung by Venus and of a reply by Cupid
after the song 'Love, thy powerful hand withdraw'. See Introduction, 14, 50.

0.1. SD.] Although neither manuscript specifies a location, this scene
takes place in Venus's Temple since the Priests are either already on stage
or enter to deliver their music and song at 16. Roberts suggests that Venus's
lines follow the Priests' song (Wroth *Poems*, 215). In the 1999 performance
Venus and Cupid appeared on the main stage for these lines, retiring onto
the steps of the Temple at line 16. Venus appeared in the minstrels' gallery
in the 2018 performance to address Cupid, who entered on the stage below
since the actor doubling the role had just exited as Arcas.

1. *endured*] lasted.

3. *hold ... hand*] hold back your hand (i.e. refrain from shooting any more
arrows or causing more suffering). In the 1999 performance Venus accompanied her persuasive appeal to Cupid by placing her hand on the top of his bow.

Those whose great pride did lately scorn to bow.
Thou hast performed thy promise, and thy state   5
Now is confessed; O slacken then thy hate.
They humble do their hearts and thoughts to thee;
Behold them, and accept them, and mild be.
Thy conquest is sufficient; save thy spoils,
And let them only taken be in toils,   10
But set at liberty again to tell
Thy might and clemency, which doth excel.

Cupid. I mean to save them, but some yet must try
More pain ere they their blessings may come nigh;
But in the end most shall be well again,   15
And sweetest is that love obtained with pain.

The music, or song of the PRIESTS.

---

4. lately] *PM;* whilum *HM.*   6. O] *HM;* Ô *PM.*   8. accept] *PM;* ~~exce~~
accept [*inserted above*] *HM.*   and] *PM;* ~~butt or~~ and [*inserted above*] *HM.*
9. Thy] *PM;* the *HM.*   10. And let them] *PM;* and let them ['*them*' *inserted
above*] *HM.*   11. to tell] *PM;* to [*inserted above*] tell *HM.*   12. and] *PM;*
~~angh~~ and [*inserted above*] *HM.*   14. More] *PM;* ~~my~~ more [*inserted above*]
HM.   15. most] *PM;* all *HM.*   16. pain.] paine: / *PM.*   16.1. SD.] *PM;*
~~Venus / Love a god did slander beare / gainst his person and his power / butt~~
Musique *HM;* [*Enter*] PRIESTS [*to music, singing*] *CWD.*

---

4. *lately*] Wroth substituted this word for the more archaic term 'whilom'
(meaning 'formerly', *OED*, adj. 2), which is found in *HM.*

bow] i.e. in acknowledgement of Venus's power.

5–6. *state ... confessed*] sovereignty (and power) is now acknowledged.

9. *spoils*] Venus refers to Cupid's captives as the spoils of war.

10. *toils*] netting, as would be used to trap animals; cf. 'Cupid's net' in
1.1.38.

15. *most*] A significant difference from 'all' in *HM;* as *CWD* points out,
'most' acknowledges that not all the characters will gain their loves by the
end of Act 5 (*CWD*, 207n.101).

16. *pain*] A small oblique / mark in *PM* here may cue the music at this
point, and perhaps also indicates the beginning of a separate sheet of manuscript on which the song lyrics are written. There is another stronger oblique
line in *PM* and an *S fermé* in *HM*, marking the end of the song (38).

16.1. SD.] *HM* has inserted the beginning of a speech by Venus which
was then erased but is still visible: 'Love a god did slander bear / gained his
person and his power / but'. This is followed by the word 'music'.

Priests. [*Sing.*]
 Love, thy powerful hand withdraw,
 All do yield unto thy law.
 Rebels now thy subjects be;
 Bound they are who late were free.   20
 Most confess thy power and might,
 All hearts yield unto thy right.
 Thoughts directed are by thee,
 Souls do strive thy joys to see.
 Pity then, and mercy give   25
 To those hearts where you do live.
 They your images do prove,
 In them may you see great love:
 They your mirrors, you their eyes,
 By which they true love do spy.   30
 Ease awhile their cruel smarts,
 And behold humble hearts;

---

20. *were*] PM; ~~was~~ were [*inserted above*] HM. 24. *see.*] see. = [*end of page*] PM. 26. *To those hearts*] PM; unto them HM. 27. *images*] HM; Images PM. 29. *mirrors*] Mirrors PM; mirours HM. *eyes*] PM; eye HM. 30. *By ... spy*] PM; ~~wher~~ by wch [*inserted above*] they ~~may~~ true love doe ['*doe' inserted above*] ~~descry~~ spy HM. 31. *Ease*] PM; ~~s~~ cease HM. 32. *humble*] PM; theyr yeelding HM.

17–38.] We have no extant score for this lyric. The 1999 production replayed 'Staines Morris', the tune used to accompany the Priests' song in 2.3, with synthesised organ accompaniment. The 2018 performance also reused the Priests' tune from 2.3; Venus exited and the Priests sang from the minstrels' gallery to Cupid below, who commanded the performance space alone on stage and basked in their praise.

27. images ... prove] become copies of you (i.e. have become lovers). The metaphor comes from Christian belief that humans are made in the image of God. In *PM* 'images' has an emphatic capital, as does 'mirrors' (29) – this may be due to the religious context of the song.

29. They ... eyes] i.e. they are reflections of you, and they look with your eyes. The metaphor of the mirror was often used of the soul in Christian tradition, as in the young Elizabeth I's radical manuscript translation of Marguerite de Navarre's poem 'The Glass of the Sinful Soul' (1544 and subsequent editions up to 1590). See *Elizabeth's Glass with 'The Glass of the Sinful Soul' (1544) by Elizabeth I*, ed. Marc Shell (Lincoln and London: University of Nebraska Press, 1993).

Greater glory 'tis to save
When that you the conquest have,
Than with tyranny to press,   35
Which still makes the honour less.
Gods do princes' hearts direct,
Then to these have some respect.   [*Exeunt.*]

---

34. *the*] *PM; a HM.*   37. *Gods ... princes'*] *HM; Gods ... Princes PM.*
hearts] *PM;* hands *HM.*   38. *respect.*] respect; / [*flourish below*] *PM;* respect,
[*S fermé*] *HM.*   38. *HM adds* Cupid ~~Now your part coms to play / in this~~
~~you must somthing sway / soe you shall, and I your child / when you bid can~~
~~soone bee milde~~ [*S fermé*] *after this line.* SD.] *CWD.*

33–6.] Calvin's sermons explain that the Gospels show God's intent 'to
set the greater glory upon his mercy' as a model for humans (*The Sermons
of M. John Calvin, Upon the Epistle of S. Paul to the Ephesians. Translated out
of French into English by Arthur Golding* (T. Dawson for L. Harrison and G
Bishop, 1577), 115). On the relationship between sovereign power and mercy
see K.J. Kesselring, *Mercy and Authority in the Tudor State* (Cambridge:
Cambridge University Press, 2003), 126–62. Straznicky has argued that this
is 'the play's most transparent passage of political allegory' (*SM*, 40).

37–8. *Gods ... respect*] See 1.4.31n. on the power of Cupid over princes
as well as shepherds. 'Princes' is capitalized in *HM*, and 'these' could refer
to the gods (advising those present to respect their power), the characters
on stage (telling spectators to pay attention to their fate) or to members of
the imagined courtly audience (which perhaps included princes).

38. In *HM* an additional four lines, attributed to Cupid, are written and
then deleted: 'Now your part comes to play / in this you must somthing sway
/ soe you shall, and I your child / when you bid can soone bee milde.'
Straznicky suggests that there is an opportunity here for the actor to 'reach
out' to spectators, 'inviting them' to play their part 'in subduing Cupid's
power and ending the shepherds' torment' (*SM*, 40). See Introduction, 50.

Act 5

[The meadows]

[Enter] MUSELLA *and* SIMEANA.

Musella. O eyes that day can see, and cannot mend
    What my joys poison; must my wretched end
    Proceed from love? And yet my true love crossed,
    Neglected for base gain, and all worth lost
    For riches? Then 'tis time for good to die,   5
    When wealth must wed us to all misery.

0.0. [ACT 5 SCENE 1]] *CWD;* The fift Act *PM;* The 5 Act; / *HM.* 0.1.
SD.] *This ed.* 0.2. SD.] *CWD;* Musella, and Simena: / *PM;* Musella,
Simena; *HM.* 1. O] *HM;* Ô *PM.* eyes] *HM;* Eyes *PM.* cannot] *PM;*
can not *HM.*

0.1.] The setting of this scene is not indicated in either manuscript or
specified by anything in the spoken text, though it must be outdoors to allow
Philisses as well as Simeana free access to Musella. By the end of the scene
their conversation is disturbed by the arrival of the others, so it probably
takes place in the meadows (though, alternatively, Musella may have
retreated to the place where she and Philisses declared their love). It is also
within walking distance of the Temple of Venus, to which the characters
exit – and presumably the Temple of Diana, where Climeana says that
Musella and Simeana are going in 5.3.20–4.

  1. *O eyes*] 'Ô' and 'Eyes' with a capital in *PM* emphasize Musella's apo-
strophic address, presumably to her own eyes but perhaps also invoking the
eyes of the spectators who must witness what will happen. In the 1999
performance Musella entered weeping and rubbing her eyes as she sat on a
bank, while in 2018 she spoke these lines out to the audience. See 1.3.31n.
on the importance of eyes in Wroth's writing.

  4–5. *worth ... riches*] As well as referring literally to Musella's arranged
marriage to Rustic in the dramatic plot, puns on worth/Wroth and 'riches'
could allude to recent Sidney family history, namely the author's arranged
marriage to Robert Wroth, and Philip Sidney's frustrated love for Penelope
Devereux, who married Lord Rich. *CWD* points out Wroth's use of the pun
on her own name at 3.1.95, 4.1.36 and 396, 5.1.4, 5.5.45–6 and 115 and
5.7.92. Cf. *PA*, especially Sonnet 3 in the 'Crown of Sonnets' in which 'the
worth of love' is 'blown by desires / Strengthened by worth' (Wroth *Poems*,
104, 137–8, 140).

Simeana. If you will but stoutly tell your mother
         You hate him, and will match with any other,
         She cannot, nor will go about to cross
         Your liking, so to bring your endless loss.   10
Musella. Alas, I've urged her, till that she with tears
         Did vow and grieve she could not mend my state,
         Agreed on by my father's will which bears
         Sway in her breast, and duty in me: Fate
         Must have her courses, while that wretched I   15
         Wish but so good a fate as now to die.
Simeana. Wish not such ill which all we suffer must,
         But take some hope, the gods are not unjust.

---

9. cannot] *PM;* can not. *HM.*   11. I've] I'have *PM;* I have *HM.*   till
that] till yᵗ *PM;* till *HM.*   15. that] *PM;* most *HM.*   17. ill] *PM;* [*inserted
above*] *HM.*   18. gods] Gods *PM, HM.*

---

   7. *stoutly*] bravely, resolutely (*OED*, adv.1 and 3), also connoting vigorously (*OED*, 5) and stubbornly (*OED*, 4). In *Urania II* the female ruler of
the islands, who stands her ground against her husband Lamurandus, is
described as 'being as stout and fiercely strong for her sex as he was for his'
(188.29–30).
   8. *him*] 'him' refers to Rustic, but his identity as Musella's promised
husband is not made clear until 45.
   match with] be engaged or betrothed to.
   12. *state*] condition (i.e. as Rustic's fiancée).
   13. *will*] a reference to her father's wishes, and possibly also to his formal
bequest of property on death. *CWD* (207n.6) points out the parallel with
Shakespeare's *Merchant of Venice* 1.2.20–6. Cf. the Queen of Argos's marriage arranged by her father against her and her mother's wishes (*Urania
II*, 94) and Beverly M. Van Note's view that 'Wroth clearly argues the
necessity of the woman's active role in choosing a spouse as fitter means
for marriage'. See 'Performing "fitter means": Marriage and Authorship in
Love's Victory', in *Re-Reading Mary Wroth*, ed. Katherine R. Larson and
Naomi J. Miller with Andrew Strycharski (Houndmills: Palgrave Macmillan,
2015), 69–81, 75.
   14. *sway*] power, authority, influence.
   14–15. *Fate … courses*] Personified as a goddess, Fate decides particular
destinies or 'courses' for mortals and is linked to the 'fatal sisters' (see below
31n.). For Wroth's use of this personification see, for example, *Urania I*
where Veralinda says she is 'left a poor example of the Fates' tyranny'
(435.26), and Emelina believes that Fate has ordained her destiny and – as
Musella does – wishes to die (300.11–18, *Poems*, 163). William Herbert's
lament 'Muse, get thee to a cell' also complains that 'fate bound me' and
forced him and his beloved to match with others (WH *Poems*, 28).
   15. *while that*] while.

My mind doth give me yet you shall be blessed,
And seldom do I miss; then quiet rest.					20
Musella. Rest quiet? (O heavens!) Have you ever known
The pains of Love, and been by him o'erthrown,
To give this counsel, and advise your friend
T'impossibilities? Why, to what end
Speak you thus madly? Can it e'er be thought					25
That quiet, or least rest, can now be brought
To me while dear Philisses thus is crossed,
Whom missing, all my happiness is lost?
Simeana. You have not missed, nor lost him yet.
Musella.						I must,
And that's enough. Did I my blessings trust					30
In your kind breasts, you fatal sisters? Now
By your decree to be bestowed? And bow
To base unworthy riches? Oh my heart,
That breaks not, but can suffer all this smart.

---

19. me] *PM;* mee [*inserted above*] *HM.*   20. miss] *PM;* faile *HM.*   21. (O heavens!)] (O heavns) *PM;* (o! heavens) *HM.*   22. Love] love *PM, HM.* o'erthrown] orethrowne = [*end of page*] *PM.*   23. and] *PM;* to *HM.*   24. T'impossibilities?] *PM;* to'impossibilities, *HM.*   25. madly] *PM;* idly *HM.*   26. be] *PM;* bee [*inserted above*] *HM.*   27. To ... while] to mee? while *PM;* to mee, while *HM.*   28. Whom] *PM;* who *HM.*   32. decree] *PM;* ~~hard harts~~ decree [*inserted above*] *HM.*   33. riches? Oh] riches: O *PM;* riches, O! *HM.*   34. but] *PM;* ~~yet~~ butt [*inserted above*] *HM.*   smart.] smart: / *PM.*

---

19. *My ... blessed*] My mind still tells me that that you shall be blessed. Simeana's continued belief in a happy ending for her brother Philisses and Musella is shaken by their resolution later in the scene (105).

20. *miss*] mistake, get things wrong.

24. *T'impossibilities*] to impossibilities. Musella finds it impossible to 'rest quiet' in the faith that everything will turn out well for her. See Veralinda's exclamation 'fie upon this strange love, which makes me so strangely love as to affect impossibilities' when she meets Leonius (*Urania I*, 431.25–6), and the Song in *Urania I* where a woman bluntly tells her aged suitor not to follow her 'As if impossibilities to shake. / For sure I hate you still' (607.18–19, *Poems*, 182).

31. *fatal sisters*] a reference to the three Fates, who in classical mythology had the power over the thread of life. Cf. *MND*, 'O sisters three, / Come, come to me' (5.1.331–68). In the 2018 performance Nichole Bird spoke these lines angrily and tearfully, raising her hands towards the roof of the Baron's Hall.

33. *riches*] As *CWD* notes (207n.15), this is a possible allusion to the match between Penelope Devereux (often identified as the beloved Stella of Philip Sidney's sonnet sequence *Astrophil and Stella*) and Lord Rich.

Simeana. Have patience.

Musella.   I can not, nor I will not.   35
    Patient be? Ay me, and bear this ill lot?
    No; I will grieve in spite of grief, and mourn
    To make those mad who now to pleasure turn.

[Enter PHILISSES.]

Philisses. My dear Musella, what is it doth grieve
    Your heart thus much? Tell me, and still believe   40
    While you complain, I must tormented be;
    Your sighs, and tears, alas do bleed in me.
Musella. I know it, 'tis your loss I thus lament.
    I must be married; would my days were spent.
Philisses. Married?
Musella.   To Rustic. My mother so commands,   45
    Who I must yield to, being in her hands.
Philisses. But will you marry? Or show love to me,
    Or her obey, and make me wretched be.
Musella. Alas Philisses, will you this doubt make?
    I would my life to pleasure you forsake.   50
    Hath not my firmness hitherto made known
    My faith and love? Which yet should more be shown
    If I might govern but my mother's will;
    Yet this last question e'en my heart doth kill.

---

36. ill] *PM;* hard *HM.*   lot?] *This ed.;* lott *PM, HM.*   38. turn.] turne;
/ *PM.*   38.1. SD.] *CWD.*   42. alas] *PM;* (alas) *HM.*   44. my days were
spent.] *PM;* my [d]ay [*words missing on damaged page*] [sp]ent. *HM.*   45.
Married?] *PM;* married! *HM.*   52. more be] *PM;* bee more *HM.*

---

40. *still believe*] remain assured.

44. *days ... spent*] life was over (*OED*, adj. 2a,3). Cf. Anthony Chute,
Beauty Dishonoured, written under the title of Shore's Wife (London: J. Windet
for John Wolfe, 1593): 'Threatening my misery ere my days were spent' (29).

46. *in ... hands*] in her custody, under her authority. Wroth refers to the
early modern convention that parental wishes were the primary authority in
the choice of a marriage partner.

47–8. *Or ... or*] Either show love to me or obey her and make me
wretched. Wroth makes multiple use of 'or' to demonstrate the entrapment
of a speaker in the opening poem of her 'Crown of Sonnets': 'Thus let me
take the right, or left hand way, / Go forward, or stand still, or back retire /
I must these doubts endure without allay' (*Poems*, 128).

50. *I ... forsake*] I would give up my life to please you.

Philisses. Grieve not my dearest, I speak but for love;   55
    Then let not love your trouble so far move.
    You weep not that it wounds not hapless me,
    Nor sigh but in me all those sorrows be:
    You never cry but groans most truly show
    From deepest of my heart I feel your woe.   60
    Then heap not now more sorrows on my heart
    By these dear tears, which taste of endless smart;
    No grief can be which I have not sustained,
    And must, for now despair hath conquest gained.
    Yet let your love in me still steady rest,   65
    And in that I sufficiently am blessed.
    But must you marry? Oh those words deny,
    Or here behold your poor Philisses die.
Musella. I would I could deny the words I spake
    When I did Rustic's marriage offer take.   70
    Hopeless of you, I gave my ill consent,

---

55. speak] *PM;* spake *HM.*   62. taste ... endless] *PM;* tasteth of all *HM.*
67. Oh those words deny,] Ô those words deny *PM;* Mu: allas my deere, I
must. *HM.*   68–74. Or ... grave] *Not in HM.*

57–8. *You ... me*] Obscure. Possibly 'You do not weep without it wounding me, and do not sigh without me experiencing all your sorrows'. Philisses
elaborates on the sympathies between their shared hearts and feelings in the
following lines.
    64. *despair*] Despair was regarded as a sin in early modern England (see
3.2.15n.). Philisses's use of the term looks forward to a further sin of self-
murder, or suicide, through his sacrifice of himself for Musella. A love poem
by William Herbert claims he is torn 'with hopes, doubts, and despairs', and
fears he will 'grieve and die / For thee' (WH *Poems,* 36); Wroth's Urania
counsels the despairing Amphilanthus (an avatar of Herbert) to 'overmaster'
the passion to commit suicide, because 'to fall into so poor a business' would
'make men think he had no sense (not so much as of Religion, doing contrary
to the poorest Christians)' (*Urania II,* 172.25–8).
    67–74.] Philisses's half line 'But must you marry?' is followed in *HM* by
Musella's 'alas my dear I must', reinforcing the finality of Philisses's next
line: 'I hear and see my end' (*SM,* 5.1.82–3). However, in *PM* there are seven
more lines of dialogue not found in *HM:* in this context Philisses's protest
at Musella's betrothal ('Oh those words deny / Or here behold your poor
Philisses die') allows Musella to explain and express her own guilt about
giving her consent to marry Rustic (69–74).
    71. *ill*] unfortunate (*CWD,* 207n.21).

And we contracted were, which I repent.
The time now curse, my tongue wish out which gave
Me to that clown with whom I wed my grave.
Philisses. I hear, and see my end. O Love unjust,   75
And careless of my heart put in your trust,
Ungrateful, and forgetful of the good
From me received, by whom thy fame hath stood,
Thy honour been maintained, thy name adored
Which by all others with disgrace was stored.   80
Is this the great reward I shall receive
For all my service? Will you thus deceive
My hopes, and joys?
Musella.   Yet let me one thing crave.
Philisses. Ask my poor life; all else long since I gave.

75. O Love] O love *PM, HM.*   76. And ... trust] and ... trust = [*end of
page*] *PM; line not in HM.*   78. me] *PM;* us *HM.*   79. been] *PM;* still
HM.   81. I shall] *PM;* wee must *HM.*   82. my] *PM;* our *HM.*   you]
[*inserted above*] *PM.*   83. My] *PM;* our *HM.*   let me] *PM;* shall I *HM.*
84. long since I] *PM;* I long since *HM.*

72. *contracted*] betrothed; a formal, binding process of alliance in marriage in early modern England. See David Cressy, *Birth, Marriage and Death:
Ritual, Religion and the Life-Cycle in Tudor and Stuart England* (Oxford:
Oxford University Press, 1997), 266–81.
    74. *clown*] Significantly, Musella identifies Rustic as a clown rather than
a villain, as do Lacon (5.3.12) and Lissius (5.5.103). As well as a possible
comment on Rustic's buffoonish character, 'clown' is also an early modern
term for 'countryman, rustic, or peasant' (*OED*, 1a) – cf. 'But all come in,
the farmer and the clown' (48) in Ben Jonson's 'To Penshurst' (1612), published in *The Forest* (1616).
    75–83.] In the 2018 performance Philisses (Robert Heard) moved down-
stage, away from Musella, and shouted these lines upwards in bitter accusa-
tion at Cupid's injustice.
    76.] This line is missing in *HM*, which follows line 67 with line 75 to
provide a rhyme with 'must'.
    78–83.] In *HM* the pronouns in these lines are in the first person plural
('from *us* received'; '*we* must receive'; 'all *our* service'; '*our* hopes'), thus
acknowledging the pain both Philisses and Musella suffer from the arranged
marriage. *PM*'s use of the first person singular implies a more solipsistic
outlook on Philisses's part, and creates the potential for more friction
between the lovers.

Musella. That will I ask, and yours requite with mine,   85
    For mine cannot be, if not joined to thine.
    Go with me to the Temple, and there we
    Will bind our lives, or else our lives make free.
Philisses. To die for thee, a new life I should gain,
    But to die with thee were eternal pain.   90
    So you will promise me that you will live
    I willingly will go, and my life give.
    You may be happy.
Musella.   Happy without thee?
    O let me rather wretched, and thine be.
    Without thee no life can be, nor least joy,   95
    Nor thought but how a sad end to enjoy.
    But promise me yourself you will not harm
    As you love me.
Philisses.   Let me impose that charm

---

85. will I] *PM;* I will *HM.*   86. cannot] *PM;* can nott *HM.*   87. Temple]
PM; temple *HM.*   89. for thee] *PM;* for you *HM.*   94. Oh ... wretched] Ô
[*in margin*] lett me rather wreched, *PM;* lett mee bee rather wreched *HM.*
95. thee] *PM;* [*inserted above*] *HM.*   96. Nor] *PM;* noe *HM.*   98. impose]
HM; impose ['*o*' *inserted above*] *PM.*

---

85. *That ... mine*] In asking Philisses for his life and pledging her own,
Musella simultaneously introduces a proposal of suicide and marriage
in these lines. Although it was unusual for female characters to propose,
precedents in drama include Webster's Duchess of Malfi (1.1.441–59) and
Shakespeare's Miranda (*Temp.* 3.1.81–6).

86. *mine ... thine*] i.e. I cannot live without you.

88. *bind ... free*] i.e. bind ourselves together in marriage or free ourselves
from unwanted bonds. Musella hints that they will free themselves by killing
themselves.

89–90.] Obscure; Philisses appears to be considering the consequences of
single or double suicide, weighing the Christian tradition of self-sacrifice
against the church's prohibition of self-murder (see R.A. Houston, *Punishing
the Dead? Suicide, Lordship and Community in Britain, 1500–1830* (Oxford:
Oxford University Press, 2010). In sacrificing himself for her future, he
would gain immortality (new life), and Musella could start her life anew,
but, if she kills herself for him as well, this will cause him the 'eternal pain'
of having destroyed her and himself.

91. *So*] Provided that. Philisses rejects the idea of a double suicide, insisting that Musella will live while he sacrifices himself for love.

97–9. *But ... agreed*] Both lovers pledge not to harm themselves, suicide
being a mortal sin (see notes to 64 and 89–90 above, and 105 below). In the
2018 production Musella and Philisses came together and took each other's
hands as they spoke these words.

Likewise on you.

Musella.   Content, I am agreed.

Philisses. Let's go alone, no company we need.   100

Musella. Simeana, she shall go, and so may tell
  The good or heavy chance that us befell.

Philisses. I am content; your will shall be obeyed
  Till this life change, and I in earth am laid.

Simeana. I fear the worst; but what will you two do?   105
  Both die, and me, poor maiden, quite undo?

Philisses. Die? No, we go for ever more to live,
  And to our loves a sacrifice to give.

Musella. Our tears and sorrows we will offer there,
  And of our offerings you shall witness bear.   110
  The truest, and most constant love there shall
  In your sight end, and yet shall never fall.

Philisses. Such faith we'll sacrifice as none can touch,
  Which once reporting there could be too much.

Simeana. I know not what you mean, but I'll along.   115

Philisses. Let's haste, for here come some may do us wrong.

                                        Exeunt.

103–4. I ... laid] *This ed.;* I ... layd; / *PM;* wᵗ all my hart Si: butt what
will you tow doe [*104 missing*] *HM.*   105. I fear ... worst] *PM; missing in*
HM.   107. SP. *Philisses.* Die?] *PM;*Phi:[*manuscript ends*] *HM.*   114. be] bee
[*inserted above*] *PM.*

100.1. SP.] In *HM* this is inserted above, at a later juncture, in very small
writing.

105. *I ... do*] Simeana acts as an audience surrogate here, as Philisses and
Musella's intentions are obscure. Having agreed not to harm themselves
(97–9), Philisses's claim that they are going 'for ever more to live' implies
that they aim to secure eternal life through dying. Musella's statement that
her and Philisses's love shall 'In your sight end, and yet shall never fall' (112)
is also ambiguous (perhaps deliberately, either on the character's part or
Wroth's); it is unclear whether it is the couple's love or lives that will end at
the Temple.

106. *undo*] This is where the Huntington Manuscript ends, although it
looks as though pages have been removed from the end of the manuscript.
See Introduction, 49.

113–14. *Such ... much*] Obscure; i.e. 'We will make such an exceptional
proof of faith in our sacrifice to love that it will exceed all attempts to report
it or repeat it' (cf. *WT* 5.2.21–3).

115. *I ... mean*] again, Simeana's confusion may anticipate that of audience members, given the lack of clarity around the precise intentions of
Musella and Philisses.

[ACT 5 SCENE 2]

[*The meadows*]

[*Enter*] LISSIUS, DALINA, ARCAS [*and separately*]
RUSTIC.

Lissius. Arcas, is't possible it is today?
Arcas. It is, Musella now can bear no sway.
 Rustic shall have her, he's the blessèd man,
 Yet cannot get her love, do what he can.
Dalina. I'm sorry for Philisses.
Lissius.   Truly so am I.   5
 What than a lost love is more misery?
Rustic. Lissius, Dalina, Arcas, well met. Today
 I must be married; pray be not away
 But see us joined, and after dine with us.
 Where is Philisses? I hope he'll not miss;   10
 This is a jolly day, this my day is.
Lissius. I will not fail; must we not fetch the bride?
Rustic. Yes, marry, from her mother's where we abide. *Exit.*
Dalina. How well this business doth become this man!

0.0. [ACT 5 SCENE 2]] *CWD.* 0.1. SD.] *This ed.* 0.2–3. SD.] *This
ed.;* Lissius, Dalina, Arcas, Rustick [*on line below*] *PM;* [*Enter*] LISSIUS,
DALINA [*and*] ARCAS *CWD.* 6.] *CWD adds* SD [*Enter* RUSTIC] *after this
line.* 9. us] us = [*end of page*] *PM.* 13. we abide] w'abide *PM.*

0.1. SD.] *PM* gives no location for this scene but it evidently takes place
immediately after the previous one, in the same open, public location. *PM*
lists all the characters entering at once, albeit Rustic is listed on the line
below the others; as he does not greet them until 7, he may enter separately
or from a different side of the stage. Rustic could be coming from Musella
and her mother's house, since he says this is 'where we abide' (13). If Rustic
enters at the same time as the others, the actor may employ some stage
business, such as paying attention to his wedding attire, to occupy himself
while they are speaking. In the 2018 production he entered slightly later.
 6. *What … misery*] This line might be directed at Arcas, given his
attempted interference in Lissius and Simeana's relationship (4.1.271–8).
 13. *marry*] As *CWD* points out (207n.29), this is a shortened version of
the oath 'By Mary' – its sound creates a pun with the occasion preoccupying
everyone here. Male characters use it infrequently in *Urania I* (268.41,
346.27).

How well he speaks word 'marriage', and began   15
In as good form his neighbours to invite
As if he studied manners; yet at night
I'll undertake much mirth will not appear
In fair Musella; she'll show heavy cheer.
Arcas. This 'tis to look so high, and to despise   20
All loves that rose not pleasing in her eyes.
Now she that soared aloft all day, at night
Must roost in a poor bush with small delight.
Lissius. I never knew this in her; but 'tis true
She liked not of the love proffered by you,   25
And for refusing that she could not like
No man ought blame her, or her mind dislike.
But you have other qualities to move
A just dislike: you love cross-baits in love.

---

15. 'marriage'] *CWD;* marriage? *PM.*   27. ought] *this ed.;* aught *PM;*
ought to *CWD.*   29. cross-baits] *CWD;* cross baites *PM.*

---

15. *speaks ... 'marriage'*] speaks the word 'marriage'. In performance
Dalina's lines here could expresses surprise at, or perhaps disdain for,
Rustic's pronunciation and knowledge of social mores; cf. their exchange in
4.1.401–7.

17. *night*] Dalina alludes to the wedding night and sexual consummation
of the marriage as an unpleasant prospect for Musella. Her words are echoed
by Arcas (22–3).

24. *this ... her*] i.e. that she was proud and despised those whose love did
not please her, as Arcas alleges in 20–1.

25. *love ... you*] Arcas's love for Musella is not mentioned before, but see
his praise of beauty (2.1.129–32) and complaint of misfortune (2.1.208).

27. *ought*] *PM's* spelling 'aught' could also mean she should not be
blamed for anything.

28–9. *qualities ... dislike*] characteristics which, justifiably, make others
dislike you.

29. *cross-baits*] Lissius's metaphor refers to Arcas's love of thwarting
romantic love with his plots. A cross-bait, used by fishermen to trap oyster-
catchers, crows and even kites, consisted of two crossed willow branches
covered with bird-lime, the sticky substance used to trap birds, with a third
short stick, baited and tied to the end of the crossed twigs. See Leonard
Mascall, *A Book of Fishing with Hook & Line, and Of All Other Instruments
Thereunto Belonging* (London: John Wolfe for Edward White, 1590), 33.

I was beholding to you when time was,   30
But I enjoy her now.
Dalina.   Come, let that pass.
Arcas is known, and I dare lay my life
You have been meddling, and have caused some strife
Lately about Musella. But take heed:
If it prove so, perchance you'll want your meed.   35
Lissius. If it be found, thou shalt no longer live
Than while thou dost her satisfaction give.
Arcas. Be not so choleric, till you know the truth.
I have left that foul error of my youth.
Dalina. Hardly, I doubt, for I saw you last day   40
Sneaking and prying all along this way.
'Twas for no goodness, that I'm very sure,
For from a child you could not that endure.   *Exeunt.*

---

32. is] *CWD;* in *PM.*   36. live] live = [*end of page*] *PM.*   37. Than] *CWD;*
then *PM.*   43. endure.] endure; / *PM.*

30–1. *beholding ... now*] Lissius blames Arcas for the former difficulties
he (Lissius) faced with Simeana, but says he enjoys her love now.
32. *lay ... life*] bet my life.
35. *perchance ... meed*] perhaps you will miss out on your reward.
36–7. *If ... give*] If it is proved that you have been interfering, your life
will only last as long as Musella pleases.
38. *choleric*] angry. Choler was one of the four humours thought to make
up a person's emotional character in early modern physiology and medi-
cine – see note to 1.2.67. Cf. *Urania II*, where the foolish, rejected Follietto
is called 'good and choleric Follietto' for his tendency to 'fume and fret'
(61.2–6).
39. *that ... youth*] i.e. his tendency to meddle, or possibly his love of
Musella.
40. *last day*] yesterday.
41. *this way*] Dalina refers to the path outside Musella's mother's house.
43. *that endure*] i.e. goodness. Dalina suggests that Arcas was disposed to
evil from his youth.

[ACT 5 SCENE 3]

[Under the trees]

[Enter] CLIMEANA *[and]* LACON [SILVESTA *following,*
overhearing their conversation].

Climeana. Lacon, how fare you now? Musella must
    This day be married. Is not Love unjust
    To suffer this distasteful match to be
    Against her choice, and most against poor thee?
Lacon. Not against me. I never hoped; then how   5
    Doth Cupid wrong me though she marry now?
    Yet thus is Love unjust: to let her wed
    One who she never sees, but wisheth dead.
    So I, although for her I oft have died,
    Grieve for her loss, not that I was denied;   10
    I was unworthy of her, and she far
    Too worthy for this clown. Oh she, the star
    Of light and beauty, must she – lovely she! –
    Be matched to Rustic, base, unworthy he?

0.0. [ACT 5 SCENE 3]] *CWD.* 0.1. SD.] *This ed.* 0.2–3. SD.] *This ed.;* Climena, Lacon *PM;* [*Enter*] CLIMEANA, LACON [*and*] SILVESTA *CWD.* 7. Love] *CWD;* love *PM.* 12. Oh] *This ed.;* Ô *PM.* 13. she ... she! –] she, lovely she? *PM.* 14. unworthy he] *PM;* *CWD adds* SD [*Enter* SILVESTA.] *after this line.*

0.1. SD.] *PM* gives no location for this scene, which may follow immediately in the same open location as the previous one or take place under the trees rather than in the meadows, since the woods are the abode of Silvesta, who overhears Climeana comforting Lacon. The shade is associated with grieving (e.g. 4.1.10), so the edge of the woods would also be an appropriate place for Lacon. In the 2018 production Arcas (who doubled with Cupid) exited with a smile at Lacon's distress, as he entered.
    8. *One ... dead*] one whom Musella never sees without wishing him dead. It is worth noting that Musella never wishes Rustic's death; she only riddles that she 'shun[s]' him (4.1.367), and instead foresees her own death (5.1.5, 16 and 74).
    9. *oft ... died*] See 2.1.10n. and Introduction, 14.
    12. *clown ... star*] Lacon sets Musella's celestial qualities against Rustic's baseness in order to emphasise the inappropriateness of the match between them, which will be far from a marriage of true minds. For 'clown' see 5.1.74n. 'Star' alludes back to Philisses's riddle (4.1.381) and to Stella in Philip Sidney's *AS*. In the 1999 and 2018 performances Lacon dissolved into tears at this point and was comforted by Climeana; this business was used to occupy them during Silvesta's speech 15–18.

Silvesta. [*Aside*] Musella to be forced, and made to tie   15
Her faith to one she hates, and still did fly?
It should not be, nor shall be. No, no, I
Will rescue her, or for her sake will die.
[*To* CLIMEANA *and* LACON] Have you yet seen Musella
here today?

Climeana. No, but I hear she passèd by this way   20
With fair Simeana, both by break of morn,
With humble minds far from their wonted scorn
To offer their last rites of maiden thought
To your chaste mistress. Venus now hath bought
Their future time; how think you of this change?   25
'Tis better, sure, than still alone to range.

Silvesta. It's well you think so, yet methinks you can
Make a clean shift to live without a man.   *Exeunt.*

---

15. SD.] *CWD.*   16. fly?] fly? = [*end of page*] *PM.*   19. SD.] *CWD.*   24.
mistress] *This ed.;* Mistress *PM.*

---

22. *wonted scorn*] accustomed disdain (i.e. for love). Climeana's line
reminds spectators of Venus's overarching goal to reform the mortals who
'scorn our will' (1.1.2).

23. *chaste mistress*] Diana, goddess of virgins. 'Mistress' is capitalized in
PM. Musella and Simeana are going to offer their last rites to Diana, as
virgins, before they become wives. Emilia does this in 5.3 of *Two Noble
Kinsmen*, praying to Diana 'O mistress, / Thou hast discharged me – I shall
be gathered' (5.3.33–5).

24–5. *Venus ... time*] As wives, they will be bound to Venus – goddess of
love – in the future, rather than to Diana. The word 'bought' might allude
to the financial basis of the arranged marriage between Musella and Rustic,
and/or the fact that Venus has had to invest time and energy, via Cupid, to
'buy' the worship of the mortals. In the 1999 performance Climeana went
to the back of the stage as she spoke these lines and opened the curtains
revealing the Temple of Love and the actor playing Venus on the first (downstage) step, with Cupid on the top step behind.

26. *'Tis ... range*] Climeana pointedly criticizes Silvesta's independent
and unconventional lifestyle of chastity. Cf. 1.2.83–90 and Introduction, 19.

28. *make ... shift*] to make a change (*OED*, 7) or attain one's goal by con-
trivance or effort (*OED*, 6ab), the word 'clean' avoiding the word's pejorative
sense of subterfuge (*OED*, 4). 'Clean shift' may also refer to an undergar-
ment (a shift), its whiteness referring to Silvesta as a chaste follower of Diana.

28. SD.] Silvesta goes to rescue Musella, whereas Climeana and Lacon
continue on their way; the actors may exit at opposite sides, physically
echoing the different attitudes expressed in the last three lines. In the 1999
production Silvesta (Jordana Chapman) began to exit downstage but then
turned upstage to the Temple, where Venus handed her the potion that she
will later give to Musella and Philisses, acknowledging her help with a nod
of the head.

[ACT 5 SCENE 4]

[*Enter*] PHILISSES [*and*] MUSELLA *offering in*
the Temple of Love [*and* SIMEANA].

[*Philisses and Musella.*]
    Venus, and great Cupid here,

0.0. [ACT 5 SCENE 4]] *CWD.* 0.1-2. SD.] *This ed.;* Philisses, Musella
offring in the Temple of Love; *PM;* [*Enter*] PHILISSES [*and*] MUSELLA
offering in the Temple of Love CWD. 1. SP.] *CWD.* here] *This ed.;* heere
PM; hear *CWD.*

0.1–2. SD.] The setting of Venus's Temple, the short rhyming verse and
the references to 'rites' (3) and 'relics' (5) give this scene the quality of a
religious ceremony, linked simultaneously to marriage (in the sense of giving
a pledge of permanent, indissoluble affection – see *OED*, v.3,7) and sacrifice.
In the 1999 production, the actors playing Venus and Cupid posed as living
statues at the top of the steps, which represented the Temple at the back of
the stage.

0.2. SD.] *PM* has no stage direction to explicitly indicate when Simeana
enters the scene. Philisses and Musella ask Simeana to accompany them to
the Temple as a witness to their offerings to Love (5.1.110) and to report
their actions (5.1.101–2), and she agrees to go along (5.1.115); Climeana also
witnesses her going to the Temple with Musella (5.3.20–4). It is thus likely
that she enters at the beginning of the scene.

1. SP.] There is no prefix to these lines apart from the SD above ('Philisses
and Musella offering in the Temple of Love'), so it is not clear whether the
protagonists sing or speak these lines, although we can assume that they
express themselves in unison in 1–12. *PM*'s lack of clear written direction
may be an indication that Wroth was present to direct a performance based
on this manuscript, or that the manuscript is intended to serve as a record
of a performance. See Introduction, 51–4. As in 2.3, the seven-syllable couplets have a liturgical quality which echoes that of Mary and Philip's translations of the *Psalms* (e.g. Psalm 44, *Psalms*, 84–7), and suggests they could
be sung or chanted like the Psalms. In the 1999 and 2018 productions all
the lines were sung, albeit the 1999 performance cut 17–22 and 27–32, whilst
the 2018 performance repeated 11–12, slowing the pace of the scene. In 1999,
Philisses and Musella entered hand in hand, singing, and kneeled before the
steps, facing each other and holding hands, to mimic a marriage ceremony.
The 2014 staged reading used a mixture of song and speech: Musella and
Philisses sang the first 12 lines together, spoke their individual lines to Venus
and to Cupid, and then sang 37–8 together. This edition's use of non-italic
script for the speeches is designed to leave the mode of delivery open for
interpretation in future performances.

1. *here*] In *PM* the spelling is 'heere', which invokes the homophone
'hear', giving the line a double sense of invocation (prayers to Venus and
Cupid) and presentation, and drawing spectators' attention to the presence
of the supernatural characters, perhaps on stage in an upper balcony or on
an elevated altar, as was the case in the 1999 performance.

Take our sacrifices clear,
Where not rites we only give,
But our hearts wherein you live;
Those true relics of firm love   5
On your altar still to move,
Where none such, none so sincere,
To your triumph light did bear.
Yours they lived while joy had life,
Dying, here will end all strife.   10
Truer love, or truer hearts
Never perished by your darts.
Philisses to VENUS.
Venus, only queen of love,
Take these passions which I prove:
Take these tears, this vow take,   15
Which my death shall perfect make.

---

3. rites] *CWD;* rights *PM.*   12. darts.] darts; / *PM.*   13. queen of love]
This ed.; Queene of love *PM.*   14. prove] prove = [*end of page*] *PM.*

5–6. *relics … move*] relics of true love, perhaps suggesting that the hearts
they promise to leave on the altar will move others to praise Love. Relics
were an important part of Catholic devotion, appropriated by poets such as
in 'The Relic' by John Donne, born into a Catholic family but from 1615 a
Protestant and from 1621 Dean of St Paul's (*Donne*, 130). The heart of Sir
Henry Sidney, grandfather of Lady Mary Wroth, was buried in a lead casket
in the tomb of his daughter Ambrosia in St Laurence's Church in Ludlow.

13. SP.] *PM*'s treatment of Philisses's speech here and that of Musella to
speak 'to Cupid' may suggest that, in performance, the two gods have separate altars, as in *Two Noble Kinsmen* when Arcite, Palamon and Emilia pray
to Mars, Venus and Diana, respectively. Venus and Cupid could be represented by symbolic props on the altar(s), or by the actors playing Venus and
Cupid. In the 2014 staged reading at Penshurst Place the actors playing
Musella and Philisses moved to opposite sides of the stage area and directed
their lines to the back of the Baron's Hall. The separate vows suggest that
each lover is still thinking of suicide separately so that the other may live;
on this reading, their reference to 'dying' hearts in 10–12 is purely metaphorical. Cf. 45–6 and 51–3. The 1999 performance created a different kinaes-
thetic effect by having Philisses and Musella (still kneeling and facing each
other) direct their songs upwards and across the Temple steps to the statues
of Venus and Cupid, creating a chiasmic pattern.

14. *prove*] See 1.2.4n. Here, and in Musella's dedication to Cupid, the
transitive verbs present Philisses's and Musella's suicides as sacrifices *to*
Venus and Cupid as well as *for* each other, thus proving their reverence for
love's power.

But Musella my heart loved,
Her loss hath my joy removed.
Hers I lived, hers now I die,
Crowned with fame's eternity.   20
Thus your force shall glory have
By Philisses' loving grave.

Musella to CUPID.

Cupid, lord of love and hearts,
King of thoughts, and loving smarts,
Take these offerings which I give   25
And my life which new shall live.
Earth, too mean for such a truth,
Shall in death have lasting youth,
No decay, no strife, no fate
Shall disturb that 'during state.   30
Life I offer to true love;
Then accept this end I prove.
Time none such did know, nor shall
See so willingly to fall.
In Philisses I did live,   35
He departing, life I give.

Philisses [and] Musella.

Fame hereafter swell with pride,
Never love thus lived, thus died.

Philisses. Now my Musella, and in death but mine,

---

23. lord] *This ed.;* Lord *PM.*   30. 'during] *CWD;* during *PM.*

17. *But*] Only.

18. *Her loss*] i.e. losing her either to Rustic or to death.

20. *fame's eternity*] Philisses's statement echoes the opening of Petrarch's *Triumph of Fame,* translated by Henry Parker (1555), in which the 'bright star' of Fame is a being 'that man's life for ever doth save / And pulleth him out alive from his grave' (Jiv). Cf. Musella, 48.

27–8. *Earth ... youth*] Earth, too base for such transcendent love, shall be rejuvenated by my death.

30. *'during state*] enduring state (i.e. of youth and passionate love). Cf. the immortality of Romeo and Juliet (esp. 5.3.299–303).

39. *Now ... mine*] In the 1999 production, Philisses took Musella's hands as he spoke this vow, and the couple (still kneeling) clasped hands around a knife, blade pointing upwards.

Take this last farewell in which glories shine.   40
Love but to you could never be so true,
And death than life I choose, since 'tis for you.
My life in you I had, my joy, my bliss,
And now for you, and by you my end is.
Yet keep your promise, ever happy be;   45
You may be fortunate, and outlive me.
Musella. That I believe, when I do thee outlive
Shame shall instead of fame my triumph give.
I loved as firmly as thou couldst me love,
And can as willingly a death's wound prove.   50
But you forget the promise you did make,
And since, condition made, yourself first break,
I am released, your word forgot, and broke.
My hand shall first conclude that blessèd stroke

---

40. shine] shine [*mark at end of page – possibly abandoned catchword,* 'l[ove]']
PM.   41. Love] Love *PM.*   42. than] *CWD;* then *PM.*

---

44. *by you*] This line is ambiguous, and could mean 'caused by you', because you gave your consent to marry Rustic; 'by your side', as in here with you; and 'alongside you' (since Philisses knows that she too has implied that she will commit suicide). The latter sense of a double 'death' may invoke connotations of death as sexual climax.

47-8. *That ... give*] i.e. 'This I believe: if I outlive you, I will be proclaimed as an example of shame's triumph, instead of a famous example of the triumph of true love.' A triumph was also a type of entertainment, 'a pageant or commemorative show', as *CWD* points out (207n.47). In *Urania II*, 'all the day was spent in the triumphs and entertainments' at the return of 'the magnanimous Emperor Amphilanthus' to his kingdom (294.2–11). Shakespeare's Cleopatra chooses suicide and love rather than the shame of being led in triumph through Rome as a prisoner (*AC* 5.2.203–16).

51-3. *But ... broke*] Musella argues that since Philisses is going to kill himself rather than keep his promise not to harm himself (5.1.97–8), then she is released from her promise to him, freeing her to initiate a double suicide. The speed with which Musella and Philisses's agreement not to harm themselves becomes a suicide pact is remarkable.

54. *first conclude*] Musella's line suggests she takes the lead in raising a dagger.

blessèd stroke] Musella's welcoming of the fatal blow is a forceful contrast to the condemnation of suicide in Christian doctrine. Cf. 68.

Unto thy love, and mine since it is thus.   55
Farewell poor world, life's living bides in us.

    [*She raises a dagger.* SILVESTA *enters with a potion.*]

Silvesta. Oh hold your hands! I knew your minds, and have
    Brought fitter means to wed you to your grave.
    Let not those hands be spotted with your blood,
    But since your destiny is not withstood,   60
    Drink this sweet potion, then take leave, and die;
    Embracing thus, you dead shall buried lie.
Philisses. Friendship, what greater blessing than thou art
    Can once descend into a mortal heart?
    Silvesta friend and priest doth now appear,   65
    And as our loves, let this thy deed shine clear.
Musella. Never more fit did friendship meet with need.
    Blessed be thy days, most blessèd be this deed.

56.1. SD.] *This ed.;* [*She raises a dagger. Enter* SILVESTA] *CWD.*   57. Oh]
This ed.; O *PM.*   62. lie] ly; - [*horizontal mark*] *PM.*   68.1. SD.] *This ed.;*
[*They drink the potion and fall*] *CWD.*

   56.1. SD.] Musella's propensity for taking the initiative was emphasized
in the 1999 production where there was only one dagger, which she took
from Philisses and raised as though to kill him first. In 2018, Philisses held
Musella from behind so that both would be struck when she put the dagger
to her chest. As the time of Silvesta's entrance is not specified in the text,
in performance it could be prompted by Musella's raising the dagger. In
1999 Silvesta ran in only just in time to grasp Musella's hand and prevent
her from stabbing Philisses; in 2018, a pause after Silvesta held out the potion
raised tension as to whether Musella would put down the knife and take the
potion instead.
   58. *fitter*] more appropriate. Cf. 5.5.90. Avoiding penetration by the two
sharp knives metaphorically preserves the chastity of the lovers, so poison is
a fitting alternative for Silvesta to offer.
   wed ... grave] Cf. *RJ* 3.5.140.
   60. *since ... withstood*] since nothing stands in the way of your destiny (i.e.
Silvesta declares she is not going to prevent their suicide – perhaps speaking
as Venus's 'instrument').
   61. *sweet potion*] Cf. Juliet and Romeo's use of potion and poison, *RJ*
4.3.23–55 and 5.3.162–6.
   die] In *PM* this word is followed by a faint horizontal mark on the page
which may direct an action or may possibly be just a pen mark.
   67. *fit*] fittingly.
   68. *Blessed ... deed*] Musella's blessing of Silvesta and of her and Philisses's
suicides flies in the face of Christian doctrine condemning murder and
suicide as mortal sins.

[*They each drink the potion and fall.*]

Simeana. What, have you killed them? For this you must
   die.
Silvesta. And dying for them, I die happily.   70
   Who would outlive them? Who would dying fly
   That here beheld love, and love's tragedy?
   But first upon Love's altar let's them lay,

---

73. Love's] *CWD;* loves *PM.*

68.1. SD.] *PM* gives no directions as to the staging here, leaving opportunities for creative interpretation in performance. In the 1999 production,
Musella took the potion from Silvesta, ascended to the second step of the
Temple, sat facing stage left, drank and then kissed Philisses, who sat on the
step below her facing stage right. Both lovers stretched out full-length, apparently lifeless, on the steps. By contrast, Philisses took charge of the potion
in the 2014 staged reading, taking it to an improvised altar at stage left while
Musella embraced Silvesta; Musella joined him and the two lay down
together on the altar and drank the potion. The 2018 staging emphasized
deliberation and ritual: Musella and Philisses climbed up and stood facing
each other on the 'altar' or top step of the rostrum; Musella drank first and
then handed the vial to Philisses, who drained it and returned it to Silvesta.
The lovers took hands, embraced on the altar as the potion took effect, and
collapsed entwined in each other's arms.
   69. *What ... them?*] Simeana's reaction could be explained as the result
of her having just entered or re-entered, or, if she has been onstage from the
beginning of the scene, as a shocked reaction that Silvesta's intervention has
not prevented, but rather seems to have enabled, the suicides.
   71–2. *Who ... tragedy*] Silvesta's acceptance of death as result of her love
for Musella and Philisses, and their own sacrifices to love, suggests that the
progress to love's victory is also towards tragedy. *CWD* (208n.49) points out
that Silvesta's phrase 'love's tragedy' highlights the difference between the
events on stage and the promise inherent in the play's title. The sleepless
Pamphilia imagines losing Amphilanthus in a night 'wherein the blacker
tragedy is to be acted' (*Urania II*, 107.17–18).
   73. *let's ... lay*] In performance, the difficulty of Silvesta and Simeana
physically moving two bodies without disrupting the mood of the scene is
obviated if the lovers have collapsed on or near the altar (see 68.1 SDn.), or
if there is a break in the action at the end of the scene. Different effects are
achieved if the bodies remain on stage until Act 5 Scene 7. In 2018 Silvesta
and Simena covered the bodies with a shroud-like cloth, and the altar and
shrouded bodies, in full view of spectators, contributed silently but significantly to the sense of foreboding in Rustic's question ''Tis not fatal, is't?'
(5.5.9), and Simeana and Silvesta's accounts of the lovers' deaths later in
that scene (5.5.29–32 and 49–98).

There to abide till their new marriage day.
Then lead me to those who my life must take,   75
But ere I die some joyful heart shall ache.   *Exeunt.*

[ACT 5 SCENE 5]

[*Outside, near* MUSELLA*'s* MOTHER*'s house*]

[*Enter*] RUSTIC *with shepherds* [LISSIUS, LACON] *and*
shepherdesses [DALINA, CLIMEANA, *and* FILLIS] *ready*
to fetch the bride.

Rustic. Now is the time approached; what think you now?
    Is't not a trim day? What cloud shows a brow?

0.0. [ACT 5 SCENE 5]] *CWD.*   0.1. SD.] *This ed.*   0.2–4. SD.] *This ed.;*
Rustick wth shepherds, and shepherdesses redy to fetch the bride; / PM.

---

74. *new … day*] These words constitute another challenge to Christian
thought, in which marriage is believed to last 'till death us do part' rather
than being eternal, something that may have been registered by Wroth's early
modern readers or audience members.
    76. *some … ache*] Which heart Silvesta imagines will ache is left ambigu-
ous; the most obvious candidate for such grief is Rustic, though she may
also be referring to the Forester. Zelmane (the disguised Pyrocles) warns
that kings' crowns cannot save them 'from cruel heartache' (*Arcadia*, I.194),
and in *Urania I* the evil Clotorindus tells Rosindy that 'thy heart shall ache
more' in the loss of his beloved Meriana than at the loss of any battle or
territory (158.3).

0.1–4. SD.] *PM* does not give a location, but this scene probably takes
place in the open air near to Musella's mother's house. The assembled community gathered in anticipation of the wedding may include both onstage
actors and members of the audience. Given the shared antipathy to the
arranged marriage expressed by the shepherds and shepherdesses in the
lines which follow, they may distance themselves from Rustic once they
are on stage.
    2. *trim*] suitable, with connotations of well-prepared (*OED*, 1a) and finely
dressed (*OED*, 2), possibly referring to the wedding clothes he and probably
the other characters are wearing. Rustic displayed his lavish, shiny green
costume and cape with flamboyant pleasure in the 2018 production, having
entered from the back of the hall amidst the congregation of audience
members. In the light of 'love's tragedy' (5.4.72) just staged, Rustic's jovial
wedding-morning visit is as unsuitable as that of Paris in *Romeo and Juliet*
4.4.
    shows … brow] i.e. frowns (over the sunlit sky).

All at my fortune clear, all smile with joy,
Sheep, goats and cattle, glad that I enjoy.
Dalina. [*To others*] I never loved him, now I hate him. Fie,   5
To think Musella by this beast must lie.
Rustic. Come, let's along, and quickly fetch the bride,
Methinks I long to have her by my side.
[*He stumbles.*] How now? What, stumble? 'Tis not fatal,
is't?
Lissius. Good luck that you to kiss the ground have missed.   10
Dalina. A far worse sign than this it doth foretell,

---

3. clear] *This ed.;* cleere *PM;* cheer *CWD.*   5. SD.] *This ed.*   8.] *CWD*
adds SD [*They see* MUSELLA *and* PHILISSES] *after this line.*   9. SD.] *This*
ed.   10. kiss] *This ed.;* kis *PM;* his *R;* him *CWD.*   11. foretell,] foretell =
[*end of page*] *PM.*

3. *clear*] Logically, this refers to Rustic's 'clear' good fortune, or possibly
back to the clear weather mentioned in the previous phrase. A possible editorial emendation to 'cheer', to make the word refer to the group of people
gathered with Rustic, seems strained. It would have to be justified in terms
of Rustic's ignorance, since the shepherds and shepherdesses clearly feel
sorry for Musella and Philisses and so are unlikely to cheer at his fortune.
He continues to refer to the natural environment, his animals smiling for
joy, in the following phrase.

5. *I ... him*] Dalina's outspoken opinion on Rustic is addressed to the
other shepherds, with whom she is probably standing in a group at a distance
from Rustic. Her hatred for Rustic here contrasts with the development of
their relationship in 5.7.

6. *beast*] Wroth uses this term to describe wild and farm animals and,
opprobriously, men and women lacking in civility. In *Urania I*, for example,
Philarchos fights with a 'creature' who is likened to his horse: 'never were
two beasts better matched; none fit to ride the one, but he who was fittest
to be master of the other' (203.1–7). The term is especially appropriate for
Rustic, given his preoccupation with his cattle in the following lines.

9. *What ... is't*] i.e. 'What, have I tripped up! That's not a bad omen, the
act of fate, is it?' Rustic's superstitious nature (cf. 4.1.389–406) makes him
see bad luck in having stumbled. To modern ears, his superstition makes a
strange contrast to his very materialistic attitude, but these would not have
been so incompatible in early modern England.

10. *Good ... missed*] i.e. 'It's good luck that you didn't fall and hit the
ground face down.' In *PM* Wroth's handwriting of 'kis' resembles that at
5.6.7 (*PM*, fol. 45), though the 'k' is slightly less distinctive (as it is in 'kiss'
on *HM*, fol. 18r and in 'kill' on fol. 38r of *PM*). Kissing the ground is an
expression of extreme humility often associated with religious practice.
Possibly Lissius hints that it would be more fitting for Rustic to kiss the
ground than to kiss Musella.

But yet have courage, all things may prove well.
Rustic. Nay, pray resolve me, I begin to fear.
Lissius. To fear? Fie man, can trips make hope forbear?
    On, on, have mettle, will you now wax faint?   15
    You who to us a happy life must paint?
Rustic. This is not all, this morn a cow did low,
    And that ill luck foretells I truly know.
Dalina. Had she not lost her calf?
Rustic.   Her calf? Fie, no,
    She had a dainty one – as I will show   20
    At my return – and they together came,
    And while she lowed the youngling sucked her dam.
Lissius. And so might hurt her, whereat she did cry,
    And for your help did low so bitterly.
Rustic. Well, come what will, we now may not go back.   25
Dalina. Yes, very well, for her consent you lack.
Rustic. Come then, away, the precious time doth waste.

        [*Enter*] SIMEANA [*and*] SILVESTA.

Simeana. Hear first my news, for it may stay your haste.
    Your bride a bridegroom new with joy hath gained,

12-32. But ... breath.] *These lines (fol. 42b of PM) are mistakenly transcribed at 34 in CWD, and 33-54 (fol. 43a of PM) inserted here instead.* 17. cow] Cowe *PM.* 27.1. SD.] *This ed.;* Simeana, Sillvesta *PM.*

---

14. *trips ... forbear*] Can trips cancel out hope?
15. *mettle*] courage (*CWD*, 208n.57).
wax faint] grow weak, lose your nerve. Lissius's reference to the bridegroom's nervousness may provoke some sympathy for Rustic.
16. *who ... paint*] who should set us an example of a happy life.
17. *low*] moo (i.e. make a low resonant sound), one which could be interpreted as mournful.
20. *dainty*] choice, pretty, valuable, but also with connotations of tastiness (*OED*, adj.1, 3).
22. *youngling ... dam*] young calf sucked her mother.
23-4. *And ... bitterly*] i.e. the cow lowed for help at the hurt caused by the young calf's suckling.
26. *very ... lack*] Dalina contradicts Rustic, saying it would be highly appropriate to turn back on his wedding plans since he does not have Musella's consent (though she admits she has given her 'ill consent' at 5.1.71).
28. *haste*] Several early English proverbs counselled against haste in marriage: see, for example, 'In haste to wedding, your haste to withhold' in John Heywood, *A Dialogue Containing the Number in Effect of All the Proverbs in the English Tongue* (London: Thomas Berthelet, 1546, A3v).

And both for wedding-bed a tomb obtained.   30
[*Indicating* SILVESTA] Here is the priest that married
   them to death,
And I the witness of their passing breath.
Rustic. How, is she married, and thus cozened me?
   And dead, and buried? How can all this be?
Silvesta. Fetch forth her mother, and you then shall know   35
   The cause and actor of this cruel blow.
                         [*Exit* RUSTIC.]
Lissius. O heaven, was she too rare a prize for earth,
   Or were we only happy in her birth?
Dalina. Only made rich enjoying of her sight;
   She gone, expect we nothing but sad night.   40
Fillis. What glory day did give us was to show
   The virtue in her beauty seemed to grow.
Climeana. Sweet love and friendship in her shinèd bright,
   Now dimmed are both since darkened is her light.
Lacon. No worth did live which in her had not spring,   45
   And she thus gone, to her grave worth doth bring.

    [*Re-enter* RUSTIC *with* MUSELLA'*s* MOTHER.]

Rustic. I liked her well, but she ne'er cared for me;
   Yet am I sorry we thus parted be.

---

31. SD.] *This ed.*   36. SD.] *This ed.*   46.1. SD.] *This ed.*   48. be] bee: /
PM.

33. *cozened*] tricked.
36. *cause … actor*] Silvesta's lines implicitly shift the blame for Musella's
death to her mother's – and possibly her dead father's – actions.
37–8.] Cf. John Donne's celebrated 'Elegy' and 'Anniversary' poems on
the death of the young Elizabeth Drury, written and circulated from 1610,
which were probably known to Lady Mary Wroth (*Donne*, 204–31).
46. *And … bring*] She has done honour to her memory in the manner of
her death. Another allusion to the pun on Wroth's name.
46.1. SD.] *PM* gives no indication as to how long it takes Rustic to fetch
Musella's mother from the house, and therefore how much of the other
shepherds' mourning they hear as they come on stage, but Simeana's line
'Now hear of me' suggests that their entrance is the cue for her to begin her
speech. Clad in black in the 2018 performance, the Mother's slow walk down
a central aisle of the Baron's Hall, with the shepherds and shepherdesses
bowing reverentially as she sat on one of the tree stumps, brought a quiet
gravity to the scene.
48–50. In *PM* the diacritical marks ('/') after 'prove' and between the lines
ending 'me' and 'be' (47–8) may be evidence that these marks are stage

Simeana. Now hear of me the mournfullest end of love,
    That heart for heart could find, and heartless prove.   50
    Philisses and Musella had loved long,
    And long unknown, which bred their only wrong.
    At last discovered to their greatest joy,
    This match came cross their dear hopes to destroy.
    For she (alas) despairing of her bliss,   55
    Agreed to marry Rustic, and to miss
    No cross, nor froward hap, which sure with him
    She must encounter if in this stream swim.
    When this was done, they knew each other's heart,
    And by it knew the thread which led to smart.   60
    They yet awhile rejoicèd in their love
    But too, too soon there followed this remove:
    Her mother, hasty to conclude her will,
    Appointed this sad day should that fulfil,
    Which hath indeed fulfilled a greater harm   65
    Than spite itself could purchase with her charm.
    Musella, finding that her given consent
    Proved thus her hell, her soul did then lament,
    Yet could not gain release but that she must

---

50. heartless prove] hartles [*inserted above*] prove: / *PM*

directions for the start and completion of Rustic and Mother's entrance. The second '/' occurs within rather than at the end of Simeana's speech, and mark an appropriate moment for her to start her narrative.

    54. *cross*] untowardly.

    57. *froward hap*] perverse fortune.

    58. *if … swim*] i.e. if she were to proceed in this course (of becoming Rustic's wife).

    59. *When … done*] i.e. after Musella had given her consent to marry Rustic. See Introduction, 22.

    60. *thread … smart*] i.e. the thread of fate that would lead to pain. Another image relating to labyrinths, in this case the thread that enables Theseus to find his way out of the labyrinth after defeating the Minotaur.

    65. *fulfilled … harm*] brought about a greater wrong (i.e. the deaths of Musella and Philisses).

    66. *spite … charm*] an unusual characterization of spite, associated with the charm of cunning deception. Cf. Greville, *Mustapha*: 'this charm of cunning spite' (London: John Windet for Nathaniel Butter, 1609, D2), and *PA*, Sonnet 12: 'black as spite' (92).

Look as her mother liked (oh force unjust!).   70
Yet so it was, and this procured her end.
Her mother grown her foe, and death her friend,
Her friend she chose. Philisses, who did love
As much as she, and she as much did prove
Of love and pain as he who felt all smart,   75
Vowed since they might not join but rather part,
They yet as most unfeignèd lovers would
Lovingly die, and so firm lovers should.
Unto the Temple then they took their way,
Together wept, together did they pray,   80
Together offered; now Silvesta, you
Must tell the hapless end which did ensue.
Silvesta. And so I will. Their loves they gave, and lives,
Which should have finished been by two sharp knives

---

70. oh] *This ed.;* O *PM.*   84. two] *This ed.;* too *PM*

70. *Look ... liked*] Cf. Wroth's fantasy depiction of the opposite perspective in an anecdote in *Urania II*, where 'The Lady, who saw but with her daughter's eyes' consents to her daughter's marriage with the knight Parismeria (317.6).

(*oh ... unjust!*)] In the 2018 performance Laura Soper's fine, emotionally charged performance of Simeana's speech was delivered from centre stage, directly at the Mother, and Simeana was forced to pause and swallow her resentment and grief at this line before continuing, whereas in 1999 Paula McGovern took a step towards the Mother and hissed the lines in her face. Rustic, however, stood protectively next to the Mother, with his arm around her to comfort her in her grief.

72. *mother ... friend*] Cf. Philippe De Mornay's description of Death as a caring, maternal figure who 'stretcheth out her arms to pull us into port, when after so many dangerous passages' she 'would conduct us to our true home and resting place' in Mary Sidney Herbert's translation of *A Discourse of Life and Death* (MSH *Works I*, 229).

73–5.] Philisses (who loved as much as she did) and Musella (who experienced as much pain and love as he felt injury). In the 2018 performance Simeana's focus on her brother provoked another wave of grief and anger from her at this point.

76. *Vowed ... part*] Vowed, since they could not marry, but instead were forced to part.

77. *unfeignèd*] true, genuine.

78. *Lovingly die*] Laura Soper's Simeana (2018) had to pause again, fighting her tears, before she could say these words.

84. *two sharp*] with a pun on 'too sharp', highlighted by the spelling 'too' in *PM*.

Provided closely those two to have killed,   85
Who have the world with love and wonder filled.
But I came in and hindered that sharp blow,
Though not their wills. More honour I did owe
To that (in love alone) unhappy pair,
And brought their ends more quiet, and more fair.   90
A drink I gave them made their souls to meet
Which in their clayey cages could not. Sweet
Was their farewell, while Sorrow then used art
To flatter Joy till they no more should part.
Their bodies, likewise joined by us, are placed   95
Upon Love's altar, nor from thence displaced
By vow must be till all you lovers lay
This love-killed couple in their biding clay.
This I have done, and here am I to die
If so you please, and take it willingly.   100
Rustic. Nay, if she loved another, farewell she;
I'm glad she by her death hath made me free.
Lissius. Is this your care? O clownish part, can you
For shame not sorrow when our hearts do rue?
Rustic. I'm free, I care not.
Silvesta.   The like is she then now.   105

---

85. two] *CWD;* too *PM.*   86. love and] [*inserted above*] *PM.*   93. while]
[*inserted above*] *PM.*   Sorrow] *This ed.;* sorrow *PM.*   94. Joy] *This ed.;* joy
PM.   96. Love's] *CWD;* loves *PM.*   98. love-killed] *CWD;* love kild *PM.*

---

92. *clayey ... not*] Silvesta explains that their souls could not meet when
imprisoned in their bodies ('clayey cages'). Cf. Shakespeare's love-birds, the
phoenix and turtle dove, who have 'hearts remote yet not asunder' and are
joined in death and love where 'Either was the other's mine' (*PT,* 29–36).

93–4. *Sorrow ... part*] Sorrow, personified, wooed Joy with such art as to
create an everlasting bond between them. This abstraction allegorizes the
protagonists' own bitter-sweet love story and the tragicomic plot of *Love's
Victory.*

95–6. *joined ... altar*] Silvesta states that she and Simeana have placed the
bodies of Musella and Philisses together on Love's altar.

98. *biding ... clay*] i.e. the graves where they will remain.

103. *clownish part*] *OED* defines 'clownish' as like a clown or peasant,
boorish and uncultivated (adj. 1,2); see 5.1.74n. The reference to 'part'
highlights Rustic's status as a clown of pastoral tradition, although Lissius's
meaning here is clearly more pejorative given the tragic context of the scene.

104. *rue*] grieve, regret what has happened. Cf. 1.2.190n.

Rustic. She is for me, and here I disavow
    All promises which have between us passed,
    Or have been made by her, at first or last,
    To me; and thus I do release her. Now
    May I seek one and please myself in love;   110
    I'll none but such whose heart my love shall move.
                                         Exit.

Silvesta. She's happy yet in death that she is free
    From such a worthless creature. Can this be?
    Such virtue should in her fair breast abound,
    Yet to be tied where no worth could be found?   115
Lissius. [*To* MOTHER] Thus have your years your happiness
        outworn,
    And brought untimely death to your first-born.
    Can you endure this change, and hear us say
    Your forcèd marriage brought her funeral day?
Mother. If the true grief I feel could be expressed   120
    By words, or sighs, I should myself detest.
    Sorrow in heart and soul doth only bide,
    And in them shall my woe be justly tried.
    Yet justice do I crave of this vile pair
    Which were the founders of my endless care: 125

---

110. one] [*inserted above*] *PM*.   112. SP.] *CWD;* Si: *PM*.   116. SD.] *This ed.; [To* MUSELLA'S MOTHER] *CWD*.

111. *Exit*] Rustic's abrupt exit, cued in *PM*, emphasizes his careless sense of liberty.

112–15. The speech heading for these lines in *PM* reads 'Si:', so possibly these lines are spoken by Simeana.

113–15. *worthless … worth*] two more puns on Wroth's name. Cf. 3.1.95; 4.1.36; 5.3.11–14 and 5.1.4–5n.

116. *outworn*] outlasted.

117. *first-born*] *CWD* identifies an autobiographical reference to Wroth here, as the first-born child of Robert Sidney and Barbara Gamage. See Introduction, 42, for biographical readings of the play. The significance of the dynastic loss was emphasized in the 2018 Penshurst production when Lissius delivered these lines to the Mother (Virginia Denham) with a bow. In response, she offered her hand and he helped her to her feet. Denham spoke her responding lines with a cracked voice, slowly and remorsefully, giving a very moving effect in performance.

122–3. *Sorrow … tried*] i.e. only sorrow remains in my heart and soul, and in them will my remorse be rightly judged.

124. *vile pair*] i.e. Arcas and Silvesta.

Arcas first plotted it with skilful art
To ruin me, and living eat my heart.
He told me that Musella wantonly
Did seek Philisses' love; alas, only
The speech of that did inly wound me so,   130
As stay I could not, nor the time let go,
But sent for her, and forced her to consent
To finish that which makes us all lament,
And me to die, oh me, with grief and shame
That thus deservedly I bear this blame.   135
Silvesta, who their lives brought to an end,
Must also suffer. Death, alone my friend,
Shall me release. These things I hope you'll do,
Which done with age and grief, I'll suffer too.
Lissius. These must and shall be done, and rites   140
Performed to their dear bodies, and their sprites.
Now to the Temple, and their bodies view,
Then give these judgement, bidding joy adieu.   *Exeunt.*

---

134. oh] *This ed.;* O *PM.*   139. too.] too; / *PM.*

127. *ruin*] dishonour (cf. 134), but possibly also to reduce to poverty, an early modern usage (*OED*, 2b), by destroying the match with Rustic.

eat ... heart] The Mother claims that Arcas is eating her heart while she is alive, possibly a variation on the proverbial phrase 'to eat one's heart out'; meaning be consumed or sick with remorse or worry 'which an ancient writer termed to eat out one's heart' (*OED*, n.P3b(a)). Cf. George Chapman, *The Iliads of Homer, Prince of Poets* (London: Richard Field for Nathaniel Butter, 1611), bk 24, where Thetis asks Achilles 'How long time wilt thou thus eat thy heart?' (329).

128. *wantonly*] 'both without her mother's consent and with a sense of impropriety' (*CWD*, 208n.76).

133. *that ... lament*] i.e. the arranged marriage which has brought about the tragedy.

137. *death ... friend*] Cf. Simeana's words about Musella, which the mother echoes here (72 and n. above).

139. *suffer too*] The Mother suggests that she will suffer death as well as Silvesta.

143. *these*] i.e. Arcas and Silvesta. In the 2018 performance Lissius formally offered the Mother his hand and led her off stage to the funeral in silence, followed by the other characters.

[ACT 5 SCENE 6]

[*Outside, close to the Temple*]

[*Enter*] *The* FORESTER.

Forester. Under a hedge, all dead, to rest I laid,
My body by despair wholly decayed,
When sleep no sooner did my eyelids close
But half distracted with a dream, I rose.
Methought I saw Silvesta's fair hands tied   5

0.0. [ACT 5 SCENE 6]] *CWD.* 0.1. SD.] *This ed.* 0.2. SD.] *This ed.; [Enter* FORESTER] *CWD.* 8. Virtue] vertu *PM;* virtue *CWD.* 14. SD.] *CWD.*

0.1. SD.] *PM* gives no location for this short scene, which takes place somewhere close to the Temple since the Forester can see Silvesta being led there.

1–14. *Under ... throw*] The Forester's soliloquy is fourteen lines long, forming another complete sonnet, typical of his rhetorical style as a courtly lover.

1. *hedge ... dead*] a dead hedge is either one that has died and is then interwoven with new plants or one that is constructed out of dead wood. John Norden's *The Surveyor's Dialogue: Divided into Five Books* (London: Simon Stafford for Hugh Astley, 1607), points out that a 'dead fence' can be 'made one year, and pulled down another' and is 'common upon the downs in many countries' (238), but warns that 'Quick-set hedges' are preferable 'to repair decayed places' because 'they increase & yield profit and supply' while 'dead hedges or hays devour and spend' (239). The dead hedge, which 'devours' money or energy, is thus an appropriate place for the Forester, who is consumed by his love for Silvesta. The detail looks forward to his willingness to lay down his life to save hers.

2. *decayed*] wasted. Cf. 1 above and *Urania I*, where Princess Emmilena's beauty is 'decayed as love was withered to her' (300.31–2).

5–7. *tied ... limbs*] The Forester dreams of Silvesta being tied to a stake and burned, a common fate of Christian martyrs, as immortalized in John Foxe's much-reprinted Protestant polemic *The Book of Martyrs* (*Acts and Monuments of these Latter Perilous Days Touching Matters of the Church* (London, John Day, 1563), with expanded editions in 1583, 1596–97 and a sixth edition in 1610). The Petrarchan trope of burning to death as a sacrifice to love takes on a material form through this image. It is also found in Lindavera's song 'Behold this sacred fire' where she imagines the 'fiery rays' of her love will consume her on love's altar (*Urania II*, 102–3). Those found guilty of witchcraft or offences such as killing others by poison, as Silvesta appears to have done, were also burned at the stake in continental Europe (though usually hanged in England). Wroth may be alluding obliquely to the dramatic increase in prosecutions for witchcraft in Denmark following King Christian IV's 1617 Ordinance Against Witches (see Louise

Fast to a stake where fire burned in all pride,
To kiss with heat those most unmatchèd limbs
Where Virtue with her shape like habits trims
Herself with her, while she, alas, fair she
Should to those flames a sacred offering be.   10
This dream persuaded me to seek her out,
And save her, or to free me from the doubt.
And there I see her to the Temple go;
I'll after, and my life at her feet throw.   [*Exit.*]

[ACT 5 SCENE 7]

The Temple, and the dead bodies [MUSELLA *and*
PHILISSES] *on the altar.* [*Enter*] *the shepherds*
[LISSIUS, LACON, ARCAS] *and shepherdesses*
[SIMEANA, CLIMEANA, DALINA, FILLIS] *casting flowers
on them* [*with* SILVESTA, MOTHER, RUSTIC *and
the* PRIESTS] *and while* VENUS *appears in glory they sing
this song.*

0.0. [ACT 5 SCENE 7]] *CWD.*   0.1–7. SD.] *This ed.;* The Temple, and
the dead bodys on the Aulter, the sheapherds and sheapherdesses casting
flowers on them & while Venus apeers in glory they sing this song; / [', &'
and 'they sing this song; /' possibly added later] *PM;* The temple, the dead bodies on
the altar. Enter the SHEPHERDS *and* SHEPHERDESSES, *casting flowers on them;*
VENUS, [*who*] *appears in glory;* [CUPID *and the* PRIESTS]. *CWD.*

Nyholm Kallestrap, *Agents of Witchcraft in Early Modern Italy and Denmark*,
Houndmills: Palgrave, 2015, n.239). The nightmarish quality of the Forester's
dream was effectively conveyed in the 1999 performance by the diminutive
Helen Walden, who delivered the lines in a breathless, frightened tone.
        7. *unmatchèd*] unparalleled (i.e. in their beauty); probably implying their
whiteness as a mark of purity since Urania's hands are 'to be adored' for
their 'unmatched whiteness' (*Urania I*, 639.7–8).
        8–9. *Virtue ... her*] The Forester implies that Virtue clothes Silvesta,
fitting her as closely as garments do.
        10. *sacred offering*] These words identify Silvesta more closely with reli-
gious sacrifices such as those of Iphigenia in Euripides' *Iphigenia at Aulis*,
first translated into English by Lady Jane Lumley (*c.* 1557), or Christian
martyrs (cf. the sentence given in 5.7.15–18).

        0.1. SD.] This scene takes place in the Temple of Venus, as suggested
by the Forester's penultimate line in the previous scene. In *PM* part of the
SD ('&' and 'They sing this song: /') appears to have been added later. In

Sorrow, now conclude thy hate,
More can not be done by fate.
Grief, abandon thy cursed skill,
Love hath now found means to kill.
Lovers here example take: 5
Faith in love should never shake.
Only Death hath force to part
Lovers' bodies by his dart,
But their spirits higher fly;
Death can never make them die,   10
But their souls with pure love's fire
Will to heavenly bliss aspire.

Priests. Now must we judge the offenders for this deed,
      And each one punish; thus it is decreed.
      Silvesta, greatest in the fault, must bend   15
      Her spirit first unto her own sought end:

---

1. *Sorrow*] Sorow *PM.* 3. *Grief*] Griefe *PM.* 4. *Love*] love *PM.* 5.
Lovers] Lovers *PM.* 7. *Only Death*] *CWD;* Only death *PM.* 12. *aspire*]
aspire; / *PM*

the 1999 production the Priests opened the curtains to reveal the Temple
with Philisses and Musella's bodies on the steps, and the shepherds and
shepherdesses walked past in single file, singing and placing white roses on
the bodies. In the 2014 staged reading the shepherds and shepherdesses were
simply spaced across the stage area facing the altar stage left; in the 2018
production they filed into the Temple while singing, and were followed by
the Priests who removed a covering from the bodies on the altar and draped
them with garlands of fabric flowers in silence at the end of the song.

7–9. Only ... fly] 'Only' is perhaps used here to create a double meaning:
that 'only Death's arrow can part the true lovers' bodies' and that it can part
'only' their bodies, not their spirits which transcend death. On Death's arrow
or dart see 2.2.12n.

13. SP.] The speech heading 'The Priests' in *PM* does not indicate
whether the lines are intoned in unison by the Priests of Venus or split
between them. A single priest pronounced the lines in the 1999 production
and in the 2014 staged reading; in the 2018 production the lines were divided
between the two priests, who delivered them in couplets.

judge] In *Urania I* the priest of Venus explains that the palace of Venus
depicted in the engraved title page by Simon Van Passe is the 'trial of false
or faithful lovers' (48.35).

15–16. *bend ... spirit*] A phrase commonly used in religious discourse or
prayer. See, for example, 'Yet according to thy commandment, I will thor-
ough thy grace wholly bend my spirit to serve thee', Richard Kilby, *Hallelujah,
Praise Ye the Lord* (Cambridge: Cantrell Legge, 1618, 118). Mary Sidney's

With flames of fire, as she with flames of zeal
Did act this, she must now her last day seal.
Death she procured, and for death, life shall give.
Silvesta. 'Tis justice, thus by death anew I live.   20
My name by this will win eternity,
For no true heart will let my merit die.

[*Enter* FORESTER.]

Forester. I must enjoy my death ere this be done!
Bright Venus, I beseech thee, and thy son
To look on me, your true, though luckless slave,   25
And view the heart my faith to firm love gave.
Save sweet Silvesta, whose youth framed this deed;
Let not her virtue as offences speed,

---

17. zeal] Zeale *PM*.   22.1. SD.] *CWD*.

translation of Psalm 119, verse 'O', concludes with the heart 'which still doth
bend, / And only bend to do what thou dost will / And do it in the end'
(*Psalms*, 239).
   17. *zeal*] passion, often used in religious discourse, and so linked to
Silvesta's role as 'friend and priest' to Philisses and Musella (5.4.65).
   18. *seal*] finish.
   19. *Death ... give*] Cf. Matthew 7:2 and *MM* 5.1.41.
   21. *win eternity*] achieve immortality (as an example of self-sacrifice for
love and friendship).
   23–36. *I must ... strife*] Again the Forester expresses his love in the form
of a sonnet. In the 2018 production he rushed on and fell to his knees, centre
stage, delivering his lines to the minstrels' gallery on which Venus stood
above him.
   23. *enjoy*] The use of this verb by both the Forester and Venus (at 40)
conjures up 'the high privilege of the Christian, to enjoy death' (see Francis
Rous, *Meditations of instruction, of exhortation, of reproof endeavouring the
edification and reparation of the house of God* (London: I. L[egat] for George
Gibbs and Francis Constable, 1616, 217), since, for the believer (and especially for a martyr) 'death can be but sweet and agreeable: knowing that
through it he is to enter into a place of all joys' (*MSH Works I*, 252). The
word also carries connotations of bliss or sexual fulfilment. Cf. 1.1.29–30n.
and 1.3.59n.
   25. *slave*] Like 'vassal' (cf. 1.4.10 and 4.1.220) this word exemplifies the
Forester's abjection to Venus and Cupid as a slave of love.
   27. *youth*] The Forester appears to mount a defence of diminished
responsibility on Silvesta's behalf on account of her youth, raising the possibility that he is older than her. See Introduction, 23.
   28. *Let ... speed*] i.e. Do not mistake her virtuous deeds for offences.

Or, though by law she have deserved this doom,
Let me for her obtain her 'pointed tomb.　　　　　30
I am more fit to die and suffer far,
Life with my sorrows are at endless war.
Besides the law allows if one will die
For other's fault, his death may their life buy.
Let me first beg it, pay it then with life,　　　　　35
Death for her sake shall please, and end the strife.
Venus. Poor Forester, thy love deserveth more,
For in thy heart true firmness lived in store.
But since you will her life with your life buy
You must enjoy death. We can none deny　　　　　40
That thus do claim it; she's by you made free,
And you for her must now my offering be.
Forester. Goddess of hearts, you thus have done me right,
Now shall my faith to honour you shine bright.
Silvesta. Thanks is your due for saving me from death;　　　　　45
Did I not rather hate than love this breath?

---

34. his] [*inserted above*] *P.M.*

30. *obtain ... tomb*] be given her appointed grave.

33–4. *law ... buy*] Self-sacrifice is the basic principle of Christian law, as in the Bible verse 'Greater love hath no man than this; that a man lay down his life for his friends' (John 15:13); Wroth may draw on the classical example of Alcestis who 'chose to die thereby to deliver her said husband from death', celebrated by Euripides and Seneca. This was recommended as a model of supreme love for Princess Elizabeth (daughter of James I) and Prince Frederick whom Robert Sidney escorted to Germany after their marriage in 1613: 'such unquenched fire as once the breasts did burn / Of Admetus and his Alcestis dear / Burn both your breasts till both to ashes turn' (James Maxwell, *A Monument of Remembrance erected in Albion* (London: Nicholas Okes for Henry Bell, 1613), E3).

35. *beg it*] In the 2014 staged reading the Forester entered from amidst the spectators, kneeled and raised his hands to Venus and the minstrels' gallery on this line.

37. *Poor Forester*] In the 2018 production Venus's spoken response alerted other characters on stage to her presence, and all fell to their knees to reverence her.

38. *firmness ... store*] constancy existed in abundance.

46. *Did ... breath*] This line is ambiguous: Silvesta could be referring either to her own breath ('did I not want to die rather than live?') or could be questioning her previous opinion of the Forester (i.e. 'did I not hate rather than love this [the Forester's] breath?'). In the 2014 reading Silvesta and the Forester were positioned at opposite sides of the stage, with a considerable distance between them. In 2018 Silvesta expressed heartfelt pity for the Forester, clutching her arm to her chest.

Yet shall this bounty gain in my chaste heart
To your deserts a kind and thankful part.
Forester. Death, happy death, since she for whom I die
Doth pity me, and weighs my constancy. 50
Could I live ages, 'twould not be so good
As now to die, with thanks given for my blood.
Then farewell world; death welcome as new life.
Silvesta thanks me, and gives me this wife.
Mother. You sacred priests, perform the latest due 55
To their dead bodies, and my joys adieu.
Priests. Rustic, before us here disclaim the right
In life was tied to you, now to her sprite.
Rustic. I love no sprites, nor those affect not me,
She loved Philisses; therefore she is free. 60
Were she alive, she were her own to choose,
Thus here to her all claim I do refuse.
Priests. Philisses, of us take Musella fair.
We join your hands, rise and abandon care.
Venus hath caused this wonder for her glory. 65
And the triumph of love's victory.

---

48. part] part; – *PM.* 53. life.] lyfe [*possible diagonal / mark*] *PM.* 55.
priests] Priests *PM.* 66. triumph] Triumph *PM.*

---

47. *bounty*] this generosity (i.e. his offering to die in her place).

50. *weighs*] values – a continuation of the mercantile trope in 'bounty'.

53. In *PM* a small but deliberate pen stroke appears at the end of the line
after 'life'. It may link with the point below or as an exclamation mark or as a
semi colon, but would be unlike any other diacritical marks in *PM.*
Alternatively, it could be a small version of the slash / mark Wroth seems to
have occasionally used to indicate the end of a speech.

54. *this wife*] Since Silvesta will not give him her love, the Forester imagines Death as his bride – cf. *MM* (3.1.82) and *A&C* (4.14.99–100). His joy
at the prospect of death was highly pronounced in the 2018 production.

57–8. *disclaim … sprite*] Rustic is asked to disclaim the right he had to
Musella in life, as a declaration to her spirit that it is now free. For obvious
reasons, the Priest asks for this formal, public surrender before Musella (and
Philisses) can be 'revived'.

59. *I … me*] I don't love ghosts, or those who don't love me. Rustic
confirms his materialist outlook.

66. *triumph … victory*] an allusion to the title of the play and to Petrarch's
Triumph of Love. See Parker, A4–D4v.

[PHILISSES *and* MUSELLA *arise from the altar.*]

Venus. Lovers, be not amazed, this is my deed,
　　Who could not suffer your dear hearts to bleed.
　　Come forth, and joy your faith hath been thus tried,
　　Who truly would for true love's sake have died.　　　　70
　　Silvesta was my instrument ordained
　　To kill and save her friends, by which sh'hath gained
　　Immortal fame, and bands of firmest love
　　In their kind breasts where true affections move.
　　Then all rejoice, and with a loving song　　　　　　　　75
　　Conclude the joy hath been kept down too long.
Mother. Joy now as great as was my former woe
　　Shuts up my speech from speaking what I owe
　　To all but mine, for mine I joy you are,
　　And love and bliss maintain you from all care.　　　　80
　　Pardon my fault, enjoy, and blessèd be,
　　And children, and their children's children see.
Musella. Pardon me first who have your sorrow wrought,
　　Then take our thanks, whose good your care hath
　　　　brought.
　　Silvesta, next to you our lives are bound,　　　　　　　85
　　For in you only was true friendship found.

66.1. SD.] *CWD.*　74. move] move; / *PM.*　76. long] long; / *PM.*　84.
brought] brought [*'ht' inserted above*] *PM.*

---

67. *Lovers ... amazed*] Venus's line was given extra force in the 2014
reading where, having descended from the gallery, she appeared amongst
the mortals on the main stage, entering at stage right.

71. *instrument ordained*] appointed means, with the implication of a call
to holy orders (i.e. the priesthood of Venus).

72. *sh'hath*] she hath [has]; elided to a single syllable to conform to the
ten-syllable line length.

75–6.] In the 2018 production Venus proclaimed these celebratory lines
with her hands raised in blessing over all the mortals.

78–9. *Shuts ... mine*] prevents me from speaking my apologies and thanks
to anyone but my own daughter. Virginia Denman, playing the Mother in
the 2018 production, moved centre stage while Musella and Philisses kneeled
for her blessing. She clasped Musella's hands in her own and spoke these
words slowly and with a moving sense of wonder at the miraculously restored
gift of her daughter.

84. *whose ... brought*] whose protection [good] has brought you so much
trouble, or possibly 'those whose benefit has been brought by your care'.

Philisses. Mother, for so your gift makes me you call,
    Receive my humble thanks which ever shall
    With faithful love and duty you attend,
    Till death our lives bring to a final end.   90
    And chaste Silvesta, take my life when I
    Ungrateful prove to your worth-binding tie.
Silvesta. Venus the praise must have, whose love to you
    Made her descend on earth, and your cares view.
    She sent the drink hath wedded you to joy,   95
    And in joy live, and happiness enjoy.
    Chaste love relieved you, in chaste love still live,
    And each to other true affections give.
    For you, kind Forester, my chaste love take,
    And know I grieve now only for your sake.   *Exit.* 100

---

92. worth-binding tie] worth=binding ty; / *PM. A second = is written parallel to Silvesta's speech heading, as though Wroth decided to add another speech
heading and line at the bottom of the page.*

---

87. *so ... call*] so your gift [i.e. of her daughter] makes me call you.
Philisses addresses the Mother as his mother-in-law.

91–2. *take ... tie*] Philisses invites Silvesta to kill him if he is ever ungrateful for her sacrifice; alternatively, 'worth-binding tie' could refer to Philisses's
union with Musella, with a possible additional allusion to Wroth's own
marriage through the pun on 'worth'/'Wroth'. 'Worth=binding' has a double
hyphen in *PM* and is followed by a second =, the symbol used by Wroth to
mark the end of a page in *PM*. In this case it is written parallel to Silvesta's
speech heading, suggesting that Wroth then decided to add another speech
heading and line of script at the bottom of the page.

94. *descend on earth*] As noted, in the 2014 staged reading Venus did
descend from the minstrels' gallery on line 67 ('Lovers be not amazed'), and
remained on the main stage until the end of the play. In the 1999 production
Venus invited Philisses and Musella, followed by all the other mortals, to sit
on the steps of the Temple at 94.

97. *chaste ... live*] See Introduction, 15, Nathaniel Baxter's praise of Wroth
as 'Chaste, holy modest, divine and perfect' in *Sir Philip Sidney's Ourania,
that is Endymion's Song and Tragedy* (London: E. Allde for Edward White,
1606) and Ben Jonson's 'To Penshurst', 90–2, on the importance placed on
chastity in marriage.

100. *grieve ... sake*] i.e. perhaps because she only cares about him, or
because she can only offer chaste love, or perhaps – given the sentence of
death is not explicitly reprieved by Venus – because he has not been par-
doned, though imminent sacrifice seems unlikely given Venus's command
to 'all rejoice'. Silvesta's exit at this point in the text conveys her intention
to remain chaste and unmarried, a point underlined in the 2018 production
by the firm manner of her departure.

Forester. My joys increase, she grieves now for my pain;
 Ah, happy proffered life which this can gain.
 Now shall I go contented to my grave
 Though no more happiness I ever have.
Lissius. Now let me ask my joy, which you must give: 105
 Philisses, you may make me die, or live.
 Your sister for my wife I seek, alone
 I crave but her, and love makes her mine own;
 Two bodies we are yet have but one heart,
 Then rather join than let such dear love part.   110
Philisses. Myself from bliss I sooner will divide
 Than cross your loves. Then henceforth thus abide
 Joined in firm love, and happiness attend
 Your days on earth until your lives do end.
Dalina. Rustic, what think you, is this called fair play?   115
Rustic. When Venus wills, men can not but obey.
 Yet this I'll swear, I'm plainly cozened here;
 But 'tis all one, the bargain may prove dear.
Dalina. Yet you have not lost all: this wreath you see
 Is proved your garland, this fair willow tree   120
 You now must reverence, and bravely wear.
Rustic. I'll sooner die than such disgrace to bear.

---

104. have] have; / *PM.* 107. sister] Sister *PM.*

102. *proffered life*] i.e. his own life, which he has offered to save hers.

103–4. *shall … have*] The Forester's words may still carry the possibility of him being literally sacrificed, but his anticipation of going contentedly to his grave carries the stronger suggestion of a longer future of limited happiness or 'content' with Silvesta's chaste love and pity. In the 2018 production the Forester exited full of celebratory laughter.

107–8. *alone … her*] I crave only her, i.e. with the possible implication that Lissius is not seeking a dowry, and therefore that this is not a material match, in contrast to that planned between Rustic and Musella.

109. *Two … heart*] Cf. *MND* 2.2.47–50.

118. *the … dear*] Using characteristically materialistic terms, Rustic suggests, perhaps bad-temperedly, that Musella and Philisses' match may prove costly to them.

120. *willow tree*] Rustic is finally forced into the role of courtly lover, having to wear the willow garland, a symbol of unrequited love, because he has been 'cozened' or tricked out of his bride. In *Urania I* Princess Emelina's dress is of brown and willow colour and 'embroidered with willow garlands' to show her unrequited love for Amphilanthus (300.36).

    Nay, sooner marry, and that now I deem
    Far worse than death, though slighter in esteem.
Dalina. I would I might but name the happy maid   125
    Should be your wife.
Rustic.   Yourself name and all's said.
Dalina. Will you have me then?
Rustic.   Rather than my life.
Dalina. In troth, agreed. I'll prove a loving wife.
Rustic. 'Tis all I seek. Now, god give you all joy,
    And blessed am I who this sweet lass enjoy.   130
Musella. A good exchange, and everyone agreed.   .
Philisses. And as we love and like so let us speed.
Venus. Now sing a song, both priests and all, for joy,
    And cursed be they your blessèd states annoy.

The song.

Cupid. Now my wars in love hath end: 135
    Each one here enjoys their friend,
    And so all shall henceforth say
    Who my laws will still obey.
    Mother, now judge Arcas' fault,
    All things else your will hath wrought.   140

---

126. said] sayd ['*d*' *inserted above*] *PM*.   127. then] [*inserted above*] *PM*.
134.1. SD.] the song; / *PM* [*followed by a blank space on the page*].   139.
Mother] Mother *PM*.   140. wrought] wrought; / *PM*.

---

123. *that*] i.e. marriage.

128. *in troth*] in truth, but also carrying the meaning of betrothal.

129. *god*] This reference to a single Christian deity seems oddly out of place in a scene where Venus and Cupid are on stage as presiding deities, but Rustic may just be using the commonplace salutation 'God give you joy'.

130–1. *enjoy … exchange*] The sudden nature of Dalina and Rustic's engagement, conveyed by the rather blunt tone of this exchange between Dalina and Rustic in the 2018 production, contrasted with a long and vigorous kiss enjoyed by the couple after they agreed to marry. This prompted Musella's remark 'a good exchange', and caused amused embarrassment amongst the other characters.

134.1. *The song*] *PM* has a blank space indicating that a song should be inserted here. To cover the absence, Cupid sang 135–8 in the 2018 production.

Venus. Arcas, think not your villainy's forgot;
    But since each now enjoys, the better lot
    Doth fall to you. You here must still abide
    In these fair plains, where you shall never hide
    The shame of falsehood printed in your face,   145
    Nor hence remove, but in the self-same place
    You did commit that error foul and ill.
    There your days left, with grief and shame shall fill
    Your gnawing conscience; this shall be your doom.
Arcas. O sacred goddess, let my heart's suit come   150
    Before your eyes: rather O let me die
    Than here remain with shame and infamy.
    This dying life (alas) than death is worse,
    Nor can you lay on me a greater curse.
Venus. Your doom is giv'n, it may not be recalled,   155
    But with your treachery you must be thralled.
    And now all duties are performed to Love;
    Look that no more our powers by scorn you move,
    But be the treasures of love's lasting glory,
    And I your princess, crowned with victory.   160

---

148. days] [*inserted above*] *PM.*   150. goddess] Goddess *PM.*   151. O] ô
PM; o *CWD.*   160. princess crowned] Princess Crownd *PM.*   victory.]
Victory; / *PM.*

---

145. *shame ... face*] As *CWD* points out (208n.104), this is possibly an
allusion to the mark of Cain, the first murderer, in the Bible (Genesis 4:15);
alternatively Venus may be sentencing Arcas to be branded on the face – as
Clare Dawkins notes, this was a possible punishment for slander or sedition
when Wroth was writing ('Victorious Service in Lady Mary Wroth's Love's
Victory', *SJ*, 31:1 (2013) 131–49, 147).

149. *doom*] Arcas was effectively condemned by all the mortals in the
1999 performance, who were sitting in judgement on him on the steps of
Venus's Temple as she spoke, and silently raised their arms to point at him
on this word.

150. *goddess*] 'goddess' has a capital in *PM* which, given that Arcas is
speaking to Venus, may indicate his respect for her.

156. *thralled*] enslaved. Arcas explicitly acknowledged his inescapable
guilt in the 1999 performance by curling up with his head bowed as he sat
alone at centre stage, facing the audience.

160. *princess ... victory*] In *PM* both Princess and Crowned have emphatic
capitals as if to mark Venus's triumph, and even the smaller 'v' in 'victory'
has a leading stroke like the capital for Venus. To emphasize her triumph,
the 1999 performance finished with a short extract from Robert van
Leeuwen's song 'Venus' as the actors took their bows.

Arcas. Thus still is sin rewarded with all shame,
    And so let all be that deserve like blame.
    I have offended in the basest kind,
    And more ill do deserve than ill can find.
    I traitor was to Love, and to my love;   165
    Those who shall thus offend, like me, shame prove.

                                        Exeunt.

                        Finis.

---

166. prove] prove; [*S fermé*] *PM.*   166.1. *Finis.*] Finis [*flourish below*] *PM.*

161–6. Arcas's shaming confession, delivered out to members of the audience in both the 1999 and 2018 performances, and the lack of pardon he receives (from Venus at least), create a harsh warning note at the end of the play, perhaps reflecting an intention on Wroth's behalf to mimic Venus by shaming traitors to love amongst her contemporaries.

Appendix I

Poetic Justice Theatre Company, *Love's Victory*, directed by Stephanie Hodgson-Wright
Bede Tower Studio, University of Sunderland, November 1999.

Cast
Venus – Christine Wolfendale
Cupid / Lacon – Richard Tattersall
Priest / Climeana – Hilary Crowe
Priest / Arcas – Andrew Slade
Philisses – Kevin Hogarth
Lissius – Colin Reid
Silvesta – Jordana Chapman
Forester – Helen Walden
Dalina – Emma Lancaster
Musella – Susie Smith
Rustic – Scott Wilson
Simeana – Paula McGovern
Musella's Mother – Claire Thirlwell

Music by Alison Findlay with additional music by Kevin Hogarth
and Simon Taylor
Video – Sophie Chapple (University of Gloucestershire)
With thanks to the University of Sunderland.

Appendix II

The Urania Company, *Love's Victory*, directed by Martin Hodgson
The Baron's Hall, Penshurst Place, 16 September 2018.

Cast (in alphabetical order)
Musella – Nichole Bird
Mother – Virginia Denham
Cupid / Arcas – Zak Douglas
Rustic – Dylan Frankland
Philisses – Robert Heard
Forester – Andrew Hodges
Lissius – Jonny McPherson
Venus / Fillis – Charlie Mulliner
Silvesta – Anne-Marie Piazza
Lacon / Priest of Venus – Joel Sams
Climeana / Priest of Venus – Nadia Shash
Simeana – Laura Soper
Dalina – Rachel Winters

Music by Martin Hodgson, arranged by Sam Goble
Musical Director: Sam Goble
Cornetto – Sam Goble
Lute and Theorbo – Robin Jeffrey
Lute – Lynda Sayce
Company Stage Managers: Harriet Saffin and Jonny Gosling

The performance was produced by Alison Findlay in collaboration
with Penshurst Place, with funding from the Arts and Humanities
Research Council and Lancaster University.

Index

Note: this index incorporates a glossarial index, listing the first uses of unusual words, or words used in a particular sense. It also references historical persons, characters, authors and critics. The entries for these give page numbers followed by note numbers (e.g. 3n66, 71n1-32). Bold indicates page numbers where a character is on stage, with the Act and Scene in brackets. The appearances of songs and the Book of Fortunes in the play are also marked in bold.

Lightning Source UK Ltd.
Milton Keynes UK
UKHW021459291122
413059UK00037B/573

THE REVELS PLAYS

Former general editors
Clifford Leech
F. David Hoeniger
E. A. J. Honigmann
J. R. Mulryne
Eugene M. Waith

General editors
David Bevington, Richard Dutton, Alison Findlay,
Helen Ostovich and Martin White

LOVE'S VICTORY

Manchester University Press

THE REVELS PLAYS